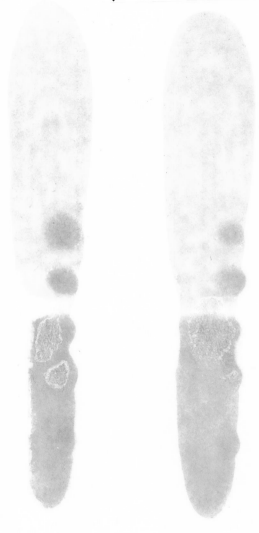

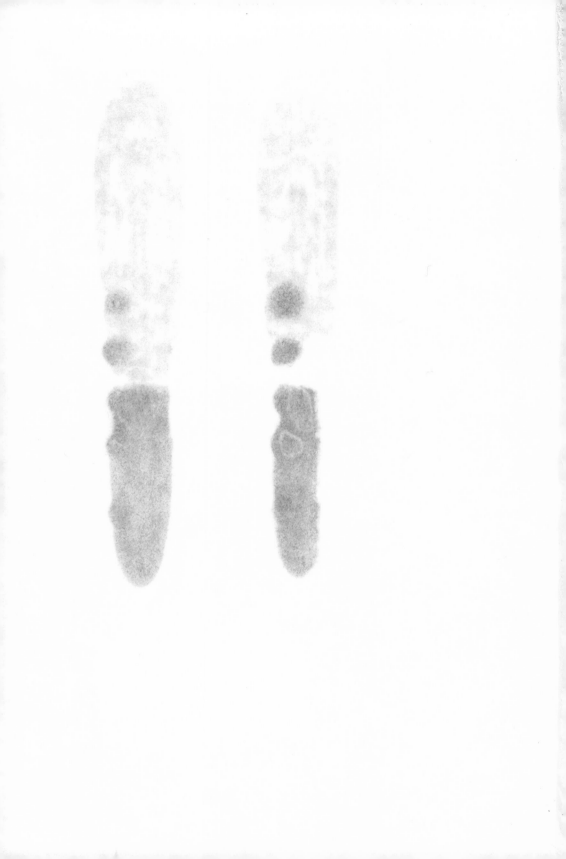

SELLING AT THE TOP

SELLING AT THE TOP

THE 100 BEST COMPANIES IN AMERICA TO SELL FOR

WILLIAM J. BIRNES

GARY MARKMAN

A Shadow Lawn Press Book

1817

HARPER & ROW, PUBLISHERS, New York
Cambridge, Philadelphia, San Francisco, London
Mexico City, São Paulo, Singapore, Sydney

For Kathe,
Thank you
for being you
G.M.

Portions of the chapter on advertising are reprinted from *We Sell, or Else,*
© Ogilvy & Mather Direct, and are used by permission of Ogilvy & Mather
Direct.

FIRST EDITION

Designer: Dorothy L. Amsden

Library of Congress Cataloging in Publication Data

Birnes, William J.
    Selling at the top.

    1. Sales personnel--United States--Salaries,
commissions, etc.   I. Markman, Gary.   II. Title.
HF5439.7.B57   1985   331.2'0973   84-48579
ISBN 0-06-015424-1

85 86 87 88 89 RRD 10 9 8 7 6 5 4 3 2 1

Contents

ACKNOWLEDGMENTS   vii
FOREWORD   ix
INTRODUCTION   xi

Section ONE: SERVICE

1 ADVERTISING   3
2 BANKING   21
3 EDUCATION PRODUCTS   37
4 INSURANCE   53
5 REAL ESTATE   69

Section TWO: CONSUMER GOODS

1 AUTOMOBILES   85
2 BOOK PUBLISHING   103
3 FOOD   127
4 MICROCOMPUTERS   143
5 RETAIL   161

Section THREE: LIGHT INDUSTRY

1 MAINFRAME COMPUTERS   177
2 MEDICAL EQUIPMENT   195
3 OFFICE FURNITURE   211
4 PHARMACEUTICALS   225

SECTION FOUR: HEAVY INDUSTRY

1	AEROSPACE	241
2	BUILDING	257
3	INDUSTRIAL CHEMICALS	273
4	HEAVY MACHINERY	287
5	PAPER	303
6	PRINTING	315
	INDEX	329
	INDEX OF THE 100 TOP COMPANIES	334

Acknowledgments

O ne of the most difficult tasks facing us when writing *Selling at the Top* was getting an accurate overview of the sales profession. We needed to consult with someone who is intimately involved in sales as a professional, yet not involved in the same way as the salespeople and managers we were interviewing. Although we knew that a sales headhunter would fit the bill, we were reluctant to speak to one. We'd heard so many headhunters describe their profession as a numbers game based on the philosophy, "The more resumes you throw against the wall, the more that will stick." Thus, we approached Richard Harris with considerable hesitation. However, after speaking with him for three hours at our first fifteen-minute interview, we knew that we would never label him a "headhunter." Richie—as he likes to be called—confirmed then and at many subsequent meetings that he is a recruitment professional in every sense of the word. Richie's unique view of sales recruitment, his meticulous research, and his absolute commitment to both his clients and candidates, showed us the world of sales recruitment as it ought to be.

But as much help as Richie gave us with the book, he confirmed something which is even more valuable to us personally. Richie Harris showed us once again that nice guys finish first.

In addition, we would like to thank the following:

AT&T; Advanced Systems, Inc.; Air Products and Chemicals, Inc.; Jackie Alaimo; Allstate Insurance Co.; Ally & Gargano Inc.; Altos Computer Systems; American Cyanamid Company; Apollo Computer Inc.; Apple Computer, Inc.; Ellen Atkinson; BBDO, Inc.; BankAmerica Corporation; Bell & Howell: Better Homes & Gardens Real Estate; Big Three Industries, Inc.;

Blount, Inc.; The Boeing Company; Bowne & Co., Inc.; CYMA; Carter Hawley Hale Stores Inc.; Cencor, Inc.; Centex Corporation; Century 21 Real Estate Corp.; Champion International Corp.; Chrysler Corp.; Citicorp; Compaq; Connecticut General Life Insurance Co.; Control Data Corp.; Joel Coopersmith; Leslie Coopersmith; Cordis Corporation; D. V. Schiavello Enterprises; Henry Daze; Joseph DePaul; Della Femina, Travisano & Partners; De Luxe Check Printers, Inc.; Dexter Corp.; John Dickinson; Digital Equipment Corp.; R. R. Donnelley & Sons Co.; Terry Donovan; Mike Edelhardt; Eli Lilly and Company; Executive Compensation Service, Inc.; Farmers Group Inc.; Fleming Companies, Inc.; Ford Motor Co.; GF Corporation; General Dynamics Corp.; General Motors Corp.; Gourmet Dinner Club; Great Northern Nekoosa Corp.; Grumman Corp.; Hammermill Paper Co.; Harper & Row Publishers, Inc.; Haworth, Inc.; Herman Miller Inc.; Hewlett-Packard Co.; Holt, Rinehart & Winston; Honda Motor Co., Ltd.; Mel Hornick; Houghton Mifflin Company; IBM Corp.; IVAC; International Paper Co.; K mart Corp.; Kaufman and Broad, Inc.; Ronnie Kavner; Kathe Kendall; Koger Properties, Inc.; Lockheed Corp.; R. H. Macy & Co., Inc.; Glenn Marcus; Peter McAlister; McDonnell Douglas Corp.; McGraw-Hill Inc.; The Mead Corporation; Medtronic, Inc.; Merck & Co., Inc.; Merrill Lynch & Co., Inc.; Metropolitan Life Insurance Co.; Steve Mirsky; Mike Mitchell; Monsanto Company; Moore Business Forms, Inc.; John Munroe; Ogilvy & Mather International, Inc.; Pandick, Inc.; Paramus Honda; Pfizer Inc.; Lee Pierson; Ron Pisaturo; Potamkin Cadillac; Prentice-Hall, Inc.; The Prudential Life Insurance Co. of America; Pulte Home Corp.; Jane Rafal; John W. Rafal Associates, Inc.; Ken Rutledge; Ryan Homes, Inc.; Rykoff-Sexton, Inc.; Ryland Group Inc.; Sales Recruiters International, Ltd.; Robert Santa-Morena; Stan Scherer; G. D. Searle & Co.; Sears Merchandise Group; Security Pacific Corp.; Shearson Lehman Brothers, Inc.; Squibb Corp.; Steelcase Inc.; Joseph Stevens; Robert Sturtevant; Super Valu Stores, Inc.; Sysco Corp.; TECA Corp.; TeleVideo Systems, Inc.; Toyota Motor Corp.; U.S. Home Corp.; The Upjohn Co.; William Usher; Paul Vasi; Charles Walther; Wang Laboratories Inc.; Nancy Waack; Westinghouse Electric Corp.; Westwood Lincoln Mercury; Wetterau Incorporated; Richard Wohl; Bill Woodall; F. W. Woolworth Co.; Xerox Corp.; Young & Rubicam Inc.

and

Sales Personnel Report, Twenty-ninth Edition, 1984/85
Executive Compensation Service, Inc.
a subsidiary of The Wyatt Company
Two Executive Drive
Fort Lee, N.J. 07024

Foreword

Selling is the bedrock of American industry. Good products have failed in the marketplace and products of lesser quality have succeeded due to the ability—or lack of same—of the sales force. Highly qualified people have been rejected as candidates for jobs because they couldn't sell themselves effectively, and candidates with lesser qualifications have been hired because they could. Products are sold. Services are sold. People are sold. But what is selling all about? Is there a single, universal way to sell? Can soda be sold the same way that beer can be sold? Can cars be sold the same way that F-111 fighters can be sold? Are there universal principles of selling that apply across the board? Do principles of selling change through the years or are there immutable truths?

I got my start in advertising by selling myself: my abilities, my enthusiasm, my dedication. But I've said that if today I were to interview Jerry Della Femina when he was first starting out, I wouldn't hire him. Why not? Selling—both in and out of the advertising industry—has become highly specialized. The science of demographics has been refined to an art. Technology has impacted on advertising as well as on every other industry. If you want to sell—products, services, yourself—you've got to keep current. You've got to know what's happening today. It's been said that you don't really sell; you find out what people want and what they need. And then they'll come to you for it. But the key is to find out what people want and need. One of the bedrock principles of my agency is that we talk to people—the people who are buying the products and services our clients are selling. We talk to our clients about their business. I insist that my people learn our clients' business well enough to go work for the client. It's hard work, and you've got to be creative—and original. Creativity is the key ingredient in all selling—not only in advertising. Stale doesn't sell bread and it won't sell anything else either. It's been said that in advertising all your creativity is gone by the time you're thirty-five. I say that creativity—independent thought and original ideas—can be eternal. As eternal as the spirit of the men and women who are willing to dedicate themselves to being the best that they can be, and who are willing to get up every morning and do their jobs with the same bright enthusiasm that they had their very first day. Creativity is not a gift. You won't find it under your Christmas tree. You can't buy it. Creativity is effort . . . and sweat. Creativity comes from the willingness to fail and to pull yourself up and try again. Creativity comes from the willingness to hear a thousand no's and to keep striving for that one yes. Creativity is guts.

JERRY DELLA FEMINA
President,
Della Femina, Travisano & Partners

Introduction

The research for *Selling at the Top* has focused on the most important aspects of how we rated the individual companies: salary and commission, company support for representatives in the field, and the trends within the individual company which will affect the sales representatives favorably or unfavorably. The purely financial aspects of selling, such as salaries, commissions, and direct bonuses and cash incentives, are easily added up and averaged and thus can be used as common denominators. But other areas, such as the support a sales representative on the road receives from the home office or the direct access he or she has to the service manager or engineer to answer a client's technical questions, can't be reduced to simple numbers. For these, we have relied on what salespeople have told us about their companies.

What we learned from our interviews with the individual representatives allowed us to develop our across-the-board common demoninators. Our first is compensation: a hybrid figure that consists of straight salary and bonus/commission. The compensation figure varied from industry to industry because there is no separation of salary from bonus/commission in some industries. Consequently, only total compensation—the hybrid figures—were available. In other industries: auto sales, for example, different companies treat salary in different ways. One dealership pays its sales personnel a small salary but supplements their income with an advance against future commissions. Other dealerships provide their salespeople with company cars, gasoline, and a large expense account. Still others provide their salespeople with sales incentives such as bonus points and commission escalators, but pay them no salary at all and charge them rental demonstration cars from the dealership. Our industry comparisons had to account for such differences between companies and between industries. Consequently, the figures are listed in two forms.

For each industry, a median figure is listed that reflects the salary plus bonus/commission of a prototypical sales representative. In some industries such as medical supplies and pharmaceuticals, the prototypical sales representative has been with his or her company for two years. Thus, the median figure reflects the total compensation of a sales person after two years on the job. In the medical equipment industry, a sales person who has been in the industry for two years earns a median compensation of $32,100, and the median commission rate is 2 percent. How a company fares against this "standard" determines its place in the industry rankings. If a company's combined salary and bonus/commission compensation package is more than 10 percent above the median, the company receives a 5. If it is more than 10 percent below, the company receives a 1. The other rankings fall between the two:

RANK	MEANING
1	*The company's figure is more than 10 percent below the industry median figure.*
2	*The company's figure is more than 5 percent but less than 10 percent below the industry median.*
3	*The company's figure is within (plus or minus) 5 percent of the industry median.*
4	*The company's figure is more than 5 percent but less than 10 percent above the industry median.*
5	*The company's figure is more than 10 percent above the industry median figure.*

It is important to note that the company rankings are only relative to one another within the same industry and cannot be used to compare companies in different industries. For example, in the most obvious instance, Company "A" in pharmaceuticals may have a compensation ranking of 3, while Company "B" in retailing may have a compensation ranking of 5. But because of the differences in the industry medians between the pharmaceutical and retailing industries, Company A's compensation, reflected in dollar figures, may actually be higher. In a less obvious instance, it would be inappropriate to compare AT&T, one of the major companies in the mainframe computer and office automation industry, with Compaq or Apple, even though the two companies compete within the small business office environment. AT&T's primary market at this time is focused on the large corporate networked office environment, while both Compaq and Apple are selling desktop personal computers that either stand alone and run commercially packaged software or are lassoed into very elementary multiterminal configurations. Neither computer company at this time is selling a product based on the strength of a resident network that links different terminals within a large multiuser environment. Therefore, AT&T and Compaq are in different industries according to our survey rankings, although both sell computers that run the same software. Industries, and therefore companies within different industries, can be compared by looking at the industry median and using the rankings as they apply to the industry median.

In our survey, sales representatives cited the following as important factors in the area of company support: classroom training, field training, internship on the job, technical informational support, direct product support, clerical and administrative support within the company offices, and the use of a company car. We used these as the basic support factors in determining the best companies to sell for. Because the support factors are necessarily objective, the companies are not ranked against one another directly, but are measured against the objective standard as if it were a benchmark. In other words, our respondents were asked how many of these support factors are provided by their companies. It is possible that every company within a given industry might receive a rank of "0" simply because it is not standard practice in that industry for the company to provide almost all of the support. This doesn't mean that the company is not a good company to work for; it only means that this level of support, albeit low, is the industry standard.

The rankings are on a scale of from 0 to 5, with 0 indicating the "zero support condition," in which the company provides absolutely no support whatsoever. This would apply to independent commission representatives who must function as independent distributors supplying their own marketing and product support.

RANK	MEANING
0	*Company offers no support; the sales person provides and pays for everything.*
1	*Company only supplies one of the support factors.*
2	*Company supplies two support factors.*
3	*Company supplies most support factors, but a major factor is missing.*
4	*Company supplies most support factors, but a minor factor is still missing.*
5	*Company supplies all support factors.*

In addition to the support rankings, we have added explanatory comments where we felt the rankings themselves require some elaboration.

This brings us to the issue of intangible factors. Our research revealed that intangible factors are important because with a simple total of numbers and rankings there was often something still missing from the full picture of some of the companies within the industry. These intangibles varied from company to company, but almost always had to do with the trends within an industry or the trends within a specific company. We listed the intangibles in this way:

RANK	MEANING
[− −]	*There is an additional factor which may have a strong negative impact on a sales representation for this company.*
[−]	*There is an additional factor which may have some negative impact on a sales representation for this company.*
[+]	*There is an additional factor which may have some positive impact on a sales representation for this company.*
[+ +]	*There is an additional factor which may have a strong positive impact on a sales representation for this company.*

As an example, let's say that Company "A" is rumored to be merging with Company "B," and that if the merger goes through, 50 percent of Company A's sales representatives will be laid off while Company B's sales people will pick up additional product to sell. In a case such as this, Company A would receive a [− −] and Company "B" a [+ +] if the rumor is considered strong and reliable, whereas their respective rankings would be [−] and [+] if the rumor is considered possible, but not strong. Whenever an intangible indication is made, an explanation follows. However, if no intangible indication is made, it simply means that there are no additional factors that should be considered in evaluating the particular company.

We have attempted to present the most complete industry and company picture possible, utilizing clearly objective standards where possible, such as compensation figures, and using objective standards to explain the inherently subjective responses given by our survey population wherever necessary.

SECTION ONE:
S E R V I C E

ADVERTISING

BANKING

EDUCATION
PRODUCTS

INSURANCE

REAL ESTATE

ADVERTISING

THE TOP FIVE:

1 Ogilvy & Mather, Int'l., Inc.

2 BBDO, Inc.

3 Della Femina, Travisano & Partners

4 Ally & Gargano, Inc.

5 Young & Rubicam Inc.

The advertising industry has become one of the most important services of the post-World War II economy. It encompasses a very broad spectrum of services from representatives who sell space in magazines or newspapers or time slots on radio and television, to representatives for agencies who sell custom market research and targeted advertising to their clients. At the highest levels of the advertising industry, sales representatives for networks and major publications deal directly with the top agencies such as Ogilvy & Mather or Della Femina, Travisano & Partners. At intermediate levels, media representatives deal with the in-house advertising departments of businesses. Nonetheless, at all levels, advertising is an aggressive and important factor in the modern industrial economy.

An executive at Young & Rubicam says, "Advertising is one industry where anonymity is undesirable. Obviously you have to make a splash for your clients. You want the public to know who your clients are. And you want businesses to know who you are." In other words, in the advertising business it pays to advertise yourself, and that is why advertising is an industry of personalities. There are many different facets of advertising sales and these include selling the company to potential clients, selling the client to the public, and selling broadcast time and magazine space to potential advertisers. The advertising sales representative, unlike the representative who sells chemicals and industrial gases or the book rep who sells his trade list to independent bookstores, is a combination of salesman, buyer, and business manager. Often, in small and highly creative advertising firms, the principals do most of the selling as well as the artistic design and the buying of time or space. In the smaller ad agencies, the principals are also the senior managers who make the personnel and financial decisions at the same time they are selling, buying, and creating concepts for their clients. It is no small wonder that in the advertising industry only the most dynamic and driven people survive. In this chapter, we will be describing one of those individuals, Jerry Della Femina, the president of Della Femina, Travisano, our number-three ranked advertising firm.

The advertising industry as a whole is a unique mix of buying and selling. In no other industry described in this book can one find the style of interaction between buyers and sellers that exists in advertising. Buyers of advertising are usually companies that are selling a product or service, and of course, sellers of advertising are representatives of the media—television, radio, newspapers, and magazines—who derive a significant source of income from advertising dollars. Where do advertising agencies fit into this picture? They are the experts; they are the intermediate salespeople who coordinate the interests of the ultimate buyers and the initial sellers of time or space in order to create an effective presentation, a presentation that will sell the product.

Stan Scherer, the president of Pharmaceutical Media, an advertising representative firm for over forty medical and pharmaceutical journals, tells us that even with regard to payment for services, there is a unique interaction between the client company, the ad space seller, and the ad agency. "Although the advertising agencies are being paid by the client companies for the services they render, they usually receive a 15 percent fee from the advertising space sellers for advertising placed." For example, if an ad agency buys $10,000 of advertising space from a magazine, the client company would pay the ad agency $10,000 and the agency would pay the magazine $8,500, leaving a $1,500 fee for the ad agency. Because the advertising agencies are the main cog in the advertising process—selling their clients and buying the services of other sales people—we've focused this chapter on selling at the advertising agencies while simultaneously presenting a picture of block time and space sales from the media representative's perspective.

There are three basic job "tracks" in the advertising industry and, depending on the particular agency, the tracks may or may not cross. The creative track consists of copywriters, copy supervisors, associate creative directors, and creative directors. The creative director is in charge of the entire creative effort of an ad campaign. Although he or she delegates the daily activity, the creative director is ultimately responsible for seeing that ad copy is written, that artwork is done, that media production schedules are kept, and that the physical advertisement is completed on schedule. One creative director comments, "It's an exciting, interesting job, but I use a lot of Rolaids."

Joseph Goldstein, an advertising sales representative for a major television network, explains that selling your services in the advertising industry is

> "I know deep down people are people, but in this business it's hard not to come away with the feeling that they're all scatterbrained idiots."

really selling a product that the account can change at will. He reports that most people buy an advertising agency's expertise to sell their product, but in the creative processes that follow, the client can become so involved that he actually starts calling the shots. Joseph talks about the many deals that have fallen to pieces because the agency representative, the creative staff, and the client all approached the contract from different perspectives, and none of them ever sat on the same side of the table. "I know that deep down people are people, but in this business it's really hard not to come away with the feeling that they're all scatterbrained idiots." This story illustrates Joseph's point: "We had a big account for a nonprescription stomach-soothing medication. It was our first time working for this company's account, and we knew that if we delivered we stood a good chance of getting the company's entire product line. By the way, we're talking about a company worth well over one hundred million dollars. We had a meeting with all of the principals, including the president of both the client company and of our firm, and the client company's ad agency, and we came to an understanding of how the advertising campaign was to be structured. The campaign was to be television intensive, and part of the TV presentation was going to be a computer-generated graphic that showed a man in obvious digestive distress. The computer graphic would show the man waving back and forth and fading in and out to illustrate a queasy feeling. It was going to be a surrealistic effect. Everyone who had to approve anything gave their approvals and we were humming along right on schedule. In fact, it was so smooth I knew something was going to hit the fan. Well, the big day came. The TV spot was done and the agency was ready to present it to the client. Everybody at the agency was really proud of the work, particularly because it was the first time they had ever done anything with computer-generated graphics. And computer graphics in advertising were new to me too. I'll never forget what the client firm's president said after viewing the tape. 'It's great, but I don't like the whole guy waving back and forth. Let's just have his stomach wave back and forth.' Sounded easy, right? Well, you wouldn't believe what they had to go through for that one insignificant change." As it turned out, the responsibility fell upon Joseph's shoulders and he had a considerable amount of legwork to do in order to hold the account together. Often it falls to the representative to step in and pull the contract back together.

Joseph Goldstein explains how he saved the "digestive distress" account at the last minute when all parties were ready to head for the exits: "The agency's media department had hired a computer graphics company to do the work for this commercial, so naturally we went back to them for the changes. They told us it would take three weeks, and trying to be as gentle as possible, we told them they had three hours. Now, you have to understand, computer graphics in advertising was relatively new and no one at the agency really understood the process. The way this type of graphic is created is to create individual frames with the computer and then shoot the frames one at a time. The process is time consuming (in industry jargon it's 'tape intensive,' which means that the bulk of the work is done by editing tape). Even though we told the computer people that we were likely to lose a multi-million-dollar account if they couldn't deliver and although we offered to pay them accordingly, they told us it just couldn't be done. As I was leaving their office, it seemed that the toughest decision I had to make was whether I should just commit suicide or murder everyone in the ad agency first and then commit suicide. Then out of the blue one of the computer jocks stopped us and handed us a slip of paper. It was just like a spy movie. It said something like, 'Call this number. They'll do it.' And he disappeared back inside. The place we called was in Ohio, and that's when we learned about the computer graphics business."

Joseph and the agency entourage flew out to Ohio the next day. They were met "by a bunch of kids. I swear some of these guys must have been in high school." After a two-hour demonstration of what this company's analog computer could do for their client, they had the client fly out and actually be part of the process. "It was incredible. Here's this kid sitting in front of this big box twisting dials like crazy. It was like a Flash Gordon movie. The client is peering over the kid's shoulder, saying, 'Start the wiggle higher—no, lower.' And the kid would just keep twisting dials. Finally, the client was satisfied, and they just printed the damn thing right then and there. And we had our TV spot."

The agency representatives will often blame their accounts for most of the problems that occur. Sharon Miller, an associate creative director for a large New York agency, says: "The problem is that people change their minds. Most of our clients simply don't understand the problems they can create with minor changes, and if we try to tell them, they think we're telling them that we know more about their business than they do." Bruce Wright, an art director, says, "It can get discouraging. I've lost a lot of good artists who couldn't take the way their work was being bastardized. What many commercial artists don't realize is that commercial art is commercial first and art second." Sharon adds, "The advertising business is highly competitive and your big accounts know that they can hold that over your head. Although I've seen our senior management people tell an account to take his business and put it where the sun doesn't shine, that has to be a management call from the very top. We creative folks just get paid to create."

But sometimes the clients are right. The Frank Perdue story is famous in industry circles. One source at a small New York agency describes Frank Perdue as "uglier than yesterday's dinner," and complains, "He could possibly sell chickens, but only to another chicken." According to the story, Frank Perdue insisted that he could sell chickens and persisted in being included in the ad campaign. Despite early opposition, his advertising campaign has been a major success by all standard product and character recognition indexes and by the resulting growth in sales. Of course, Frank Perdue now has one of the most recognized faces in the United States. Yet, as Sharon says, "By and large, the client is an anathema to the creative departments."

Advertising agencies sell space as well as air time. Joseph Goldstein's counterpart in the magazine advertising industry is Ellen Atkinson, a district advertising sales manager for Ziff-Davis' *PC Magazine*, one of the leading computer magazines in the IBM PC and PC-compatible environment. Ellen comments on high-tech advertising: "Reps must be educators. What has happened in the computer and other high-tech industries is that some companies have really made it quite big. Apple Computer is probably the best-known computer hardware company which went from a basement-garage operation to a multibillion-dollar business, and there are many software companies which have also made it quite big, including companies such as VisiCorp, Lotus, and Microsoft, just to name a few. As these companies grew, the markets they attempted to reach grew and so did their advertising needs. Typically, these companies started out by using either in-house advertising people or small advertising firms, but as their business expanded, they went to larger, better-known and more established advertising agencies." As Ellen discovered, however, some of the largest and best ad agencies, while being exceptionally proficient at advertising, were not very knowledgeable about computers. Ellen says, "It takes quite a bit of time working with computers to really understand some of the subtleties, and typically the large ad agencies didn't have staff people who had worked with computers." An advertising industry source agrees. "When the computer hardware and software industry boomed to its current level, its presence was forcibly thrust upon many industries that hadn't been paying much attention to the high-tech goings-on. Advertising was one of those industries." Jean Templeton at Ogilvy & Mather, our number-one rated advertising agency, points out, "Now we have staff people who are knowledgeable about all aspects of computers. In the early stages of the computer industry boom we didn't, but we learn fast." Ellen adds that in some cases, ad agencies didn't learn fast

"Selling for magazines like Time *is extremely prestigious. It's different from selling for a trade publication or . . . other well-known magazines . . ."*

enough, and she recounts a story in which she saved one account executive from making a very costly mistake: "At *PC Magazine*, my staff and I always stay on top of the latest developments in the computer field. It's our job. I'd heard about a new software product that was going to revolutionize the microcomputer industry. I called on the advertising firm that was representing the company and met with the product's account executive, a very intelligent and dedicated woman. I gave her all the reasons why she should advertise in *PC Magazine*, but she just shook her head. She had already committed her print advertising budget and said that I was too late." So what did Ellen do? "I had a feeling that this lady wasn't too knowledgeable about the computer side of the ad business, so I asked her to show me the list of magazines she'd placed ads in." Ellen was surprised to find that nearly half of the magazines were specific to the Apple computer line! What was so surprising? "The software would not run on an Apple computer. It was designed strictly for IBM and IBM-compatible computers. Not only would the advertising dollars have been wasted, but the software company would have had the additional, and expensive, problem of dealing with a lot of very irate Apple computer owners who had ordered the software. When I explained the problem to the account executive, she was so grateful that I not only got that account but many more accounts she has since sent my way." Ellen points out that trade magazines tend to pay sales reps better than the more traditional and better established magazines. Rob Stevens, a space sales representative for *Time* magazine, agrees. "True, but when you sell for a magazine like *Time*, there are quite a few perks that come along with the territory." And an industry analyst adds, "Selling for magazines like *Time* is extremely prestigious. It's completely different from selling for a trade publication or even selling for other well-known magazines such as *Glamour, Mademoiselle, Vogue, Redbook, Ladies' Home Journal,* and *Better Homes and Gardens.*" And Ellen adds, "Our sales reps can earn in the mid-to-high five figures."

The advertising market is as aggressive in the numerous smaller publications as in the major magazines. And in a highly competitive market, the smaller magazines encounter many of the same problems in selling advertising space to customers and agencies that the major magazines do. Stan explains how his company is able to offer magazine clients benefits that would be unavailable to them if they used an in-house advertising sales staff: "Because we represent forty-three journals and trade publications, we can sell an advertiser a package. Instead of investigating and spending time listening to presentations from many independent publications, an advertiser can speak to one of our sales reps and be convinced that his product is receiving the widest coverage possible. The concept of a rep service is valuable to our clients because in many instances we are able to sell space in their journal as part of a complete coverage package that they might not be able to sell on their own as a single publication. The service is also valuable to advertisers and their agencies because we can offer complete coverage with one sales call."

Stan comments on financial compensation for sales people in the print market: "Space sales reps selling for consumer publications can earn more than the publisher and, in fact, if you look at most of the publishers today, you'll see that they've come up through the sales ranks." And at Stan's company, PMI? "The first-year people I hire earn between $45,000 and $50,000. My sales reps work on a straight commission basis. We charge our client publications between 10 and 20 percent on the advertising space we sell, and our reps earn between 5 and 7 percent of what they sell. That's on net advertising dollars minus the standard 15 percent agency fee."

For comparison, the salaries on the agency side of advertising range from $40,000 to $45,000, (not including bonuses, which vary considerably) for a creative director to $15,000 to $20,000 for a copywriter.

Considerable attention in advertising has been centered on Jerry Della Femina, the president and chief sales representative of our number-three ranked company, Della Femina, Travisano, and Partners. Jerry authored the foreword to this book. It took Jerry Della Femina a long time to break into the advertising business and a long time after that to represent his own company. The story of how Jerry broke into the business is an interesting one. After a number of unsuccessful interviews, he decided to take a dramatic approach to represent his ability to sell. For four successive days he mailed ads he'd created to the chairmen of different ad agencies, signing them only J.D.F.: no other identification. On the fifth day, he hand-delivered his ad personally. On receiving the fifth ad in five days, Daniel Karsh of Daniel and Charles Inc. wanted to know who the hell J.D.F. was. Shortly thereafter, Karsh received a call: "Hi. I'm J.D.F. When can I come in for an interview?" An unusual but effective door-opener. At his interview, Jerry offered to work for free for three months as a trial period to prove himself. Instead, he received a token salary of one hundred dollars a week. This was more money than he'd ever made in his life, and the rest of the story is advertising history.

Jerry Della Femina says, "You see, the advertising business has changed. Advertising agencies used to take chances, but not any more. Today I wouldn't hire myself as I was hired back then because the ads I created then were selling the ad agencies. Today, advertising agencies don't want to see ads selling agencies. They know how to do that. They want to see ads selling products." Jerry continues: "If Jerry Della Femina were to break into advertising today, he would have to put together a portfolio of twenty product ads and pound the Madison Avenue pavement until he connected. He'd be looking to go to work for a large agency to learn the ropes. The key to advertising today is learning about your client's business. Right now, if I wanted to, I could go to work in a number of different fields just because I've studied them extensively. If you don't understand your client's business, how can you possibly sell for him?"

Youth is a primary characteristic of the successful representative in today's advertising companies. The people selling and creating ads look to the center of the spending market for their target buyers and today at that center are the children of the baby boom generation, consuming products and spending their parents' money. Young representatives can talk to this market and can relate to the types of music, art, design, and products that are capturing center stage. Representatives who have lost touch with that market because of age soon find themselves out of the mainstream of advertising activity. The slogan of the late '60s—"don't trust anyone over thirty"— has reemerged in today's advertising world with a new meaning. In advertising today, thirty is often considered the age of graceful retirement, and it is assumed that most creativity is gone by thirty-five. Jerry Della Femina laughs, "I'm ancient in this business. Last month some of my people came to me all excited because they had just signed a rock band for one of our accounts. It's a big, popular band, but I'd never heard of them. When they first mentioned its name I thought they were talking about a disease."

Successful agency representatives are taught early in their careers to speak directly to consumers before developing any elaborate sales pitches. And it is a piece of advice that Jerry Della Femina points to time and again as a centerpiece of any successful representative's campaign. "The one way to really know what people want is to ask them," he says. For example, a representative for another major advertising agency cites the famous General Foods campaign in which consumer testing discovered that the public wanted less rather than more. General Foods had developed a new cake mix to which only water needed to be added. This type of product is generally an agency or manufacturer's representative's dream because it means that the mix is easy to use, even for, in one industry representative's words, "the functionally incompetent." A source at General Foods confirms the enthusiasm for the product's early promoters. "We were really excited. It was a breakthrough." But the new cake mix was the biggest dud to hit the market

—"don't trust anyone over 30"— has new meaning. In advertising today, 30 is often considered the age of graceful retirement, and ... most creativity is gone by 35.

in years; it literally died on the store shelves. "We were baffled," our source at General Foods reported. "We knew the product was good and our older product, which this one replaced, had been a very big seller." "To find the problem, we test marketed the product," says the representative for the advertising agency, "and the result was so amazing, we had to laugh. Housewives, who of course are our prototypical purchasers of the cake mix, were used to adding an egg to their cake mixes. Even though our mix already had the egg in it, housewives still felt that they were shortchanging their families by not adding their own fresh eggs, and so they didn't buy it. However, the problem was easily solved. We just remanufactured the mix without the egg, so the egg had to be added along with the water." And sales skyrocketed. This, according to Jerry Della Femina, is an example of listening to the buyer's concerns before rushing to market with a new campaign.

For an agency representative (also called an account executive), the primary job according to Jerry Della Femina, is not to get new accounts, but "to be damn sure you don't lose the old ones." While all companies try to land as many new accounts as they can, the running accounts represent a continued source of income. Therefore, maintaining these accounts and making sure that the client is satisfied with the representative's concern for the product and the agency's ability to deliver the services must be the highest priority of the account executive. "The ideal account executive," says Jerry, "should have a college degree with a business background, and should have worked in a business other than advertising for a few years. The theme of 'know your client's business' always comes across loud and clear when any agency managers or their representatives talk about the industry. The account executive is a planner, a coordinator, and a worrier. I know when my account executives are doing an excellent job. The client wants to hire them away."

A good account executive can earn about $35,000 a year plus a healthy $2,000 to $5,000 bonus. Although some firms like to hire account executives directly from other businesses or from contacts with their clients, others begin their account executives on a lower rung of the ladder. These positions as junior or assistant account executives or account coordinators pay an average of $20,000. They are "dues paying" as well as learning positions, with the junior account executive frequently doing the nitty-gritty business such as working up budget numbers and making sure that the details of the account are taken care of. Marlene Dymond, a junior account executive at BBDO International, our number-two ranked company, says she's just a "glorified gofer." However, she expects that the experience she is getting from working with BBDO's accounts will enable her to make the jump to another agency as a full-fledged sales representative.

Two members of our list of top five companies—Della Femina, Travisano & Partners and Ally & Gargano—earned their places as numbers three and four respectively for their intensive focus on the creative side of the industry. In a business where creativity becomes a type of competition between representatives, both companies have been able to create exciting and accomplished campaigns for their clients and develop an aggressive sales-oriented style.

In the advertising industry, the representative must carry much of the burden for the success or failure of his agency. A measure of a representative's success is his or her ability to keep the client satisfied while bringing new accounts into the agency. This is the heart and soul of the account executive's work, and to accomplish it, the account executive has to work very closely with the other departments of the agency. As an executive at Ogilvy & Mather says, "In this business you don't work in a vacuum. Perhaps more than in any other industry, advertising is team effort." An account executive at BBDO agrees. "When I started at another agency I lost an account because my creative people blew it. Not only could they not come up with what the client wanted, but they were subtly trying to sell her away from her idea. Selling was my responsibility." This was a violation of the team concept. The creative staff needs to organize presentations with the management staff, as this example from our BBDO account rep illustrates: "I was handling an account for a major domestic wine producer. We had worked up an idea that was good but which we all felt was lacking something. Then our creative staff came to me with what seemed like a great idea: an ad in which our client's wine beat competing German wines in a wine taste-off at a mock country fair in Germany complete with oompah bands and authentic German flavor. Fortunately, they ran the idea past management before they presented to the client, and that was when they learned that our client's main competition was from French wines. Mistakes like that can sometimes be laughed at and then corrected, but sometimes the effects can be fatal to the account. Management also filled us in on the personal background of our clients: during World War II they had been members of the French underground and they'd all lost family members in very tragic ways. To this day they felt that Germany should have been turned into a parking lot after the war. Somehow I don't think that they'd have been laughing at our misdirected ad campaign." But even without this kind of unusual personal involvement, the client is likely to feel that the agency is simply not doing its job. "In making a mistake like that you're saying two things to your client: 'Your account isn't important enough to me to know who your main competition is, and 'We're so disorganized here that our creative department doesn't talk to our management.' " As Jerry Della Femina adds, "Our cardinal rule is to know the client well enough to be able to work for him, and to make a significant contribution to his business." Thus, in order to survive in the midst of all the competition in the industry, an account executive must be a team player who can coordinate the functions of the entire agency and he must be sure he knows the client's business inside out.

Though Della Femina, Travisano prides itself on its creativity, clients don't get lost there. An account executive within the firm confirms, "Who in this industry is going to have more appreciation and understanding of the creative process than Jerry?" An associate creative director at Della Femina, Travisano & Partners agrees. "Jerry's strength is in his ability to let you run with your ideas. He trusts his people."

The creative side of the business can be the launching pad for careers in high-level management. Amil Gargano, the president and chief executive officer of Ally & Gargano, got his start on the creative side of the business, and it's not surprising that an industry source comments, "Ally & Gargano is one of the best places for creative people to work. They give their creative staff a lot of room to be innovative, and they're small enough that you don't get lost there. If you watch the TV ads for Calvin Klein, Federal Express, and MCI, you can see that Ally & Gargano uses a wide variety of creative approaches in selling."

"We sell, or else" is the title of the tenth anniversary issue of Ogilvy & Mather's catalog for its Direct International Division. Ogilvy & Mather Direct is the largest direct-response advertising agency in the world with offices in San Francisco, Houston, New York, Kuala Lumpur, and Amsterdam, as well as many places in-between. One of the reasons Ogilvy & Mather earned our number-one rating is its company's attitude toward the profession which is communicated by everyone in the organization. It can best be described by David Ogilvy himself. "However many awards we win for creativity, we either

> *... the future of the industry was finally determined when the last holdout among the major advertising agencies started a direct-response division. This was critical because it committed them to a computer-intensive, analysis-oriented technology.*

sell or we get fired." An account executive says, "We're very results conscious. With the sophisticated techniques of demographic analysis that our clients use, we have to be." David Ogilvy adds, "Our clients know to a dollar how much each of our advertisements, TV commercials, and direct mail packages sells."

Direct advertising makes its pitch at its audience, encouraging sales by including coupons or toll-free phone numbers in the advertisement. Unlike media ad campaigns, there is no issue of image building, and the goal is very simple: get the customer to place an order, according to Jean Templeton, an account supervisor at Ogilvy & Mather. Direct-response advertising can reach the customer through the use of the mail, toll-free telephone numbers, coupons, print, radio, and television. At American Express, an executive says, "Two of our most successful ad campaigns have been soliciting credit cards through the mail and via coupons placed at outlets accepting the American Express card." Jean Templeton adds, "The 'take-one-it's-free' coupon approach is very successful because there's not very much waste."

Typically, direct mail advertising is expensive because of the postage and the fact that the returns are usually very low compared to other direct-response methods. "We use bill stuffers a lot. We know that the bill is one envelope the customer is going to open, so by using this method we're able to get past the first hurdle, which is getting the customer to look at the ad and read what the offer is."

The future of advertising lies in the direct-response technology that is now being incorporated into the operations of all of the major advertising agencies and departments within large corporations. According to Jerry Pickholz, president of Ogilvy & Mather Direct/U.S., the future of the industry was finally determined when the last holdout among the major advertising agencies started a direct-response division. This was a critical juncture because it committed the industry to a computer-intensive, analysis-oriented technology. This technology will enable an account executive to say to a prospective client that the agency can communicate directly or interactively with that client's buyer. Imagine a two-way telephone conversation between seller and buyer, with the agency as the intermediary structuring the message, collecting the responses, and interpreting them for the seller. This is what the account executive will be able to offer his clients.

Commenting on the support that direct-response advertising is receiving from broadcasters, another industry analyst says, "As I'm talking to you now, IBM is working on an interactive cable system. Someday it will be commonplace to communicate through your television with a variety of services." An executive at Cablevision of Westchester agrees. "A few years ago CBS Communications lost a bundle on a test package involving interactive cable television. The time wasn't right and there were some technical problems to be worked out. Now that IBM has entered the fray, everybody in the cable industry is convinced we'll have interactive in five years. And it will revolutionize the cable industry. We'll be able to sell direct-response advertising to local establishments and with the telecommunications industry booming, everybody will be shopping via TV. You'll see catalog ordering done through TV on a local basis." A Wall Street analyst agrees: "The Street is watching the cable industry very carefully. Once IBM entered the picture, everyone took notice."

Computers obviously play a very big part in direct-mail advertising because they can identify and isolate a target audience. A manager at Young & Rubicam says, "We bought a demographics computer package with capabilities you wouldn't believe. We can analyze results of our ad campaigns by any zip code in the country." Jean Templeton adds, "We know that our clients can do the same demographic analyses that we can, so we have to be one step ahead in the technology."

Direct-response print ads were the first attempt to communicate interactively with a target audience and have been used by specialty companies, local community advertising agencies, and book clubs for years. After early results showed that direct-response ads could increase sales dramatically, the technology to design, place, and collate the information received became an important part of an account executive's message to prospective clients. An account executive at Ogilvy & Mather says, "We've been using them for a long time and we've learned a lot. For example, ads on the back page of magazines and newspapers draw more than one and a half times the response that the same ad draws when it's inside the publication." Other advertising agencies and media consultants point to the high rate of success direct-response print ads have had in a wide variety of industries. "Designed and placed correctly," another Ogilvy & Mather representative points out, "direct-response ads can even create markets that traditional analyses have overlooked."

Coupon insertion is another effective direct-advertising technique. An account executive at Young & Rubicam explains that although magazine coupons are effective, the most effective coupons are product related. An executive at McGraw-Hill agrees: "We got some phenomenal results selling book/software packages in the computer book industry's heyday of 1982 and 1983. We sold the book/software packages two ways: as a package containing both the book and the software supplement; or as a book alone with a coupon inside the book entitling the purchaser to a discount on the software component." An executive at Hayden Book Company, a publisher of computer books, adds, "We also had great success with the coupon campaign. Customers were tripping over themselves to get those coupons in because it saved them a lot of keypunch time." He was referring to the fact that Hayden sold a number of computer books for beginners in which computer program listings appeared. The reader had the option of keyboarding the programs into the computer himself, or buying the programs already written on a magnetic media disk or tape and entering them that way.

Ogilvy & Mather's Jean Templeton describes how her agency combined different forms of direct-response and highly technical evaluation methods to represent AT&T during the critical divestiture period when the communications giant's customers were concerned about loss of services, and the company was concerned about competition in the hardware and long-distance services market. "AT&T was our most complex account to date. The divestiture was a confusing issue in a lot of ways and AT&T management was very concerned that the public be informed properly and in a completely nonthreatening way about what was going to happen." She adds, "Now that the telephone industry is so competitive, we're working very hard to keep AT&T in the public's eye in a very positive way." She also explains the difficulties in communicating market theory to a company which had previously owned its market through government regulation. "AT&T is an engineering-driven company, and this helps us in two ways.

First, their primary expertise is not marketing because they never had to go out and build a new clientele until now. Therefore, they come to us because marketing is certainly our expertise. Second, because they are an engineering-driven company, their products are always technically superior to the competition's. Let's face it—AT&T is the world leader in communications technology. If anyone is going to have the best-quality product, it's going to be them."

Jean describes the way Ogilvy & Mather used the business executive's need for immediate access to communications technology to sell AT&T's services. "People are mobile and people need to communicate, and the installation of multiple-capability computer telephones in high-traffic public areas such as airports provided Ogilvy & Mather with a handle on selling AT&T. We've mailed over twelve million AT&T credit cards to business customers who were selected from lists supplied by American Express, the *Official Airline Guide*, and selected magazine subscribers. The idea of the cards is to make it as simple as possible to use the computer phones. The cardholder simply inserts the card, reads the instructions, and punches the numbers. Of course, one of the goals of the card campaign is to have the cardholders bypass the discount services such as MCI and SPRINT. The phones also accept American Express cards and soon will also take Visa and

> *. . . the modus operandi of a company comes from the top, and at Della Femina, Travisano & Partners is a man who is a legend. His credo is: "Treat your clients like family."*

MasterCard. This is a type of direct-response in which the means to use the product is placed directly in the buyer's hand. All he had to do was push the buttons, and he was buying AT&T."

Training in the advertising industry varies considerably, and usually depends on the size of the agency. Jerry Della Femina reports, "We try to hire experienced people. We're not set up to do training." At Ogilvy & Mather, Jean Templeton says, "Training is very thorough and is an ongoing process. When I joined the company, I attended three classes a week for three months." Jerry Pickholz adds, "We exchange information with our offices all over the world through our international newsletter, *The Courier*. We share what we have learned with clients and with our network offices."

As indicated earlier, the advertising industry posed unique problems in our evaluation of the industry from the point of view of the account executive or sales representative. The account executive is not an independent representative in the same way that a real estate agent is a representative of the agency and the seller of a piece of property. Advertising is very much a team game, so an account executive without the proper creative support is like a skillful ship captain without a ship. He or she will not fare as well economically or professionally as his or her counterpart at an agency where creative support abounds. Because of this, we have carefully evaluated the creative support offered by the agencies we investigated.

This quote from Stan Winston, the executive creative director at Ogilvy & Mather Direct, best explains why his company was awarded our top spot: "If you're interested in safety and security, then always follow the rules. It's not very challenging, and it's not much fun, but you'll stay out of trouble. If you want to be rich and famous, you'll have to take a riskier path. Challenge the myths. Break the rules. You'll occasionally be labeled an amateur, a lunatic, or worse. But you'll have more fun and your clients will prosper."

We believe that the style with which a business operates on a daily basis and the concern with which a business views and treats its clients starts from the top. If we knew nothing about Ogilvy & Mather other than this quote from an upper echelon manager, we would already have a strong inclination to rate this company highly in the industry. But add to that the strong support the company has from its personnel, its innovative ideas (particularly in looking toward technological progress), and its obvious success rate—both as a corporation and as an employer—and it is clear why they have earned our number-one ranking.

Our number-two spot goes to BBDO International, another giant that cultivates its creative staff. Allen Rosenshine, the company's soon-to-be president and chief executive officer, broke into the business as a copywriter and worked his way up the creative ladder. BBDO's billings increased over 25 percent from 1983 to 1984, and with their large, very successful ad cam-

"Designed and placed correctly . . . direct-response ads can even create markets that traditional analyses have overlooked."

paigns for Dodge, Black & Decker, and Pepsi scheduled for major revisions, they are going to be well set for the rest of 1985. In addition, their commitment to the technological advances that the industry is about to experience makes them an excellent choice for account executives, and deserving of our number-two ranking.

The number-three position was virtually a toss-up between two of the industry's smaller yet most innovative companies: Della Femina, Travisano

> *Advertising is very much a team game, so an account executive without the proper creative support is like a ship's captain without a ship. He will not fare as well economically . . .*

& Partners, and Ally & Gargano. Both companies are known for their exceptional creativity, support for their creative staffs, and a positive work atmosphere. And both companies are growing, with 1984 billings over the quarter-billion-dollar level. However, only one of the companies has a man with the charisma and reputation of Jerry Della Femina. As we stated earlier, the modus operandi of a company comes from the top, and at Della Femina, Travisano & Partners, at the "top" is a man who is a legend in the industry. His credo is: "Treat your clients like they're your family. Be honest and candid with your clients and they'll respect both you and your opinion." When a philosophy like this guides the way business is done, you have an advertising agency that is an excellent place to work.

Our number-five spot goes to Young & Rubicam, another industry giant. They have over sixty years of expertise in the advertising business, combined with a concern for their employees that is unusual in a company this size, and in an industry as temperamental as advertising. An account executive at Y&R says, "In the advertising business, if an account exec loses an account he's usually going to be in the market for a new head, much less a new job. But here, unless you've really screwed up royally, they'll turn you onto another account." Because a company's attitude toward its employees and the attitudes of employees toward their company have been a very important standard by which we've judged the companies in our survey, we believe Young & Rubicam has earned our number-five rank.

ADVERTISING	COMPENSATION	COMMISSION	SUPPORT	INTANGIBLE
1 Ogilvy & Mather, Int'l., Inc.	4		5	
2 BBDO, Inc.	4		5	
3 Della Femina, Travisano & Partners	5		4	
4 Ally & Gargano, Inc.	5		4	
5 Young & Rubicam Inc.	4		5	

The position we used as a basis to compute our rankings is a two-year account executive. The industry median compensation figure is $31,100, including yearly bonus.

BANKING

THE TOP FIVE:

1. Citicorp
2. Merrill Lynch & Co., Inc.
3. Security Pacific Corp.
4. Shearson Lehman Brothers, Inc.
5. BankAmerica Corp.

T he actual roots of modern banking go back to the Middle Ages when institutions such as the Knights Templar transported gold and silver across Europe just after the Crusades. There were banking and lending institutions in Renaissance Italian cities, and these banking houses helped inspire the growth of the merchant class. In the United States today, the banking industry is only just emerging from the restrictions of the New Deal regulatory legislation that was enacted in reaction to banking practices that the government saw as too speculative. Today's account executive is as much a sales representative as he is a loan officer, aggressively seeking new customers for financing packages, leases, and other commercial services.

"Banking is becoming more like an ice cream parlor every day, with a changing menu of rates," according to Alan Jenkins, an account officer with BankAmerica. Jenkins explains that his job is to sell banking services—he calls them financial services—to his commercial accounts. "Selling financial services is what we do in banking because if you can't bring in new customers, the bank won't make any money." According to Jenkins, the industry is changing dramatically to keep up with other financial service institutions. "At BankAmerica we have a lot of flexibility in setting prices for each deal we make. We accommodate our customers as much as we can while staying within the limits of our corporate rate policy." Jenkins describes an equipment leasing arrangement he is putting together for a large industrial client: "The terms of the lease depend largely upon where the customer is financially. We can give him our standard plain vanilla package or show him a menu of different options. The point is that we can give him any flavor he wants that will suit his financial situation."

An industry source reports that because so many bank officers are becoming financial package sales representatives for their institutions, the term "banking" as we understand it may soon be obsolete. The buzzword today is "financial planning." Peter McAllister, an assistant vice-president at Citicorp, agrees. "A financial revolution is under way. The winners will be those banks who are willing to be in the forefront of the move to diversify," he says. And John Rafal, a financial consultant in Connecticut, adds: "It's not just the banks. The revolution is encompassing the entire financial service industry from banks to brokerage houses to insurance companies. The name of the game is diversification. The survivors will be the companies that can offer complete financial services."

Selling financial services is one of the newest sales industries in the United States. From bankers, who are coming out from behind their desks to join a growing financial services sales force, to account representatives from large insurance companies, stockbrokerage houses, and major accounting firms, new professionals are entering the financial service sales industry every month. The industry itself is a hybrid of old fashioned savings and thrift institutions, insurance services, and stock portfolio management combined with newer instruments such as CDs, money market funds, and stock options. Salespeople in this industry work with both the commercial and personal markets, offering combinations of savings, investment, risk management, and financing options that are tailored to individual customer needs. The bottom line, however, is sales and commissions. And the successful sales representative is the one who can show the customer how to make money using the service package offered by his company rather than someone else's. These account representatives sell a service: the growth management of money. And this is a vital service to an entire generation that knows money is more than something to be saved or spent and recognizes it as a form of leverage, a fulcrum that can move even greater amounts of money. Therefore, the account representatives who sell financial services sell the promise of making more money to their customers.

Another key to successful sales in this industry is the diversification of the package the salesperson offers. A package that's weighted too strongly in one direction or another can make a potential investor fearful that his

> *... the term "banking" as we understand it may soon be obsolete. The buzzword today is "financial planning."*

investment will be lost should a particular market weaken. Because diversification is so important and because banking and investment companies are approaching the same customers with the same incentive of combining all financial needs into one package, we have combined the banking and brokerage institutions under one umbrella. The five companies at the top— Citicorp, Merrill Lynch, Security Pacific, Shearson Lehman/American Express, and BankAmerica—have each earned their ranking for their commitment to being on the frontier of the financial services industry as well as for the compensation packages they offer to their account representatives.

Ron Pisaturo, a management consultant and former manager at Citicorp, describes how banking was conducted before the advent of the financial services industry: "Initially, banks sold money and customers came to the bank to buy the money. It was totally a sellers' market. The price the customers paid for the money was, of course, the interest, and the interest was the bank's main source of revenue as well as their biggest expense to depositors." But things have changed considerably. "Today," he continues, "banks have to sell people on depositing funds at their bank, and we've all seen the tremendous proliferation of advertising directed at the individual consumer since banking deregulation took effect."

The interest crunch of the 1970s shook up a lot of people, and some of the people who were the most shaken were the people who ran the banks. Richard Harris, president of Sales Recruiters International, says, "The interest crisis of the late '70s caught a lot of businesses unprepared. It was probably the biggest single factor that triggered the move to diversification in the industry today." John Rafal agrees: "For one, insurance companies got killed. People borrowed against their life insurance policies at 4 percent interest and deposited the money in accounts paying three times that amount or more." Ron Pisaturo adds, "And even some banks got hurt. Some banks had outstanding long-term loans which were bringing in 6, 7, and 8 percent, while the money they were paying to depositors was at the 10 to 12 percent level." Peter McAllister points out, "The credit card industry was also hit very hard. In most states the banks were locked into an 18 percent interest rate by state usury laws, but since they were paying out double-digit interest, they were barely supporting their credit card business. One industry source believes that it was definitely the interest crunch that spurred American Express to diversify in order to protect itself. So the die was cast in the late '70s. The survivors were to be the multifaceted financial institutions that were flexible enough to weather developments in a fluctuating economic climate. The big winners were to be the companies that would use the defense of diversification as an offensive weapon in the 1980s.

Because of the emphasis on sales techniques and the development of client relationships, training in the industry today is unrecognizable compared to what it was even ten years ago. Alan Jenkins recalls that training used to be strictly on the job: "Promotions were usually from within at Bank-America. Those were the days when a bank was a bank. If you'd seen one, you'd seen them all." Peter McAllister adds, "The loan officer of yesteryear has been replaced by what amounts to an account executive: a sales representative who deals with customers as buyers." And because of the need to sell services, there is a new focus on sales training. This professional training reflects the new complexity in the industry. Alan Reeves, a junior relationship manager at Citicorp, says, "They want professionals. I have an MBA from Wharton, and every single person in my training class had at least two years of experience in the field and an MBA. Only one guy wasn't from the Ivies." Nancy Justin, a junior account rep at Shearson Lehman, adds, "In our training class, we were all pretty high-powered people—a few years' experience in the business, some MBAs. Yet the very first thing they told us in training was to forget everything that we had learned in school because now we were really going to learn about finance." Peter McAllister points out how competitive the industry is becoming: "At Citicorp, we give a lot of preference to graduates of certain business schools. The Ivies and Stanford are pretty good door-openers as long as the candidate has an MBA." The training program at Citicorp for junior relationship managers usually lasts between six and nine months. The relationship manager position at Citicorp is like a senior or supervising account executive position at other financial institutions. Alan Reeves explains that relationship managers are in charge of an account. For example, an individual might manage the entire Ford Motor Company account, delegating different aspects of putting together the financial instruments to junior relationship managers.

For new sales representatives at most of the major financial services companies, learning is on a rotating basis. At Shearson Lehman, reps learn by rotating from one type of account to another. One week they may be involved with brokering a municipal bond package for a large construction company and the next week with helping to set up the underwriting for a small computer software company. Alan Jenkins summarizes the change in the industry: "Years ago, it was almost unheard of to bring in outsiders. Promotion was always from within. Now the competition for qualified account managers is incredible. A friend of mine went from making $32,000 a year three years ago to $55,000 now. He was hired away from us by another bank, and after two years somebody else grabbed him."

Computerization and cost cutting are the new watchwords in the financial industry and affect the way account representatives sell their services. As Jim DiOrio, an assistant account executive at Merrill Lynch, says, "We installed fifty new computer terminals in our office so that the terminal sits on a ledge between two of us and swivels. That way we're cutting in half the cost of terminals." An executive at Merrill Lynch reports buying a thousand fast terminals to replace two thousand slow ones. After trade-in, the cost to the company was $100,000, but with the increased speed Merrill Lynch anticipates increasing its business by between $3 million and $6 million. Companies are cutting costs and upgrading their data management facilities to improve their sales and sales support. Faster access time at the terminal means that a single account representative can do more work, service more clients, and sell more complete financial packages. In the financial industry, the product is information, and the sales representatives market this information. Account executives from most of the major companies report that the majority of their working time is spent either on the telephone or in front of a terminal, usually both at the same time. This new type of sales person is the harbinger of a new type of American economy, one based not on the production and sales of manufactured goods but on the delivery of information-based services and advice. This trend is reflected in the gross national product which reveals that a greater portion of the product sold in the United States is service-oriented rather than manufactured product.

The selling of loans and other financial packages directly to the American business and private consumer was, in part, a direct outgrowth not only of the inflationary 1970s but also of the deteriorating international financial marketplace at that time. Ron Pisaturo discusses Citicorp's outstanding foreign loan situation in the early and mid '70s: "The domestic corporate loan market was becoming highly competitive, particularly with the entry of the brokerage houses. It's just as easy for a corporation to float stock or bonds as it is to carry loans." Citicorp started to look at the consumer market with an eye to selling not only traditional banking services in that arena, but comprehensive investment and loan packages as well. Citicorp planned its entry into the consumer banking market very carefully. John

Reed, who was in charge of all back office operations for corporate accounts, and at thirty-one, the youngest vice president in the history of Citicorp, was asked to take two years off to research consumer banking. John's research project was so successful that Citicorp was soon organized into two separate divisions, corporate and consumer, and John was made the head of the consumer division.

Today John Reed is the chairman of the board largely because he helped to shape a financial sales marketplace at a time when there was an unrecognized but pent-up consumer demand for it. And although it may be unrealistic for most Citicorp personnel to aspire to the chairmanship of the corporation, if it can be done, it will be done through the sales career track as John Reed demonstrated. One executive points out that the ranks of senior management are filled with people who have been with the bank throughout their entire careers. But there are some exceptions. If there is a critical need for immediate expertise, particularly in the areas of sales and marketing, the bank will hire from outside, but it's an unusual situation. Corporate policy is similarly structured at Security Pacific, according to an executive there. Their long-standing tradition is one of rewarding longevity with the company but there are instances when they also have to go outside. The banking business today is too complex to expect that all your top people can advance from within. Other sources confirm that the impact of sales and marketing is so strong that the commercial banks, normally the most traditional of financial institutions, are restructuring their management to bring profit-oriented executives up through the ranks quickly. It seems that the thrift institutions have just discovered sales, and they can't get enough of them.

Innovations in banking services actually began on the corporate side of the market, according to an executive at BankAmerica. Ron Pisaturo agrees: "It used to be that banks sold corporate loans only for the interest, but within the last ten or fifteen years that began to change. Banks seemed to realize, as did successful businesses in many other industries, that their customers had

> *And although it may be unrealistic for most Citicorp personnel to aspire to the chairmanship of the corporation, if it can be done, it will be done on the sales career track . . .*

needs, and that if they could meet those needs, there would be profit for all."
So today, it is quite common to find banks supplying corporations with
collection services, letters of credit, factoring, and credit checking services,
all for a fee and all as part of a larger financial services package. For example,
if Calvin Klein receives a $10,000 order from a new customer, the manufac-
turing company doesn't want to be bothered with the expense and additional
work of credit checking. So they turn to their bank for these services. The
bank may advance Calvin Klein the $10,000 with a 1 percent discount sub-
tracted as a service fee and within a specified time period, they repay the full
$10,000 to the bank. In another variation of this arrangement, the bank may
actually buy the account receivable for the full $10,000, with the understand-
ing that they will actually pay Calvin Klein the $10,000 when the receivable
falls due, usually after thirty days. Neither the customer nor Calvin Klein
would pay the bank any interest in this type of arrangement. However, in
exchange for validating the customer's credit rating and collecting the
money, the bank has interest-free use of the $10,000 for thirty days. In this
way, the bank has acted as Calvin Klein's collection agency and accounts
manager and in return has been granted free use of Calvin Klein's money. In
reality, the bank has free use of at least two or three million dollars from a
number of customers which could be invested, loaned to other banks or corporations, or moved in and out of international money markets for thirty
days. When the account falls due, the bank might be able to repay Calvin
Klein with money from another account or it might roll over its investments
in other markets to pay Calvin Klein and invest somewhere else. Throughout
the course of a year, the bank can make a sizable profit with very little risk
because it is not using any of its own money. These are the types of
arrangements that the account representative can bring in to benefit both
the client and the bank. This new banking is changing the face of the entire
financial industry. As BankAmerica's Alan Jenkins says, "Any variation of
this bank-to-client arrangement that you can imagine is probably done, and
it's up to the account representative to structure the deal in the bank's
best interest."

Ron Pisaturo comments on selling collateral loans to industry. "Typically banks will lend money up to 50 percent of the value of inventory but
they have to check to make sure the inventory is real. This is also part of the
account representative's job. In addition to selling the customer on the bank
and the terms of the financial package, the representative has to manage the
credit evaluation and the valuation of the inventory. This is especially difficult
when the collateral is something other than a depreciable asset. When it
comes to checking the receivables that a company wants to use as collateral, many banks set up dummy corporations whose sole purpose is to
call the company's clients and verify that, in fact, the merchandise was
ordered. To do this without embarrassing their client, they may make believe

they're an independent auditing company. They may represent themselves as XYZ auditors doing ABC company's annual audit and confirming an order for ten thousand widgets on April 29." But as it turns out, sometimes the banks get fooled. A banking executive recalls one of the big scams in the industry: "It involved a loan to an olive oil importing company based on their inventory of X tons of olive oil. The olive oil was stored in a huge tank, much like a water tank. The account representative actually had to go out to the location of the tank, put on a hard hat, and climb up the ladder to the top and see for himself that there was olive oil there. Can you guess the scam? Ninety percent of the tank was filled with water, and the ten percent that was olive oil rose to the top."

Lease packaging is another popular sales item on the corporate or commercial side of the banking and finance industry. The sales of lease packages can run into the hundreds of millions of dollars and can be an important component of any financial arrangement sold by a senior account representative to a new corporate client. Because leasing arrangements are becoming increasingly common throughout a variety of industries, banks and their subsidiary leasing companies are becoming the largest single property owners in the United States today. Who owns the largest fleet of nonmilitary commercial aircraft? United Airlines? American? TWA? In fact, the answer is Citicorp.

Citicorp's account executives have been very successful in the leasing market because they can command the large sums of money necessary to buy the products from the manufacturers, and they can push leases in a very hungry corporate market. Large corporations don't like to sink huge sums of capital into property, especially high maintenance property such as aircraft. Leasing has become a popular alternative to outright ownership in business today because it does not tie up capital unnecessarily and because favorable tax laws allow for write-offs that exceed normal depreciation schedules. Banks typically carry the paper on large leases and their account representatives solicit potential customers among major corporations. A typical leasing arrangement usually begins when a carrier such as American Airlines submits a proposal to Boeing for twenty 767 aircraft. But if American doesn't want to pay cash for the planes and Boeing doesn't want to carry the paper, American and Boeing can go to their account manager at Citicorp who structures the lease package. Under the terms of the package the account manager designs, Citicorp will borrow the money from its correspondent banks or from the Fed, buy the planes from Boeing, retaining title to them, and then will lease them to American. At the expiration of the lease, American can either buy them outright for a cash settlement or can work with the Citicorp representative to sell the 767s to an airline from a third world country or to a smaller regional carrier. With this arrangement, American gets their aircraft with a comparatively small financial drain on the company, Boeing gets paid up front from Citicorp, and Citicorp earns double or triple its cash outlay on the lease. Thus, as an executive at American says, "Nobody on earth owns anything except the banks."

The transformation of bank executives into account executives and the aggressive growth of financial services sales among investment bankers and brokerage houses has created a new industry and new opportunities for bankers turned sales representatives. This growth has been pushed along not only by the high interest rates of the middle to late 1970s, but by the federal government's deregulation of the entire financial industry. And the move toward further deregulation continues.

The history of almost all current financial regulation begins with the Glass-Steagall Act of 1934 which created a de facto separation between the banking industry and the investment brokerages. Ironically, the beginning of federal regulation was a reaction to the stock market crash of 1929 which, according to Merrill Lynch, was attributed incorrectly to overzealousness on the part of stock sales representatives at the major brokerages. The government pointed the finger at the account executives for being too aggressive and at the brokerages themselves for giving away credit and holding too small a margin. A Merrill Lynch financial manager says the market collapsed because there was too little cash to support it and as a result, "the feds tied our hands and put the bankers behind the desks. Investment and thrift became two different entities that weren't allowed to mix. Now it's all chang-

> ... as an executive at American says, "Nobody on earth owns anything except the banks."

ing and bankers are becoming salesmen again." Due to deregulation, an account manager at Merrill Lynch explains, the law has been interpreted almost out of existence. He believes the tendency in the financial industry today is toward further and further deregulation, and although the Glass-Steagall Act is not likely to be repealed, it may literally be interpreted to death. The net result is an aggressive sales campaign that combines the elements of thrift and investment. The Merrill Lynch manager adds: "You can see it in the television ads that tell you to come and meet your personal banker. The personal banker is really the bank's sales representative who's going to sell you services. NOW accounts, equity line financing, CD checking, consumer loans, IRAs—these are all consumer financial items. Banks sell them just like we sell our investment packages. The key is full-service financial planning. We're selling it at Merrill Lynch just like they're selling it at Shearson Lehman and at Sears."

The cardinal rule of banking, or of any other industry, is to take in more capital than you spend. And, as one industry analyst indicates, some banks are in danger of violating that rule. "There are a number of banks whose international account representatives have been so successful overseas that the banks are now overexposed to foreign debt, particularly in OPEC and third world countries which have almost no resiliency in their economies." With oil prices falling, the OPEC countries are finding their fragile econ-

> *"The service reps who are the most diligent, ambitious, and hardworking are exploring other avenues of financial vehicles for their clients, and when they gain the confidence to provide the full range of financial vehicles, they leave to go out on their own."*

omies overextended by the costs of industrial development, and the third world countries have consistent problems with debt service. Some U.S. banks have recognized this as a serious problem and have directed their account representatives to reduce their considerable liabilities overseas. But other banks, such as Continental Illinois, have been battered by problems stemming from bad loans.

The fallout from the changes and expansion in the banking and finance industry could be widespread, according to account representatives. Unchecked sales or sales not regulated by any governing body could conceivably start a run on mutually dependent banks. If banks, overextended by sales of bad loans to developing countries, are threatened with collapse and turn to their correspondent banks for help, the resulting wave of insolvency could spread back across the ocean right up the money chain to the neighborhood commercial bank on Main Street. Even now there are doomsayers in the banking and finance industry who predict a collapse of a major U.S. bank before the next decade. As a banking officer comments, "You can't have your loans backed by prayers and get away with it forever."

The aggressive selling of banking and financial packages is also making it easier for large interstate banking corporations to swallow up local commercial or neighborhood banks. But according to Mike Conte, an account manager at Merrill Lynch, banking laws designed to protect the local institutions from the big fish are anachronisms. "Interstate banking laws, especially the regulations which were supposed to keep community banks alive, are being interpreted away by the courts." He points to the McFadden Act, which specifically prohibits banks from having interstate branches. "If McFadden were enforced, salesmen like me wouldn't be able to operate between New York and New Jersey. If you lived in New Jersey you could bank in New Jersey, and if you worked in New York you could bank in New York, but the same bank couldn't have branches in both states. Now the whole concept of bank branch offices is changing because of electronic fund transfers, and the small banks are going to go the way of the steam engine." Alan Jenkins points to the role of the banking services account executive as a catalyst in the transformation of modern banking. Because a bank representative can sell "over-the-phone" banking as part of a special customer service to draw new clients into savings-checking-investment-loan packages, it almost doesn't matter what happens with the banking laws. The future will see electronic funds transfer on a national scale between many full-service divisions of the same financial corporation. People will sit at home at their personal computer terminals and transfer funds from their money market accounts into their checking accounts to purchase municipal bonds. To them, the transactions will all be taking place on the screen, but on paper the transactions will be taking place in three different states. One financial services industry analyst predicts that local and community banks will not be able to compete with this range of services and packaged offerings and will find themselves gobbled up by the new national banks.

The importance of offering full service financial packages is reflected in the shift of personnel away from traditional financial service companies to the full service organizations. John Rafal reports that many smaller financial service organizations are losing their best people because they don't offer a complete line of services: "The service reps who are the most diligent, ambitious, and hardworking are exploring other avenues of financial vehicles for their clients, and when they gain the confidence that they are able to provide the full range of financial vehicles, they leave and go out on their own. Many companies don't seem to realize that there is an element of personal pride for service reps. They want to do right—one hundred percent right—by their clients."

The most successful financial service institutions are the ones that will offer complete financial planning packages to their clients. "Full service banking" is much more than a slogan. Industry representatives believe it is helping to shape the present and will definitely be the wave of the future. The rankings of the top five companies in banking and finance have been based on that belief. Because services offered by banks and financial brokerage houses overlap considerably, our survey has combined both in the category of "financial service institutions."

Although the banks and brokerage houses we have rated are considered to be excellent in terms of compensation, support, and intangibles, we gave Citicorp a slight edge over Merrill Lynch for two reasons. First, Citicorp is moving very aggressively into the financial services marketplace, and although Merrill Lynch has been there for a long time, we feel that Citicorp's rapid expansion gives their prototypical two-year representative a slight advantage over Merrill Lynch. We see more advancement opportunities at Citicorp. Second, Citicorp's commitment to politically vulnerable foreign investments has decreased recently. In the last year Citicorp has focused an increasing amount of corporate attention on the more stable domestic consumer market, and shored up its overseas positions, particularly in Brazil, so that its position in foreign markets is much stronger.

> *The only title that seems to be lost in the wave of the full service financial institutions is loan officer. The account executive . . . is primarily a sales rep who sells financial packages.*

Merrill Lynch earned the number-two ranking by being both the industry leader and the industry innovator among the brokerage houses. Merrill Lynch's innovations in the development of financial instruments have created a climate of growth and flexibility that should allow account executives to thrive.

Positions three, four, and five in our survey were very close. Security Pacific placed third because of its aggressive commitment to flexibility in the financial markets and also its commitment to employees. Shearson Lehman/American Express edged out BankAmerica primarily because of its great marketing tool—American Express' base of upscale credit card users. BankAmerica Corporation, although a strong contender, and certainly deserving of its position in our survey, has earned the fifth position because of its somewhat less aggressive posture in pursuing growth and diversification in the financial marketplace.

Because the full service banking institution is a relatively new concept in an industry long bound by tradition, the titles describing the employment positions vary widely from banking house to banking house and among the different financial companies. For example, at Merrill Lynch the key position for the basis of our prototypical two-year sales representative was the assistant account executive, while at other brokerage houses it was the junior account executive. At Citicorp, the position had the unique title, junior relationship manager, while at other banking institutions the title was account representative. The only title that seems to be lost in the wave of the full service financial institutions is loan officer. The account executives explained that the traditional loan officer, still an important position in most local and community banks, evaluates loan applicants with an eye to making traditionally secured or otherwise collateralized loans. The account executive, on the other hand, is primarily a sales representative who sells financial packages, including loans and leases, to prospective clients. For a two-year junior (assistant) account representative without an MBA, the industry median compensation package is $28,900.

	BANKING	COMPENSATION	COMMISSION	SUPPORT	INTANGIBLE
1	Citicorp	4		5	++
2	Merrill Lynch & Co., Inc.	4		5	++
3	Security Pacific Corp.	4		5	++
4	Shearson Lehman Brothers, Inc.	3		5	+
5	BankAmerica Corp.	4		5	+

Citicorp [++]

Citicorp has earned our number-one spot by being in the vanguard of the financial revolution. The company has carefully positioned itself to take advantage of the climate of deregulation, so that it is able to capitalize on every possible opportunity available to the banking industry. As mentioned earlier, the McFadden Act is under pressure and although interstate banking is still only de facto, Citicorp has taken advantage of the reciprocal interstate banking laws which do permit consolidation. In 1982, Citicorp acquired Fidelity Savings, a California bank, and renamed it Citicorp Savings. Citicorp has also opened offices to take advantage of the more liberal banking laws in states such as South Dakota which permit banks to offer insurance. While other banks have taken the acquisition and merger route to expand their basic financial services into other areas of the financial marketplace, Citicorp has developed its own financial management services which rival those of the major brokerage houses. It is currently positioned to be a major underwriter of corporate securities as well, but only when the FDIC gives the go-ahead. Once the Federal Reserve Board flashed the green light, Citicorp expanded into the area of data processing services, and is now offering its customers the benefits of electronic funds transfer through its subsidiary, Citishare Corporation. And Citicorp obviously knows how to do things right. Whereas Chemical Bank of New York established an electronic funds transfer capability for its customers by utilizing a specific home computer (the often troubled Atari line), Citicorp's system is computer-independent. When the Export Trading Act was passed, Citicorp was there to take full advantage by establishing productive business relationships with export trading companies. And Citicorp now offers asset management accounts through its affiliation with Lehman Brothers.

The message to potential account officers is that at Citicorp you will receive the training and support you need to become a versatile financial planner and a success in this industry in the years ahead. Citicorp is letting the financial industry know that it intends not only to be around for a very long time, but to be at the top.

Merrill Lynch [+ +]

Merrill Lynch has been called the industry's financial department store, and although that description may not sound very exotic, it has been said with great respect. They are the largest brokerage house in the U.S., with approximately 1,000 offices, over 10,000 registered representatives, and 40,000 employees. The top eight brokerage houses control over six billion investment dollars, and Merrill Lynch accounts for nearly 30 percent of that total. Merrill Lynch has long been an industry leader in both performance and innovation. They have been the pioneers of diversified investment services, and we have every reason to believe that they will continue to dominate. They are industry leaders in the use of technology in their daily business and are rumored to be speaking with AT&T about a major leap in communications technology. For account representatives, Merrill Lynch provides a stable environment in what can often be a wild and crazy industry and the opportunity to learn the business from the very best in the world. Their commitment to growth and diversification also provides their representatives with opportunities that would simply not be available at smaller or more conservative brokerage houses.

Security Pacific [++]

California's largest bank holding company is following Citicorp's lead and jumping into the financial services markets. Security Pacific recently purchased a seat on the New York Stock Exchange and has bought out a number of bond brokerage firms. Security Pacific has also taken advantage of the Export Trading Act and become more active in the international trading scene. They have expanded their operation into the insurance business by taking advantage of South Dakota's liberal banking policy, which permits banks to broker the full complement of insurance instruments. In our rankings, they have earned a [++] and just barely edged out Shearson Lehman/ American Express for two reasons. The first is Security's move into the highly lucrative bond market. How lucrative is the corporate and municipal bond market? One account representative for a major New York bond brokerage house was heard to comment recently that this year had been a real wipeout and he'd be lucky to make one eighth of what he made last year. It turned out that during the year he was complaining about, he'd made just under one million dollars including bonuses. The second reason behind their [++] rating is their commitment to their employees. For years, Security Pacific has been a leader in California in employee relations. They utilize many of the techniques made popular in Japanese industry for making employees an integral part of the operation. Although Security Pacific's focus in employee relations has been primarily on the employees at the lower echelon of the pay scale, their pro-employee attitudes carry over into the higher level positions as well. For example, 50 percent of promotions at Security Pacific are from within.

As with the other companies in our top five positions, Security Pacific earned their place in the sun by their commitment to stay on the frontier of the industry by aggressively packaging and selling diversified financial services in the corporate and consumer markets. And now, particularly because of their penetration into the bond brokerage markets, they are offering their account representatives some very lucrative opportunities.

Shearson Lehman Brothers, Inc. [+]

American Express reacted to the wild interest fluctuations that began in the late 1970s by attempting to protect themselves from as many negative economic influences as possible. By their recent purchase of Lehman Brothers, they have solidified their position in the financial securities market and served notice that they are a force to be reckoned with. Account representatives at Shearson Lehman/American Express have the advantage of the huge, upscale Amex credit card customer base, which the company is calling on extensively to market its financial services. For many of the same reasons that representatives with Merrill Lynch are in an excellent position to expand along the cutting edge of the industry, so too are account executives at Amex financial services. Of the top eight brokerage houses, Shearson Lehman/American Express controls 17 percent of the investment dollars. At present, remuneration for our prototypical representative is lagging only somewhat behind the rest of the industry, and that is the only factor which is keeping Amex's rating in the intangibles at [+] instead of [++].

BankAmerica Corp. [+]

BankAmerica jumped into the diversification fray in 1982 when it acquired Charles Schwab & Company. As is the case with all of the top five, especially Citicorp and Security Pacific, BankAmerica has diversified into the foreign trade arena by taking advantage of the Export Trading Act. However, unlike the others, BankAmerica has shown a more conservative tendency toward diversification, and while it seems committed to the principle, it hasn't moved as firmly as the others in the industry. For example, there has been no indication that BankAmerica plans to expand into the insurance end of the business, a critical aspect of the financial service industry. Although both training and its structure are highly beneficial to their service officers (account reps), we feel that the areas in which we have found Bank-America lacking warrant a [+] rather than a [++].

EDUCATION PRODUCTS

THE TOP FIVE:

1 Xerox Corp.
2 Bell & Howell
3 Control Data Corp.
4 Cencor Inc.
5 Advanced Systems, Inc.

T he sales of educational services grew out of a need to provide a product that wasn't traditionally provided by public education. High intensity reading and mathematics programs, compressed tutorials for the state bar exams, and self-contained computer resource laboratories are among the products and services sold by private vendors to individual and corporate consumers. There is an even larger market for industrial training and on-site institutional education programs such as occupational health and safety awareness or other compliance-based activities. These services can range from orienting sales personnel to new products to testing the skill levels of professionals. These types of private educational service programs are among the most important in the education industry.

Sales in the education industry cover a wide range of services which include specialized instruction for individuals preparing for standardized tests such as the SAT or the bar examination, educational support facilities for public and private schools, continuing education and vocational education for nontraditional students, and industrial education for on-site instruction or preparation for licensing examinations. There are even salespeople for private schools, specific types of preschool programs, companies that build and staff private schools overseas, and companies that sell administrative and educational consulting to school boards. The concept of sales in the education industry has expanded rapidly over the past ten years as the demand for individuals with specialized training has increased and the sources of funding—both public and private—have developed to support those needs. There is also a ready pool of individuals, many of whom were teachers and have had extensive graduate training, who are creating their own independent companies that sell products and services to the educational market.

In the United States today, there are few industries that are as controversial as the education industry. The bedrock of the industry is the public school system, supported by local, state, and federal tax revenues. Everybody pays for maintaining and administering this system whether they have children in the schools or not. Even people who send their children to private or parochial schools must pay for public education. This makes public education, and the state and direction of the public school systems, a vital political issue that often dominates state and local campaigns. Recently, the condition of American education generally and of the public schools specifically has become a national political issue receiving increasing public awareness. National political exposure has meant free publicity for the representatives who sell education to consumers, to industry, and to the schools themselves.

The education industry, like all of Gaul, is divided into three basic parts: the sale of educational services to schools; the sale of educational services—including private school education, test preparation, and vocational training—directly to the public; and the sale of industrial education and training programs to businesses. Within these three areas are many subareas which range all the way from formal academic degree programs to one- and two-person consulting firms that provide highly specialized training to individuals. And each segment of this market has its unique way of selling itself to a potential customer. From the television announcer in coveralls for Apex Tech in New York, who promises that "no salesman will call," to the private school recruiter who earns a commission on the tuition of each student he or she signs up, sales in the education-for-pay markets are as aggressive and competitive as they are in any other sales-oriented industry in the United States.

Some of the growth areas in the sales of educational services developed out of the need for industries to upgrade the skills of their employees or to familiarize employees with new products. Other areas in educational sales developed out of the need for advanced specialized training to meet licensing or certification examinations. Private classes are offered to students about to take the SATs, the LSATs, the Med Boards, and of course, the state bar examinations. And still other growth areas are emerging in the fields of public school support services. These types of services offer schools complete remedial and enrichment programs at a fraction of the cost it would take for a school to develop them. Some of the educational service companies like New Century and WICAT even offer completely integrated computer facilities that serve as student work stations and manage student progress in the areas of reading and mathematics. And finally, private school

> *Each segment of this market has its unique way of selling itself, from the television announcer in coveralls who promises that "No salesman will call," to the private school recruiter who earns a commission on each student he or she signs up.*

education itself, long considered to be the exclusive prerogative of the very wealthy, has emerged as one of the newer areas of educational sales. Representatives for preschool education centers can offer two-career families the day care they are looking for in programs enhanced by an early childhood curriculum that stimulates the preschooler at the most critical period of his or her intellectual development. This is a powerful marketing claim.

However, none of these services developed in a complete vacuum. They emerged because there existed in the education marketplace a need for information or administrative products that simply was not being filled by the existing educational system. And as in any industry where serious gaps exist, businesses will spring up to fill them. The education industry, although one of the oldest industries in the United States, is no exception. To supplement the public schools or to provide an alternative to them, there are formal private school programs at all grade levels; to fill the need for on-site training and employee education, there are industrial training programs. To meet the growing need for adult retraining or simply to provide a method of keeping in touch with the professional knowledge base, there are continuing education and adult education extension services that are administered at a local, municipal, or state level, and through private agencies such as colleges and universities; and finally, to fill the need for test preparation or

> "By 1986, industrial education alone will be a multibillion-dollar industry."

certification requirements, there are career-oriented education programs such as SAT or LSAT. In each of these situations a fee is paid to the school or educational organization either by the student or by his or her company and a sale of educational product has taken place. And more often than not, the sale was made through a representative of the company—a sales rep.

An industry analyst explains, "Educational sales reps are an informal lot. The job of educational sales representative is not a clearly identifiable position in an organization as, for example, a new car salesman is in a showroom." Some representatives can earn as much as a 15 percent commission for each fee-paying student they bring into an organization. The same source says, "The concept in industrial education is somewhat different. You're bringing the school or the educational materials directly to the student rather than the student to the school." And he adds, "By 1986, industrial education alone will be a multibillion-dollar industry."

Mel Hornick, author of *The Successful Marketing of Schools*, suggests that one of the problems of public education is that schools do not have to compete with one another for students, nor, because of compulsory education laws, do they have to compete with other sectors of the marketplace for attendees. He argues that there should be no "guaranteed enrollment" for schools. Hornick successfully practiced what he preached by developing The Connecticut Center for Continuing Education, which according to one industry source is one of the most successful operations of its kind in the country and probably the world.

Of all the pay-for-education services covered in this chapter, industrial education has the largest market share by far. Companies such as our number-two ranked Bell & Howell with 1984 educational sales of $117 million, number-five ranked Advanced Systems with 1984 sales of $38 million, and number-four ranked Cencor Corporation with 1984 educational sales of $10 million, are industry leaders in professional and employee training systems. The aggressive Control Data Corporation, number three in the educational sales industry (and also one of our top five companies in the mini-mainframe computer market), has been successfully marketing their PLATO educational system for many years in the industrial marketplace and is now selling to the primary and secondary education markets. PLATO is a Computer Assisted Instruction (CAI) system which is used for industrial as well as academic training. From its origins as a mainframe-based, on-line system, it has been expanded into the world of microcomputers, so that today PLATO is used by students at home on stand-alone microcomputers, on classroom microcomputers and on-line terminals, and by employees training in many major corporations. The development of the PLATO system is one of the few examples of the interaction between private corporations and the public education system. In PLATO's development, the Minneapolis-based Control Data utilized the educational expertise of the Minnesota Educational Computing Consortium (MECC). Not surprisingly, Minnesota, with both MECC and CDC, is considered the leading state in the use of CAI in the public school system.

A spokesman for MECC says, "CAI systems are excellent learning tools. They are nonjudgmental and they permit the student to learn at his or her own pace." A former editor for educational software at McGraw-Hill agrees. "In the early days of CAI, programs were quite simple and not very interactive. Kids were implicitly taught to be passive because the software did all the work. But today the product is much better developed. It involves the user in an ongoing thought process and it is more sophisticated so it has become a better learning tool." With the growing use of computer-aided instructional programs in industry and the classroom, companies that are developing materials in this area, and companies like CDC that sell authoring systems to create CAI materials, will be in the vanguard of educational resource development. These CAI materials, both curriculum resources and the actual software, are being developed by a variety of private organizations ranging from large corporations such as CDC, Bell & Howell, and Xerox, to small private entrepreneurial companies, and everything in between. They are servicing the growing market created by the demand for new instructional methodologies and educational services.

Our research shows that the educational services industry is highly diverse and includes major corporations such as Xerox and Control Data; middle-sized companies such as WICAT Systems, Prescription Learning, and New Century Education Corporation; and small cottage industry operations. Educational services also include private schools and specialized career betterment and certification training programs. Therefore, in order to cover the full range of services within the education-for-pay industry, we've chosen to evaluate each of the major areas within the industry by analyzing one of its major companies as a representative of that area. However, for the all-important and constantly growing field of industrial education, we have ranked the top five companies that represent the most aggressive educational service delivery companies in America today and whose sales forces are at work in all segments of the economy.

Educational resource and service companies such as New Century Education Corporation, WICAT Systems, Computer Curriculum Corporation, and Prescription Learning sell complete learning packages directly to schools. The packages cover a very broad range of educational materials, but all of them supplement, support, or in some cases, actually replace the traditional curriculum materials used by the school district. IBM, AT&T, Control Data, and Bell & Howell are also actively involved in the sales of educational resources to schools.

According to Charles Walther, president of New Century and developer of its sales strategies and materials, there is an abundant interest on the part of public school superintendents in educational resource companies that can produce student performance results on a variety of standardized tests. First of all, he points out, many school districts rely on a system of standardized testing to measure the performance of students and schools against the district at large as well as against comparative age and grade groups nationally. Therefore, learning programs that help students increase their scores as well as remediate specific weaknesses in academic subjects are attractive to school superintendents. New Century has been one of the important companies in the educational services industry for the past twenty years. With a program designed by B. F. Skinner, the celebrated behavioral psychologist, New Century was one of the pioneers of student performance-oriented remedial systems with visual and auditory reinforcement. New Century's reading and mathematics learning centers, which combine audio tape cassettes with computer work stations for displaying lesson frames and logging student responses, are currently under development.

Charles Walther hires former school superintendents and principals as sales representatives to work in conjunction with New Century's sales office. He explains that selling to schools requires such a deep level of understanding and sympathy with the problems of school administrators that, more often than not, only other administrators can communicate effectively. The cost of the learning centers is also a factor in new sales initiatives. New Century usually bypasses the acquisitions and purchasing offices of school districts and goes directly to the school superintendent or the other leaders of the school district. "This implies," Charles says, "that our sales personnel must be people who have served as CEOs in a district or who have reported directly to the superintendent. This type of sales recruitment is not as limiting as it seems because school superintendents are highly mobile professionals who rarely stay in the same job for more than five years. We approach the ones we want to hire when they are between jobs or close to retirement."

Selling learning centers is not like selling pencils or workbooks. The latter items are bought in bulk by school or district purchasing agents, often after a rigorous bidding process. Selling learning centers complete with an integrated computer network, student work stations, tape players and thousands of audio cassettes, and the training program for schoolteachers to staff the centers, requires a complex marketing approach that is targeted directly at the key executives in a school district. New Century doesn't sell hardware or software, but rather, according to Charles, it sells student progress. New Century stipulates that students attending its reading and math learning centers for remediation of specific skills will pick up those skills much faster than they would in a normal classroom. But, as he explains, selling progress is not like selling pencils or pens because you have no product you can hand over for inspection. "To sell complex instructional systems to schools, you must violate a lot of standard consumer marketing rules and create new ones. For example, we learned many years ago that we should never give a school administrator a written or graphic description of a learning center before he sees one in action." Consequently, the New Century sales representative simply hands the school principal evaluations and reports of student progress at existing centers. By the time the prospective clients visit a learning center site, they understand how the center functions

> *". . . selling progress is not like selling pencils or pens. To sell complex industrial systems, you must violate a lot of standard consumer marketing rules and create new ones."*

and what they should be looking for. Once prospective clients see the learning center during a typical class period, according to Charles, they can't help but be impressed by the entire operation. He says that New Century's selling method involves "getting school adminstrators to see an operating learning center, having them talk to satisfied users about its benefits, and having someone they know and feel comfortable with ask for the order. It sounds easy, but it's hard work, usually completed over a two-year period."

An industry analyst says, "Private schools used to be a status symbol for the wealthy. Today they are rapidly becoming a necessity." Dr. Lee Pierson, a cognitive psychologist, agrees: "Parents are simply not willing to subject their children to years of boredom and frustration and the result is that private school education is about to explode. And when tuition tax credits are finally legislated into reality, private school education will become commonplace."

Private schools are traditionally nonprofit organizations. But at the American Renaissance School (ARS) the operating officers don't try to hide the fact that they expect to make a profit by administering a first-class educational establishment. According to an educator from a major northeastern university, "The school is unique in many ways. It's extremely student oriented, whereas most schools are teacher and administration oriented." Massachusetts Institute of Technology was so impressed with the quality of education offered at ARS that they've offered one of the school's first graduates an early admissions acceptance to their prestigious Cambridge campus.

ARS is a business, and it makes money by attracting parents who are motivated to enroll their children. This means that the school's services and its promises of scholastic success have to be promoted and sold. This is typical of the independent school community, especially schools that do not belong to the New England or Northeastern prep school establishment which includes Choate, Andover, St. Paul's, Lawrenceville, Dalton, Peddie, Princeton Day School, and others. ARS is different; they have to promote their delivery of services. When asked how they "sell" education to students and parents, Dr. Glenn Marcus, vice-president of ARS, answers: "Our position is that we are selling an excellent product—namely, education. We expect our students' parents to pay for the product, and we in turn expect to pay our teachers to deliver the product. As in any organization which delivers a product to the public, we have to sell ours, and we advertise in the media and also pay field reps to do just that."

The product that parents pay for is experienced teachers who can communicate their professional expertise to their students. Dr. Marcus explains why this is an important feature of ARS: "Our teachers are all involved in the outside world. We have a math teacher who runs a computer business. One of our history teachers is also a novelist. One of our karate instructors is a bank vice-president. Another of our teachers writes business books, and every one of our teachers has either a master's degree or a Ph.D." He asserts that because ARS teachers are actively involved in practicing the skills of their professions, they are better instructors than teachers who have been isolated in the classrooms.

Selling private school education is not an easy task according to a representative of a private New York City school. "We compete with some real heavyweights—very prestigious private schools who turn down more students than apply to us." At the same time, private schools must compete against the free public education system. An industry source illustrates the problem this way: "There aren't many industries I know in which a business is expected to be able to fund a start-up operation while simultaneously funding its competition's business to a level where the competition can offer the product for free, but the start-up business has to charge." In order to get buyers, private schools use traditional promotion and marketing tools such as advertising, professional recruiters, and, in the case of ARS, field representatives. Other private schools are experimenting with using field representatives and professional recruiters. At one private school in New York for example, everyone who is connected with the school becomes a commission-based field representative as soon as he or she signs up a new student. As the administrator explains, "Everyone sells the school—teachers, administrators, and other students. We offer a finder's fee for each new student who registers."

Industrial education is the most institutionalized segment of the industry. It is significantly different conceptually from the other segments of the education market in a number of ways. For one, the learning environment comes to the student, not the other way around. For another, the tab is almost always paid by a corporation, not the student. And three, the education is almost devoid of a teacher in the traditional sense of the word. The training is materials intensive, not teacher intensive. For representatives, this is the most lucrative aspect of the education market.

Marsha Altman, a rep for Xerox, says, "The industrial training industry is really exploding. It seems that every former educator who kissed off traditional teaching is developing training materials." And apparently, some of those training materials are quite good, because Xerox recently spent $6 million on a new sales training package written by some former educators. An industry analyst adds: "The growth of the industrial training industry is directly proportional to the growth of the telecommunications industry." Why? "Because every Tom, Dick, and Jane with a home computer and a VCR is putting together training materials." Marsha agrees: "There is a growing number of companies who are acting as independent reps for the cottage industry aspect of industrial training."

Milton Beamon, the director of a behavioral training center in New Jersey, says, "Our company was always in the black, but it was always a struggle. We had therapists for private and group sessions in behavior modification, and we also ran training programs for professionals." But Milton could see that he was never going to get rich from the center. "One day, I was approached by a sales rep who had training materials that were better than some of the things we were doing. I was so impressed that I got in touch with the company and became a dealer for their line. I began by hiring three commissioned representatives, two former sales reps and a former schoolteacher." Milton's price for the training courses is 35 percent off list, with the list prices ranging from $1,000 to $5,000, depending on the course. The representatives are paid a flat 10 percent commission on the net sale dollars, and Milton reimburses them for traveling expenses. This means that on a sale of a $1,000 training course, Milton pays the company $650 and his representative earns $100. So Milton's company makes $250 minus overhead expenses. But often the numbers don't work out that way. "The industry is very competitive, so to compete with the Xeroxes and Bell & Howells, I have to give up some points and discount the product. The average discount is 10 percent."

Marsha says, "The Xerox name gets us in the door," but Milton concedes, "My reps have to be pretty creative." Joan Reynolds, an independent representative specializing in microcomputer-based training, understands this approach. "Frankly, I'll do whatever it takes to get my foot in the door," she says. And Joan isn't kidding. "The craziest sale I ever made was to a major corporation in New York City. I knew they were having a horrendous time with their word processing package. I was selling a training course combined with a different word processing package, and I knew it would be perfect for this company." But Joan couldn't get in to see the right people. "I even had a friend who worked there get me a referral, and that didn't work. It turns out that the person responsible for making the decision didn't care about the computer problems. He was just focused on production." As Joan indicates, his approach was not very scientific. "He just assumed that the amount of time it would take to install a new system and train his people on it would make it very expensive." So in desperation, Joan borrowed a scene from a grade B movie. "I dressed up as a cleaning woman and walked into Mr. Jones's office in the middle of the day. I made believe I was cleaning and I deliberately made a big fuss—a lot of noise and I knocked a few things down." And how did Mr. Jones react to all this? "He didn't say anything for the first few minutes and then he had a fit. One of the things he said was, 'Do you know how much time you've cost me?' " And at that, Joan launched into her sales pitch. "I told him who I was and I said, 'If you're so damn worried about time, how come your secretaries waste three man-days a month with that screwed-up word processing system you have and your management information systems people waste one man-week a month trying to fix it, when I can save you all that time and more?' At that point he was beet red and he just shoved me out the door, but not before I half threw my presentation at him." And Joan had done her homework. "I had all the facts and figures to show him just how much money he would save in no more than a year by using the word processing and training system I was selling. In addition, the training system alone was so good that the information management people would never have to get involved in training," she said. Was Joan dejected at getting thrown out? "Absolutely not. I don't sell schlock. By the time I'm ready to close on a company, I know that they're fools if they don't go with my systems, so if they don't, my attitude is that it's their loss." But a funny thing happened on the way to Rejectionland. "I got a call about three days later from the VP of the MIS department. I went in to see him, and half an hour later I walked out with a $30,000 sale. I never saw Mr. Jones, and his name was never mentioned to me."

Lilly Sullivan, a representative for Control Data, comments on Joan's story: "That's pretty extreme, but when I was working for a small company

> *"I dressed up as a cleaning woman*
> *and walked into Mr. Jones's office*
> *in the middle of the day.*
> *I made believe*
> *I was cleaning . . ."*

selling management training, we had to use some creative door-opening techniques too." But Lilly adds, "The CDC name is our door opener now."

Our research has shown that the industrial training field is unusual because it encompasses huge corporations such as Xerox, Bell & Howell, and Control Data, each with sales within the industry in the seven-figure range, as well as a thriving cottage industry operation. Milton Beamon comments, "There's a lot of new blood in the world of business management, and they're very fact oriented. If a product is going to save or make a lot of money for a company, they'll buy it whether it's being sold by Xerox or by Podunk & Sons."

Because many schools, especially privately funded institutions, are looking for ways to make money, the continuing education concept has expanded dramatically in recent years. One industry source says, "It's very hard to measure the dollar size of the industry because there are so many versions of continuing education." But this same source says, "If you include every aspect of continuing education, from local church courses to major programs such as those at NYU or at other major universities, then I'd have to say you're looking at a quarter- to half-billion-dollar industry right now."

The term "continuing education" refers to any courses taken that are not part of a degree program. These can include courses that might normally be part of a degree program, such as math, as well as courses such as drama, guitar playing, ceramics, and computer literacy. One industry source advised us that any research on continuing education had to include a talk to Mel Hornick, the man who is credited with establishing the most successful continuing education of its time. Mel, who wrote *The Successful Marketing of Schools* about his phenomenal success in establishing the Connecticut Center for Continuing Education, describes his experience: "Establishing the Center really seemed easy once I found out how to sell the concept." And

> *"Paul Newman and Joanne Woodward came to speak to our students, and later on Tennessee Williams lectured."*

how did he find out? "First we surveyed our market, which of course, had to be fairly local. We found out that the people who were most interested were adults, and their interest was primarily in arts courses. Once we identified our market, we went after it the way you go after any market." As you'll see, Mel's approach was professional. "We did a slick four-color brochure, got a number of mailing lists, and also advertised locally in newspapers and on radio." Mel admits having some help with the advertising. "I met Charlie Feldman, the senior creative director at Young & Rubicam. He was fascinated with what we were trying to do so he volunteered his expertise. His help with the advertising was invaluable to us." And how did the operation actually work? "We started with courses in theater, acting, and film. The fee for students was $100 for a sixteen-week course that met once a week." And teachers? "That was amazing. Our philosophy was that, as with any educational program, the course is only as good as the teacher, so we were paying teachers $50 an hour, which was an excellent salary then (1973-77). I called the chairpersons at major universities such as Yale and asked if they could recommend any faculty members from their respective departments. More often than not, we got the chairman himself." The Center was established with the reputation of having some fine teachers and the effect snowballed. "Through various high-powered contacts we were able to have Paul Newman and Joanne Woodward come to speak to our students, and later on Tennessee Williams lectured." But didn't these big names require some big fees? "Not at all. They were delighted to do it for free. The Newmans lived in the community and wanted to help, and Mr. Williams helped us as a favor to a friend." Thus, the arts courses clearly got the Center on its way, but Mel had bigger plans. "With the reputation we now had, expanding the programs was easy. We developed a number of certificate programs, including the first one in graphic design and one of the first in paralegal training." And where is the Center today? Mel, like many creative people we met, got bored. "I'd taken the center as far as I could without having it turn into a business for me. Up to that point it was a lot of fun, but I realized that to continue building it, I'd have to be more removed from the daily goings-on and become more of a business executive. I didn't want that, so I sold the whole package to Fairfield University in 1977."

About continuing education today, Mel says, "It's really big business. Almost every major university has a continuing education program." Roger Friedman, an administrator at the New School in New York City, agrees. "Schools realized that they had a big, empty building which was sitting there collecting dust for one-third of every day. So why not put it to use?" Mel adds, "Continuing education has also taken on a social aspect. A lot of people have the attitude, 'I'll go take a course to meet people, and if I happen to learn something besides, all the better.' "

The personal and career-betterment segment of the education-for-pay market is similar in structure to continuing education in that the students come to a school, and the courses taken are not part of a degree program. However, at this point the similarities end. An industry source says, "This is clearly the smallest segment of the education market with most estimates placing the figure at between $50 and $100 million."

Dr. Lee Pierson, a cognitive psychologist and developer of the TIPS (Training by Interactive Problem Solving) program, agrees: "The market

> *"Our research has indicated that students want us to structure their test preparation. They want to be drilled on the actual kinds of questions they will be asked on the real exams. So we stress the exams themselves and not the theory . . ."*

consists primarily of exam-preparation centers, such as SAT and GRE preparation, and self-improvement institutes such as the Evelyn Wood reading classes." Dr. Pierson is affiliated with the Sexton Educational Centers, which specialize in preparing students for standardized exams such as SAT, GRE, LSAT, and GMAT. He says, "We also offer tutoring in specific courses such as math and English." The approach of the Sexton schools is unique among the exam preparation centers we researched because, as Dr. Pierson says, "We stress learning whereas most of the other centers stress drill." He adds, "Our educational philosophy is that students will do better on exams if they understand the reasoning behind the questions." And he uses his TIPS program in the course of exam preparation. "TIPS is a formal learning system in which students are taught to verbalize their thinking and problem-solving processes. I found that having students work in pairs, so that one student critiques the other, is a powerful aid to the learning process." There are now twenty franchised Sexton Centers throughout the U.S. The franchise owners pay a start-up fee to the home office and also a percentage of gross earnings.

James Klein, a spokesman for the Stanley Kaplan Centers, the largest examination preparatory center in the country, says, "Our research has indicated that students want us to structure their test preparation. They want to be drilled on the actual kinds of questions they will be asked on the real exams. So we stress the exams themselves and not the theory behind the questions on the exams." The Stanley Kaplan Centers have been in existence over half a century, and were recently sold to the *Washington Post.*

Mr. Klein comments about selling the courses, "We're sufficiently established so our program is really sold by word of mouth. We do advertise in newspapers, ranging from the *New York Times* to local college and high school papers." Dr. Pierson adds: "We also advertise, mostly in newspapers, but we also try to establish affiliations with local colleges. The Sexton Centers nationwide are franchised, and the home office supplies the centers with a number of boilerplate ads, but the individual franchises are responsible for placing and paying for local ads."

Because the diverse structure of this industry does not lend itself to our usual ranking analysis, we have adjusted our rankings as follows: for industrial training—the one industry area in which commissioned sales representatives are employed—we have ranked the top five companies as we have in the other industries in our survey. However, in other areas of the educational sales industry where the sales representative organization lacks a formal structure, we have discussed a typical company to illustrate how sales are made and how business is conducted in general. Keep in mind that for all industry segments which we've discussed in this chapter (with the exception of industrial training), there are no formal commissioned representatives, but rather representatives who spend most of their time wearing two hats: administrator and salesperson, or teacher and salesperson. As a result, a rep for a private school will derive a very small portion of his income from selling. The bulk of his income will be derived from his other "hat," for instance, his administrative salary. However, the sale of private educational services or of continuing or career advancement education courses has become so important in today's educational market that these aspects of the industry warrant inclusion in the industry overview even though they do not lend themselves to our usual evaluation procedures.

EDUCATION PRODUCTS	COMPENSATION	COMMISSION	SUPPORT	INTANGIBLE
1 Xerox Corp.	4		5	+
2 Bell & Howell	4		5	+
3 Control Data Corp.	4		5	−
4 Cencor Inc.	4		4	
5 Advanced Systems, Inc.	4		4	

The median salary for a two-year rep is $25,200. Since commission rates vary considerably, we are ranking the compensation figure without breaking it down into salary and commission.

Xerox [+]

Some companies have names that are door-openers. Xerox reps can knock the door down. That reason alone earns Xerox a [+]. In addition, Xerox is not shy about going after—and getting—the best training materials available, even to the tune of $6 million. Add to this the Xerox presence—dominance is a better word—in the office automation market and you have a picture which should have Xerox representatives smiling for years to come.

Bell & Howell [+]

This industry giant with 1984 sales of nearly three-quarters of a billion dollars finds itself being pulled more and more in the direction of education and training. From their early ventures putting together AV displays using the early Apple II computers, Bell & Howell has continued to support the education/training arm of its business. We see this, as well as the continued strengthening of its position in the marketplace, as being very positive indications for B&H reps.

Control Data Corp [−]

CDC is a good company, with many good products. However, there are signs that the company may experience a massive reorganization. If this occurs, what will happen to PLATO, and how will all this impact on CDC representatives? We don't profess to know. However, we do know that CDC reps need to consider the changes and uncertainty that a reorganization may bring.

INSURANCE

THE TOP FIVE:

1 Connecticut General Life Ins. Co.

2 Allstate Ins. Co.

3 Metropolitan Life Ins. Co.

4 Farmers Group, Inc.

5 The Prudential Ins. Co. of America

F ew people know that the earliest policies were written in 1000 B.C. by the Phoenicians and Greeks to cover ships and marine expeditions. Life insurance policies as we know them today were written during the ancient Roman Empire. In fact, there was even an elementary mortality table that dates back to the earliest days of the emperors. Today's insurance company representatives sell much more than simple life policies. In today's market, the insurance companies sell comprehensive financial plans that cover not only basic risks, but provide for retirement income, college tuition, and real growth of assets. In short, insurance has become an important tool for today's investor.

Insurance policy salespeople are expendable. Many are recruited directly out of college and, following a company training period, are sent into the thick of a sales campaign. Novice insurance salespeople are encouraged to sell to family and friends first and told that once they've gotten the hang of it, they'll be able to sell to anyone. As former sales representatives describe the experience, they were trained to believe that selling insurance was more like an act of charity than an act of business. According to Margaret Carter, a former representative for Metropolitan Life, "I was at loose ends jobwise. I'd been laid off at my former job, so I thought I'd try insurance. I left my interview with Metropolitan shaking my head because, frankly, I didn't see how the interview was going to help them make any decision about hiring me." Margaret had entered the first phase of a marketing strategy that Metropolitan Life had used for many years, but that recently has started to change. "The next thing I knew, I was attending a two-week training session. I thought I was going to learn about insurance, but what I learned about was selling." And what she learned was: "Selling isn't the most important thing—closing is."

"You'll be a godsend to your family and friends," I was told. "The trainers actually had us convinced that because of our newfound expertise in insurance, we would be doing our families and friends a favor by selling them insurance policies. We weren't salespeople; we were benefactors." Peter Bennett, a sales representative for Prudential, had a similar story. "At Prudential, we were encouraged to go to our families and friends and make a pitch like we were doing them a favor. I didn't sell diddly at first and I temporarily lost a few friends." Margaret adds, "If you think about it, it's pretty presumptuous to show up at your cousin's house for dinner and in effect tell him that he doesn't know how to plan for his future. That's what I did. I'm not the kind of person who talks down to people, but after thinking about the way I was coming across, I know I was being perceived that way." And Peter concludes, "They had us believing we were missionaries, and I approached the task with a missionary's fervor. For me it was the wrong way to sell." And so it was for most of the new reps hired during the life insurance blitzkrieg of recent years which saw, according to a Metroplitan rep, a turnover rate of over 80 percent among new sales representatives.

Other representatives and former representatives have had similar experiences in hiring and training. "Sell your family and friends" seemed to be the selling battle cry for the new reps hired by many life insurance companies seeking to expand both their sales force and the number of policies sold by hiring individuals to sell within their own discrete spheres of influence. Barry Hoffer, a district manager for Metropolitan, comments on the blitzkrieg policy: "Basically it's true. The company policy—and it wasn't just us—was to hire a million reps and spring them on their families. Some reps couldn't sell even to their own families, but a lot of them did. Either way, most quit after a few months. The turnover rate was truly astronomical." The "sell your family" approach to life insurance required a relatively low cash outlay on the part of the companies, and they reaped a hefty return on the premiums from the reps' families since they didn't have to pay a commission once the rep had quit. But Barry is

> "They had us believing we were missionaries, and I approached the task with a missionary's fervor. For me it was the wrong way to sell."

quick to add, "Even though you may think the practice of hiring reps while knowing they would most likely sell only to their families and then quit was shady, it really wasn't. For one thing, people need insurance, so it wasn't as though people were buying a fraudulent product. The product wasn't like a used car with its odometer turned back." He also points out that the representatives themselves weren't actually exploited. "There are some reps working today earning over sixty grand a year who sold their first policies to their folks."

Both the sales strategies and the types of commission vary according to the kind of policies that the insurance representatives offer. For example, a company representative may earn a commission of from 10 to 15 percent on the customer's premium while selling casualty insurance, but a commission of 50 percent on the first-year premium for a whole life policy. Also, as in each of the industries we've covered in our survey, independent agents earn significantly higher commissions than company representatives, but this can be offset by the higher overhead that most independent agencies support. Not only do commission rates vary quite a bit from one type of insurance to another, but so do the sales strategies of representatives in different areas of insurance. For example, representatives who sell car insurance or any other type of limited-risk policies generally focus their client's attention directly upon the risks covered by the insurance. The amount of car insurance one carries and the cost of the policy is directly related to the type of car, the ages, occupations, and records of the drivers, and the areas in which the cars will be driven. Many states also have mandatory coverage requirements, and all of these will affect the representative's approach to his or her clients and, of course, the amount of commission the salesperson will eventually earn. Home or dwelling insurance policies offer more flexibilty, but these too are affected by a number of predetermined factors, including the amount of the mortgage, the size of the dwellng and its replacement value, and the nearest supply of municipal water for fire emergencies.

However, it is in the whole-life and retirement policies that the greatest amount of flexibility exists because this type of insurance is usually regarded by both sales representative and buyer as a form of investment. In fact, in recent years, the borderline between insurance as pure risk management and insurance as a component of a family financial plan has begun to blur. As an executive for Connecticut General says, "In the insurance industry we really pioneered the idea of selling insurance as one aspect of financial planning." And a sales manager for Northwestern who has been familiar with the problems of selling against Connecticut General says, "Ten years ago CG hired lawyers and accountants to sell insurance because the company believed that professionals could best sell to professionals in related fields."

Salesmanship versus selling is what is taught at Connecticut General, according to Bob Weingarten, a CG manager. He describes his company's unique sales philosophy: "We teach our reps that they're not selling insurance; they're selling commitment. We've always had a very long-range view of this business, and over 90 percent of our business is from either referrals or repeat business." John Agramonte, a rep for Connecticut General, says, "If you listened to my conversation on a first sales call, you wouldn't know I was a salesman." Connecticut General's usual procedure is to have the rep spend the first sales call explaining what he or she sells, how sales are made, and how he or she is paid. Then the representative helps the client identify those problems in the client's business that Connecticut General's experience can help to solve. Bob Weingarten explains that at first glance this seems an unproductive sales approach. But, he points out, "Remember, we're in this for the long haul. When you're dealing with businesses, you have to look ahead and consider their long-range financial picture. Our techniques may be unusual, but they're very successful."

At first glance, it seems to most observers that CG representatives take a very indirect approach to selling insurance. Bob Weingarten agrees, but explains that the sale of insurance takes place after the representative has sold his or her own business expertise and CG's ability to solve problems. "On average, our reps spend two to four hours with the client at a second meeting in which the bulk of time is spent gathering data about the operation of the prospective client's business, plant, or office operation, and any other issues relevant to putting together a financial/insurance package. Our reps try to get to know the principals of the business to find out their goals. and even their dreams." In successive meetings, Bob explains, the sales representatives put themselves in a position of authority. The result is a very successful sales record. "Our statistics show that when a rep has a second meeting with a client, he or she has a three-to-one chance of closing the sale eventually and a better than two-to-one chance of closing the sale at the next meeting." And by the third meeting, both sales representative and prospective client are discussing solutions to the most critical problems that are confronting the client's business. As John Agramonte indicates, the solutions can often be complex and time-consuming. "It's not unusual for me to work with my client's attorney, putting together buy and sell agreements, wills, and trusts, in addition to satisfying the client's insurance requirements."

Connecticut General's methods are so successful that the insurance representative becomes a business consultant in his or her own right. A former CG representative, John Rafal, started an independent business by building on his CG training and experience. "Selling insurance was the last thing I wanted to do," John explains. He is the president of John W. Rafal & Associates in New Haven, Connecticut, a firm that specializes in financial planning for businesses and individuals. He recalls his beginnings in the insurance business over ten years ago. "A friend of mine, working for Connecticut General, had earned over $40,000 back in the mid '70s. I'd just graduated from law school and I wanted to get into corporate law. The kind of position I was looking for was pretty scarce at the time, so I figured I'd earn some money first and then reevaluate the legal profession. The thing that turned me on to Connecticut General, in addition to my friend's earning power, was what I'd heard about their training. CG's training program is unbelievable. They trained me for three months before I even went out on a call. I majored in business administration but I learned more in three months at Connecticut General than I did in four years in college."

Bob Weingarten says that CG's training program directly affects the way their representatives approach prospective clients. He explains what he believes is special about CG's training: "We care about the rep as a person. We believe the rep is going to treat his clients the way we treat the rep. You'll really understand where we're coming from in training and in sales if you'll keep two words in mind: 'long-range.' All the steps we take today, whether they are in training, sales, or the insurance and financial instruments we employ, are designed to produce results in ten years as well as right at the present. We don't see any contradictions between long- and short-range planning." According to John Rafal, "They trained us beyond their ability to support us with products and services. They trained us to be tax shelter salesmen, but we didn't have the full product line of tax shelters. We were trained to be investment salesmen but we didn't have a full supply of investment products. They taught us to serve our clients well." For John Rafal this meant that he needed to expand his horizons. "So after a while I realized that in order to serve the clients well I had to sell them non-Connecticut General products. And at that point I left the company and went on my own."

Bob Weingarten explains that the thoroughness of CG's training is not as self-defeating as it may seem. It is not the company's intent, he contends, to train representatives so well that when they reach the point where

> ... a company representative may earn a commission of from 10 to 15 percent on the customer's premium while selling casualty insurance, but a commission of 50 percent on the first-year premium for a whole life policy.

they are in the best position to sell the most for the company, they leave. He says, "We really have no problem with salespeople leaving because we trained them too well." He suggests that every industry has talented sales representatives who know the industry so well that they are more effective as independent agents than as company employees. "Frankly," he says, "in any industry, guys like John Rafal are going to go on their own. But every rep we hire isn't a John Rafal. There are plenty of guys who are making good money with the company and who are giving their clients everything they need. Not every client needs the kind of sophisticated services that John is providing."

John Rafal's odyssey from attorney to CG representative to independent financial planner is an example of how the business and commercial insurance industry has become an integral part of the financial industry as a whole. But even the personal and life insurance sector of the industry, which deals primarily with individual policies, is not immune to fluctuations and major trends in the business cycle. Interest rates, for example, are just one of the many factors that can dramatically affect the value of personal insurance. Janine Wilson, a rep for Metropolitan, explains that the entire insurance industry is so sensitive to interest rates that even the value of commissions will vary according to the public's perception of interest trends.

"Selling a whole-life policy is very lucrative," Janine says. "We get 50 percent of the first year's premium, 11 percent of the annual premium for each of the next four years, and then 2 percent per year after that." But, as Janine and the rest of the industry discovered, interest rates have a tremendous effect on the the public's perception of insurance. One industry analyst explains, "The interest crisis of the late '70s was a rude awakening for the insurance industry. People who had accumulated cash value in their policies were borrowing heavily against them and investing the newly borrowed funds at interest rates which were five times higher than they were earning on their policies." Janine remarks that the '70s were a difficult time for anyone dealing in financial instruments. It was a particularly difficult time for insurance representatives because they could never be sure of the future of their commissions. For example, she says, after selling a nice, fat whole-life policy and making a mental and financial adjustment to the 11 percent commissions it would earn for four years, many a new insurance representative settled into a more prosperous lifestyle. This is what Janine did. However, when the interest rates skyrocketed, representatives found that many of the expensive whole-life policies were being canceled in favor of their cash value and were replaced by the far less expensive, and less lucrative, term-life policies. This made more cash available to the policy owner who could invest it in higher interest-yielding instruments. When the policies were canceled, so were the representatives' commissions, and the agents found that their personal financial circumstances had not lived up to expectations.

Janine learned the hard way. "I bought a new car based on the commissions I was going to receive from the policies I'd sold. I had so many cancellations it really scared me to death. I was afraid that I couldn't make the car payments." But her personal experience reflects what soon turned out to be a complete industry shakeout. An industry source says, "It wasn't just the reps who were in trouble. At that point, the industry as a whole was in serious jeopardy. The insurance industry professionals used to amortize the policy acquisition costs over years. Now they needed to write them off immediately." He suggests that the interest crisis forced insurance planners to rethink many of the axioms they had believed in since the New Deal.

The insurance industry responded to the unique changes that were occurring in the industry with a new product called universal life insurance. Universal life insurance offers competitive rates of return on monies invested in the policy, plus adjustable premium payment and death benefits. It's also possible for the insured to "invest" money above and beyond the premium payments, and in some cases, the interest rates are so attractive that it pays to do this. Alicia Rodriguez, an analyst with Prudential, says, "The industry has changed so much that shopping for life insurance is like going to the supermarket. There's something for everybody. Each company has its own policy provisions. Some companies offer 'perks' in the interest rates. Others offer more flexible premium payment plans. The industry just isn't the staid, lethargic monolith people have become used to. Competition has changed all that."

One of the major changes, according to Alicia Rodriguez, is that companies are turning their backs on short-term profits in order to build their larger customer base. USLIFE Corporation is the best known of the companies adopting this approach. Ms. Rodriguez says, "They have made their intentions clear by encouraging the conversion of whole-life policies to their universal life policy. They believe that if they don't encourage this type of conversion, their customer base will be lost. It's a gamble that may not make their stockholders happy right now, but I think it's the correct approach in the long run." And it appears that Ms. Rodriguez's analysis is borne out as USLIFE's universal life policy, the Medalist, is winning converts in record numbers.

The average insurance representative has gone through a roller coaster ride over the past five years, according to Janine Wilson. She explains, "Selling insurance got pretty hairy for awhile. I had a lot of learning to do about the new instruments, especially universal life, but it's all paying off." She remarks that the changes in types of insurance policies and the new approaches adopted by companies for the full-service financial marketplace mean that insurance representatives have to become comprehensive financial analysts for their clients.

Insurance company representatives work very hard in this new marketplace. They have a more flexible portfolio of policy options and a highly automated system of customer data basing, but they still have to learn about what they're selling. Carol Bandy, a Metropolitan rep for six years, says, "My typical twelve-hour day starts and ends at 8:30, and I work an average of two weekend days a month. Metropolitan expects us to do a lot on our own but after training, you get used to that." She continues: "For me, training mainly consisted of getting a truckload of books we were expected to learn on our own. We then had to license ourselves in life, health, and casualty insurance." Metropolitan's recent computer upgrade, called SONIC, is making Carol's life easier and targeting her sales approach more directly to the right clients. This is the kind of office support that many companies are adopting for their representatives. "It's great," Carol says. "Where we used to wait eight to ten days for an insurance model illustration, we can get it now in an hour. This quick response to a client's financial needs means that I can service individual clients faster and add more sales calls to my week."

X-Dating business is one of Carol's least favorite, but most productive prospecting tools. "We obtain lists of premium renewal dates for our competition's casualty insurers, mostly auto. We have a big book with names and the dates by which the insured need to renew their casualty policies. I'll call Mr. Jones two months before his renewal date and say something like, 'Mr. Jones, this is Carol Bandy from Metropolitan. I see that your auto insurance is due for renewal. Would you let me have two minutes of your time to explain why it would be to your advantage to renew with Metropolitan?' If he says yes, I tell him. And if he says no, I ask if he'd mind if I call back in a month when he's closer to making a decision about renewal." The term X-Dating refers to nothing more complicated than placing an "X" next to Mr. Jones's name with the date on which the next call is to be made. Carol adds, "Now X-Dating is a breeze. We just key the data into SONIC as we go along and at the end of each day we get a print-out of the X-Date calls to make for the following day.

X-Dating, fast insurance modeling, word processing, and customer data basing are the tools of the insurance representative of the '80s. They allow the representative to process the high volume of business that the commission structure of the insurance industry requires. Barry Hoffer, Carol's district manager at Metropolitan, explains the commission struc-

> *"The interest crisis of the late '70s was a rude awakening for the insurance industry. People who had accumulated cash value in their policies were borrowing against them and investing the funds at interest rates which were five times higher..."*

ture: "On casualty insurance, the reps get between 10 and 15 percent of the first year's premium, and then approximately 7.5 percent on re-newals." He adds that the branch manager gets an override—a commission on a commission—of 16 percent of each rep's commission, and the district manager gets an override of 8 to 10 percent of each rep's commission. For a typical family auto policy with a premium of $1,200, the representative would receive a commission of between $120 and $180, the branch manager would receive an override of between $19.20 and $28.80, and the district manager would receive an override of between $9.60 and $18.00. Clearly, selling this kind of insurance requires a high-volume approach if these commissions are going to amount to a substantial income. At the same time, insurance companies are cutting costs by running a much tighter ship than they ever have before. In fact, according to one industry analyst, there is an informal competition among the big companies in the area of cost cutting and financial management. Unfortunately, Carol Bandy's branch manager received a graphic illustration of this fact as Metropolitan began to phase out the position of branch manager on a companywide basis.

Carol comments on the belt tightening at Metropolitan: "Every year the company sets a maintenance figure for reps. (The maintenance figure is the amount of money it costs Metropolitan to service a rep for a year.) It was $8,000 in 1984. It's going to be $10,000 in '85 and rumor has it that it'll be $17,000 in '86." A rep who doesn't earn the maintenance figure for the company can be fired. Carol says, "We think Metropolitan is raising the maintenance number to be able to fire people. You know, when they fire a rep, they keep the commissions." She was referring to what's known in the business as an orphan agency. When a representative leaves the com-

> *"The industry just isn't the staid, lethargic monolith people have become used to. Competition has changed all that."*

pany, voluntarily or not, his or her accounts are distributed among other representatives. But the other representatives don't receive a commission for the premiums since they didn't generate the business, hence the term "orphan." An executive at Metropolitan responds to Carol's claim that the company is raising the maintenance figure in order to be able to fire representatives who don't meet it: "It's not true. The maintenance figures are calculated by a formula which includes what it costs Metropolitan to run the business. We don't just invent numbers. By the way, one of those costs was a two-million-dollar computer system designed specifically to help the reps become more efficient and productive."

As insurance representatives gain experience in selling the variety of policies their companies underwrite, they become specialists in one or more areas of risk or financial planning. Each type of policy generates its own specialist and each type of insurance specialist soon develops his or her own way of selling policies. Life insurance representatives operate differently from auto insurance salespeople, and commercial casualty insurance specialists approach sales from a different perspective than home insurance salesmen. According to Metropolitan Life's Barry Hoffer, "Each rep has his or her own favorite policy types. It's really just going with what you know best and are most comfortable with. Each kind of insurance selling has its pluses and minuses." For example, life insurance representatives always concentrate on new business since life insurance doesn't require much servicing of existing accounts, and the new life policies pay lucrative commissions the first five years. "I have reps who pretty much just sell life insurance and they're pulling down $35,000 to $40,000 a year. I also have other reps making $400 a week from casualty insurance renewals." Casualty insurance, such as automobile coverage, is a service-intensive sale in which the representative must be ready to deal with many problems that more often than not involve intimate family situations.

Casualty representatives can become like members of the family, according to many casualty insurance salespeople. A rep for Allstate reports, "The stuff you see in the TV ads is true. I've had grown men break down and cry on my shoulder when I showed up and handed them a check in settlement for their house that burned down." A Prudential representative adds, "I lost an account because every time I went to the client's home, he'd spend two hours showing pictures of his last trip to the Grand Canyon. It got so I couldn't afford the time to service the account, and I just couldn't turn the guy off no matter what I did."

Barry Hoffer comments that insurance representatives do more than simply sell policies, service renewals, and move on to other customers. He explains that in the service-intensive policies such as automobile and personal liability, sales representatives are often plunged into the middle of family situations for which no degree of professional training will ever prepare them. As an example, he cites the story of a client who, because of his less than careful attorney, found himself in the middle of a major lawsuit when by rights he bore no responsibility for damages whatsoever. "One of my reps," Barry explains, "got in the middle of a really crazy situation. A young man my rep had insured went to break up a fight between his girlfriend and another girl. In the process, the other girl hit her head and received a mild concussion. Next, our insured client was picked up by the cops and charged with hit-and-run driving. Now, all this had happened without my insurance rep knowing about it. The lawyer for our client told him that the girl had witnesses who would swear that he hit her with the car, and our client replied that he had witnesses who would swear that the girl and her friends were lying. But the lawyer advised that even though he'd probably win in court, it would be a long, drawn-out trial, and would cost a lot of money in legal and investigative fees. The lawyer also told our client that he could get the DA to agree to a plea bargain of leaving the scene of an accident, which is a misdemeanor carrying a $50 fine and two points on the license. So the client and his folks decided that was the easy way out, and for fifty bucks he copped a plea and it was over. Except it wasn't over. By pleading guilty, he had implicitly admitted that he had hit the girl with his car, and he stood convicted in the eyes of the law. The next complication was a little notice he received in the mail informing him that the girl is suing for three quarters of a million dollars in damages. My rep received a panic-stricken call from the client's father and the net result was that Metropolitan and the family were all in the middle of this mess together."

Lawyers are the bane of the insurance business, according to an executive at Allstate. He quickly qualifies his opinion: "Don't get me wrong. Most lawyers are ethical. It's just that getting involved with a lawyer is like seeing a doctor—it usually means something's wrong. And it usually costs a lot of money. We spend a fortune each year in investigations alone. The costs of investigating and adjudicating a claim are so high that in many instances it pays for us to simply settle out of court even when we believe we're right." And this points to the central feature of most insurance company management operations: they manage money by controlling expenses and increasing their revenues. And this methodology applies to controlling the dollar amount of court settlements, where applicable, as well as to restructuring the entire sales representation and compensation operation.

Compensation in the insurance industry has traditionally been on a straight commission basis, with companies arranging a "financing plan" with their representatives. The financing plan amounted to a draw against future commissions, and the sum was agreed upon by the representative and management based on what both sides saw as the projected commission earnings of the rep. Although this arrangement is still typical in the industry, some companies, such as Connecticut General, are also hiring salaried (that is, noncommissioned) financial planners to handle financial planning and other aspects of the insurance business. Since an agent's commissions are typically 50 percent of the premiums in the financial planning end of the insurance business, it's not surprising that a company such as Connecticut General is phasing out its agent operations.

In fact, according to Alicia Rodriguez at Prudential, company agents are becoming an endangered species. She explains that since cost cutting is very important in today's economy, many insurance companies, such as GEICO and Life of Virginia, sell directly to the public. And companies such as Prudential and Metropolitan, which used to use agents extensively, are phasing out the agent operation in favor of brokers. Brokers are straight commission reps who are licensed to sell the kind of policies that are being underwritten by a particular insurance company. Since brokers maintain their own independent office operation and overhead, insurance companies can deal with brokers on a straight commission basis. And the commission can run as high as 90 percent of the premium, depending on the company, the policies, and the broker. According to Stan Waldmere at Connecticut General, "We know we have a great training system for our reps. I think half the brokers hanging a shingle in the state are former Connecticut General reps." John Rafal testifies to this: "During my first year I thought I knew it all. I didn't follow recommended selling procedures, and I didn't earn a whole lot of money either. My second year I wised up a bit and decided to talk to some of the reps who were successful. In each case—and I'm not exaggerating—the advice they gave me was the same advice I'd learned in training." So John implemented CG's training policies and today he is an extremely successful independent financial planner.

According to one industry source, insurance is being sold like soap in retail operations such as Sears/Allstate where people can literally walk in off the street and buy insurance. David Nunzio, an Allstate rep, says, "Working here in a Sears store certainly solves the referral problem that some reps face in prospecting for new business, but Sears is extremely volume

> "The stuff you see in the TV ads is true. I've had grown men break down and cry on my shoulder when I show up and hand them a check in settlement for their house that burned down."

conscious." David explains that his management expects his book of business to reach between 3,000 and 4,000 clients in ten years. Commenting on that number, David says, "That means I need to write an average of more than one new policy a day." Alicia Rodriguez says, "That's okay. Writing a new policy each day can be done. It's not as outrageous as it sounds."

For many new Allstate salespeople, the booths at Sears are stepping stones in their careers. For reps who are successful selling off-the-street policies, the next step at Allstate is a local agency. Fran Manfra has just been moved to a local Allstate office in Westchester County, New York. She says, "That's how I got started. You learn a lot in those little booths.

You learn how to get right to the point. Sometimes they're stacked six deep at the booth, so you need to really zero in on who is a hot prospect and who's just passing the time."

Another important, but simple, method representatives use when reaching for new business is keeping their existing customers happy so that they will refer potential clients. In fact, referrals are the checks and balances of the insurance industry, according to John Rafal. "There is no substitute for a satisfied customer. He or she will help generate new business without fail." And according to an executive at Metropolitan, "Referrals are a very wholesome part of the industry. In order to get referrals, you need to have a satisfied customer. And in order to have a satisfied customer, you need to do a good job. So, to the insurance industry, referrals create a checks and balances system in which competence and hard work are rewarded." However, to a neophyte insurance rep, the referral system can be a Catch-22 situation. How do you get referrals before you have any satisfied customers who can refer you? According to Barry Hoffer, "Basically, you do the insurance rep's version of pounding the pavement. You do a lot of cold calling on the telephone. You write a lot of introductory letters. You've got to be pleasantly persistent. There are no shortcuts in this business—it takes a lot of hard work."

In rating the top five companies, we were faced with a bit of a dilemma. Insurance sales vary greatly in different areas of the industry. Selling life insurance to individuals is very different from selling financial planning to Fortune 500 executives, and even selling automobile insurance is very different from selling life insurance. Would it benefit our readers if we separated the rankings of the insurance companies into different categories? And if we did, what would we do in the case of the diversified companies such as Metropolitan? Our alternative was to rank the different kinds of companies together—thereby possibly falling into the trap of comparing apples and oranges.

We decided on the latter course and chose to rank all insurance companies in one category. Our main reason is that we intend this book to serve as a guide to sales reps and potential reps who are investigating what selling is like in a given industry. Thus, we decided that it would be beneficial to compare a company such as Connecticut General, which specializes in financial planning, with diversified companies such as Metropolitan and Prudential.

Normally, we award individual companies pluses or minuses on intangible industry or corporate factors. In the case of insurance, we are giving the entire industry a [−]. We want to call your attention to the fact that the complexion of the insurance industry has changed dramatically in the last five years, and industry analysts expect that the changes affecting the industry will continue for some time to come.

If industry planners could report on the future, they might say that someday insurance salesmen will be as much of an anachronism as the bakery deliveryman who brought fresh hot loaves to the doorstep every morning. Gone are the days of the kindly old "Father Knows Best" insurance agent dropping by for a cup of coffee and an afternoon chat, a look at the latest family snapshots, and almost as an afterthought, a renewal of the family's policy. This old-fashioned agent is rapidly being replaced by insurance reps who sell in volume in department stores like Sears; he is being replaced by direct-sales insurance companies such as GEICO; and he is being replaced by independent brokers who are full-service family and commercial financial planners such as John Rafal. Once getting a job selling insurance was easy, but now the market is highly competitive. Companies no longer care that you can sell a policy to six relatives by next Friday. That type of policy sale has been replaced by the long-term view which sees insurance as a part of the larger financial picture. One industry source says, "Just as the horse and buggy were replaced by the automobile, so will the insurance salesman be replaced by the financial planner." Alicia Rodriguez adds, "Tomorrow's insurance salesperson will have a degree in business and will probably need an MBA to really go anywhere in the insurance field." Because we believe this is an accurate picture of the industry's future and the changes that will occur, we feel that prospective job seekers should take a long, hard look at what the industry will hold for them and what they will need to succeed in it.

INSURANCE	COMPENSATION	COMMISSION	SUPPORT	INTANGIBLE
1 Connecticut General Life Ins. Co.	5		4	+
2 Allstate Ins. Co.	4		4	+
3 Metropolitan Life Ins. Co.	3		4	
4 Farmers Group, Inc.	3		4	–
5 The Prudential Ins. Co. of America	3		3	

Compensation in the insurance industry is strictly on a commission basis. An exception: salaried financial planners who are being hired by Connecticut General and other companies. This is a new concept in the industry, however, so our compensation rankings were computed on commission earnings alone. The industry median annual compensation for a rep who's been in the industry for two years is $24,900.

Connecticut General [+]

Their compensation plans and support, their philosophy of business and education, and their fine reputation have earned Connecticut General our number-one ranking. Connecticut General continues to offer an outstanding training program which is invaluable to their reps. In addition, their excellent reputation in the business community not only opens many doors, but it also generates sales.

Allstate [+]

With the insurance industry becoming so highly competitive, we believe that companies need a special niche in order to succeed. Through their Sears affiliation, Allstate has established a niche which is guaranteed to generate business for reps.

REAL ESTATE

THE TOP FIVE:

1 Centex Corp.
2 Ryan Homes, Inc.
3 Ryland Group Inc.
4 Century 21 Real Estate Corp.
5 The Meredith Corp.

S omewhere between 20 to 25 percent of all American families are on the move each year, most of them selling or buying their own properties. Over 98 percent of these transactions involve a local real estate agent. Similarly, the recent boom in office properties involve the listing and sales facilities of the local commercial real estate brokerage. Increasingly, as homeowners realize the need to sell and buy quickly they are utilizing the services of national franchises such as Century 21 and Better Homes and Gardens that combine the intimacy of the local community real estate broker with the power of national property listings and ties to major lenders. This is changing the entire shape of the real estate industry.

"Every July I want to quit." So said Kira Saydek, an independent real estate agent working for one of the Better Homes and Gardens franchise agencies, our number-five rated company. "July always seems to be the toughest month for me. Schools are out and people with kids are stepping up their search for a house because they want everything in place by the time school begins again in September." Kira is an energetic, experienced real estate agent who has set her own standards in the business. "My way to sell real estate is certainly not necessarily the 'right way,' and Lord knows most agents don't agree with my methods, but it works for me. I'm comfortable with it." Kira takes a personal interest in her clients. "I always conduct an interview in which I find out my clients' likes and dislikes, particularly how their habits and personal tastes are likely to affect the kind of house they're looking for."

In some cases she even violates the unwritten rule of real estate selling and turns away sales. "When I was selling in Rockland County, New York, I could have closed on a house with a middle-aged couple who'd lived in the city all their lives. Their only child had just entered college, and they were looking for their dream house in 'the country.' " But something was bothering Kira. "The man was a high-powered executive, the kind of guy who schedules everything to within five minutes. During my first interview, he made a wisecrack about hating to wait in line. 'If I'm ever captured by the enemy and they want to get information from me, all they have to do is make me stand in line for an hour and I'll do anything they want,' he said." Kira knew that after this house sale he'd be standing in line for more than an hour twice a day. "There are two ways to get to the city from Rockland County: auto and train. He hated to drive, and the train commute was easily two hours each way—that is if the trains were running. On their last visit to the house, I told them I wasn't going to sell them the house and I explained why. The man stared at me as if I'd just turned into a creature from *Star Wars*, and I thought his wife was going to cry." But Kira had an alternative plan. "Better Homes and Gardens has offices all over the place. I located a house for them in Westchester County—an easier commute to New York. They had to give up a little bit on the house because real estate values are higher in Westchester, but the commute was under an hour on trains that were reliable."

Kira says, "Most people think that real estate agents get a 6 percent commission on what they sell. In fact, I frequently get asked to cut my commission." But the numbers can be quite misleading because, according to Kira, most agencies use a listing service, which gets 3 percent of the 6 percent commission. State and local taxes take $4\frac{1}{2}$ percent of the 6 percent commission in Rockland County. The parent organization, Better Homes and Gardens, gets 5 percent. This leaves a commission of $5\frac{1}{4}$ percent which is split evenly between the agency and the individual agent. So, in this scenario, the agent earns a commission of $2\frac{5}{8}$ percent on the sale. But Kira points out,

"We usually don't see the money for three or four months because that's how long all the paper takes to clear after a title closing."

In the case of referrals from other agencies, commissions are even lower. Because residential real estate sales are typically made by a local agency, Kira points out that it's a fairly common practice for agencies to refer clients to each other when a client moves to a different locale. In this case, the typical commission split is 70 percent to the selling broker and 30 percent to the referring broker. So when Kira referred her clients to the agent in Westchester County, the Westchester agent earned a commission of 1⅜ percent and Kira received a commission of ⅞ percent. The selling price was $230,000, so Kira made a little over $2,000 and the agent in Westchester made over $3,000. Thus, Kira's concern for her clients cost her $1,000. However, she wasn't dismayed. "It's worth a heck of a lot more than $1,000 to me to know that I'm doing my job the way I think it should be done." And it seems that nice guys don't always finish last. "The gentleman who bought the house in Westchester County has since referred three other sales to me. Two of the sales I made in Rockland and I got a referral fee on one because the house was purchased elsewhere."

> *In some cases she even violates the unwritten rule of real estate selling and turns away sales.*

Joseph Petri, an agent for Century 21, our number-four ranked company and also a franchise operation, says, "Referrals are the lifeblood of this business. I had a case where a client didn't even buy from the agent I sent him to, but he was so grateful for the help I gave him that he referred his whole office to me. They were relocating in the Southwest and just by making some calls, I wound up with a $10,000 commission."

Our research reveals that the real estate industry is one of the most diverse of the service trades when it comes to sales techniques and styles of presentation. On one end of the scale there are representatives such as Kira Saydek, who take a personal interest in clients, and at the other end there are what the trade calls the "barracudas," who will do anything to make a sale. Mike Taggart, a representative for the Ryland Group, our number-three ranked company, tells one of the most incredible "barracuda" stories in the annals of real estate agenting. Mike begins: "An agent I know was ready to close a sale with the owner of a house. She had a buyer who made a fair offer. When she went to propose it to the owner, he had a heart attack right in front of her. As he was being wheeled outside to the ambulance, she had him sign the contract agreeing to the sale." And according to Mike, "She wasn't ashamed. In fact she's proud of the sale. She'd tell you that she did the guy a favor because he wouldn't have to worry about selling his house anymore while he was recuperating, and if he died, his wife and kids wouldn't have the hassle of the house hanging over their heads." Postscript: The man recovered and was so incensed at the agent that he sued her and her agency for damages.

There are four distinct segments within the real estate sales industry. There are corporations such as Centex, Ryan Homes, and The Ryland Group, our number-one, two-, and three-ranked companies respectively, each of which specializes in a soup-to-nuts menu of real estate, buildings, and mortgages or mortgage brokering. A second segment consists of regional land developers such as AMREP, Deltona, Fairfield, and Horizon. These companies specialize in land development for residential and recreational communities in regions such as Florida and the Southwest. Another segment consists of franchise operations such as Century 21, our number-four ranked company and a subsidiary of TWA, and Better Homes and Gardens, our fifth-ranked company and a subsidiary of the Meredith Publishing Group. The last segment consists of small, independent real estate agencies, whose numbers, according to one nervous industry source, seem to be multiplying like rabbits.

> "People became very creative in financing houses. In many cases, the banks were simply eliminated from the transactions."

The Dallas-based Centex Corporation had gross sales of $1.3 billion in 1984 and has earned our number-one ranking primarily for their far-sighted, comprehensive approach to the sale of residential real estate. Some name corporations such as Deltona and Horizon have focused on the regional markets of Florida and the Southwest respectively, and according to an industry analyst, have not done as well as Centex, which has established its base of operations in key growth areas all over the U.S. While Deltona reported a 20 percent drop in gross sales and Horizon a 30 percent drop in the 1983 to 1984 bear market, Centex itself has reported a more than 10 percent increase.

"Having a billion dollars behind you gives you a very warm feeling," says Ralph Bradley, a Centex rep in Chicago. He continues, "When we go into a community, we take care of everything: land, building, financing." He compares working for Centex to his experience with a small, independent real estate agency. "The complexities were enormous. We had to arrange for financing with an independent bank. The banks were experiencing growing pains and that affected the way they were handling mortgages. In one case, I had a deal all lined up with a bank in Indiana for a buyer in Cicero which is just outside Chicago, but the sale hinged on getting a 15-year, fixed-rate mortgage at a maximum of 13 percent. The local banks were offering rates in the 13.9 to 14½ percent range, so I jumped at this bank in Indiana." But unfortunately, as Ralph discovered, Murphy's Law always seems to be in operation when mortgage money is involved. "When I was ready to finalize the mortgage, the bank balked at the fact that the house wasn't in Indiana. They said they were only offering mortgages to houses within the state." Yet Ralph swears, "I told them right up front where the house was, and all the details." An industry source adds, "Frankly, many local banks didn't know what they were doing. Policy sometimes changed twice a week, and very often the new mortgage policy wasn't based on any information that would have impacted on the bank's position." Ralph adds, "I figured that the Indiana bank thought they could increase the mortgage by a point or so, but they couldn't tell me that so they just backed off." Art Needy, a mortgage officer in a New Jersey bank, agrees. "We'd have meetings almost every day during the crazy mortgage times in the early '80s. You could see that the officers were scared. They didn't know what to do." And what happened to Ralph's sale? "I lost it. A buyer came along and offered the owner 50 percent down if the owner would hold a 12 percent mortgage for ten years." Art adds, "People became very creative in financing houses. In many cases, the banks were simply eliminated from the transactions."

And how are things for Ralph at Centex? "Fantastic. Of course we're dealing with new construction so the problem of representing many different sellers, each with his own needs, is eliminated. And Centex can arrange very flexible financing. Having a billion dollars behind you means never having to say 'I'm sorry.' " Centex's billion-dollar sales come from a variety of operations, including the production of construction materials. We believe this offers Centex resiliency in a bear market for home construction, and should be comforting news for their representatives.

Ryan Homes, a Pittsburgh-based company, saw sales rise by an incredible 50 percent during the 1982-83 bear market. They have earned our number-two ranking primarily because of their very broad-based approach to the residential real estate market. One industry analyst says, "No matter what the real estate market does, Ryan will win." The company is involved in the construction and sale of single-family houses, townhouses, garden apartments, and low-rise condominiums. They also build low-income housing units under various government-subsidized programs. The same industry analyst says, "Ryan really tightened up their operation after the 1980 debacle." He was referring to the 25 percent industrywide drop in single-family housing starts in the 1979-80 period during which Ryan's sales dropped nearly 15 percent. After this, Ryan pursued the market aggressively. And aggressively means going into the financing end of home buying. Frank Shore, a Ryan sales representative in Philadelphia, says, "The company has been exceptionally creative when it comes to financing. They were one of the first to generate mortgage funds by selling investor bonds backed by the properties and by U.S. government securities." An industry source states, "A number of companies were using the investor bond technique to generate private mortgage funds. But one of the problems was that investors were nervous about the viability of the mortgages in view of the wild interest swings." He adds, "Ryan was the first company I know that backed the bonds partially with U.S. government securities." And as a result, they generated considerable capital which in turn enabled them to sell houses. Frank adds, "There's simply no comparison in working for a company like Ryan versus one of the small independent agencies." He explains: "We at Ryan know it's in our interest to cut points on the financing side because we're going to make it up on the selling side. What's in it for your neighborhood bank to cut points?" Kira agrees. "It's true. Banks are selling money, period. Ryan is selling houses and money, so they can lose on one and make it up on the other."

The Ryland Group has earned our number-three ranking, just barely losing out to Ryan Homes for the number-two spot. It was Ryan's growth record of 62 percent in the 1981-83 bear market and their innovative financing packages that earned them the number-two spot, but Ryland is not far behind. Like Ryan, Ryland has become involved in the financing side of the real estate business through their subsidiary, the Ryland Mortgage Company. This Maryland-based company realized a 91 percent spurt in sales (to $395 million) in 1983 after seeing sales fall by over 20 percent ($258 million to $206 million) in the 1980-82 bear market.

A Ryland spokesman comments, "Because of the interest rate fluctuations, more and more companies are acting like banks in the secondary mortgage markets." This secondary market operates when companies, individuals, or government agencies buy either the actual mortgage from a company such as Ryland, or buy securities backed by the mortgages held by Ryland. Some examples of government-sponsored secondary mortgage programs are: Fannie Mae, the Federal National Mortgage Association; Ginnie Mae, the Government National Mortgage Association; and Freddie Mac, the Federal Home Loan Mortgage Corporation. Without getting into the technical banking aspects of the secondary mortgage market, it is sufficient to say that it serves as an insurance program to the mortgage originators, usually banks, but more recently to companies such as Ryland, who want to limit their risks in mortgage originations. The impact of these mortgage plans on sales can be dramatic because real estate buyers can shop for a house and for a mortgage at the same time. In addition, it offers an agency representative a significant amount of leverage over a real estate broker from a small or an independent agency with no supplementary source of mortgage money. A representative from a local real estate agency in western New Jersey laments, "While I have to beg for an edge on mortgage points from one of the local banks, these reps from the national real estate groups can walk in and spread money around like fertilizer. The 'sold' signs spring up like April grass."

Commenting on the dramatic growth in the secondary mortgage market after the recession of 1981-82, one industry analyst says that it was just a matter of time before the secondary mortgage market expanded beyond the federally backed associations and into the private sector. The dramatic fluctuations in the interest rates and resulting impact on housing starts in the late '70s and early '80s created a revolution in the mortgage concept itself.

> "Ryan is selling houses and money, so they can lose on one and make it up on the other."

An industry wit commented that Century 21 is the only company in the business that is definitely going to have to change its name in the years to come. Of course, he may not be around to find out what the new name is. Century 21 is the largest real estate franchise company in the United States. One industry source says, "They didn't pioneer the concept of the franchised agencies but they sure did perfect it." Century 21 agencies pay top dollar for the franchise: where Better Homes and Gardens charges member agencies a 5 percent commission on sales, Century 21 charges their agencies 8 percent. Betty Richards, an agent at a Century 21 agency in New Jersey, says, "They're well worth the price. Their network system is the most sophisticated in the country." The computerization of the real estate industry has expanded the markets for many local agencies. Due to the referral system, by which a real estate agent can earn a commission, usually in the ½ to 1 percent range, having a strong national network can result in a referral fee for an agent who otherwise wouldn't be in that particular out-of-town market. Betty adds that last year she earned over $8,000 in referral fees alone. She reports that when she used to work for a local nonfranchised agency several years ago, she was lucky if her referral income was $500 a year.

> *"Are you working for me or against me?" the seller often asks the agent. "It's pretty easy to feel sympathetic to the buyer because you're working so closely with him," agents report.*

The Century 21 concept is simple but effective. It transforms a local real estate agency, usually an agency that already has strong ties to a community, into a point of entry into a nationwide real estate network within which agents can co-broke a sale in different parts of the country as easily as two agents can co-broke a sale in different parts of the same county. According to an industry source, "The goal of TWA, Century 21's parent company, was to provide the same kind of personalized service on a nationwide basis that independent real estate agencies have been providing on a local basis for many years." An industry analyst agrees, adding that modern technology, specifically telecommunications, has made such coordination possible. And Betty adds, "I was a little nervous about using the computer system, but now I honestly don't know how I worked without it." Randolph Meade, a partner in a Century 21 agency in New York, says, "We can handle absolutely every aspect of a standard buy-sell situation. For example, I had a client come in off the street. He'd just found out that he was being transferred to St. Louis in a month and he wanted to talk about selling his house. When I pulled up a listing on the computer of the homes which were available in the St. Louis area, I thought his eyes were going to pop right out of his head. And how did it all work out? I sold his New York house and got a referral fee on his St. Louis house."

"Are you working for me or against me?" is a question real estate agents are hearing more and more. Randolph says, "Most people don't think of this aspect of selling real estate, but it's a very unusual aspect. We are actually working for the seller, but we spend most of the time with the buyer." Kira agrees. "I may spend half an hour with a seller, visiting his house and deciding on a selling price. But before I've sold the house, I've usually spent days with the buyer. I've gotten to know him, his wife, his kids, and even his personal habits." Betty adds, "Sometimes it's pretty hard. For example, I had a lovely young family in last week. They were on a very strict budget and could not afford more than a $1,100 monthly payment for a mortgage. We work pretty closely with a local bank, and I was able to get them a twenty-five-year variable rate mortgage at 11.8 percent the first year, with an increase up to only 13 percent the third year. But the numbers just didn't quite make it. Unfortunately, the price of the house was $25,000 too high. I went back to the owner, and in effect, pleaded the case for this family. He just stared at me, and after a full minute he said, 'Are you working for me or against me?' " Betty realized her mistake. "I apologized to him. He was right. The problem is that it's pretty easy to feel sympathetic to the buyer because you're working so closely with him."

The two hats a real estate agent must wear have caused problems in the industry because the agent represents both buyer and seller at the same time. A spokesman for the National Board of Realtors says, "This is a big problem in the real estate sales industry. We have had more than one meeting about how to handle the duality of the real estate agent's role in selling." He adds, "There is definitely a movement in the works to have the buyer pay the realtor's commission. I don't know if that will be the outcome, but I do believe you'll see a change in the agent-buyer-seller system in the not-too-distant future." An additional aspect of this problem, according to many real estate agents, is the intimacy they must share with both buyer and seller. The seller, one listing agent explains, has often invested most of the family's savings in a house. "He's made the most important commitment of his life, and I'm supposed to represent that commitment to a buyer. I don't take that task lightly." On the other hand, buyers show up at an agency door and put their dreams right on the table. As a Princeton, New Jersey, broker explains, "I meet people who would give anything for a house in Princeton, which is considered a prestigious town. Yet, when they see the numbers in black and white, they're out in one of the townships and counting pennies just to make the down payment. I get to know their kids, ride in their station wagons, and shake hands with their dogs. I know these families and I hate to see despair in their faces when they realize they just can't afford the house of their dreams. I like selling houses, and I love selling houses in Princeton, but I hate not being able to sell the right house to the right person every time."

The psychology of real estate can be very strange, according to Randolph Meade, our Century 21 partner. "I don't think it's a good idea in any business to get involved in a client's personal life, but unfortunately in the real estate business it's often very difficult to avoid." Betty Richards agrees. "Look, I've had to move with a husband and two kids myself, so I know what it's like. Clients like to feel understood." Rodney Sanders, a Los Angeles psychologist, adds, "A house is the single most personal purchase a person is going to make. It's almost as personal a choice as choosing a mate, and can be filled with considerable trauma for a lot of people." Dr. Sanders emphasizes, "During the crazy inflationary spiral in the late '70s, real estate values here in Southern California went through the roof. I treated a number of patients for severe depression, and in each case the onset of the depression was triggered by different aspects of the real estate problem." During this period, certain properties tripled in price in the space of a year, and many people who were waiting to buy a house simply got shut out of the market. Dr. Sanders adds, "I also treated people who were having a very big problem with the fact that they sold their properties before the boom hit. It's generally agreed among mental health professionals that moving generates a level of stress second only to that of losing a spouse. I certainly don't envy real estate agents. They definitely earn their keep."

And he won't get an argument from Betty Richards: "The psychology of real estate is fascinating. My worst case involved a very well-to-do California couple. They had bought their dream house in California and had lived in it for just two months when the husband was transferred to New York City. The wife was an interior decorator, which is tough enough on real estate agents, but to make matters worse, she had just found a great job and her career was really taking off." Betty smiles sadly. "She left a fingernail trail all the way from California to New York." Betty recalls their initial meeting. "Her very first words to me were, 'How much are you willing to cut your commission?' I thought to myself, Maybe this is just a bad dream. The alarm will go off soon. I'll wake up. And hopefully I can start the day over." But that was not to be the case. "Things were so bad that if I pointed up and said, 'That's the ceiling,' she'd say, 'No it isn't. It's the floor.' " Finally Betty had had enough. "I read her the riot act—nicely, of course." And the result? "I made the sale, but she still doesn't like me." Dr. Sanders points out: "In a case like that, it's not uncommon for the uprooted partner to be furious with the spouse, who is already scared witless about the job change, and trying to put up a brave front. Neither one of them wants to move, and they feel trapped. So who gets dumped on? The family dog and the real estate agent." And, according to Dr. Sanders, not necessarily in that order.

> *"While I have to beg for an edge on mortgage points from one of the local banks, these reps from the national real estate groups can walk in and spread money around like fertilizer . . . 'sold' signs spring up like April grass."*

Better Homes and Gardens Realty is a subsidiary of The Meredith Corporation, publishers of the venerable *Better Homes and Gardens* magazine, and was formed to capitalize on the booming real estate market as well as the huge circulation of the magazine (currently about eight million readers). They have received our number-five ranking for much the same reason that Century 21 was awarded our number-four spot. BH&G, like Century 21, is using modern computer network technology to create a national market for its local agencies. Utilizing this new technology to generate sales requires considerable training, and BH&G representatives are trained extensively.

Kira Saydek comments on the company's training, which is similar to the rest of the industry's today. "Training is very definitely up to the individual, although many agencies will sponsor training programs." And who actually does the training? The Board of Realtors has established the Graduate Realtor Institute which offers courses. The courses are usually held at hotels, local colleges, and in some cases at agencies. The first step in the training program is to get the state broker's license. After that, requirements differ from state to state. In New York, brokers are required to take at least one course every four years to keep current with the goings-on in the industry." George Kendall, an agent for another local BH&G agency, adds, "Any agent worth his or her salt will be taking more than the required courses. The business is changing too fast." Kira agrees. "I got my CRS (Certified Residential Specialist) certificate. I feel that more paper credentials will make me a better agent." And George adds, "Usually our clients think so too." Some of the most valuable training is in the area of financing. George says, "With interest rates as volatile as they are these days, if you're a real estate agent and don't know the financing end of the business, you're not going to be in business very long." Kira adds, "At Better Homes we're strongly encouraged to take seminars in financing. In many cases, the agency holds them right at the local office. Once you can see financing from the bank officer's point of view and can understand the fine points of the deal, you do a better job for both the buyer and the seller. Clients really do appreciate that, and the more deals you can pull together, the more commissions you can make."

"Financing can make or break a sale," George Kendall confirms. "One sale that I remember involved an elderly gentleman who had owned his house for over thirty years. His mortgage was paid up, and he wanted to sell and retire to Florida. His asking price was about $35,000 too high for my buyer, who was relying on normal financing arrangements." But George's financial training at the local Better Homes and Gardens agency had served him well. "The seller wanted $175,000 for the house. The buyer could make a $50,000 down payment from selling his own house, but couldn't get a bank to give him a mortgage for the balance of $125,000." So George called some banks. "I arranged for the seller to remortgage his house immediately for $55,000 at 12 percent for ten years. The seller then agreed to hold a $55,000 mortgage for the buyer at 12 percent for twenty years. The buyer then took out a mortgage of his own for the $70,000 balance." And so everyone was happy. "The seller got the $105,000 in cash which he wanted. The buyer's bank was willing to give him a mortgage for $70,000 while they weren't willing to give a mortgage for $125,000 and the buyer was able to get a mortgage for $55,000 at 12 percent for twenty years." If you think that sounds complicated, George claims, "That was simple. When you factor in variable rate mortgages and balloon mortgages on top of the self-financing concepts, it's almost like you're a financial analyst, not a real estate broker."

"When is creative selling not creative selling?" asks Kira. "When no one acknowledges that there is a sale." She points out that many people are becoming quite creative when it comes to the taxation aspects of selling houses. "One buyer I found owned a car dealership. He struck a deal with the seller of the house for a new car every two years for twenty years. Off the books of course." And how is Kira affected by a deal of this type? "First of all, I'm obligated by law to point out that such an arrangement is illegal. After that, I have nothing to do with it. If someone wants to sell a $200,000 house for $140,000, that's their business." And what about Kira's commission? "In a deal like this, I make an arrangement for a special fee, so I don't lose." She hastily adds, "Please understand that I do not encourage this kind of an arrangement. However, if my client comes to me and tells me that this is the way the sale is going to be made, I am not about to walk out the door."

Kira's aggressive presence in the sales arena is typical of many local

SECTION TWO:
CONSUMER GOODS

AUTOMOBILES

BOOK
PUBLISHING

FOOD

MICRO-
COMPUTERS

RETAIL

AUTOMOBILES

THE TOP FIVE:

1 Honda Motor Co., Ltd.
2 Ford Motor Co.
3 Chrysler Corp.
4 General Motors Corp.
5 Toyota Motor Co.

The automobile industry is one of the backbone manufacturing and sales industries in the skeleton of the American economy. With over two million cars and trucks on the road and about fifty thousand automobile sales franchises, the industry is a giant employer. Yet, notwithstanding its size and power, the automobile manufacturing and sales is only a 75- to 80-year old industry, with real commercial growth occurring within the past 60 years. And like the aerospace industry, automobile manufacturing and sales is a product of the 20th century that is founded on 18th and 19th century technology. Automobiles are America's dream machines, and automobile sales people help make those dreams into reality.

Like the residential real estate industry and many other franchised businesses in the country, the automobile sales industry is made up of locally owned, independent showroom dealerships that buy from the manufacturer or trade among one another and sell directly to the customer. At these dealerships, sales commission and compensation figures vary widely, and this makes comparisons among them very difficult to establish. However, there have been general trends throughout the auto sales industry which indicate profound changes over the past twenty-five years and which point to a very different car sales market in the near future. Any analysis of automobile sales, therefore, must begin with the market terrain as it existed twenty-five years ago.

Twenty-five years ago, there were very few dealerships which sold more than one make of car and, likewise, there were not as many low-end foreign car dealerships as there are today. Large, single-car franchises which traded in American-made automobiles were the only game in town in most metropolitan areas, and they held a complete monopoly over all new car sales. American cars were big twenty-five years ago, and they were delivered to the dealer's lot as a basic unit with an engine, a chassis, a stock interior, a three-speed, wheel-mounted manual transmission, and a steering wheel, all sitting on a frame. Everything else, including power steering, automatic transmission, power brakes, an AM radio, seat belts, long-life tires, and a padded dashboard, was a factory or dealer-installed option which formed a major component of the salesman's commission.

Twenty-five years ago, the traditional Volkswagen Beetle was the largest-selling foreign car, but full-service dealerships and service facilities were limited to major metropolitan areas. There was virtually no Japanese penetration of the American market; Renault was more of an oddity than a car, and only the very rich could afford a Mercedes or a Porsche. The British cars couldn't start in damp weather. Twenty-five years ago, most of the huge fins had disappeared from the rear decks of Detroit's cars in favor of a lower, rounder look, and gasoline could be purchased for under twenty-five cents a gallon along most of the major highways. The Ford Thunderbird had been toned down considerably from its rakish 1956 and 1957 models; the Edsel was just an unhappy memory, and the Mustang, the Pontiac GTO, and the Bonneville were events just waiting to happen.

Twenty-five years ago, only the futurists were predicting the possibility of major oil shortages or the complete domination of the American small car market by the Germans and the Japanese. Only the psychically prescient could have foreseen the skyrocketing interest rates that so depressed new car sales that Chrysler had to beg for loan guarantees from the federal government just to stay alive long enough to develop and sell cars based on a technology that ten years earlier had been laughed at by most American car manufacturers. And twenty-five years ago, Elliott Katz glued a giant cardboard skate key to the rear of his black Volkswagen Beetle and drove around the flagpole in front of Forest Hills High School during fourth period lunch. Everybody, including Mrs. Weil, ran out to see what the commotion was, and Elliott Katz got detention. That was twenty-five years ago.

> "I grew up thinking that 'planned obsolescence' was an obscenity . . ."

Today the automobile sales industry is undergoing a rapid change in the way it delivers its product to its customers and in the types of products it delivers. Automobile showroom dealers who sell American-made cars exclusively are facing some of the stiffest competition they have ever faced and are reconsidering their chosen vocation in the light of foreign car sales in the small- to medium-sized model range. The structure of the dealership organization itself, which has changed very little from what it was twenty-five years ago, has now begun to evolve. Dealers who had relied on the one-car franchise have now begun to look at multi-manufacturer showrooms, and dealers who relegated their used car sales to a well-concealed corner of the lot have moved them up to center stage as a way of attracting a younger, less affluent buyer who might someday become a steady "forty-eight month rollover" buyer who trades in his new car every time his four-year car loan has fully amortized.

"My Dad used to fight like hell with our family car," remembers Steve Marks, a New York resident and prototypical car buyer. In the early 1980s, Steve was in the market for a small car. He hadn't bought a car since 1975, at which time he bought a VW Rabbit—since deceased along with a sizable number of other VW Rabbits from that first model year, and according to Steve, deservedly so. His car purchase prior to the ill-fated Rabbit had been a 1971 Buick Estate Wagon which, Steve says, "had the handling characteristics of the Queen Elizabeth II. Every time I was ready to park I kept looking for little tugboats to help me." Steve adds, "My father was a very kind man, not given to violence. But I have vivid childhood memories of him trying to pick a fight with our family car. He used to yell at it and then act as if it were yelling back. I grew up thinking that 'planned obsolescence' was an obscenity because I always heard the phrase 'bleeping planned obsolescence' as he angrily slammed the car door and stomped off to call our garage."

Steve, like many Americans, was fed up with the American cars he had seen in the '60s and '70s. Steve says, "After the A-frame on the right rear of my Estate Wagon cracked three months after the warranty expired, I swore off American cars." Steve bought his Buick Estate Wagon in 1971, the car's first model year. It was billed by Buick as their top-of-the-line wagon, with the same features and identical body as their top sedan, the Electra. Steve says, "I was furious. I paid $5,000, which was a lot of money back then, for that car precisely because I was sick and tired of car problems. I wanted the best." A Buick spokesman says, "There was a problem with the frame back then but the company did take care of it." Steve agrees reluctantly. "Sure they took care of it. After three months of screaming bloody murder to every Buick and GM official from here to Detroit. The manager at my dealership told me it was my fault that the frame cracked. What did he think I was doing—transporting elephants for the circus?" The Buick spokesman says, "We can't speak for our individual dealers, but I do know that we at Buick weren't aware of the problem until we'd received a number of complaints, so that's probably why it took so long for him to get a response from the company." A spokesman for Mark Buick, a very large dealership in Yonkers, New York, says, "You have to understand that anytime anything goes wrong with a car, the customer wants to blame the car or the dealer. But 95 percent of the time the problem is due to the customer's misuse or failure to service the car properly." Steve smiles. "Now that I think of it, he's probably right. I would drive into a service station and say, 'Fill it up with premium and check the oil.' I confess: I forgot to ask to have the frame checked too."

Steve says, "I thought Honda was a motorcycle when I began looking for a new car in the early '80s. But I kept hearing good things about their cars, so I went to a Honda dealer near my Manhattan office. I saw the Prelude and it was love at first sight." But he wasn't about to jump into anything. "I decided to do my homework. I read about the car. I asked mechanics. And I nearly killed myself once because I would stop Honda owners as they were driving and ask them about the car. There were no exceptions. Every report I got said, 'This is a great car.' " And so Steve went to negotiate his deal.

"What's your best deal?" That's probably the question most often heard by automobile sales representatives. In a typical scenario, a customer walks into a showroom, casually peruses the sticker prices on some of the cars he is considering, and walks over to a showroom floor representative when he is ready, believing that the salesman will quote a price at least 10 percent under the sticker price. Our car buyer also believes that through some hard-nosed bargaining, the salesman might drop the final price down another 10 percent. But, as Steve Marks found out, times have changed.

"I can get you a car by Christmas," was what Steve heard from the salesman. "It was early July. I thought he was kidding." But as Steve found out, the Japanese had studied the American market quite carefully and had begun producing small, fuel-efficient cars that didn't know the meaning of the word "obsolescence." And Steve says, "He wasn't kidding. Their backlog was that long." And what about price? "They were quite up-front about it. They had a seller's market. The sticker price was the price of the car." A Honda spokesman says, "The laws of supply and demand are always in operation. We have the best product in the marketplace. We can sell more cars than we have. If we lose a sale because of price, we just go to our waiting list and call up the customer at the top of the list. And I guarantee he or she will be at our showroom, checkbook in hand. within the hour."

> *It is easier to sell a Honda than just about any other automobile in its class. Prospective buyers in one state plan trips to other states for the sole purpose of trading their old cars and driving their new Hondas . . .*

The federal government soon came to the rescue. By 1980, with sales of imported cars skyrocketing from 17 percent of the market in 1978 to 23 percent in 1979, and with the Japanese imports leading the pack, the American automakers' lobby in Congress was screaming for import quotas. Under that kind of pressure, the Japanese automakers, led by our number-two and five ranked companies, Honda and Toyota, negotiated a voluntary import quota which limited the number of Japanese exports to the U.S. to 1.68 million cars. Even operating under the restrictions of the quota, Japanese imports accounted for approximately 85 percent of the import market in 1983. It's clear, therefore, that the entrance of the Japanese automakers into the bread and butter American marketplace has changed the entire complexion of the new car industry and instilled a real fear among U.S. car manufacturers. This fear is quite justified as William Hoglund, vice president and general manager of Pontiac, discovered in 1981 when he called a conference to find out where his Pontiac customers were going. "What we really found out was that the buyer had gone to the imports. Our dealer network was severely damaged and we had a big morale problem." What the Detroit Big Three did was to incorporate, wherever possible, the design attributes of their Japanese competitors' cars, such as front-wheel drive, five-speed overdrive transmissions, fuel-injected and turbo-boosted engines, and complete options packages that projected efficiency, sportiness, or luxury. The target of their national sales pitch was the younger and more aggressive car buyers who, over the long haul, will turn out to be the largest money-spending group in the economy for years to come. The results of these changes in design and marketing are turning up positive results for the U.S. automakers. However, two foreign companies, Honda and Toyota, still dominate the American markets and are cited as our number-one and five-ranked companies, respectively.

Honda is ranked first in our survey for many reasons, all stemming from the simple but undisputable fact that Honda's products are consistently ranked in the the top five of their class year after year by such prestigious automobile rating surveys such as those found in *Car & Driver*. Consequently, Honda dealers and showroom salesmen report that it is easier to sell a Honda than just about any other automobile in its class. Honda dealers tell stories about prospective buyers in one state who plan trips to other states for the sole purpose of trading their old cars and driving their new Hondas home. Honda management gives strong support to their dealers through their devotion to the reputation of quality which has become synonymous with Japanese industry, and their strategies which circumvent some of the U.S. import duties. For example, Hondas are shipped to the U.S. as essentially stripped vehicles. In other words, the actual car that arrives on the dock in the U.S. is devoid of any luxury options such as air conditioning, or even many of the standard features such as light packages and basic accessories. These add-ons are shipped separately in kit form to be installed by the Honda dealers as optional packages in the new cars. One of the benefits of this method is that the value of the car passing through U.S. customs is far less than the value of the car fully assembled, and therefore the import duties are less. The duties on the separately shipped parts fall under a different, and lower, import duty structure. A spokesman for a Honda dealer in Rochester, New York, says, "It's great for the dealers. We don't have to worry about all kinds of crazy combinations of options. Most of the equipment and color combinations are standard. It makes life for the dealers and their representatives very easy."

Steve continues with his Honda story. "I needed a car right then in early July, not just in time for Christmas. So I got my hands on a book containing all the Honda dealers in the country, and I literally called every single dealer in New York state, New Jersey, eastern Pennsylvania, Connecticut, and Massachusetts. I wanted a blue Prelude with a five-speed stick and air conditioning. Of over fifty dealers called, I found three who had a Prelude in stock, but none were what I wanted. And each of the three said I'd have to sign the deal that day or the car would be gone." So what did Steve do? "I found a dealer in Rochester, New York, who was getting a shipment at the end of July. I wired him a $500 deposit, and when the time came, I flew up to Rochester and drove the car back." And how does Steve like his Prelude? "I have 80,000 miles on it and all I've ever had done is standard maintenance. I love it." Steve will probably buy another Honda because he, like many other Honda owners, has become spoiled by the ease of owning the car. This, Honda dealers say, is what makes selling Hondas as easy as filling out an order slip and cashing the customer's check.

The Honda Motor Company's approach to manufacturing, promotion, and sales has made Honda dealers in America devoted fans of the way the Japanese manufacturer does business. Many dealers who were struggling with their American car franchises have found that by switching to Honda's cars, they have been able to turn marginal profits or, in more than one instance, outright losses into solid year-after-year profits. Thomas J. Peters and Robert H. Waterman, Jr., coauthors of In Search of Excellence, suggest that the success of the Japanese imports is due more to management techniques than to technological advances. As an example of contrasting managerial structures, they point out that Ford Motor Company has seventeen layers of management while Toyota has five, and that Honda doesn't even refer to a formal managerial structure but focuses instead on project teams.

How does this affect Honda's American dealerships? Carl Iten, a Honda sales representative in northern New Jersey, says, "I used to be a salesman. Now I'm an order taker." Carl used to work for an Oldsmobile dealer in the Bronx. "At Olds, we actually used to do some prospecting. I'd call on leasing companies or corporations. I really hustled for the big sales. Even for the walk-ins, customers who'd stop in right off the street as if they had decided 'today is the day I'm buying that Olds,' you really had to sell. We were selling against Buick and Pontiac. When a customer walked in, nine times out of ten he was not sold on an Olds." And at Honda? "Nine out of ten customers who walk in are sold on a Honda. And the ones who aren't are more often than not setting us up against Toyota and Datsun, or in a rare case against the VW Scirocco. But," Carl continues, "usually they're here to buy and since nobody's discounting the cars, the only unresolved issue in the sale is delivery, and there's not much negotiating there either."

Still, Carl has developed a few techniques to increase his volume. "We get a lot of repeat customers. Most of my people won't drive anything else after they've had a Honda, unless they step up to the luxury lines like Mercedes." So Carl stays in touch with his customers. "We use a computer to track our sales, and some of the statistics we get are quite useful. My average customer trades his car in every two to three years. So at six-month intervals, we send out correspondence to our customers advertising our cars and letting them know how long a wait there is for new cars. That way, if they want to order one, they can plan ahead. It saves the customer the hassle of running around to Honda dealers all over the place, and of course, it's business for us." Carl also adds a personal touch for his customers by sending out birthday and Christmas cards. Carl's reasoning is interesting. "In a dealer's market like ours, it's easy for the customer to feel like you're doing him a favor and he's in your debt just for having the opportunity to buy a Honda. That's not what Honda is all about." Carl also pointed out the obvious. "Just because somebody buys a Honda doesn't mean I'm going to do well. I want that customer to buy that Honda from me."

Carl earns a commission of between 20 to 22 percent of the net profit on each car he sells. For example, if a Prelude sells for $14,000 and the dealer pays Honda $11,500 for the car, then the net profit is $2,500. Carl's commission is based on that figure, so his commission is between $500 and $550 on the sale. Carl adds, "Depending on fluctuations in the market, we at this dealership have been adding premiums of up to $1,500 on top of the sticker price." This would put another $300 to $330 in Carl's pocket. In addition, Carl drives an Accord, Honda's top-of-the-line sedan. He says, "Everyone gets a company car, but the model depends on your production and how long you've been with the dealership. Carl reports that four salesmen in his dealership made over $60,000 last year.

> *The handwriting first appeared on the wall during the oil shortages of the early '70s. The first message was that cars had to be made more fuel efficient. But when the Japanese imports invaded, another message appeared . . . "You've also got to make them better."*

Honda deserves our number-one ranking on the basis of both the present reputation it enjoys and the future reputation it will build. For showroom dealers today, having the kind of seller's market that Honda enjoys clearly makes selling Hondas a salesman's dream, and the dedication to excellence that is exemplified by the Honda organization itself bodes well for Honda's representatives. *Car & Driver* and *Road & Track* reviews consistently rate Hondas among the top five automobiles in their class, so customers keep on pouring through the doors. New Jersey Honda salesmen report that they spend much of their time trading among themselves to balance out the available supply of cars to meet the customer demand.

There is only one potentially negative aspect to this rosy picture for Honda sales representatives and it is politically based and not a reflection of anything that Honda has or has not done. It is the trade climate that exists between the United States and Japan. If the U.S. and Japan cannot agree on lifting certain trade restrictions that Japan has placed on specific American products, it is likely that the Reagan administration will retaliate by imposing certain restrictions on Japanese products. Thus, Honda showrooms in the U.S. could face serious new product rationing and even parts shortages if trade relations between the U.S. and Japan are allowed to deteriorate. This intangible is, of course, considered in our rankings.

The Big Three American carmakers have had to play catch-up with the Japanese and the Germans ever since the market shifted out from under them. Most American car dealers still remember the early 1970s as a period of rude awakening. A showroom salesman for a sprawling Ford dealership in Trenton, New Jersey, recalls that when the first Hondas arrived in America, the tiny Civics were not considered real road vehicles and were quickly dismissed by at least one of the consumer products review magazines. Another salesman for a Pennsylvania dealership, one of the largest multi-car franchises in the U.S., remembers test driving the early Datsun and Toyota subcompacts and worrying more about the future of the Beetle than about the future of American small cars. However, the American car salesman's confidence in his product was so shaken during the 1970s that many large suburban car dealerships borrowed whatever money they could to buy a sales franchise for whatever Japanese car they could. And ultimately the American car manufacturers themselves bought into the Japanese manufacturing environment and began selling imports under an American trade name.

The handwriting first appeared on the wall during the oil shortages of the early '70s. The first message was that cars had to be made more fuel efficient, *much* more fuel efficient. But when the Japanese imports invaded, another message appeared on the industry wall. "You've also got to make them better," an industry analyst says. "Planned obsolescence was not a myth. Not only was it a fact, but it fueled the Japanese invasion. Planned obsolescence is so diametrically opposite to the Japanese way of doing business, I don't think they could operate that way if they wanted to." There's a cliché about building a better mousetrap, and if the world will flock to your door for a mousetrap, what will the response be to a car? "The actions taken by the U.S. auto industry were unprecedented. They were at war, and they knew it. They were in a lot of trouble and they pulled out all the stops. 'Buy American' campaigns weren't enough, so they had to petition Congress for legislative help." Steve Marks adds, "The one thing the U.S. automakers never said was, 'Buy our cars because they're better.' " But, our analyst adds,

"Fortunately they seem to have learned their lesson. They're starting to turn it around."

GM finally saw the light and adapted an "If you can't beat 'em, join 'em," approach to the competition. They formed a controversial affiliation with Toyota, our number-five ranked company, for the production of small, energy-efficient cars at a factory site in the United States that is managed according to a Japanese organizational model. Other U.S. manufacturers have also taken stock of their operations and have made a number of changes, the net result of which, according to an industry source, "Promises to produce better, more cost effective cars for years to come. Planned obsolescence is a thing of the past. You'll never see it again because the public knows they don't have to take it, and the automakers know that the Japanese are always ready." According to industry sources, the most significant changes made by U.S. automakers have been in cost cutting and efficiency. Older plants have been shut down and parts and equipment have been redesigned, but the most signficant development of all is standardization. The U.S. automakers are designing a basic model and sticking with it. They'll make improvements along the way, but they're not starting from scratch every two years the way they used to.

Cooperation among the different divisions of American automobile manufacturers is quite commonplace now, according to many salesmen who see the results in the types of cars that are shipped and the types of options that are supplied to them by the different manufacturing divisions. A Ford dealer says, "The Ford LTD and the Mercury Marquis are, for all intents and purposes, the same car. Ditto, the Thunderbird and Cougar, and the LTD Grand Victoria and the Mercury Grand Marquis." Similar economies have been reported among GM's divisions, particularly Oldsmobile, Buick, and Pontiac, and at Chrysler's Dodge and Plymouth divisions. According to a Buick dealer, "This means that we're not competing as much against one another as we used to, but against the cars from a different manufacturer. Years ago, I used to feel the heat from the top-of-the-line Chevy Caprice and maybe the Olds Toronado or the Ninety-eight. Now, I get the pressure from the Chryslers and the Mercurys. At the lower end of my line, I have to fight the Toyota and Datsun wagons. Next year, I think the luxury Hondas will be in the competition too. But at least I can hold my own; five years ago it was a different story."

In the four-year period from January 1979 to January 1983, the total number of GM dealerships was reduced by 12 percent. At Ford the reduction was 18 percent, and the financially troubled Chrysler dealerships had shrunk by 24 percent. However, after the shakeout, the news became encouraging. Domestic new car sales rose sharply by 1.2 million between 1982 and 1983 to 6.7 million (an increase of 22 percent), and to 8 million units in 1984 (an increase of 48 percent from 1982 and 19 percent from

1983). This upswing indicated that the buying public's perception of American cars had finally turned the corner.

Ford has earned our number-two ranking by being an industry leader in quality workmanship and customer service and support. In 1984, an industry survey of the most reliable cars ranked Lincoln-Mercury number seven and Ford number eleven. These were the only two American manufacturers ranked in the first dozen. Ron Kavner, a salesman for Westwood Lincoln-Mercury in Emerson, New Jersey, exemplifies the attitude and dedication that earned this division of Ford the number-two slot in our survey. Ron has worked as a sales representative for three years. In 1983, he received the Master Sales Club award, and in 1984 he was ranked in the top 4 percent of all 8,000 Lincoln-Mercury reps nationwide. Ron explains his way of selling: "First of all, you have to be comfortable with your approach to selling. I've seen sales reps sell 'by the book' and not last in the business because they weren't comfortable with their approach. They tried to do it from a book." The atmosphere at Westwood Lincoln-Mercury is very informal and low-key. Sales reps are willing to spend time with customers to explain things. Ron says, "I treat all my customers the same whether they buy a Lynx, Mercury's lowest price model, or a Mark VII, Lincoln's top of the line. Frankly, I never thought about my style being a sales approach. It's just the way I like to do business." And Ron's way of doing business has proved highly successful for him. Ron continues, "I don't mind going out of my way for people because I find that when I do, they go out of their way for me." Over 50 percent of Ron's sales come from repeat business and referrals. "I sold a car to a gentleman who was ill, and because he needed help I delivered the car personally to him on my own time. I really didn't think that much about it at the time, but he's wound up referring over twenty-five sales to me."

Commissions at Westwood Lincoln-Mercury are in the industry's standard range of 20 to 25 percent net profit. Ron says, "Most people think that the profit on a car is a lot higher than it really is." And he says that promotions and the laws of supply and demand have a big effect on the selling price of a car. "When we were selling the Grand Marquis, our top-of-the-line, full-size car, for $9,995, sales reps made between $50 and $75 on each sale." He adds, "Dealerships are quite independent when it comes to setting policy, although there are always broad corporate guidelines which come from Ford."

Ford's recent history is an interesting one. Lee Iacocca, the former president of Ford who is credited with some of the industry's most innovative approaches to automobile packaging, revolutionized the development and sale of small cars in America in the 1960s with the introduction of the personally customized Mustang kit. Sales of the Mustang set records and today the car is considered a classic, which in restored, "mint" condition can sell for over $10,000. Ford hoped history would repeat itself in the 1970s with the

Maverick and Pinto, but serious design flaws and the emerging foreign car market worked against them. An industry source says, "The lesson that Ford should have learned from the Mustang's success is that a good-looking, good-driving, buyer-oriented product will sell itself. The Mustang was a car that truly could be user customized with a wide variety of options that ranged from fuel efficiency to high performance and elegance." The Mustang was a gamble for Ford because it was a departure in design and marketing strategy from the conservative image that the manufacturer had been cultivating in its product line up to that time. It was even more of a gamble since the Mustang debuted a scant five years after the Edsel fiasco. But Ford's gamble paid off this time, and a dealer in Trenton, New Jersey, smiling fondly at the memory, says, "I was selling Mustangs as they rolled off the truck."

The industry shakeout of the early '70s was precipitated by the oil shortages, gasoline lines, the influx of foreign cars, and the disastrous sales decline that raged from the 1979 sales year (sales down one million units industrywide) through the 1982 sales year (sales down 3.8 million units industrywide from the 1978 base year). After the shakeout, Ford made a strategic decision to redesign their basic automobile from stem to stern, or, as one industry analyst put it, "from frame to finish." They abandoned the traditional box shape with its long front and rear decks and sharp angles because their research showed that this design was most popular with older Ford buyers who were tending to spend less on the cars they bought and holding on to them longer. They were losing the younger, first-time buyers to the Japanese, and Ford wanted desperately to capture this market because they knew it represented the future rather than the past.

> "I've seen sales reps sell 'by the book' and not last in the business because they weren't comfortable with their approach."

One Ford dealer says, "We were pretty scared. A lot of us were looking to jump ship and pick up other lines." And in many cases that's exactly what happened as Ford lost over one sixth of its dealers. A Ford executive agrees, "The company mood was very low, and not just at the dealer level. The troops at the home office in Dearborn were pretty glum as well." In addition to all the other problems, Ford had an image problem to overcome. One dealer says, "There was a time when the public perceived 'Ford' as meaning 'Fixed or Repaired Daily.'" Although this image wasn't accurate, it was being fed by the labor problems at Ford's eastern manufacturing plants where, rumor had it, the cars were being assembled so badly that, as the same Ford dealer says, "People believed the cars were rolling off the assembly line and into the repair shop."

Ford attacked its image problems—stodgy cars and poor workmanship—on two fronts. On the design front, they went with the sporty European look for their '83 and '84 cars, led by the Topaz and Tempo models. On the quality-control front, Ford borrowed a page from the Japanese book of operations and established in-plant, labor-management, quality control teams. This emphasis on quality control has already worked to redefine the company's image as a manufacturer of well-designed, well-engineered automobiles across its entire range of automobile lines from the low-end Escort right up to the Lincolns. And Ford's sales figures for 1983 and 1984 have reflected the new company strategy with '83 sales in at $44.5 billion and '84 sales at $53 billion.

But Ford isn't stopping there. An industry source says, "The Ford people have become aggressive in their approach to the market and to their dealers. They are moving more in the direction of the Japanese companies and are involving their dealers in the pre-release phases of a new product. Ron Kavner agrees. "Last month I was out test driving the new Merkur." Manufactured by Ford in Germany, the Merkur is a high-performance sports car which will compete against Porsche and Audi. Ron says, "The car is fantastic. I'm not a sports car buff, but I was on the test track with the test driver doing the actual driving, of course, and that thing was flying, doing three-sixties, and handling it all beautifully." And how was driving it? "They let me drive it under less acrobatic conditions, and it is incredibly smooth and powerful." The same industry source adds, "The Merkur is a very well-engineered car."

Ford has made convincing improvements to its cars and to its production of cars, as well as well-planned and significant changes in management philosophy, a new and very visible commitment to quality, and an aggressive support for their dealers that is reflected in dealer loyalty to the company and in salesman support for the dealer. "You have to realize," our Ford dealer in Trenton explains, "that in the car sales industry, there is no such thing as a national dealership. Each dealer is an independent. When I sell Fords, I'm one of Ford's dealers, but I also sell other cars. Sure I'm loyal to Ford, but the industry's changed since the days of the single-brand-only dealership. I can look down Route 1 and point to dealers who fifteen years ago sold only Buicks or Oldsmobiles and who today are selling Hondas, Subarus, and Saabs. The thing with Ford is that they turned everything around, especially the quality. Ten years ago, I would sell what we call an "estate wagon," and two weeks later the customer would be back in the shop with a long list of things to fix. This bulb was out, that switch didn't work, the brakes pulled, the engine felt like it was skipping, the seat adjustment lever broke off—I could go on for an hour. Some of it was our fault, and you can believe I burned the ears off my service manager for it. But most of it was factory stuff. I had no control over that, but I had to eat most of the expense. Today somebody buys a Tempo and two weeks later his best friend walks in to buy the same car in a different color. I'm sure not complaining."

> *"We screamed our heads off to Detroit . . . I think that Iacocca might have heard us."*

Chrysler has earned the number-three spot in our survey. Frankly, had we looked at Chrysler a scant eight years ago, we'd have projected that they would be the prime example in a how-not-to-do-it story. But while many industry analysts had the company dead and buried in the late '70s, a funny thing happened on the way to the cemetery. The coffin slowly opened and up popped Chrysler.

It is said that Chrysler is a salesman's company, and with good reason. Lee Iacocca, the president of Chrysler who waved the magic wand and brought the auto giant back from the brink of disaster, started his career as a salesman. But no selling job that Iacocca did on the lot will ever match the job he did on the United Auto Workers, on the Congress of the United States, and on the American public. He sold the UAW on participatory management in return for union givebacks and a postponement of contractual benefits. He sold the Carter administration and Congress, a very antibusiness Congress at the time, on loan guarantees to keep the company afloat. And he sold the American public on the quality and engineering of Chrysler's new products with a big-name advertising campaign and an early commitment to European front-wheel-drive technology. Chrysler's K cars scored early gains against the other domestic automakers and went on to establish a standard for American car design. The K cars were Chrysler's preemptive strike against the Japanese goal to take over the American midsized market.

A Washington source reports on Iacocca's approach to Congress to get his loan guarantees: "The Congress was in no mood to be bailing out

American business. They didn't want another Lockheed, and they were afraid of public sentiment which they perceived as being decidedly antibusiness, particularly in the high-inflation economy of the time." But Iacocca wasn't easily dissuaded. "At first they turned him down. Then he really went after them. He told them, in effect, 'You guys throw money away all over the globe and you never get a nickel back. I'm the only one who's ever going to pay you back—and with interest—and you won't give me a loan. You're so damn worried about public sentiment? How will the public react when I have to close the doors and all the workers are unemployed?' "

The K cars got off to a rocky start when they were first introduced because the people at Chrysler followed a traditional American sales approach of delivering a stripped-down version of the car to the customer and making him pay extra for even the most basic add-ons. The public was highly resistant to this marketing because, as Johnny Komjatti, a Chrysler-Plymouth dealer near Princeton, New Jersey, explains, "They were all spoiled by the Japanese. You could go down Route 1 to the Toyota place or up Route 1 to Datsun, and what did you see? Cars sitting on the lot with all the extras included at no charge in the sticker price. That's what the customer saw. So, when the first K car came rolling in, my men tried to sell them just like they sold the New Yorkers and the Le Barons. It didn't work. Young couples would walk in, look at the sticker, get mad and walk out. We couldn't even get in the handshake. Why? They saw the sticker, saw how many options they weren't getting, and drove over to Toyota. We screamed our heads off to Detroit about that. I think that Iacocca might have heard us."

In fact, Chrysler management, following the lead of Iacocca, had listened to the sales representatives and found out what the public wanted. The second-edition K cars came bundled with a lot of higher-price options as standard equipment and the K cars made major inroads against the Japanese imports. "It was all in the packaging," Johnny Komjatti explains. "All they did was repackage the car and the options, play with the price, and they made my day." The success of the K cars and the positive image of Lee Iacocca's leadership fueled Chrysler's comeback to the point that the company paid off its debt early and registered 1984 sales figures of 188,000 cars sold: 42 percent higher than '83 sales figures.

A Chrysler dealer in northern New Jersey says, "Business has been fantastic. I'm making a bundle on options such as door guards, undercoating, service contracts—you name it." Another dealer, pointing to the incentives offered by the manufacturer, says, "When Chrysler offers us 9 percent financing against the street price of 13 to 15 percent that GM offers, we can clear out our showroom in a weekend." He cited a number of other dealer incentives that Chrysler uses to support their independent dealerships. "Usually dealers have to eat a lot of expenses when it comes to supporting the car. Sure we can bump back all of it, and then some, to the buyers, but with the Japanese dealers offering so many options, we take a beating. So, Chrysler offers a 9 percent financing package. They use their clout in Detroit to borrow discounted money, front-end it to the dealers who offer low-rate car loans to first-time or young family buyers, and the whole thing is applied to a K car." Chrysler's introduction of low loan rates at a time when the economy was still relatively flat helped boost the sales of the new K cars. Chrysler's sales also helped to restore public confidence in the rest of the American car market. "As far as I'm concerned," Johnny Komjatti explains, "it was Iacocca who turned the economy around, not Reagan."

Chrysler has earned our number-three place in the rankings because it has become one of the legends of American business.

It would be pretty hard to ignore General Motors, an industry leader in sales with nearly three quarters of a million units sold in '83; 870,000 units in '84, and just under an even million projected for '85. GM has earned our number-four spot on the list for performance, but there is one main reason they did not place higher: GM has too many divisions competing against each other for customers. Oldsmobile, Buick, and Pontiac go head-to-head every day right down the product line. Though Ford competes to some extent with its Lincoln-Mercury division, the competition is in the overlapping areas of the product line (the high-end LTD against the low-end Grand Marquis, for example). Even at Chrysler there is a certain amount of competition between Chrysler and Plymouth on some models. But in no other car manufacturer is the cross competition as extensive as it is at GM.

GM is clearly committed to the production of small, energy-efficient cars. Their recent affiliation with Toyota at its new California plant and in Korea backs GM's claim that it will soon be able to supply its dealers with cars that will compete with anything the Europeans or Japanese can put in U.S. showrooms. Industry analysts suggest that GM's long-term sales strategy is to match foreign imports on a model-for-model and dollar-for-dollar basis. This will attract young, first-time car buyers to GM's small cars, and as their families grow and they become more affluent, they will buy the larger, option-heavy, higher-priced and commission-rich cars. GM is banking that their sales strategy will work and they have invested heavily in electronic data processing acquisitions to incorporate high-tech marketing and project management procedures into their ongoing operations. GM's recently announced Saturn project is a good indication of what the company is expecting in terms of production. GM expects to produce 500,000 cars per site with 6,000 employees, using state-of-the-art production facilities that will be heavily dependent on robotics. The first Saturns are expected to be on the market in 1989.

Our research indicates that GM has made powerful strides toward tightening up management and improving car quality, and we think the direction GM has chosen bodes well for their stockholders, but we are not yet convinced that their marketing strategy will necessarily bode well for their dealers and sales representatives. This conversation illustrates our point: Jim Mackey, a Cadillac salesman in New York, says, "When you're selling Cadillacs, you're selling a name which has become synonymous with excellence. Most of my business is repeat business." (Jim's commission structure is within the industry standard of 20 to 25 percent of net profits.) Jim adds, "With Cadillacs, there's a virtual fortune to be made on options." But an industry source disagrees with Jim's rosy picture: "Everything he says is true, but what he isn't saying is that Cadillac is facing some fierce competition from Lincoln and Mercedes, especially Lincoln. Many people have rented a Lincoln from Budget and other rent-a-car companies, and they like it so much that they switch. You can't rent a Cadillac from those kinds of agencies." As a result, other luxury cars are challenging Cadillac's lead, especially among younger buyers who associate Cadillac not only with luxury but with stodginess and a commitment to the past rather than the future.

Training in the industry is fairly informal. However, a spokesman at Potamkin Cadillac in Manhattan says, "Each dealer has its own philosophy of selling. We provide our reps with our own training course and materials including our own sales guide." GM also has a five-day training course to which some dealers send their salespeople. In summary, GM, because it is the world's largest auto manufacturer, clearly must enjoy a place in our top five auto companies. However, as has been the case with some companies in other industries, we feel that the steps the company is taking may indicate better news for their stockholders than for their sales representatives.

For many of the same reasons that Honda has been ranked number-one in our survey, Toyota has placed in the number-five position. Although Toyota is an excellent manufacturer for reps, it is clearly lagging behind Honda, both in terms of the import market share (24 percent to Honda's 34 percent), and in reputation for quality. It's not that Toyota produces a shabby product, but Toyota's line simply doesn't measure up to Honda's award-winning entries year after year.

Roger Freehan, a Toyota salesman in a New York showroom, describes selling at Toyota. "The vast majority of sales are walk-ins, and usually our walk-in customers are comparing us to Honda." And how does Toyota do against Honda? "Well, they're number-one in our market, but we're more price sensitive than Honda. I've sold a lot of Celicas in the $10,500 to $11,500 price range to people who couldn't see spending $15,000 for an Accord." And does Toyota sell against any American competition? "No. Virtually no one walking in the door will ever compare a Toyota to any American model. It's always Honda or Nissan and sometimes VW and Subaru." Roger drives a company Celica and his commission structure is based on a salary of $100 per week plus 20 percent of net profits on the cars he sells. Roger says, "If you're willing, you can make $35,000 to $40,000 a year."

Toyota's recent agreement with GM is causing some consternation among Toyota salespeople. Roger comments, "The company says that Toyotas will not be sold anywhere but in Toyota dealerships, but GM is the kind of outfit that can make an offer Toyota can't refuse." An industry analyst says, "It's conceivable that GM might sell Toyotas someday, but I doubt it. It would be too much of an admission that American cars have lost to the Japanese. They are much more likely to keep making cars to compete with the Japanese."

	AUTOMOBILES	COMPENSATION	COMMISSION	SUPPORT	INTANGIBLE
1	Honda Motor Co., Ltd.	5	4	4	−
2	Ford Motor Co.	4	4	4	+
3	Chrysler Corp.	4	4	4	+
4	General Motors Corp.	4	4	4	
5	Toyota Motor Corp.	4	4	4	−

The compensation rankings are based on the earnings of a sales rep who has been working in the industry for two years. The median compensation is $26,100 and since, to all intents and purposes, there is no salary to speak of in the industry, we have not included salary figures in the rankings.

Honda [−] and Toyota [−]

Both companies are subject to the vagaries of American politics as they pertain to import quotas. At present, both companies have been thriving in the U.S. even with the import restrictions in place. However, with this kind of sword hanging over their heads, reps should give some thought to the possibility of import quotas becoming tighter in the latter part of this decade as competition becomes more intense.

Ford [+] and Chrysler [+]

Both companies have made great strides in turning around a negative image. Both companies have shown the American public that they can produce quality cars at reasonable prices, and both companies are very dealer and therefore sales, rep-conscious.

BOOK PUBLISHING

THE TOP FIVE:	
1	McGraw-Hill, Inc.
2	Harper & Row Pub. Inc.
3	Holt, Rinehart & Winston
4	Houghton Mifflin Co.
5	Prentice-Hall, Inc.

I f you are reading this, then you are a consumer of the book publishing industry. Along with real estate, insurance, banking, food, and printing, publishing is one of the oldest of the world's industries. Modern book publishing actually began with Gutenberg's bible, and the Bible has been the largest bestseller ever since. Joining the Bible as the biggest sellers of all time are cookbooks, gardening books, and books about manners and etiquette. Even today, if you can show someone how to do something well, you will likely have a bestseller on your hands. People tend to buy books that show them how do to something well, especially if they can make more money at it.

"One of the nicest things about Syracuse is seeing it slowly disappear in the rear view mirror as I head back down south to New Jersey," says Bruce Hecht, a traveling sales representative for Prentice Hall, our number-five ranked company in trade, college, and professional publishing. Bruce is a salesman for PH's college division, selling texts to college bookstores, and hunting up textbook adoptions from core-course faculty members in a region which includes most of New York State. Bruce Hecht, a New York City native, says, "I used to think that 'upstate' was 96th Street in Manhattan. I had no idea this state was so big."

Nomadic lifestyles are a common experience among the salespeople in the book publishing industry whose seasonal odysseys can take them anywhere from isolated college towns to major cities all over the United States. They visit with owners of independent bookstores to pitch the latest novel; they talk with the most junior of college faculty members about the problems of teaching freshman composition; and lately, they assure prospective buyers that their publisher's newest line of computer software is guaranteed PC-compatible. Known in the trade as travelers, these are the people whose enthusiasm creates the bestsellers by turning the hopes of editors and authors into cash sales. Most, according to Bruce, consider themselves the last of the itinerant harbingers of culture to the rest of the country. Their lives are spent on the road traveling between college campuses and small towns whose names most people can't pronounce, but they are bound to what they do by, quite simply, a love of the books on their publishers' lists.

"I do more driving in a month than I used to do in a year," Bruce comments. Joe Fields, a former traveler for Reston, a Prentice Hall subsidiary, whose territory included all of Texas, says, "Not being a native Texan, I have no vested interest in bragging about how big Texas is. But just to give you an idea: For one month when I started, I was only working the local Ma and Pa bookstores in the Dallas-Fort Worth area. I was pretty efficient in planning my routes and my schedule, and I patted myself on the back for saving the company time and money." At the end of the first month when he submitted his expense report to the home office in Virginia, Reston's sales manager looked at the travel and expense forms and just sat there in shock. "He couldn't believe that I was claiming to have traveled 5,000 miles in just one metropolitan area of just one state." Joe thought he was in big trouble. "Alan, my sales manager, was a very nice guy who really backed his people. He asked me straight out what the story was. I said, 'Alan, let me put it to you this way. When I got down here, I took a cab from the airport to a motel that was about a mile outside the airport. The meter read twelve bucks before I got to the airport exit, and the total fare was twenty. That's twelve bucks just to get from the flight terminal to the airport gate. This place is big.' " Bruce just laughed. "He can keep Texas. I have enough trouble just dealing with traffic on the Thruway."

Book sales representatives are an important fraternity in one of the oldest industries in the United States, and editors and publishers respect the power that they wield. Their motivation, or lack of it, to support a new title can mean the difference between a quiet midlist book that "struts and frets its hour" upon the page of a publisher's catalog, and a book "with legs" that sells so aggressively that it almost walks off the bookstore shelves. Most trade editors are unwilling to make an acquisition unless they get the green light from their sales manager about the book's prospects. And editors who prepare a profit and loss statement for each proposed title routinely write a market plan that lists the different sales opportunities the new book will provide.

> *Entire publishing divisions were created overnight, only to be dismantled less than eighteen months later.*

Sales management is so vital to the health of the publishing industry that it is customary for many publishing executives to begin their careers in sales, especially as college and school book reps. At McGraw-Hill, for example, which is ranked number one in our survey of the best publishers to sell for, the climb up the corporate ladder begins in sales and marketing. The heads of publishing divisions and group vice-presidents are almost always former salespeople whose professional expertise is in sales and marketing. Joe Fields points out that the corporate design at McGraw-Hill is typical of the industry. "Prentice Hall operates exactly the same way, and so do most of the trade houses. In a high-volume publishing operation, sales is the route to the top because sales mean profits, and profits insure the company's health. In publishing, you can lose your shirt in just a few bad quarters, and all you have left are remainders that turn up in wire bins in the drugstore." Joe points out that while all trade publishers use their editorial divisions as a source of management, editorial's concerns are acquisitions and production. "The bottom line in trade publishing is the sales force. The books have to move to the bookstores and to the consumer or nobody makes any money. And sometimes it doesn't matter what the book says; it matters that the book sells."

Bruce Hecht describes what he calls Prentice Hall's selling machine: "College sales are handled by the college sales force. They go out looking for acquisitions at colleges and schools. That type of selling is straightforward. It's in some of the trade titles, particularly in computer books, where it can get crazy. As a pre-Gulf & Western company, Prentice Hall was just a walled-in editorial and sales factory in New Jersey. It was a mini-federation composed of a large central company called Prentice Hall Publishing and its semi-independent publishing subsidiaries in different parts of the country. If you were selling at Prentice Hall, you were selling at the center of the company, but if you were selling for one of the subsidiaries, you were in Siberia. Each division had a separate sales force which, technically speaking, could manage its own efforts. But each division was absolutely required to coordinate its sales with GBM, the general book marketing division of the company, and its principal profit center. Brady, Reston, Arco, the California kids, all have their own salespeople, but when GBM drops in to push a book, everybody has to fall in line. I've seen a GBM rep walk into one of the subsidiaries, and the whole company management just rolled over and panted."

Both Bob and Joe explain that when GBM mobilizes behind a book, that book sells. Joe elaborates: "GBM puts on the big push for conventions and conferences like the American Booksellers and the COMDEX conferences for computer store owners. At COMDEX '83 in Las Vegas, while GBM was marketing PH's new book/software line, including products like *The Profit Center* and *ExecuVision*, Reston had a whole line of computer books and games including *MovieMaker*. Brady had some software, and even Arco had a little book/software package. Everybody in the organization was going to be a hitter that year, or so it seemed. The word came down from GBM: 'Max out at COMDEX.' And did we ever. We put up a whole cabana with six computers running software all the time and a giant color video monitor playing from demonstration disks. We hired special advertising people to come up with logos, and we coordinated with every division. We even got our authors and developers to spend time in the booth, and we hired Yuppie-types to make the presentations. Every evening, after some grueling days on the cement floor buttonholing computer store managers from the middle of Iowa, the head of GBM would stand up and give us his 'sell-one-for-the-Gipper speech.' I thought we were the only publishers who got that crazy, but then I found out afterwards that every other house was doing the same thing." Bob agrees: "It was all those computer books. Sales figures started going through the roof. The sales predictions put all of us on Jupiter. Normal everyday sales managers at Prentice Hall, even the guys in the direct sales division who sit in their offices and stare at their Pet Rocks all day, had dollar signs in their eyes. Prentice Hall went insane with the rest of the industry, and we were so successful that PH even made some money. And now look what happened. Gulf & Western ate them up."

The publishing industry is still reeling from the computer book boom and the devastation it caused. Entire publishing divisions were created overnight, only to be dismantled less than eighteen months later. What happened to publishing during the computer book boom is instructive because it shows in a microcosm how the industry embraced, attempted to swallow, and then almost choked on an entirely new product. The computer book frenzy is an illustrative demonstration of how publishers work, especially when they see a product which has great potential, but which they aren't geared to produce. For most of the publishing industry, the attempt to cash in on the computer book market combined elements of the "Great Race" and the "Search for the Dead Sea Scrolls," all wrapped up in one unhappy series of events.

The microcomputer revolution and its demands for instant documentation hit publishing in 1980 with the same atomic impact it had on everything else. And there were few New York book publishers in a position to make an immediate jump into the computer book profits pool that they knew was sitting there. Sales managers at the big trade houses saw the commissions they could make but, as Joe Fields remembers, "There just wasn't any product in the houses that we could push. Those little West Coast startup publishers with ties to microcomputer manufacturers had the material and the authors, and all we could do was look at them and drool."

Business managers at the major New York trade houses knew that everything they needed to put together a computer book list was just waiting for them out in California. But there weren't enough technically trained editors at the trades to evaluate the information, and there weren't enough technical authors with professional writing skills to go around. The forces were building for a new California Gold Rush of the 1980s as the publishers tried to position themselves to take advantage of a growing and fanatically hungry consumer book market. The bigger publishers simply opened new divisions, bought the product they couldn't develop overnight, and dumped the titles on their sales force. Other publishers hired both technical editors and technically trained sales managers to create the lists and push them into the stores.

Bruce remembers that in 1982, Prentice Hall was aggressively seeking sales representatives who could demonstrate software to the computer stores. "We looked for reps, preferably women, who could walk into a computer store, pop a disk into one of their machines, demo the product, and walk out with an order of twenty or thirty $150 software packages. We learned our lesson fast." Computer store owners were skeptical about buying software from publishers because they knew that the publishers had to buy them from the software companies. If things went wrong with the product, who would stand behind it, the programmer or the publisher? The sales representatives had their hands full. Their companies were busy developing books and software, the traditional bookstores had no mechanism for selling anything other than books or audio tape cassettes, and the computer store owners, many of whom had once been programmers themselves, already knew what the publishers were about to learn: unsupported software is worthless. Still, the sales managers at the major trade houses had tasted blood and in their frenzy, new lines of books were acquired overnight. McGraw-Hill, the number-one ranked publisher in our survey, turned to the West Coast computer prophet Adam Osborne, and before the competition knew what had happened, the Osborne/McGraw-Hill division was pumping out product.

But even before McGraw-Hill got into the act, a quiet, friendly little academic and electronics publisher in Rochelle Park, New Jersey, had entered the market. The Hayden Book Company, just down the highway from Prentice Hall, had been known in the trade for years as a small, albeit very successful, technical book publisher. They had only one real computer programming book, *BASIC BASIC*, first published in the early '70s, on their backlist. Although it was a good book, adopted for use as a text in many college classrooms, it was an anomaly in the publishing business, because it reached its greatest popularity ten years after it was published. *BASIC BASIC* became the generic standard for an entire line of elementary programming books for new computer owners. "Store owners compared all new books to *BASIC BASIC*," Joe Fields explains. "Prentice Hall turned over every rock they could find to get product to us. I sold my head off during that period, and I don't remember the complete name of any title, but I do know that the word 'BASIC' was always in it."

An industry analyst says, "Hayden had the computer book market by the short hairs. All of their electronics authors, who had been hiding in math departments for years, and their sources of juicy technical information, who were in place and ready to write, had become infatuated with their personal computers. Had Hayden capitalized fully on its potential, it could have dominated the market for at least a year, a geological era in computer book publishing." A former manager at Hayden explains that Hayden had captured the computer market but never penetrated the giant chain stores that had just begun to stock consumer electronics items. "The whole issue was packaging. We had the books, we were developing the software, and my salesmen could sell to any bookstore. You could find our displays in all of the computer stores on the East Coast. But it was the Jamesways and the K marts that were the market we were after with our book/software packages. We just didn't have the sales force to grab the mass market we knew was there."

Prentice Hall's Bruce Hecht just shrugs at this analysis. "Hayden did quite well during the computer boom. Maybe they could have done better, but nobody in the company was complaining." When he first broke into the industry, Bruce was a representative for Hayden, selling computer books to local bookstores in the New York/New England area. He recalls, "To describe the travel, let's just say that it was terrible. The only thing that kept me going was that I really loved selling and I loved the books." Bruce has always been an avid reader and he enjoyed learning about the booming computer industry in the early '80s. "I taught myself programming and became pretty familiar with most of the machines and software on the market. And these were books I could understand. If I could understand it, I could sell it." Bookstore managers were happy to see Bruce. "Those poor guys wouldn't know a good computer book if it bit 'em on the bottom. Those were the easiest sales I ever made. They would ask me what they should take."

A former editor for McGraw-Hill agrees with Bruce's evaluation of the first six months of the boom. "In those days, it seemed that the only qualification for writing a computer book was that you were able to utilize oxygen in your bodily processes somehow. You didn't even have to breathe. And believe me, I saw plenty of authors who didn't." Bruce adds, "The proliferation of computer books was truly outrageous. There was literally a tidal wave." And salespeople like Bruce were in demand. "Like all the other reps, I was being solicited every week by publishers and distributors who were just getting their feet wet in the field."

Computer book sales were unique in the trade book publishing field because they were technical. Bruce says, "Prior to the computer book explosion, the only technical stuff was either in textbook selling or in industrial selling. So, computer book reps had to be more than order takers. We had to know the difference between Apple's DOS 3.3 and DOS 3.2. We had to know the difference between BASIC, Pascal, and Logo. And we even had to know which side of the disk was up." Sales meetings at Hayden were pretty tense at times. "The president of the company would come to the meeting and make sure that the reps knew their stuff." Bruce adds, "Sales meetings always had been taken seriously from nine to five, but we'd all let our hair down and party a little in the evening. Nothing outrageous, but we'd have fun." And during the great computer boom? "We studied. We'd be running back and forth between each other's hotel rooms, checking out software and preparing for the next day's presentations." As one industry analyst says, "During the heyday of computer books, the number of publishers with computer books in print leaped from about twenty to over one hundred, and a cottage book industry sprang up overnight."

The needs of the sales force at Prentice Hall, McGraw-Hill, and even at Hayden were so important to the division heads that acquisition editors were told in the strongest possible terms to bring in the books. Craig McKean, a former acquisitions editor for Prentice Hall, says, "I was contacted by agents who were representing guys who couldn't speak the English language in any form that I could recognize." But could they write?

"That was sort of hard to tell. On one hand you'd have to say 'yes,' but on the other hand, there wasn't a real big market for *Programming in Finnish*." Bruce agrees: "The basic problem with the computer book industry in the early stages was that the techies were doing the writing, and they weren't writers, they were tinkerers. But who cared? At Prentice Hall we were selling everything we could put on the market." Craig smiles, recalling a time when he was wooing an author in California. "You like to go out on a Saturday night? Maybe you'll have a drink. Dance a little? These guys' idea of a big night was to replace some chips in their Apple and see if they could get it to operate faster." Bruce agrees. "But the thing was that they did get the Apple to operate faster, and publishers were flocking to their doors to get them to write about it because we could sell it by the cartload. You have to remember, bookstore owners needed product, and if Prentice Hall didn't get it to them, then dilithium or little publisher would." A computer book editor at New American Library also remembers feeling that if New York publishers hadn't entered the computer book market, at whatever cost it took to do it, then the market would have been lost to the West Coast.

"The computer publishing industry was thrice blessed by IBM," according to Bruce. As the rumors grew hotter that IBM was going to make a grand entrance, the skeptical publishers—who had stayed away from computer books because they didn't understand them and worried about immediate market saturation—swung over to the computer book and software arena overnight. IBM made computer book sellers out of people who had been laughing about the industry only three months earlier. Bruce Hecht recalls: "By the time IBM announced their PC, the computer book industry was entering its peak phase. The big guys were on the bandwagon, and the market began to become specialized. Publishers began looking for niches. The generalized, literacy books—we called them 'Dick and Janes'— which had proliferated to the point of witlessness, disappeared from bookshelves quicker than you could say 'bits and bytes.' " Gwen Anderson, a manager for a Dalton's bookstore in New York, agrees, "It was amazing. During one six-month period in 1983, computer books suddenly seemed to swing from a seller's to a buyer's market." And the book sales figures plummeted. Craig comments, "The market quickly shifted into machine-specific books. We had to be pretty creative in coming up with new angles for books." Children's books proliferated, and book/software combinations became very popular. Bruce says, "At Hayden, we did an informal testing of a book/software package. To be honest, I don't think anyone thought it would sell because the software was extremely simplistic and didn't seem to add much to the book. So we packaged the software literally in plain brown wrappers, and sent some to selected dealers. The response was unbelievable. The dealers didn't even advertise the software. They'd mention it to a few of the people who bought the books, and maybe to a few of the techies who hung out at the bookstore. And pretty soon our phones were jumping off the hook, and buyers were chasing our order people around the room." So Hayden, as well as the rest of the publishing industry, entered the book/software phase. Book sales representatives began selling software, bringing into the publishing industry an entirely new concept of product.

Over the next six to nine months, the technology of book/software products improved dramatically. The early products, such as the cassette-based *My Favorite BASIC Programs* by Kent Sandroff, Assistant Professor of Computer Science at Cayuga County Junior College, were replaced by packages like Prentice Hall's *ExecuVision* and Simon & Schuster's *Typing Tutor III*. Success stories like these prompted some publishers, most notably S&S, to develop entire electronic book and software divisions. But as Bruce remembers, "You didn't have to be a genius to see that the heyday of computer books was about to go the way of the nickel beer." And so, when the great computer book boom went bust (along with a number of smaller publishers who had overextended themselves in the area), Bruce decided that it was time to leave Hayden and get into college textbook sales at Prentice Hall, one of the biggest college textbook companies in the United States. And he claims that it was the smartest thing he ever did.

"College selling is as much like trade book selling as deep sea fishing is to fresh water fishing," says Bruce, who felt at first as if his boat was about to go down. "For openers, when I left computer book sales, I figured I was through with Syracuse forever. But as the fates and my sales manager at PH decreed it, Syracuse was the exact geographic center of my territory." According to Bruce, "It turns out that there's not much else to do in that part of the country except shovel snow and go to school." And Bruce soon found out that, "There are more than a few schools in that neck of the woods: Cornell, Ithaca, and the State University of New York, along with schools like Binghamton, Albany, Harpur, and the University of Rochester, just to name a few." And then there's Syracuse. "It almost seems as if Syracuse is the only city in the United States named after a football team. Everybody at Syracuse University is so rah-rah, even the profs, that I went out and bought a suit in Syracuse orange."

Adoptions are the name of the game in college textbook sales. Selling adoptions to college faculty members is much like selling in the pharmaceuticals industry. In both cases, the point of purchase buyer of the products—the college student or the patient needing a prescription—is not the person the sales representative makes his pitch to. In pharmaceuticals, the company representative sells to the doctor, and in college text sales, the publisher's representative sells to the professor making a required reading list for the next year. In pharmaceutical sales, it's the druggist who stocks the drug and fills the doctor's prescription, and in college sales, it's the college bookstore that fills faculty book requests and hands the course texts out to the student at the beginning of the semester.

Bruce sells science texts, mainly biology and chemistry, but some physics as well. This is a specialized market, and he knows his product as well as his competition. He points out that unlike selling trade books to store owners, he is selling directly to the people who have the power to order books by the thousands. "It's one thing to sell to a bookstore owner in the middle of Arizona who reads the weekly book reviews and *Publishers Weekly* and thinks he knows what his customers want. But it's quite another thing to sell in the college market." But one of the biggest differences between the trade and textbook market is the level of commissions that it's possible to earn in the college market. "In trade sales, one call on a store account might get a sale worth about $300 to me personally. Selling college texts is a lot better. One call could conceivably be worth $3,000 to my account."

But, he explains, the task is also more difficult. "The downside to college text selling is that there just are no guarantees when you talk to the professors. When I was in trade sales, if I walked into a bookstore—any bookstore—I was just about guaranteed to come out with a sale. In college sales, that's not at all the case." Bruce explains: "Pitching to profs is a very tough business. For one thing, most of these types are not only experts in their fields, they're sometimes on a first name basis with the author of the book. There's no feeling quite like saying to a biology professor, 'This book contains the latest research on the synthesis of DNA,' and then having him point to a colleague standing nearby, and say, 'Not so. Jerry over there just delivered a paper at the Molecular Biology Conference at Carnegie Mellon refuting that research.' " And what does a salesperson do in a situation like that? "You talk to them about it. I'd say something along the lines of, 'Really? What did your research show?' " Bruce adds, "These people love to talk, so that's an in. The one thing you don't want to do is argue with them unless you really know what you're talking about. And there's no finessing your way around either. If your act is not in gear, smile and hope for luck the next time."

Educational sales are the mainstay of the publishing industry, and those publishers with strong education lists are usually highly resistant to the kinds of cyclical market fluctuations that plague trade publishers. Educational sales representatives are quick to point out that American publishing had its roots in education sales. "Education is the bread and butter of the industry," one representative explains. "The gross unit numbers tell the whole story." He points out that when the Chicago school board, for example, adopts a particular title for sixth-grade science or eighth-grade social studies, the result is thousands of sales for that one year alone. For sales representatives who know their territories and who have developed a rapport with the curriculum planners and textbook evaluators at the various grade levels—many of whom might already serve as reviewers for the publisher—the yearly gross sales can be very substantial. "This might not be as interesting as trade," one representative suggests, "but if you like books, like traveling, enjoy talking to teachers, and have a family to feed, you can have a successful career."

The strength and importance of the education market was not lost on Gulf & Western. Within the past three years, the parent corporation of trade giant Simon & Schuster has acquired Allyn & Bacon as a part of its purchase of Esquire Inc., and Prentice Hall. This makes Gulf & Western the largest educational publisher in the country, with projected sales in the elementary to college markets of about $300 million a year. In the process, G&W also acquired Prentice Hall's professional books and vocational skills books and Arco's educational series.

Trade sales are a stark contrast to educational sales. Trade sales representatives, especially those who began as educational sales representatives, find the work more interesting even if the compensation is lower. (Trade sales reps' compensation is lower than school reps' but higher than college reps'.) Trade sales are also more difficult because the structure of the market is different. The educational sales representative is selling against the competition from other publishers. However, the book traveler pushing a trade line is often in direct competition with the distributors who can buy from the publisher in bulk and stock entire lines from competing houses. The publisher's representative can only sell what one house prints. Thus, the competition is fierce in trade books, according to the publisher at a major house who had worked his way up via the sales route: "I don't think there's another industry where, in effect, manufacturers' reps may have to go head-to-head against the distributors' reps. The publishers play both ends against the middle, and they can make out like bandits."

Because virtually all publishers utilize book distributors such as Ingram, Baker & Taylor, and Golden Lee, in addition to their own in-house sales force, they can hit the bookstore from both sides. This is a powerful strategy because, even though a publisher will sacrifice the markup in a sale to a distributor, the volume of the sales helps make the difference. Moreover, because an author's royalties are often based on the publisher's net profits, rather than the list price on the cover, the author shares the impact of the discount with the publisher. And small bookstore owners rely on their distributors for their livelihood.

"I started my entire operation courtesy of Ingram," says Gerard McKenna, owner of a small bookstore in Pennsylvania. "Ingram carries everything I could ever want, and the Ingram rep really knows his business." Ingram, the largest of the distributors, also carries a full line of computer software as well as educational materials. Paula James, who owns a family bookstore in Flemington, New Jersey, explains that her Ingram salesman put up the software display by the cash register, filled it with product, and told her to "watch it sell." "It did," she reports. "I don't know a thing about the software, I only know that the entire rack gets cleaned out by my customers before I even turn around." Bruce Hecht comments, "It really is pretty discouraging to have to pitch against the Ingrams and the Baker & Taylors. They're able to offer the bookstores a good one-stop shopping operation. If you want to start a bookstore, call Ingram, and they'll set you up." He adds, "It's the one reason I never wanted to be in trade books in the first place."

From the traveler's point of view, distributors can be a problem in trade book sales. This is compounded by Bruce's observation about publishers' trade book representatives: "You're not going to get rich." Another representative for a major trade publisher says, "Frankly, I'm only putting in my time as a trade rep because I want to get into the management side of the business. As far as earning a living goes, we trade reps are just getting by." The compensation for sales representatives at the major trade and mass market houses is quite low compared to the compensation for educational book representatives. An average trade sales representative earns between $18,000 and $21,000, plus bonuses, in a typical year. "Our biggest problem," according to a sales manager at a trade publisher, "is the distributors and the house accounts. The individual reps can't compete against the big distributors and the national accounts like Dalton and Walden Books. The trade rep gets murdered because the national chains are usually house accounts. How's a trade rep supposed to make a living selling against outfits that can pull a truck up in front of a bookstore and stock all the titles the store wants in one shot at a better price than the trade rep can give? And the publishers support it." Most of the representatives interviewed complained that Baker and Taylor, Ingram, and Golden Lee are killing small trade sales. Furthermore, the central ordering and distribution at the national bookstore franchises also operate against the individual trade representative, although publishers suggest that the effect of the major bookstore chains is largely overrated.

Trade sales may be the critical factor in a publisher's success, but high trade sales do not necessarily spell big money for the trade representative. In addition to competition from the distributors and the national bookstore chains, the trade representative also competes against the book clubs. "You'd be surprised at the effect of book clubs," Bruce explains. "Some editors will do anything to get a book in one of the clubs, particularly if it serves a specialty market. Book clubs pay an advance and they buy in pretty good numbers. A couple of book club acquisitions can more than send a book into the black and turn a marginal title into a profit. But the trade rep won't even see a dime." As a sales manager for one of the major trade houses suggests, a trade publisher simply does not need the sales force to make money. He can sell directly to distributors and sell directly to the national chains. He can push a title into as many book clubs as possible and bring down a reprint sale, neither of which involves the trade sales force.

Are trade sales an important segment of the book sales industry? According to successful trade representatives, there is always the promise of a best seller, and best sellers generate money for everybody. One representative explains, "If a title can catch fire because of a good publicity campaign or because of a name author, then all the individual bookstores want it and want it fast. When a title is wanted fast, a distributor can resupply three to five times faster than the publisher. But, he continues, the window for hardcover sales is very small. "If a title is moving that well, it'll be sold to paper quickly enough, and then sales drop. Bookstores will stock maybe two to four units after a reprint sale and wait."

Trade sales still have an important place in the industry. According to one New York publishing executive who started out as a trade representative, "In my own case, I initially got into trade sales because I love books and I love selling." But he soon realized that he wasn't making the money he wanted to make. "It didn't take me long to figure out that I wasn't going to get rich quick—or even slow—doing what I was doing. I knew I could make money selling in a different industry, but I loved publishing too much to leave. So I paid my dues for three years and worked my way up the corporate ladder." Another sales manager for a trade publisher says, "I started out by selling single units to local bookstores in Iowa. I'm not going to bore you with a rundown of my life during those years, but it was the beginning of my publishing career." Most trade representatives confirm that they are in the industry either as an entry level career position or for the love of books. No one is in it for the money.

Because of the peculiar nature of the trade sales industry in which publishers compete against their own sales forces, our rankings are weighted in favor of those publishers whose representatives are insulated as much as possible from distributor competition. All of our top five publishers—McGraw-Hill, Holt, Harper & Row, Houghton Mifflin, and Prentice-Hall—have a strong position in the college markets, and all but Harper & Row in the elementary and high school markets, in addition to powerful trade and professional lists. In fact, according to most industry sources who have followed the history of American publishing for the past century and a half, the education market is by far the strongest and most stable over the long term, even though some salespeople who are positioned in the right place at the right time can make quite a bit of money in startup areas such as computer book sales. In fact, if we were still in the midst of the great computer book boom, the five top-ranked publishers would include some of the companies publishing computer books and software exclusively. Those days are gone and some of the same publishers who were thriving in 1982 are cutting back staff or even flirting with Chapter 11 in 1985. None has made it into our top five, with one exception.

A former sales manager describes McGraw-Hill like this: "Remember the joke that went 'When a well-muscled, six-foot four-inch, 240-pound guy goes to the beach, where does he sit? Anywhere he wants.' That's the best way to describe McGraw-Hill." McGraw-Hill is so big and it has so many divisions and so many authors writing for it that it gets to sit in whatever market it wants whenever it wants, and it doesn't have to go back to a parent corporation and beg for the money. It is the one exception among many woeful computer book publishers. When some of the smaller publishers decided to get into the computer book market, they went out and hired themselves an acquisitions editor. If he or she had a strictly technical background, everybody had to wait while the person learned how to edit in the English language. If the editor had only an editorial background, then everybody waited while he or she learned the jargon and nuances of techie authors. And maybe they even hired a sales representative who had some technical experience, or at least said that he had some technical experience. Then they found some authors who claimed to be able to write and, if they were very fortunate, a year later they were selling computer books. McGraw-Hill approached the problem differently. They surveyed the situation and created an entire company called Osborne/McGraw-Hill. Three months later, they were selling the most important computer books on the market. Six months later, they had created Byte Books and had even more computer books on the market than their rivals among the trade houses. As one sales representative for one of the small computer book publishers puts it, "When we have editorial and sales meetings to plan for future titles, we're talking about two years down the road. When McGraw-Hill does the same thing, they're talking about the year 2000."

A favorite story among the sales representatives who attend computer products shows is "The Tale of Two Software Companies." As Reston's Joe Field tells it, once upon a time there were two little software companies: CYMA and ASK MICRO. Both companies developed and marketed professional accounting software, the type recognized as the most complex and treacherous of any business office software system. Both companies were small, but both companies seemed to have strong growth prospects. Both companies got lots of sunshine: CYMA was in Arizona and ASK MICRO was in California, and both companies marketed their software through independent dealers. But CYMA was a little bit different from ASK MICRO, as well as from most software companies. Most of the software companies in CYMA's category sold software that worked well enough to do the job. CYMA's software, however, not only worked well, it worked flawlessly. ASK MICRO's software didn't work well at all. Today, ASK MICRO is known in their town as "that company that went out of business," and CYMA is known in theirs as CYMA/McGraw-Hill.

When industry sales representatives comment on McGraw-Hill's Midas touch, the gist of their conversation is that McGraw-Hill always seems to be in the right market at the right time with the right money. As Joe Field explains, "The question is whether they are the IBM of the publishing industry, or is IBM the McGraw-Hill of the computer industry?" The point is that McGraw-Hill is good, it's smart, and it looks as though it's going to stay that way. In our survey, McGraw-Hill earned a 5 in both the trade books and textbook compensation categories. This means that the prototypical trade book representative at McGraw-Hill earns more than $26,620 or 10 percent above the industry median of $24,200. The prototypical college textbook representative earns more than $29,260 or 10 percent above the industry median of $26,600. Salary figures in this chapter reflect the average for all reps in the industry, not just for reps with two years' experience.

> *"The computer publishing industry was thrice blessed by IBM. As the rumors grew hotter that IBM was going to make a grand entrance, the skeptical publishers . . . swung over to the computer book and software arena overnight."*

The company has achieved its number-one ranking the old fashioned way: They earned it. But is McGraw-Hill right for everyone? "Emphatically no!" according to George Kimball, a former McGraw-Hill salesman. "They're extremely corporate at that company, too corporate for most people. Most publishers' reps let their hair down after five. Not the MG-H boys. You could always tell the McGraw-Hill crowd at the trade shows. Everyone else was in shirtsleeves, but our reps were in their three-piece pinstripes, standing there at their booths like ramrods until somebody told them to turn it off." An industry source agrees, "Sure, there's a lot of regimentation there, and if anyone is going to balk at regimentation it's those weird California computer freaks who speak in hex code. But when McGraw-Hill beats the drum, even the California longhairs march to it. It's eerie." Walter Miller, a former McGraw-Hill editor, adds, "You don't sell a billion-plus a year by magic. But if you want to get in on the action at McGraw-Hill, you have to play their game. Your office is the same as everybody else's at your level, your carpeting is the same, and you get the same number of windows." How regimented is it at McGraw-Hill? Walter says, "I knew a guy there whose promotion was held up for months because there was no office available with the correct number of windows. And the company is addicted to schedules. If you say you're going to do something by a certain date, you either do it or you're not there the day after." If rules are not your cup of tea, McGraw-Hill is not for you.

An industry source puts it this way: "If you like books, you'll love selling at Harper & Row. They have one of the best lists in town." The oldest of the publishers in our survey—it was founded in 1817—and in many ways one of the most traditional of the major New York houses, Harper & Row has earned the number-two ranking in the industry. It edged out Holt, number three in the rankings, for four major reasons. First, as was the case with both McGraw-Hill and Holt, H&R scored a strong 5 for compensation in the sales representatives category. Second, H&R is a representative's delight because of the breadth and strength of its list. In addition to publishing a total of 1,200 titles in 1984, H&R has over 19,000 titles in print, and is also the distributor for over a dozen small publishers. Third, H&R recently sold its elementary to high school textbook operation to acquisition-happy Macmillan for a figure reported at between $20 and $25 million. We read this as a sign that H&R is planning to concentrate capital in the more profitable areas of trade and college textbook publishing, a good sign for H&R representatives. Reason number four can best be described by Sherman Lethbridge, an H&R college textbook salesman: "When I call on a professor for the first time, I'm treated as a professional because of the H&R name. It's a door opener." Sherman had worked for Holt for a number of years, and says, "Holt is certainly as well known as we are, but somehow there's an edge— some kind of intangible difference that I see from professors when I tell them I'm from Harper & Row. I think we're viewed as having a desirable amount of 'old world stability.' "

The Harper & Row college textbook list may be one of the strongest in publishing, and Harper editions of classics in all academic disciplines turn up on required reading lists at colleges throughout the country. As Sherman points out, when hundreds of thousands of students buy Harper & Row college editions every year, the dollars mount up. "That's an awful lot of sales, and those types of sales are steady. They just don't stop."

Commenting on the difference between trade and college sales at Harper & Row, Sherman says, "I started in the book selling business as a trade rep for a small house. There wasn't the kind of meat in trade sales that there is in college texts. And at Harper & Row, we have a very strong college catalog." Sherman loves education. "I respect education. I respect the process, and I think that's why I enjoy college selling as much as I do. I like the college atmosphere, and I enjoy talking to professors." Asked whether he considered trade sales to be educational as well, he replied: "Yes, but it's not the same thing. Most of the bookstore operators I met were educated people who truly did love books, but of necessity, they were also business people, and business in a small bookstore always came first." Sherman frowns, recalling his experiences with cash registers. "I got to despise those insatiable little machines. I'd be in the middle of talking to the store owner, and he'd have to go running over and tend to the bloody cash register." And how is college selling different? "The professors I speak to are not buyers in the strict sense of the word, although in a way I suppose they're surrogate buyers. But with professors, I can sit down, have a cup of tea, and talk about the books." And what about selling? "I have a unique style. I'm not a high pressure person. More often than not, professors tell me they're going to adopt one of my texts before I ask them." Is this low-key approach common among college sales people? "I honestly don't know because I don't see many reps actually in the process of selling. However, judging from some personal feedback I receive from the professors, I'd say not." Sherman concludes with the kind of observation echoed by many of the representatives interviewed across the broad span of American industry: "I like what I do."

Holt, Rinehart & Winston has earned our number-three ranking for three reasons. First, Holt representatives are well paid; the company received a 5 in the compensation category for textbook sales people, which means that their companywide average salary is more than $29,260. Second, Holt is extremely strong in textbook sales. It always has been, and gives every indication of staying that way. Reason number three is best described by Terry Brouer, a Holt representative. "With CBS behind you, how bad can things get?" The CBS publishing arms, Holt, Dryden, and Saunders, accounted for over $600 million in sales in 1984, with Holt accounting for nearly half that amount. In 1984, Holt alone published 875 titles. Although Terry Brouer's encomium to CBS has proven to be true to date, there might be a very different future if book publishing profits in any of the divisions show signs of a prolonged slump. CBS, the parent corporation, has shown in the past that it has no qualms about lopping off unprofitable ventures.

Garry Mindare, a former software acquisitions editor for one of the small computer publishers, gives an insight into some of the interesting decision making that went on at CBS in 1981-82 with the computer craze at its height. "I was contacted by a headhunter to interview at Holt. That kind of thing was quite common during the computer book insanity. I assumed that the position was to organize a startup educational software operation that Holt was looking into." But Garry soon found out that the operation was bigger than that. "They were looking to hire someone not only to head up the development of the educational software operation, but also to integrate the operation throughout the three main publishing divisions at CBS. Their idea was to have a matrix management operation in which the person they hired would be expected to make top-down recommendations to the three publishers and develop an integrated approach to educational software development, but without wielding the final authority about what was to be done. I thought they had a chance, if we could change the management structure they had in mind." So Garry made some recommendations. "I told them that the educational software market was still too young and unsophisticated and that it was unrealistic to expect that the software would be adopted along with their texts. Don't forget, that was in the days before colleges were buying microcomputers for their students, so the only microcomputers were those owned by individual students." He continues: "I told them that the way to sell educational software was to cut a deal with the hardware manufacturers and package a product in which a student buying a Holt text would get a coupon for a discount on an Apple or an IBM and the software that would go along with the text."

Did it work? "Not quite. The bottom line was that to commit to the kind of operation they wanted, there had to be some uniformity in the operation

> *"You don't sell a billion-plus a year by magic. But if you want to get in on the action at McGraw-Hill, you have to play their game. Your office is the same as everybody else's at your level, your carpeting is the same . . ."*

of the three publishers, and they were too entrenched in the idea of operating as independents." Terry Brouer adds, "I really don't think they were ready for that kind of software operation." She also says, "And I don't think it would have been very profitable." But what about the additional income for Holt representatives from the accompanying software sales? "Frankly, I really don't believe there would have been enough to make it worth our while. Do you have any idea how much time we would have had to put in learning the software, not to mention demonstrating it?" Terry feels that Holt representatives have enough to do. "We're expected to stay very much on top of the textbook business, and you can imagine what that's like. There's a lot of work to do, and an awful lot of reading. We were real happy to leave the software to the CBS software people and worry about selling our line of textbooks."

Granger Meaham, an acquisitions editor for a small educational publisher, tells a story which may best describe why Houghton Mifflin earned our number-four ranking. "I had found a group of educators at a small college in Cambridge, Massachusetts, who had some very unique talents. They were working on a Logo curriculum." Logo is a computer language which is used typically, though not exclusively, at the elementary school level for computer literacy as well as subject-area teaching. "These people were good at what they did. They really understood how kids learned, and they were designing all the materials in a very integrated way. I was really excited about the project." And he wanted to keep it quiet. "They didn't seem to be knowledgeable about the publishing industry, which made me quite happy." He quickly adds, "Not that I was going to be unfair in terms of offering them a contract, but usually in a situation like this, you wind up bidding against a lot of publishers, and I wasn't looking forward to that." He continues, "Well, we were all set to close the deal. I had given them a contract, and my GM was going to fly up and meet with them. It was going to be quite a party." But alas, it was not to be. "I got a call from the group leader, and he said, something to this effect, 'Listen, we're just about ready to sign, but my cousin told us to talk to this guy from Houghton Mifflin, so if it's okay, I'd like to postpone our meeting a day.' I wasn't too disappointed, because it still sounded good."

As it turned out, Granger was fairly new to educational publishing at the time, but his general manager wasn't. "I called into the office to postpone the meeting, and when my GM said, 'Forget it. Come home,' I damn near died. I couldn't understand it." But an analogy helped. "My GM said, 'Look, if you want to stay this one out to the bitter end, go ahead, but I'll show you what's going to happen.'" He then told Granger to go get a cotton ball and place it in his palm. "I thought he was nuts. Then he said, 'The cotton ball is us, and you're Houghton Mifflin. Now blow on the cotton ball.'" So, what did Granger do? "I stayed around. I'd worked too hard on this one to leave before somebody kicked me out." And, did somebody kick him out? "Yeah. Houghton Mifflin made an offer that I couldn't begin to compete with. The people at the college were really apologetic. They felt terrible, they said, but they weren't insane. They signed with Houghton Mifflin."

HM's sales increased by 15 percent in 1983 over 1982's figures, and 1984's sales were up another 14 percent to $250 million. With the bulk of the sales coming in from HM's educational operations, this is a good future indicator for Houghton Mifflin representatives. The optimism at Houghton Mifflin is echoed by Harry Newmar, an HM college representative in Boston, who says, "We're starting to go more high-tech now. I'm learning the engineering business, because the word is out that we're going to be pursuing engineering titles pretty hard." Harry adds, "I really don't expect to have any trouble. I have a lot of contacts among college profs." Contacts have been very useful to Harry. "I made a sale once to a small school in Illinois, and I've never been to Illinois. A prof at Boston University was so in love with one of my math texts that he called his buddy in Illinois and told him to order it. Then he handed the phone to me. I got the number for the college bookstore, and I had an order."

Houghton Mifflin has earned our number-four spot for other reasons as well. They scored a 5 on our compensation scale, which means that their prototypical college representative earns over $29,260. In addition, the HM name, which has been respected in education since 1896, is clearly a door opener. However, HM has also earned a [−] and we are raising the yellow caution flag to HM reps. Industry sources indicate that HM intends to move into the business software market with word processing and tutorial packages. There is a proliferation of business software products and it has already become extremely difficult to crack the market, even for major software companies that already have excellent name recognition from previously successful projects. We feel that this market is already oversaturated with quality products. Unless Houghton Mifflin's software products can also cook dinner and get you into Boston Celtics' games for free, it's possible that they could be making a very big and very expensive mistake. One mollifying aspect would be if Houghton Mifflin planned to enter the software business via the acquisition route, although even that would be a risky move in a market that is suffering heavy casualties.

Even though it's now become amalgamated into Gulf & Western's publishing divisions, Prentice Hall has one of the largest and most aggressive sales forces in the business and, along with McGraw-Hill and Harper & Row, has dominated the educational and professional markets for years.

"When a well-muscled, six-foot four-inch, 240-pound guy goes to the beach, where does he sit? Anywhere he wants. That's the best way to describe McGraw-Hill."

Through its ties to academic authors and through its subsidiaries, PH has flooded the computer book market with strong-selling titles since 1980.

Through its little Arco division, PH has been able to pump out a steady supply of study guides and test preparation books for every imaginable school, college, and civil service examination. Through its general book marketing division, PH has brought its *ExecuVision* graphics presentation software

> *"Hayden had the computer book market by the short hairs. All of their electronics authors, who had been hiding in math departments for years, and their sources of juicy technical information . . ."*

through the shoals of computer-store sales and into the business market. Its legal, accounting, and nursing texts are able to hold their own in their respective markets. It is no wonder that Gulf & Western, seeing the company's strength in the professional and college marketplace and its dominance in direct sales, sought to acquire it. And having acquired it, Gulf & Western moved quickly to restructure an entirely new publishing group to take advantage of the sales opportunities that the Prentice Hall list can offer.

So why isn't this new company number two, three, or four? It's primarily because of the uncertainty surrounding the company's future as it begins to square off against the former Simon & Schuster divisions. It is still too early to tell how the Prentice Hall management will fit into the Gulf & Western family. Although the separate Prentice Hall and Simon & Schuster imprints will still remain, the new publishing entity, a division of three companies—Prentice Hall, Simon & Schuster, and Allyn & Bacon—into six divisions along market lines, will need a shakedown cruise before it can sail off into a one-on-one battle against McGraw-Hill. As of this writing, it is unclear to outsiders exactly how the different sales forces might be amalgamated, although the importance of the Prentice Hall list and the aggressiveness of its sales force in the trade, education, and professional markets more than earns Prentice Hall a place in the top five, even though it has just been acquired by Gulf & Western. As reported in *The Wall Street Journal*, Gulf & Western has said that PH can keep its own management and operate as an independent, but it is not unlikely that eventually Prentice Hall will exist only as an imprint and not as a corporate entity. Time will certainly tell.

This means that Prentice Hall has earned a [−] in our intangible ratings category. The yellow flag is up because although the company's sales have been strong, it is still too early to tell what will happen. Therefore, as far as sales representatives are concerned, there's a red sky at morning. A quick summary of the positives and negatives at Prentice Hall reveals a cloudy picture. First of all, the negatives at PH are clearly not fatal. The company earned a 5 in both the trade and college text compensation categories, because the prototypical PH representative still earns more than $29,260 selling college texts and more than $24,200 in trade sales. PH sales increased by 10 percent in 1983 and again in 1984, and 1985 projections are for an 11 percent increase to $545 million. The Arco division, a leading test preparation and consumer reference publisher, published 270 titles in 1984 and has 1,000 titles in print. The company has an enormous and valuable backlist. Peter Grenquist, a Prentice Hall veteran troubleshooter and Arco's CEO, has called the company "a true cash cow." Reston, PH's computer book publishing arm, is struggling, but then, what computer book publisher isn't? The market was simply oversold and overpromoted. Prentice Hall sales representatives are still able to get their titles on the shelves, and

> *Nomadic lifestyles are a common experience among the salespeople in the book publishing industry whose seasonal odysseys can take them anywhere from isolated college towns to major cities all over the United States.*

as one of the division heads reports, PH's backlist titles continue to sell "like water dripping on a rock." In summary, the situation for Prentice Hall representatives is that it's far too early to tell how the restructured company will operate as a series of G&W divisions.

From the 50th-floor executive dining room at McGraw-Hill you can look across the Hudson River to the New Jersey Meadowlands. On a clear day you can almost see the flat Prentice Hall building surrounded by an endless parking lot. If you cross the hall at McGraw-Hill and look out the east windows, you can see the Simon & Schuster building looming above the Sixth Avenue traffic. Now the two publishers flanking McGraw-Hill have become six publishing divisions within the same parent corporation. Recently, Simon & Schuster's Dick Snyder bought a large chunk of Von Nostrand as well. Nobody's worried at McGraw-Hill, however. Insiders in sales report that McGraw-Hill's position in all of its markets will keep it in the number-one position for a long time to come.

BOOK PUBLISHING	COMPENSATION	COMMISSION	SUPPORT	INTANGIBLE
1 McGraw-Hill, Inc.	5	5	5	
2 Harper & Row Pub. Inc.	5	5	5	+
3 Holt, Rinehart & Winston	N/A	5	5	
4 Houghton Mifflin Co.	N/A	5	5	−
5 Prentice-Hall, Inc.	5	5	5	−

The industry median in trade book sales compensation for the prototypical two-year representative is $24,200 and in college text sales, it is $26,600. As has been the case in most industries, because commission rates and compensation packages are so varied, we did not split out the commission schedule.

Harper & Row [+]
Having more product to sell is good news to reps, and H&R's distribution scheme, by which they are a marketing arm for over a dozen small publishers, has earned our number-two ranked company a [+].

Houghton Mifflin [−]
Indications that HM is actively going to pursue the development and sale of business software has earned our number-four ranked company a [−]. Simply put, we think it could be a costly mistake that will not benefit HM reps, considering the already saturated market, and the time-consuming training that selling software requires.

Prentice Hall (Gulf & Western) [−]

PH would have been our number-two company had this book been written a year ago. If there is a recognizable Prentice Hall one year from now, they may well be our number-two company when we update our information. However, this book is being written neither in the past nor in the future; it's being written as Prentice Hall and Simon & Schuster are being combined into six publishing and information units within Gulf & Western, and there is currently much too much uncertainty for former PH reps for the ranking to be any higher than fifth.

FOOD

THE TOP FIVE:

1 Fleming Companies, Inc.
2 Sysco Corp.
3 Rykoff-Sexton
4 Wetterau, Inc.
5 Super Valu Stores, Inc.

L ike real estate—the brokering of shelter—food is a staple industry in most civilized nations. This is an industry whose commercial roots can be traced to the very beginning of human society when the first hunting parties contributed their goods for the nourishment and survival of the clan. Organized food purveyors have been a fixture of every historical period, and today, the food industry is one of the largest in the United States. Food sales encompass the huge wholesaling houses that supply both supermarkets, convenience stores, and fast-food restaurants as well as the little family neighborhood grocery store. In the United States, the world's largest food producer, food distribution is among the most important of industries.

The diffuse wholesale food-selling industry in the United States consists of national wholesale distribution chains such as our five top companies—Fleming, Sysco, Rykoff-Sexton, Wetterau, and Super Valu Stores—which sell food to the major retailers, and includes a food distribution chain to restaurants. The wholesale distributors are the most important link in the process of getting food from the producers to the consumers because they do the bulk buying from the food manufacturers such as Beatrice Foods, General Foods, and meat packing companies, and then deliver it to the supermarket shelves. But, although there are many forms of point-of-purchase retailing to the consumer in addition to the supermarket or convenience grocery store, the wholesalers are the focal point of distribution. And sales representatives for the wholesalers are the true food sales people in the entire food distribution industry.

The restaurant industry should also be considered in the food distribution chain because, according to an industry source, "More than one-third of every dollar spent on food in the United States is spent on food purchased away from home. This fact alone effectively adds restaurant point-of-purchase to the retail food industry. And within ten years, this figure will climb to over one-half." Therefore, any discussion of the food distribution and sales industry must include a discussion of restaurants, as buyers of food and supplies, as well as a discussion of the suppliers who provide restaurant owners with wholesale food and provisions in addition to the information they need to manage their establishments profitably and efficiently. With this in mind, we have researched the restaurant industry as well as the food wholesaling industry, and we have found some unusual and interesting stories describing how food is sold to and in restaurants.

Because the restaurant industry is so fragmented, we have made no attempt to rank major restaurants. However, we are going to report on some unusual aspects of selling in restaurants, a term that will include every type of retail food establishment from the diners along New Jersey's Route 22 to New York's "21" Club. We have omitted from the restaurant research the fast-food chains such as McDonald's, Burger King, and Wendy's, because retailing in the fast-food industry is quite different from food sales in the restaurant and hospitality industry. Fast-food franchises, unlike other types of food and hospitality establishments, rely almost exclusively on mass media advertising and other forms of promotion that have little or nothing to do with the sales and delivery of food through the wholesale distribution chain.

In the mid 1970s, Jody DiOrio, like thousands of students across the nation, was working part-time as a waitress to pay her way through graduate school. However, by applying some basic logic and some of the quantitative evaluation procedures she was learning in school, Jody combined her graduate school learning and her waitressing experience into a restaurant consulting firm that was the beginning of her career as an entrepreneur in the restaurant business. Her approach to the problems of restaurant management sheds light on the way restaurants are operated, the way they fit into the food distribution chain, and the way goods are bought and sold in restaurants. Most important, her story sheds light on the way representatives in the food distribution business can help their customers realize greater profits while moving larger amounts of food and provisions. Jody's ability to turn a part-time job into a full-time career indicates that the restaurant business is far more than the seat-of-the-pants operation that most people think it is. The business is based on very practical methodologies that Jody was able to evaluate and manipulate in much the same way that representatives from the major food wholesalers do when they convince restaurant owners to buy more rather than less.

Jody worked in one of New York's steak chain restaurants that specialized in medium-priced steaks and chops and offered a salad bar and cocktail bar. She explains, "I really counted on tips to survive, so I was always focused on the issue of my tips. I soon noticed that the tips I got on Fridays

> "... one of the biggest sore spots in many negotiations with restaurant owners is reordering."

were always about 20 percent lower than the tips during the rest of the week. This 'Friday syndrome' really puzzled me. I figured that Friday tips should be the best because typically people were relaxing after a hard work week and tended to be in a more celebratory mood than on a normal workday. I didn't really know what to make of it until one day my boyfriend said something to this effect: 'If it's okay with you, I'd rather not go out on Friday nights. Let's go out Saturday instead.' When I pressed him for a reason, he said, 'Because you're always a grouch on Fridays.' And that got me to do a little thinking and a little soul searching, the net result of which was very profitable. I realized that I was in a bitchy mood on Fridays because I was really whipped from Friday classes which ran from eight to five almost straight through. By the time I came to work, all that I wanted to do was sleep and the last thing I wanted was to listen to somebody complain about his steak being too well done." But Jody realized that her own bread and butter depended on that steak turning out just right. "I asked the other waitresses.

and wasn't surprised to find out that Friday was their best tip night of the workweek, so I was convinced that it was my problem, and not that Friday was just my unlucky day."

Joe Dotter, a representative for Sysco, our number-two rated company, adds a comment to Jody's story: "In this restaurant business I study all factors influencing a restaurant's bottom line, and one of the significant factors is the serving person's attitude. I'm not at all surprised that Jody's tips were lowest at a time when she says she was also." Joe Dotter explains that in his role as a wholesaler's representative, he is in much the same position as Jody with regard to making an independent evaluation of how a restaurant is operating. From his perspective, he points out, he is trying to sell products. But in the process, he is able to turn around an entire restaurant operation from a low-purchase, low-profit account to a high-purchase, high-profit account in much the same way that Jody turned around her profits and the profits of the rest of the staff and owner as well.

Having discovered the cause of her low tips on Friday nights, Jody decided to conduct her own study to see how much she could turn Friday around. "I didn't change anything that I'd been doing on the other nights, but I went out of my way to give super service on Fridays. And I wasn't surprised to find that after three months my tips on Fridays went from being 20 percent lower than any other day to being 30 percent higher." But Jody wasn't finished. "I started wondering what else I could do to increase my tips. Since they totalled about 15 percent of the check total, I realized that if I could get my tables to spend more, I'd make more." So, she began to do a little advertising. "I'd push cocktails. We always had a cocktail special each night, and I'd recommend it to my tables. I'd also push side dishes. People would order steak, so I'd recommend a side order of mushrooms or onion rings. And the results were phenomenal. I'd say that over 90 percent of my tables went with my suggestions, and my overall tips increased an additional 15 percent."

Joe Dotter states, "Many restaurant owners have become aware of the simple fact that for every dollar that tips increase, their gross increases by six or seven dollars. As a result, in many restaurants tips are now shared, so everyone is in a position of watching out for everyone else. It's in everyone's best interest to see that the customers are happy." And what makes customers the happiest? "Good food. If the food isn't good, tips will be down." Joe adds, "One of the ironies is that the chef was virtually never tipped, except for an occasional bottle of wine from an appreciative customer, yet the chefs make the biggest contribution to the customer's frame of mind when it comes to tipping. It's quite common now for chefs to receive between 10 and 13 percent of the day's tips in the growing number of restaurants that pool tips."

And Jody began to expand her operation. She realized that she had a service to offer: "Since my tips were increasing 15 percent, so was my boss's business from my tables. So I approached him and offered to work as a consultant with the other waitresses. He compared my current checks with those of the other waitresses and with my previous checks, and I was hired. In two months, his gross receipts were up over 20 percent, and a big part of that was liquor." Joe Dotter adds, "The liquor tab in a restaurant can range between 10 and 80 percent of gross receipts. In a restaurant like the one Jody worked in, it's normal for the liquor tab to be about 30 percent of the total receipts. And the profit margin on liquor is considerably higher than the profit margin on food."

Restaurant owners are frequently a tightly knit group and usually share ideas. So Jody's boss approached her and asked if she'd be interested in consulting and training the waiters and waitresses in a few of his friends' restaurants. "I did," says Jody, "and I was so successful that I quit both graduate school and waitressing, and started my own consulting business.

Jody's story is an example of how individual initiative in the restaurant business has increased the bottom line for restaurant owners and made entire careers for entrepreneurs. At the same time, Jody's story points to the heart of the profit machine at most restaurant operations. Restaurants are quickly becoming a major source of food distribution to consumers in the United States and will become an even greater source as families grow smaller and two-career marriages proliferate. Therefore, the way food is retailed to restaurant customers will have an important impact on the wholesale food distribution industry which generally reacts to the economics of retail distribution patterns. It almost goes without saying that whenever the economics of an industry are changing, the sales representatives, those individuals whose primary source of income is a percentage of the sale, will be among the first group affected by any changes.

Fleming Companies, an Oklahoma City-based corporation, has earned our number-one rating in the industry for a number of reasons. One industry source says, "Fleming is the most efficient, organized operation in the industry. They are the IBM of this industry. Their reps can walk into a supermarket and tell the manager within fifteen minutes exactly how to increase his bottom line. And they're right."

Fleming's sales have reflected their reputation for efficiency and aggressive management. Sales in 1983 increased by 33 percent, 1984 sales were up another 14 percent, and the 1985 projection is for an additional 25 percent increase to $7 billion. Their reputation for aggressive management is reflected in the fact that since 1982 the company has made four major acquisitions, the last of which was United Grocers, a billion-dollar-a-year California wholesale operation.

Rod Campbell, a Fleming sales representative in Oklahoma, says, "Fleming is a great company to work for for a lot of reasons, but one is that we carry just about everything." Fleming, unlike many distributors, carries most of the major brands. An industry analyst comments, "Being able to carry major brands such as Heinz, Campbell, and Gerber is a tremendous benefit to a wholesaler because those are brand names whose wholesale prices are not going to be bargained over at contract time." Rod agrees. "Do you have any idea how much money is spent by the major food and beverage companies on advertising alone? Most people don't realize that food ads both in print and on radio and television account for a major portion of the advertising that reaches consumers. Even veterans in the advertising business admit that the total dollars spent on food ads is truly staggering—over three trillion dollars every year." But Rod adds that when one considers the number of food products on the consumer market, the expenditures become more realistic. This advertising is important because it does the job for the wholesalers' representatives and for the stores. Rod explains that a company like Fleming which carries the major advertised brands is a strong company for a food salesperson to represent because he also has the benefit of over a million dollars in free advertising for the store. "It stands to reason," he points out, "that a Fleming rep will have more clout because of the quality of the manufacturers we buy from and the quantity of products we buy. We make offers that supermarkets can't refuse."

Rod explains Fleming's services: "We've got the capability to supply a supermarket from soup to nuts. We offer marketing help, inventory control systems, and floor plans. We not only stock shelf items, but we can also supply the deli, the fish market, the meats, the frozen foods, and the produce. We also have the most sophisticated computerized warehouse system in the industry." Rod's point is well made and an independent source con-

> ... a restaurateur will do better business if he is working from a higher inventory rather than a lower one, provided that he keeps in mind the law of diminishing returns. There's an upper limit to everything.

firms that Fleming distributes to nearly 5,000 supermarkets nationwide, in addition to being a major food service supplier to institutions of all sizes. Fleming expends considerable effort on training its representatives.

"The company leaves nothing to the imagination," Rod comments. "We are trained to be professionals. In addition to being sales reps, we're expected to be consultants to the store owners and operators. We have the expertise to make a supermarket business work." Wholesalers such as Fleming also offer the same professional advice and expertise to food service institutions and to the restaurants they supply. "In the food business," according to another Fleming representative, "you're working with all types of perishable items and consumables whose distribution is heavily regulated by government agencies, so you have to know what you're doing or else face some big losses. That's where working with a major wholesaler like Fleming is an advantage. Our reps have been trained to make money for their customers, whether the customer is a supermarket or a small institution."

Fleming has earned a 5 on our compensation scale, indicating that their prototypical two-year rep earns earns more than $28,490, which is more than 10 percent above the industry median of $25,900. Fleming has earned their place as our number-one company by offering their reps the ability to sell the widest, and the most lucrative, lines of merchandise and produce available anywhere in the industry.

The Houston-based Sysco Corporation is the only one of our top five companies in the industry to derive the major portion of its revenue from sales to restaurants and institutions. Sysco earned a 5 on our compensation scale, meaning that their prototypical two-year rep earns more than $28,490, over 10 percent above the industry median of $25,900. Sysco's sales were up by 21 percent in 1984 and are projected to rise by another 18 percent by the end of 1985 to $2.7 billion. Two additional noteworthy items for Sysco reps: Sysco is increasing its fresh produce line; and Sysco should soon be gaining a foothold in the multibillion-dollar Chicago food and distribution market through the acquisition of the Railton Company, which should solidify Sysco's market standing.

Joe Dotter, a Sysco rep based in New York, comments on selling to restaurants. "Restaurant owners probably get more calls from sales reps than any other category of people on earth. They are called on by reps selling everything, including new equipment, new furniture and fixtures, advertising, and of course, food. " What methods does a rep use to get in to see these owners? "Persistence is one. It's not unusual for me to make four stops or calls to a restaurant before I get to see an owner." And what about a sale? "I don't think I've made more than 10 percent of my initial sales in fewer than three calls, and that's after I get in to see the owner." Joe has some interesting observations about the restaurant business. "You'd be surprised how many restaurants are buying frozen foods, including meats and fish. Usually they don't advertise that the food is fresh, but they sure don't advertise that it's frozen." How does that affect sales? "Actually, it helps. I have some very nice accounts—restaurants that are in the mid-to-high ticket range—and their names open doors for me in the lower-priced restaurants or diners." Joe points out, "There are more restaurants in the New York City metropolitan area, including nearby New Jersey and Connecticut, than there are in any other place on earth. And there's some pretty heavy competition for a piece of the market."

Joe comments that one of the biggest sore spots in many negotiations with restaurant owners is reordering. From the sales representative's point of view, he explains, the owner should buy more rather than fewer provisions. It's to a representative's advantage for the owner to place consistently higher orders because the more food inventory the owner has, the more he tends to sell to his customers. In fact, most wholesalers' representatives agree that a restaurateur will do better business if he is working from a higher inventory rather than a lower one, provided that he keeps in mind the law of diminishing returns. "There's an upper limit to everything," Joe warns, "especially the amount of inventory a restaurant can move over a weekend." However, Joe's major reordering problems, and those of his colleagues, should be solved by the new computerized inventory systems that are being supplied to the industry by the major computer manufacturers. In fact, according to John Rogers, a representative for Seiko Computers, the restaurant business is in step with the rest of American industry and is going high-tech. "Seiko actually entered the microcomputer market based on selling to a select group of vertical markets which we researched very carefully, and the restaurant market was right up there at the top of the list."

Seiko, those wonderful folks who make the watches, entered the computer market late in 1984, and according to Dean Black, a Seiko rep, "We didn't want to become involved in the kind of crazy, destructive competition that is so prevalent today. So what we did in the restaurant industry was contract with a software developer to put together a software package running exclusively on our machines. It's an excellent package and it's selling quite well." Joe agrees: "I've seen it in a number of the restaurants I've called on. It's a great system." One of the biggest problems facing restaurant owners is theft. Joe says, "It's not difficult for a waiter or a bartender to pocket some of the receipts. Frankly, many restaurant owners have the theft problem built into their budget and only fire an employee who's stealing excessively." Dean agrees: "The first thing our research showed was that restaurant owners wanted a pilfer-proof system. The theft protection feature is one of the biggest selling points of the system." Joe adds, "It really is very impressive. If I owned a restaurant, I'd sure as hell have one." Dean explains how the system works: "The restaurant has four computer terminals at strategic points, including the bar. Waiters, waitresses, and the bartender take a customer's order and punch it into the system at one of the terminals. For food orders, the system prints a copy of the order in the kitchen, so the chef knows what to prepare. The system also automatically prints charges, so that once an item is entered as being ordered, the price will automatically appear on the customer's check. That way it's virtually impossible for the

> "... for every dollar that tips increase, their gross increases by six or seven dollars. As a result, in many restaurants tips are now shared, so everyone is in a position of watching out for everyone else."

employees to shortchange the owner. When the customer pays the bill, the system registers the amount of the check and the tip. "It can also contact the major credit card centers automatically for verification and payment authorization." Finally, the system also prints out a check for the customer.

The major feature of restaurant management software that benefits the wholesaler's representative is the inventory control system. Joe comments, "I love these systems because they keep track of inventory and expenses. When I call on an account that uses the system, all the information I need to recommend orders and make comparisons is right there, so I get no arguments from restaurant owners." Pete Siani, a chef-owner of a restaurant in New York City and one of Joe's clients, says, "I always flew by the seat of my pants when it came to ordering food and supplies. I wouldn't believe a salesman if he told me the sun was coming up tomorrow." Joe laughs at Pete's comment and reminds him, "Don't forget to tell the story of how you always used to run out of things before you got the computer." Pete responds, "Yeah, sometimes, but—" Joe interjects good-naturedly, "I know. All salesmen are thieves. But seriously," Joe continues, "if most restaurant owners knew how much money they were losing because of poor inventory management, they would be lining up outside the computer stores to get any kind of system that tracked their inventory consumption and provided them with comparisons of items. I can talk to an owner or his chef until I'm blue in the face about what they need, and I just get blank stares. With a computer system I can point to the numbers and say 'Look at this week, now look at that week. Here's what you need to order.' "

Perhaps surprisingly, Joe and his fellow representatives consider employee theft a factor that makes selling to restaurants more difficult. Restaurant owners can become cynical because they deal with people who may steal from them as soon as they get the chance. A lot of restaurant owners suspect that their employees are stealing, and they are constantly being approached by sales reps who want them to spend the money they've guarded so carefully. "While I don't really blame these guys for being cynical," Joe adds with a sigh, "it sure does make it a heck of a lot tougher to work with them."

Sysco has earned our number-two ranking primarily because they pay their representatives well, and through their expansion of profitable areas such as fresh produce and their acquisition of additional companies, they are offering their reps a solid growth opportunity. In addition, Sysco holds a very important position in the wholesale industry because of its primary market relationship with restaurants. The number of single people and families using restaurants as their primary food purchase point is increasing, and wholesalers like Sysco will be at the center of the market as the restaurant industry enters a major expansionary period in the late 1980s to early 1990s.

Rykoff-Sexton, based in Los Angeles, has earned its number-three place in our rankings for many of the same reasons that Sysco earned our number-two spot. They pay their representatives very well and they are experiencing a period of steady, even spectacular, growth with a sales increase of 62 percent in 1983 and an additional 52 percent in 1984 to $850 million. Rykoff-Sexton offers its representatives an even more diversified product line than Sysco does, and R-S reps are now selling supplies such as napkins and other paper goods as well as large equipment such as refrigerators. Company management has won accolades for the merger of the Rykoff and Sexton companies, which one industry analyst describes as "one case where one plus one equals three." By this he means that by joining forces, the merging companies were able to accomplish many economies of operation while simultaneously expanding their capital base and markets. Rykoff-Sexton barely lost out to Sysco for the number-two spot due to Sysco's position in the rapidly growing restaurant market which we see as being an exceptional growth area in the next five years.

R-S has earned a 5 on our compensation scale, indicating that a prototypical two-year rep earns more than $28,490, which is more than 10 percent above the industry median of $25,900. Sean Smythe, an R-S rep based in New York, says, "I negotiated my own compensation plan when I signed on with the company in 1984." It should be pointed out, however, that Sean is not prototypical, because he came to R-S with approximately four years of successful sales experience in a related industry.

Sean sells primarily to delis, hotels, and restaurants, and says, "In this business you really need to rely on your wits. The people you sell to are getting bombarded with sales reps of all sizes and shapes, and you've got to polish your approach and make a quick hit." He adds, "If the deli owners, restaurant managers, or hotel managers think you're giving them a line, you'll be out and they'll never talk to you again." He comments on the Rykoff-Sexton merger. "It was great for me personally because it really expanded my product line." Sean recalls one unusual sale: "I was making cold calls on some delis in my territory and I was running into a lot of resistance. In one deli I happened to notice that they had an old refrigeration unit which was leaking. I pointed it out to the owner, remarking casually about what a nuisance those things could be. He then launched into a fifteen minute diatribe about how that SOB machine was ruining his life and how he was going to shoot it and the repairman the next time he came." Sean thinks that the owner really loosened up. "Because he didn't think I was selling refrigerators, he felt safe talking about it. He didn't think I was using a sales angle in talking about the refrigeration unit." But the deli owner was in for a surprise. "I had to do some pretty quick thinking. We had just picked up Rykoff's equipment line and I knew we had a good unit, but I didn't know squat about it. So I decided to offer a combination deal. I told him that if he signed up with me for a distribution contract, I'd be able to get him a 10 percent discount on a new refrigeration unit." And the response? "He was amazed. He had no idea that we sold heavy equipment. I told him that the company was so successful that we were expanding quite a bit, and that impressed him even more. By the time I walked out of there, he really felt that he had found the answer to all his supply needs. And," Sean adds, "he was right."

Sean also comments about what it took to really get started in the industry. "You've got to be able to take rejection. It takes me between five and eight cold shots at a guy to make a sale. If you're the kind of person who will take 'no' for an answer, this isn't the job for you." He adds, "There's nothing magic about selling in this business. The heavy hitters, and I mean reps who are sitting right at the top of the sales ladder, worked their tails off to get where they are, and they usually don't slow down much even after they've made it big." Sean points out, "The industry changes too fast for anyone to be able to coast along. Also, the people we sell to are pretty hyper types. They like to be catered to." When asked whether he thought any special training was needed to be able to sell, Sean says, "Absolutely. You should practice banging your head against a wall at least three times a day." He adds, "Seriously, it's just plugging along. You have to keep hitting on your people to find an opening. It's probably like most other kinds of selling."

Sean also had some interesting comments on the entrepreneurial side of the restaurant business. "The competition among restaurant owners is pretty intense, and I sometimes get the flak from the tension that these guys are under. Because restaurants are strictly local operations, except for the famous ones like '21' and other establishments in that league, they're subject to all sorts of crazy goings-on in their local area that can really affect their operation." He gave an example of one: "A new restaurant opened up in a town in Westchester County. It gradually built up a loyal clientele by offering fabulous food and a nice atmosphere. After about two years business suddenly dropped by 30 percent." Why? "Because the town was doing construction, and the main road to the restaurant was under repair. The route that people had to take to get to the restaurant was so cumbersome that a lot of people didn't bother, and still others got lost." Sean adds, "The restaurant owner was young, with a wife and two small children, so he was pretty upset. Then, out of the blue, his fairy godfather appeared, telling him that the way to make more money was to start giving his food away for free." Having gained the undivided attention of his audience, Sean continues: "The operator of a dining club service came in and proved to the restaurant owner that he could increase business substantially by using the

> *The number of single people and families using restaurants as their primary food purchase point is increasing . . .*

dining club's two-for-one dinner concept." In other words, the restaurant owner would be able to draw more customers by offering one free meal for the full price of a regular meal, a plan that has been gaining popularity with various local credit card organizations for almost fifteen years.

Joseph DePaul, the founder of the Gourmet Dining Club, explains the concept of his marketing approach, "I'm actually a middleman between the dining public and the restaurant owners. I sell the public a book of coupons for my member restaurants. Each coupon entitles the holder to one free meal at a member restaurant with each meal that is purchased at equal or greater value. It's a two-for-one special. The advantage of the coupon from the user's point of view is that he can try a new restaurant on a reduced-risk basis since he's only paying for half the check." But what's in it for the restaurant owner? "More business," Joseph explains. "It's not unlike airline super-savers, or any other special gimmicks to drum up more business." "But," we object, "airlines don't actually give away a product; they just put people in seats that would have been empty otherwise. The restaurant actually gives away food for which it has to pay." Joseph has the answers: "Only 10 percent of the people who use my coupons order the basic meal and nothing else. The rest order drinks and other extras, so the restaurant makes money on the transaction. It also gives the restaurant an opportunity to generate repeat business. The coupons are good for only one free meal at a restaurant." He also points out, "I advertise my service in quite a few publications, so the restaurant is also getting free advertising." The restaurant doesn't pay a fee to the Gourmet Dining Club; only the people who buy the coupons actually pay the club.

In the process of researching the club, which has been in existence since 1979, Joseph developed some interesting statistics on the restaurant business in general. He asks, "Which restaurant do you think is the best to work for in terms of tips? It isn't a fancy, well-known, high-ticket Manhattan restaurant, such as '21' or the Rainbow Room, where most people will tip very generously as a rule. The best restaurant for high tips is Howard Johnson's because there is a tremendous turnover there. Typically people take forty-five minutes for dinner, and a waiter or waitress waits on five tables at once. That means that in an evening, he or she will be serving twenty tables in a three hour span. If the average table has three people, that would be sixty dinners, and if the average tab is ten dollars, the total gross tab will be $600. The tips would amount to approximately $90." Joseph compares this with an elegant restaurant: "The typical table is for one couple and although the tab might be $150, the average dinner lasts two hours. So at best, the waiter or waitress will be serving two tables at two separate sittings and the total tab for the evening will be $300, which may result in $50 or $60 in tips." Joseph also points out that waiters and waitresses frequently work off the books and live solely on tip income. These statistics do show, however, that the trend toward fast turnover of customers means both higher gross incomes for the restaurant owners and faster consumption of inventories that will be replenished by the wholesale food distributors. Thus, many representatives like Sean encourage restaurant owners to participate in the types of dining clubs that ultimately result in a greater number of customers and higher consumption of food supplies. "Everybody benefits, including the customer," Sean explains.

Wetterau, based in Missouri, has earned our number-four spot in the industry for many of the same reasons as Fleming, its predecessor in the supermarket distribution end of the business. Although Wetterau is an excellent company, it simply does not have the product line that Fleming has nor the distribution network. Wetterau, although strong, is just not quite in Fleming's league, and although we felt that Wetterau is quite close to Sysco and Rykoff-Sexton, our number-two and three ranked companies, respectively, Sysco's and Rykoff-Sexton's strong position in the burgeoning restaurant markets convinced us to rank them ahead of Wetterau.

Wetterau is pursuing considerable expansion in the market, having acquired a number of large supermarkets which it runs as supermarket-warehouses. Their proprietary position in the retail market strengthens the overall position for Wetterau sales reps. Wetterau's sales reflect the growth of the company, with a sales increase of 17 percent in 1983, another 15 percent in 1984, and a projected increase of still another 14 percent in 1985 to $3.5 billion. Brent Sowles, a Wetterau representative, comments on the company's product lines: "We've expanded beyond the scope of the super-market concept to the point where we are also merchandisers." An industry analyst adds, "This is good news for Wetterau reps since it expands their product lines." Brent continues, "We're moving in many of the same directions as Fleming. We're just not quite as big." Brent is referring to Wetterau's move to utilize computer technology to manage their ware-housing, shipping and retailing operations. In addition, "Wetterau runs their own training center for the development of modern management skills and their particular application to the industry. Wetterau scored a 5 in the compensation category, indicating that our prototypical two-year rep at Wetterau earns more than $28,490, or more than 10 percent above the industry median of $25,900.

Super Valu Stores earned our number-five rank in the industry even though it is considered by one industry source to be "the largest food wholesaler in the nation." The reason that we did not rank SV any higher is not necessarily a reflection on the company, but rather a predilection of ours. SV has the most geographically concentrated distribution network of all the companies in our survey and we consider this a disadvantage. Our point of view for sales representatives in all industries we've researched in

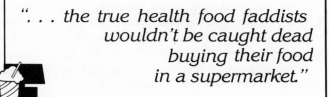

"... the true health food faddists wouldn't be caught dead buying their food in a supermarket."

the survey has been national in scope, and we feel that a more nationally focused company deserves a higher rating. In the top four rated companies, sales representatives are not concentrated in a particular geographical region and therefore are not susceptible to the economic conditions of that region. However, SV did score a 5 on our compensation scale indicating that our prototypical two-year rep at SV earns more than

$28,490, which is more than 10 percent above the industry median of $25,900. Also, the fact that SV owns over a hundred supermarkets and merchandise marts offers a stable selling environment, a big plus for sales reps.

SV sales also reflect the company's strength with a sales increase of 13 percent in 1983, another 12 percent in 1984, and a projected increase of 12 percent more by the end of 1985, to $7.4 billion. Robert Hartman, an SV representative, comments on trends in supermarkets. "We're looking seriously into expanding our coverage of 'health foods.' What began as a fad in California ten years ago is now showing signs of emerging as a significant market throughout the country." An industry analyst agrees. "As people are becoming more aware of diet and nutrition, the move toward what are generally described as health foods is increasing. However, the true health food faddists wouldn't be caught dead buying their food in a supermarket." Robert replies, "True, except our studies show that the so-called average Americans who are health food conscious are looking more and more for what they regard as healthful alternatives to the traditional fare, such as whole grain breads rather than white bread. There is strong demand now for everything without preservatives and without added sugar. Even traditionally strict health food items such as rice cakes, crunchy granola cereals, and bulk quantities of dried fruit and nuts are occupying increasingly large amounts of shelf space in supermarkets."

FOOD	COMPENSATION	COMMISSION	SUPPORT	INTANGIBLE
1 Fleming Companies, Inc.	5		5	+
2 Sysco Corp.	5		5	+
3 Rykoff-Sexton	5		5	+
4 Wetterau, Inc.	5		5	
5 Super Valu Stores, Inc.	5		5	−

The median compensation figure, including salary and bonus for our prototypical two-year industry rep is $25,900. Because compensation packages are so varied in the industry, we did not split out a separate bonus/commission figure.

Fleming [+]

For the reasons mentioned earlier, Fleming is the Cadillac of the industry, and they're growing through acquisition and use of new technology. Fleming reps should be well taken care of for the foreseeable future.

Sysco and Rykoff-Sexton [+]

Both companies have earned a [+] for their strong national position in the restaurant distribution industry.

Super Valu [−]

It's not that we're prejudiced against the Midwest and South—we like sunshine as much as anyone—but we feel that we have to treat this industry giant as a regional giant rather than a national giant. So if you don't mind relocating, or if you're lucky enough to already live in SV country, don't hesitate—they'll be around a long time.

MICROCOMPUTERS

THE TOP FIVE:

1 IBM Corp.
2 Compaq
3 Televideo Systems Inc.
4 Altos Computer Systems
5 Apple Computer Inc.

T en years ago, the only people talking about microcomputers were engineers in R&D laboratories, hobbyists, and avid readers of *Popular Electronics*. However, after the commercial development of Intel's 8-bit processor and the sale of Bill Gates' first software product to Altair—MicroSoft BASIC—an entire industry was born. Through a rapid succession of technical development cycles, what began as a home game machine has turned into a business telecommunication and data processing terminal that can track an investment through all world financial markets without the user's having to get up from his chair. The microcomputer industry has done more than pull this country out of a recession in 1981: it also promises to change the entire corporate landscape.

The microcomputer market, which seemed to rise above the depressed U.S. economy in 1981 like a giant hot-air balloon, was a long time in the making. For a full five years before personal computers made their appearance on the consumer scene, the microcomputer industry was growing and developing and improving its products. By 1981, WordStar and VisiCalc had become household words among the new generation of business and personal computer "end users," and by 1983, the IBM "power user" was talking about modeling with Lotus 1-2-3 as if it were Play-Doh. By late 1984, personal computers had become not only a factor in virtually every major business worldwide, but also the "information appliance" for millions of home users who turned to the on-line bulletin boards and computing services for their evening's socializing and electronic conversation. And while all this has been going on, fortunes are being made and lost in the industry.

The industry can be divided into the two broad categories of hardware and software. The "hardware" is the physical machines while the "software" is the instructions that make the machines work. The software comes packaged in various media, the most common of which are disks, like phonograph records, and tapes, like audio recording tapes. Computer hardware companies, such as IBM, DEC, and Hewlett-Packard, are so identified because they manufacture the actual machines and machine components. It is the computer hardware companies that will be the focus of this chapter, even though the software market is certainly as critical and as interesting as the hardware market. Keep in mind, however, that when computers are purchased, the purchaser typically buys a "package," which in industry lingo usually means the computer, one or more disk drives for storing mass quantities of data, a screen or "monitor" for seeing the data, a printer for seeing the "hard copy" of the data, and various kinds of software to perform such tasks as word processing, mathematical calculations, storing telephone lists, or playing games. The software may be sold by the hardware vendor or may be sold separately by independent software companies, which supply the computer stores or advertise and sell their product through direct mail.

Within the computer hardware industry, there are three categories of products, based on the physical size of the equipment. These are: mainframes, such as the venerable IBM 360; minicomputers, such as DEC's PDP-11; and microcomputers, such as the Apple IIe or the Atari 800-XL. The computers differ not only in physical size, which can range from room-size mainframes to refrigerator-size minis to telephone-size Timex Sinclair microcomputers, but also in the tasks each can perform. Within the traditional paradigm of computing, mainframes could perform tasks that were too large for minis or that required so much raw computing power that minicomputers were simply not the economically feasible way to process the data. Likewise, certain tasks, such as office networking and data communications, large financial calculations and probability equations, and companywide data management functions, were simply too large for desktop personal computers to handle and so minis were used. Originally, the little 48K desktop machines were just fine for spinning out letters and short reports or for assembling quick financial worksheets with a limited series of

> *". . . if you calculated the industry equivalent of the GNP generated by IBM's entry into the market, it would exceed the GNP of most countries on earth."*

numbers. However, within four years, the distinctions between the three levels of computers, and the dividing line between the applications each type of machine could handle, has blurred.

Bruce Fairleigh, an executive in the Management Information Systems (MIS) department at a major New York City bank, says, "Three years ago I thought a microcomputer was for kids. We at the bank were used to computers that you needed a crane to move. I'd have my secretary throwing out computer salesmen every hour on the hour who were all selling micros." As has so often been the case in "computer stories," a kid wound up saving the day for the beleaguered micro sales reps. "We'd been having a problem with a certain kind of sorting operation we'd been doing. The sort function tied up a lot of computer time and the rest of the MIS operation slowed down. I happened to mention it to my fifteen-year-old son. In twenty minutes he showed me a better way to do the sorting operation on his little Apple II computer." And between 1980 and 1982, Bruce Fairleigh's story was being replayed in households across the country as microcomputer users applied their home machines to solving specific business problems.

The bottom line is that bigger isn't necessarily better, and this is what Bruce learned. "It turned out that by compartmentalizing the sort into sections, the overall process went a lot quicker. But the thing that really impressed me was the message that if we used a lot of small, stand-alone, personal computers, each person could do his job independently. The idea of not having our whole MIS system dependent on one machine intrigued me. I'd been in MIS long enough to know that I had some research to do. I wasn't about to completely overhaul our system in a week." It took Bruce two years, but, "We finally got the system we wanted." Bruce's company purchased fifty PC/ATs, IBM's latest business microcomputer at that time. "My staff loves them. They acted like it was Christmas morning when the computers were delivered." And one of the things that sold Bruce on IBM was the support he got from his IBM rep. "I saw more of that guy than I did of my wife. I'm not kidding. He not only sold me computers, he gave me an education."

Unfortunately, some MIS departments had to learn about microcomputers the hard way. According to a bank executive at a major lending institution, he had heard tell of a bank that was once slapped with a series of fines by the SEC because, as he explains, their MIS department had changed over their information systems from a mainframe to a mini environment without "running parallel," or in other words, using their old computer system simultaneously with the new one for as long as it took to be sure that the new system was doing what it was supposed to do. The old system should always serve as a backup. In this instance, the new system had a problem and the managers at the bank reportedly didn't know their cash position for almost a week, and that, of course, created problems in decision making and in the reporting of figures to the regulatory agencies.

The message here for computer sales representatives is that personal computers are very powerful tools that can cause immense damage if not used properly. This means that the computer salesperson is in a very delicate position with regard to his or her client's data. Does this mean that the salesperson must be a computer jock? The industry's answer is a resounding "no." In fact, according to Janet Rushmore, a computer sales representative, "We don't want computer jocks. We won't hire computer jocks." She explains: "We found out the hard way. Computer jocks like to talk shop. They're not salespeople. What the computer industry really needs are people who can talk to people." A representative for IBM says, "Selling computers is in principle the same as any other kind of selling. The customer has to understand how the product will benefit him or her. Otherwise, there's no sale."

"Computers are blue," Janet Rushmore explains, "as in Big Blue." She describes IBM's success in the personal computer field: "I'll tell you this—their marketing is phenomenal, because their equipment isn't." Janet was expressing the frustrations she—and countless reps—have experienced trying to sell against IBM in the business micro market. Janet sells Zenith computers primarily but has recently expanded the line to include Altos systems. "The Zenith is like an IBM PC with twelve vendors added." She meant that Zenith computers come with twelve standard features that are extra-cost add-ons with the IBM PC. "And the Zeniths are faster, do better graphics, run all the IBM software, and are cheaper than the IBM PC. But what do people buy? IBM."

According to most people who know the personal computer industry, it's no secret that there are better-engineered products than the plain vanilla IBM PC. Professional programmers and sales representatives at retail outlets will explain that personal computers using the 8086 microprocessor, rather than the 8088 that IBM uses, run faster than the IBM PC. In addition, many personal computers that cost less than the IBM have standard features such as expanded memory, additional output ports, and graphics boards, that are optional equipment on the PC. Therefore, what accounts for IBM's phenomenal success? According to an executive at Hewlett-Packard: "IBM is almost chivalrous in the way they treat their customers. If you really want to know what they're all about, picture an IBM customer about to step into a puddle as he or she is crossing a street. Before a foot gets damp, an IBM rep will be there flourishing a cape à la Sir Walter Raleigh."

"IBM is a marketing-driven company. They understand that the customer is king," says George Kalafatis, a sales rep for Zenith Data Systems. "Frankly, we're an engineering-driven company. We may have built a better mousetrap, but the only ones who know it are the mice." Fran Argovitz, a rep for an independent computer sales company, relates: "When I first started selling Zenith systems I was excited. It's a very good product. But the advertising support was weak. Every bloody computer company on earth was doing major, big-ticket advertising on TV—except Zenith. I cringed every time I saw that IBM Charlie Chaplin character running all over my TV screen." Fran laments her plight at tradeshows. "People would come by the booth, see the Zenith sign, and say 'TVs? You're selling TVs?' And when I'd point out that the same company that makes the quality TV has been making computers for years, they'd smile politely and say something like 'That's interesting. I never heard of it.' " Fran got her hopes up once. "We heard that Zenith Data Systems was going to start a big advertising campaign. They were going to advertise the computers on TV along with the televisions from Zenith Radio Corporation. The first ad was supposed to appear on a Sunday afternoon during a baseball game. It was late summer, a beautiful day. My husband wanted to go to the beach, but no, I had to stay home and see this ad. After about an hour and a half, sure enough, there was the television ad. The ad was to run sixty seconds. For the first thirty seconds, there was the description of the familiar Zenith TV. Forty seconds. Fifty seconds—no computer. Finally, after fifty five seconds—and believe me, I counted—they said, in effect, 'And by the way, we also sell computers.' I almost put a chair through my TV."

Asked to comment on the apparent lack of support for dealers in the business market, a Zenith executive says: "We encourage our dealers to pursue corporate and other large accounts. We have a very solid national account system." An industry analyst says: "Zenith is quite successful selling computers. They made a corporate decision not to go head to head with IBM, DEC, Wang, and the other big guys, but Zenith computers are the number two seller in colleges behind Apple. Also, Zenith has contracts with the military worth over $100 million. They've sought out their niche and have pursued their selected markets quite successfully." But while Zenith has been successful in pursuing these areas, their failure to advertise heavily in the business market has at times left their dealers in a quandary.

Bert Grant is a dealer who recently dropped the Zenith line from his Boston store. "The way things are today, floor space is too valuable to play around with. I dropped Zenith when I found out that anybody can walk into a Heathkit store and buy a Zenith at 20 percent off list." Bert was referring to the fact that Zenith got into the computer business by buying the Heathkit

> "... picture an IBM customer about to step into a puddle. Before a foot gets damp, an IBM rep will be there flourishing a cape à la Sir Walter Raleigh."

company, and the Heathkit stores still sell Zenith computers both in kit and in finished form. Although it's not entirely true that anyone can walk in and get a 20 percent discount, it is true that if a person joins HUG, the Heath Users Group, after a ninety-day waiting period he can purchase a Zenith computer, or any other piece of equipment, at a 20 percent discount.

An industry analyst says, "If you're going to sell Zenith systems, you'd better be in the national accounts program." Another industry source remarks, "The Zenith story is indicative of the micro industry outside the IBM womb. Hardware manufacturers are scrambling for the rest of the market share, and they're selling hardware any which way they can, whether that's to national corporate accounts, to high-volume discount chains, or to foreign governments." Bert Grant says: "The micro industry is extremely price sensitive. For a store like mine to compete with Crazy Eddie, Wild Bob, and the rest of the discount houses, we have to have a gimmick. Ours is systems sales. We sell sophisticated, integrated systems to small businesses. Because we're selling a complete package, we can cut the price on our hardware and make it up in software and support. And because we're involved with support-intensive systems, over 60 percent of our revenues come from the software support side of the business."

Bert hires two tiers of sales reps. Floor sales reps, who handle walk-in business and do virtually no outside follow-up work, receive a flat commission of 4 percent on everything they sell. Bert adds: "I've been in this business since 1977, so I know how to sell systems. When I hire, I'm looking for a hungry kid who's willing to learn. I can spot a computer jock a mile away and I stay away from them. They waste too much time tinkering." Bert also has field reps who sell to small corporate accounts. "I hire specialists on a consulting basis too. Because I've been around the computer business for so long, I have a lot of contacts. When I have to put together a system for a client, I can call on people with expertise in everything from accounting packages to medical software to cataloging wines. And my field reps are all required to specialize in the name canned packages like Lotus, WordStar, and dBase III." On average, Bob's field reps make between 6 and 8 percent commission, and he adds: "The reps like to work for me because they know that they'll get the technical support from the consultants I use. The consultants are techies who are great at what they do, but who can't or won't sell themselves. So I supply them with a steady stream of work, and they supply my customers with steady support."

"Undercapitalized one-man shows give the industry a bad name," according to an industry source. "Bert's is one of the right ways to be a dealer in the business. Many businesses are going under because they don't have the resources to offer their customers the necessary support. They promise the moon and the stars to get a sale, and then they leave the customer in the lurch." Rudy Zimmerman quit his job as a rep for a small dealership in Massachusetts. "It was completely and totally bananas. I was a sales rep working on a commission. My commission structure was based on the discount level given to the customer, and without getting real complicated, it averaged out to between 5 and 6 percent. The thing was that I had no support. I was expected to qualify a customer, find out his needs, find the software to meet those needs, learn the software, customize it if necessary, and train his people. In my spare time I also had to learn about the different peripherals, such as printers, and how they interfaced with the hardware and the software packages we used. And as if that wasn't enough, if I found a new printer, for example, that the customer needed but that we didn't carry, I had to contact the manufacturer myself, locate a distributor, and cut a deal with the distributor. I quit simply as a matter of survival, but I learned so much of what not to do in this business that I now run my own consulting business."

Rudy's story is not uncommon in the industry. Many dealerships have sprung up overnight in garages and attics. Jon Randolph, the eastern region manager for a major hardware manufacturer, says: "It's not hard to become a dealer. All you need to do is get some stationery printed and give us a call. You'd have to pay for orders C.O.D. for the first six months, but if you can swing the cash flow problem, you're a dealer. Ideally we'd like to have more control, but to be honest, the industry is so cutthroat right now that we're going to sell anywhere that's legal." Jon adds, "We know that in some instances, purchasers of our equipment are getting short-changed by their dealers, but we simply can't afford the manpower to deal with that problem. Not only are we not IBM, but we have to deal with a problem that they never face. We have to compete with IBM. The situation is truly *caveat emptor*." Another industry source says, "Businesses that buy computers need to check out their dealers. The dealer is probably more important than the hardware." She adds, "One way a business has of protecting itself is for one of the principals to get involved in a local user group for the hardware manufacturer in question." And if there are no local user groups? "Let me put it this way. Would you buy a car with a diesel engine if the nearest station selling diesel fuel was a thousand miles away?"

"Learning on the job is very common," says Steve McElroy, a rep for a dealership selling Eagle, Compaq, and Columbia computers. "Because the industry is so relatively new, it's pretty much impossible to get any meaningful training beyond what you can supply for yourself. I literally taught myself almost everything I know about this business. I learned from my own mistakes, and unfortunately, they were at the customer's expense." But Steve quickly adds: "However, I never stiffed a customer. If I installed a system that wasn't doing what it was supposed to do, I came back on my own time and made sure it got fixed."

Steve's most unusual sale typified the energy, excitement, and sometimes confusion that reigned in the personal computer industry in 1984. "I'll never forget it. It was my first sales call and I was demonstrating an accounting package. Now, keep in mind I had absolutely no accounting background. I thought General Ledger was a member of the military. I'd just gotten my hands on the software the night before and was cramming for my demo. Have you ever seen a manual for accounting software? Trust me—it would have made absolutely no difference to me if they had sent the Japanese-language version." Andy Barnhard of Systems Plus, a software house based in California, confirms the difficulty of accounting software. "Of all the different types of software packages such as word processing, spreadsheets, database management, and accounting, accounting is the most difficult to design, and is also the one that is most likely to have bugs. The reason for this is that accounting software is the most complex, since the different parts of the accounting program, such as accounts receivable, sales order, payroll, accounts payable, purchase orders, and inventory, must each send data back and forth and must also communicate with the general ledger. That level of complexity is simply not found in other types of software."

A "FATAL ERROR" message is what you get after it's too late. And Steve got a graphic lesson in that fact. "As it turned out, I had to do some preliminary setup work for the demo, and since I didn't have the slightest shred of a clue as to what I was doing, I'm sure that I messed something up." Steve describes what happened at the actual demonstration. "I was showing the package to the president of the company and his bookkeeper. It was a small company and the president was a dynamic guy, always running here and there trying to solve everybody's problems. The bookkeeper was the kind of worker who has one and only one goal: leave work on time. He was as interested in my demo as I would be in haiku. As the demo was unfolding, the errors I'd made in setting it up were coming home to roost. I would press a key to generate a sales order, and instead of a sales order, the screen would go white and a brilliant, flashing 'FATAL ERROR 14' message would flash on and off." But Steve didn't panic. "The fates were really with me. I must have gotten half a dozen 'FATAL ERROR' messages, but they flashed each time the president had stepped out to handle some problem, so he never saw them. I got the sale, and to this day I have no idea if the bookkeeper also didn't see the messages or just didn't care."

According to most independent sales representatives in microcomputers, the industry picture looks like this: In business microcomputer sales, there's IBM and then there's everybody else. In no other industry is the domination of one company so complete. One industry source says: "IBM actually helped put the industry on solid footing. What they did was set a

> "We at the bank were used to computers that you needed a crane to move. I'd have my secretary throwing out computer salesmen every hour on the hour who were selling micros."

standard, in much the same way that AT&T did for telephones. For example, prior to IBM's entry there were really no universal standards for disk formatting. Apple and Commodore and Tandy had been around since the mid '70s, but they didn't establish any standards. CP/M was one standard operating system, but it was more for computer jocks."

In the early days, from 1979 to 1982, the nonstandardization in computer hardware and software made buying a business computer system a gamble that many players didn't want to make. Salespeople, especially independents, were equally nervous about the lack of recognized industrywide standards in the micro market, but relied on the emerging CP/M to set a standard protocol for software products. The appearance of CP/M, however, was more important for hardware and software companies than it was for buyers because it allowed small, undercapitalized companies to license an operating system and avoid the expense of developing their own. Buyers, on the other hand, were faced with the impossible task of having to decide among scores of small hardware and software companies without knowing any more than "it's CP/M." Bill Woodall, president of his own software company and his own sales representative, remembers, "When you bought a computer you were betting that the company would be around for awhile and would generate enough confidence so that a lot of quality software would be developed." Before IBM and it's MicroSoft operating system, that was quite a gamble. Tandy (Radio Shack) was the first company to enter the micro market. In the first year, when there were precious few microcomputers that even approached a standard, the Radio Shack people were in the right place with the right product. However, according to other industry observers, Radio Shack made a critical mistake by playing the market too conservatively.

Reportedly, Tandy at first tried to develop all their software themselves. They were reluctant to support any outside development efforts, and they

> "I never stiffed a customer. If I installed a system that wasn't doing what it was supposed to do, I came back on my own time and made sure it got fixed."

had a proprietary operating system. Because the operating system is the master set of instructions which tell the computer how to process its data, data from one operating system cannot automatically be transferred to another. It usually has to be "reformatted" so that a different operating system can understand it. Tandy's lack of immediate support for software developers not directly under contract to the company is one of the factors that opened the door for Apple, Atari, and Commodore in the late 1970s and early 1980s.

Apple was one of the companies that took advantage of outside software developers. Not only did they support independent software development; they encouraged it. Their marketing people understood that computers had to be sold to first-time and business buyers as complete systems rather than as separate components, and that the software was a critical component. Consequently, Apple normally didn't ask for anything from the outside vendors beyond standard nondisclosure agreements. The result was that Apple computer today can boast of supporting one of the largest software libraries of any computer company, a factor in making Apple one of the early beneficiaries of the educational computer market. Consequently—and this is important not only for Apple's own sales force but for independent and retail salespeople as well—the software support that Apple sought and received from third-party companies made it easy for Apple systems to be sold. This made Apple one of the largest-selling personal computers and established one of the software standards for an entire realm of software.

The story of VisiCalc is legendary in the industry to this day and shows how Apple was able to penetrate a new market. VisiCalc was the first microcomputer-based spreadsheet program. It was developed by Software Arts, the type of small, independent software company of average size for what was essentially a "garage" or "basement" industry. But as one industry source explains, "It revolutionized the industry at the time. It was the first software product which was an invaluable business tool." VisiCalc was one of the products that helped create the microcomputer revolution, and industry sources estimate that VisiCalc alone was responsible for the sale of over half a million Apple computers in the first three years of its existence. The implementation of VisiCalc on the Apple II + was a turning point which brought financial modeling to the domain of home computer users and business users with home computers. According to Bert Grant, "When I first saw the product, I was on the phone with the company in five minutes. I knew it was going to sell like potato chips. It was funny, you'd call the company and speak to the guy who designed the software. Sometimes you'd hear his dog barking in the background." But, as Bert found out, times change. "I tried to call the company three years later. I think his mother would have to go through three tiers of secretaries in order to make an appointment to speak to him."

The Commodore story is another legend in the annals of microcomputer sales. At first, Commodore International was an enigma to the industry. They were there at the beginning, like Tandy, but, as one industry source says, "They never decided on a consistent course of action. For them, long-range planning seemed to mean six months." And the results showed it. "Their first entry into the personal computer market, the PET with the built-in tape cassette storage device, had some hardware problems. But after they fixed the problems, they came out with some new machines which were not compatible with software designed for the old machines." Subsequently, Commodore settled on operating system standards for an entire line of PET computers, and changes were made to solve compatibility problems with the C-64 line. PET was one of the first best-sellers in the early 1980s. Later, VIC-20 and C-64 were among the single largest-selling small home computers ever produced to date.

The development of what has become a billion-dollar business, the microcomputer industry, started out as a helter-skelter of home computer companies like Tandy, Commodore, and Apple, all of them seeking to find bottom-line business applications for small, slow, desktop machines. Apple became one of the success stories of postwar corporate America and emerged as the big leader in the 8-bit home computer industry, due, among other things, to their very clear focus on the development of quality software for their products. Apple representative Jim Witt says, "We also took care of the compatibility problem. If you bought an Apple II + computer in 1978, you can still open any computer magazine today and see ads for hundreds of software products that will work with it." And an industry source comments "Apple's success continues to mystify many observers. They are the only major manufacturer that has not gone the IBM-compatible route, and yet they continue to be a top seller."

Microcomputers were already a big business when IBM, the most important computer and automated systems company in the world, invaded the market. An industry source says: "You couldn't really call it an invasion. The companies in the rest of the industry were like a bunch of little kids playing and squabbling. They'd keep glancing furtively over to see if Dad was watching, but Dad was too busy with grown-up things. Then, all of a sudden, Dad walked over and said, 'I'm going to play too,' and he took the ball away. Pretty soon, all the little kids gathered around, and Dad said, 'Here are the rules.' "

Many industry analysts use IBM examples extensively to illustrate the right way to run a business. In particular, they stress IBM's dedication to customer service. A representative for Compaq computers says, "The point is that IBM is doing something right, and anyone who would deny that had best not go into competition with them." Long before IBM announced their entry into the market, they had contacted the major software houses around the country and very quietly began working with them to supply software for the new IBM entry into the micro market, the IBM PC. "When the announcement was made, we weren't at all surprised that MicroSoft's operating system was the one chosen," says Bert Grant. MicroSoft is considered by many to be the premier software development company in the industry. Bert adds: "IBM had studied the market. They saw all the mistakes. And believe me, when IBM decides to go out of house for a product, they have to be convinced that it's the only way to go."

After IBM's initial entry, along with their select group of top-of-the-line software developers such as MicroSoft, the rest of the software developers and manufacturers in peripheral products industries such as printers, disk drives, modems, and logic boards joined the parade. "Everybody knew IBM

> *"Undercapitalized one-man shows give the industry a bad name. Many businesses are going under because they don't have the resources to offer the necessary support. They promise the moon and stars to get a sale, and then they leave the customer in the lurch."*

was going to sell a bushel of computers, so IBM software was being rushed to the market," says Bert. An industry source adds, "Entire companies sprang up almost overnight to manufacture hardware products to make up for the PC's shortcomings. And it was not unusual for these companies to be grossing in the high six figures after six months. There are many companies which are still living off IBM."

The IBM name had created a standard so quickly that "IBM-compatible" became a watchword first for sales representatives trying to sell business personal computers and then for manufacturers who created a secondary industry called "PC clones." Fran Argovitz says, "When I'd make a sales call, the client would show me a list of software available for the IBM. It was ridiculous—95 percent of the stuff had absolutely no bearing on the guy's business. But he still wanted to know, 'Can the Zenith run Herkimer's Interstellar Galactic Menu program? The IBM can.' " Even the computer magazines began citing products like MicroSoft's "Flight Simulator" as litmus-test programs that proved or disproved the hardware's compatibility with the IBM PC. So finally the hardware manufacturers wised up and according to Bert, "Lo and behold, a secondary market developed, consisting of IBM run-alikes. Compaq, Columbia, and Eagle marketed IBM-compatible computers to take advantage of the IBM software explosion. And in each case, the IBM clone had more computing power than the IBM." Even independent-minded Zenith caved in and came out with the Z-100 PC, a strict IBM compatible, also with more computing power than the IBM PC. Bert adds, "IBM-compatibility became a measuring stick. Some computers were 90 percent compatible, some 100 percent." And more than one manufacturer had to come out with hardware revisions in order to correct a noncompatibility problem. An executive at Zenith says, "We had to come out with a revised ROM chip because the darn thing couldn't run some games. But you know what really irks me? When we designed the 100 PC, we used the same basic technology that went into the Z-100, our earlier entry, except that we had to make it do less and run slower in order to be IBM compatible."

The IBM submarket also developed in the wake of the PC's extraordinary sales. Magazines, books, and newsletters seemed to come into existence overnight. One industry source says, "I think if you calculated the industry equivalent of the GNP generated by IBM's entry into the market, it would exceed the GNP of most countries on earth." An executive for Hayden Book Company, long a leader in the electronics book publishing business and also one of the first book publishers to produce for the microcomputer market, recalls, "We were contacted by IBM to do some technical manuals for them. We were all pretty excited. On the day the IBM people were to arrive, our offices were almost manicured clean. We were a pretty informal company style-wise, but everybody was in a gray three-piece that day." And the message was the same from other computer book publishers. "When IBM talks, people listen, usually while wearing gray

> *"Apple is the only major manufacturer that has not gone the IBM-compatible route, and yet they continue to be a top seller."*

three-piece suits." In fact, IBM's domination of the market was so complete by late 1984, salespeople for other computer companies used the IBM name as a password. When a sales rep for another computer company approached an editor at PC Magazine, a major microcomputer publication devoted to IBM and IBM-compatible computers, and pitched the virtues of his machine in the hopes of getting PC to buy it for their staff, he was met with the typical response: "I'll be glad to look at your computer, and if it's better than the IBM PC, I'll be happy to say so in the magazine. But there's no way we're going to buy anything that isn't IBM. Around here the sun sets blue."

In short order, IBM single-handedly changed the complexion of the business microcomputer industry, in some cases leaving companies who had either bucked or neglected the tide in their dust, and in other cases making companies who knew how to jump on an obvious bandwagon very wealthy. In the process they established an industrywide standard for software compatibility, made MS-DOS, MicroSoft's operating system, a household word, and brought the world of microcomputers to the mainstream of the business world.

Because selling in the microcomputer industry is done primarily through independent dealers, consultants, and distributors, rather than by manufacturers' reps, we've decided to base the rankings on the hardware sold, rather than the best company for which a rep can sell. So, by ranking computer A as number one, we're not saying that company A is the best to work for; we're saying that computer A is the best to sell. This raises the next question: "If computer A is the best to sell, for whom should I sell it?" The answer is a complex one, and although we are going to describe some productive sales scenarios, we caution you to pay attention to the stories told earlier in the chapter, which depicted some of the potential pitfalls inherent in the industry.

The ideal sales situation is to be a straight-commission rep with access to sources for a number of computers, which must include IBM, as well as sources for peripherals and software. Our research shows that straight-commission reps can earn commissions of between 10 and 15 percent, depending on how much and what kind of support they expect from their suppliers. Some commission reps work as consultants, setting up systems for clients for a fixed hourly rate, which is usually $35 to $60 per hour, against a minimum start-up charge, which usually ranges from $1,000 to $5,000, again depending on the size and scope of the operation. These reps act as a buffer between an end-user company which does not have the manpower to investigate computers, and the computer dealers and distributors who do not have the expertise to set up sophisticated systems. The key word for commission reps is expertise. In addition to being sales oriented, a commission rep must be familiar with the operation of business micros. He or she must be able to tap the sources of computer information for his client, make a responsible purchase decision, and be able to guarantee that the client's system will operate properly. That guarantee may be personal— in other words, the rep himself will take care of minor problems—or it may be via contract with appropriate third-party sources of hardware and software. Typically, commission reps have been sales reps for dealers, distributors, or manufacturers for at least two years, and can operate the name software packages on the market, such as Lotus, dBase III, and WordStar, or an equivalent word processing package. Our research also shows that if you are going to work for a dealer as a sales rep, you should be earning a commission of between 4 and 5 percent of list. Bert Grant adds, "And under no circumstances should you be expected to supply technical support to customers unless you are compensated adequately for the additional work."

Although sales opportunities abound in the still flourishing business microcomputer market, starting out can be dangerous if you make the wrong moves. For example, as Bert Grant says, "The very worst way to begin a microcomputer sales career is by taking a course in programming. It will be a complete, absolute, and total waste of time and you will learn nothing useful." He adds, "You need to get a feel for the hardware and software before you apply for a job. The best kind of job to get at first is in a retail outlet. Find a rep who knows something about computers and ask him questions. The best way to be introduced to computers is by taking a businessman's applications course at a local computer dealership. The courses are sometimes free, and at most cost fifty dollars. In these courses, a specific software package, such as Lotus 1-2-3 or dBase III, is taught at a local computer outlet. The outlet's interest in giving the course is to generate sales and according to graduates of these courses, some of them can be valuable learning experiences. Bert adds that another learning technique that works is to, "Make believe that you are interested in buying a system. Tell the sales rep that you know nothing—he'll be only too happy to explain things to you."

MICROCOMPUTERS		COMPENSATION	COMMISSION	SUPPORT	INTANGIBLE
1	IBM Corp.			5	++
2	Compaq			4	+
3	Televideo Systems Inc.			3	+
4	Altos Computer Systems			3	+
5	Apple Computer Inc.			5	−

Because the rankings are based on hardware and not on working for companies, we couldn't include definitive compensation figures as a number for each brand of computer, since compensation will always depend on whether the rep is selling as an independent or as an employee of a retail store. However, in order to fix a benchmark figure, we can report that the industry median salary for a two-year sales rep working in a retail outlet is $21,800, and the median commission is 4 percent. Also, the support category in this case does not refer to the same issues as in other industries. It refers exclusively to the technical support that a rep can expect when dealing with the hardware manufacturer. A rank of 5 indicates that the hardware manufacturer goes out of its way to support reps and dealers. A rank of 4 means that the hardware manufacturer offers adequate support. A rank of 3 means that the manufacturer supplies the dealers with support materials and expects the dealers to offer support except for unusual technical questions.

IBM [+ +]

If we haven't said enough about IBM yet, let's just add that the name will sell computers for you. One IBM rep says, "When I ask for an order I don't ask 'Yes or no?'—I ask 'How many?' " So strong is the name that any claims about IBM's weakness in engineering do not seem to have affected sales. To whatever extent other manufacturers have been able to find chinks in IBM's armor, it's been in the engineering of the computer. However, with the release of the PC/AT (for "advanced technology"), one industry source comments, "It looks like their engineers finally did something right."

Compaq [+]

Compaq has been the biggest winner to date in the IBM falloff market—and that market is substantial. The Compaq Desk Pro is more than twice as fast as the IBM PC, and the Compaqs seem to be legitimately 100 percent compatible with all IBM software.

Altos and Televideo [+]

The move in the industry today is in multi-user and network systems— that is, systems in which a number of computer users can share data. The industry as a whole—including IBM—has run into a lot of trouble getting these networks and multi-user systems to work properly. As an industry source explains, "They [the micros] were designed as stand-alone machines. You can't make a silk purse out of a sow's ear." Well, as it turns out, you can—but it's not easy. Televideo and Altos have been doing it for years, and they have a very solid market niche and excellent reputation in the multi-user end of the industry.

Apple [−]

According to an industry source, "Apple still has the name recognition, and the MacIntosh will probably get enough of the bugs worked out by the time this is published so that it will live up to its full potential—and potentially, it's a dynamite machine." The [−] is added because Apple is beginning to shift away from heavy emphasis on dealer sales in favor of large volume sales organizations. Recently, they've contracted with GE to sell the MacIntosh through GE's outlets. Also, the cancellation of the LISA/MacIntosh XL system and the reorganization of the company, according to industry publications, means that Apple may not be flying as high as it would like to be at this time. What impact will the removal of Steve Jobs from day-to-day management have on Apple? Only time will tell.

RETAIL

	THE TOP FIVE:
1	Carter Hawley Hale Stores Inc.
2	R. H. Macy & Co., Inc.
3	K mart Corp.
4	F.W. Woolworth Co.
5	Sears Merchandise Group

The retailing industry is largely a front end to a vast logistical force of product distribution which is almost totally unnoticed by the happy shopper. In fact, the mainstay of the retailing industry is not the parttime or seasonal clerk, but the veritable army of buyers, assistant buyers, store, floor and department managers, and display designers that set the stage for the point-of-purchase customer. In any retail operation, whether it is clothing, toys, hardware, or cosmetics, the decision about what products will be offered, what prices customers will pay for them, and what selection they will have is the responsibility of the retail management team, which organizes the retailing operation.

Each industry has its moment of truth, a time when the collective mettle of all its workers is tested. In the retail sales industry that moment is Christmas. The workers at retail stores prepare for and view the Christmas season as a campaign. In many retail chains and department stores, preparations for Christmas begin well before April and continue until the season actually begins. Then, while line managers brace for the onslaught of shoppers, the middle and senior retail managers prepare for the January clearance sales. One retail clerk who has worked the Christmas season exclusively for eleven years says, "I have to do it for some Christmas spending money, but you just wouldn't believe the chaos. I don't know how we all survive."

The way one sales manager explains it, "The Christmas season is to retail store managers what the hunting season is to deer." A store manager of a New York City department store comments, "When I started as a floor salesman sixteen years ago, I really liked people. Sixteen years later I believe that if beings from another planet observed one of our sale days, they would think that the earth is being used by other planets as an institution to incarcerate the functionally insane." A manager for a store dealing in mid- to low-priced items expressed similar sentiments. "Sometimes when I stand at the door as the store is being opened I know how Noah felt watching two of each kind board his ark. Retail sales managers and their assistants must have thick skin and low blood pressure."

The retail sales manager's office is where the buck stops for all the daily and nightly goings-on. And in the retail industry, it is in sales management that one's career actually begins. There are various levels of sales management, depending upon the retail outlet. At the local store level, the central figure is the store manager, while at larger retail operations, the central figure may be the department manager or the manager of a particular retail division. It is at this level that we have focused our research into the best companies to sell for, because below this level employment is fragmented and random among full- and part-time clerks and seasonal employees.

The sales manager's role is critical. Store managers, for example, must deal with an idiosyncratic public that is always right. The night manager of a soft-goods department store which caters to an affluent clientele in a New York City suburb says, "I get at least one potential lawsuit every week. Last week one of our security men saw a woman drop her purse. When she bent down to pick it up, she loosened a seam in the carpet so that the carpet was slightly raised. A few minutes later, she tripped on the carpet and claimed to have a badly twisted ankle. As we helped her to my office, the only thing she wasn't yelling was 'whiplash!' "

Security is a major component of a retail store's operation and, consequently, a major concern of every store or retail manager. As the director of a major New York City department store explains, "The success of your store security can make or break your entire operation. Shoplifting goes right to the store's bottom line." Dealing with shoplifting and customer complaints as well as the actual management of clerks and floor traffic are at the heart of the retail manager's job.

Industry sources estimate that shoplifting is a multibillion-dollar-a-year business and is by far the number-one concern of the retailing industry. It is a crime committed by store employees as well as by customers. Computerization has helped the retail industry deal with both kinds of theft. Department stores typically utilize high-tech cash register systems which track inventory, issue reports on the gross receipts of each cashier on each shift, and flag cashiers who are consistently under a predetermined average. The Caldor chain is well known in the retailing industry for its security operation. One Caldor executive reports, "We evaluate our store managers on one issue: the store's bottom line. He can run a fabulously successful store from a retailing point of view, but if he can't control the shortages he'll

> *. . . shoplifting is a multibillion-dollar-a-year business and is by far the number-one concern of the retailing industry.*

be gone." An executive at a large, well-known department store in New York City says, "We have undercover security people whom no one knows. All they do is watch our own people." At a Neiman-Marcus store in a New York City suburb, a customer wanted to pay for a purchase with an American Express Card. Instead of taking the card, the sales clerk turned on her heels and disappeared. After a few minutes, she came back with a blank American Express sales receipt. When questioned by the customer about the delay, she said, "The American Express sales tickets are in a locked box in the back. They're numbered, and we have to sign for each one we take and have a supervisor counter-sign." The store manager explains this practice: "There are people who take clerking jobs at Christmas just to be able to rip off merchandise. They run duplicate sales slips for unsuspecting customers, forge the signature, and run up huge tabs. By the time the customer gets the bill, the clerk is long gone." The store manager at a Mays department store reports, "A year ago a very well dressed woman came in with two kids and bought $600 worth of coats. She wanted to pay by check.

She had every kind of ID known to man. We even called the telephone company to verify her address. All the paper was 100 percent. But it was a fraud. It turned out she was part of a ring that traveled around the country and set up the scam."

The retail industry as a whole is sending a very strong message to potential entrants. If you are seriously thinking about going into retailing as a career, you'd better be versed in issues of store and merchandise security. As an area sales manager at Bloomingdale's in New York City reports,

> *Buyers will usually use jobbers as a buffer against this allocation situation. Jobbers have the reputation of having been in the business since most of their clients were in diapers, even if the client is sixty years old.*

"When I was interviewed, I thought that they'd made a mistake and thought I was interviewing for a security position. All they wanted to know about was my knowledge of security."

Although industry sources tend to categorize careers in the retail store industry as in the area of either store operations or purchasing, our research has shown that the two tracks do crisscross. It's not uncommon for an area sales manager in operations to become an assistant buyer, then a buyer in the purchasing division, eventually working his way up to store director where he or she will return to operations. One executive for a major department store chain in New York City boasts that he has worked his way up literally from stockboy to vice-president. Today it's almost impossible to pursue the American dream via that route. Floor sales positions earn the minimum wage and, more often than not, are dead-end positions with high turnover rates. Some stores, such as Alexander's, have begun hiring disadvantaged and unemployed workers for sales clerks positions. The government pays half the salary for people hired under this program. Presently, the position of area sales manager is the bottom rung of the ladder in the operations end of retailing. Today's area sales managers have had at least some college courses usually, but not always, in the area of business. In many cases they are college graduates. Entry-level area sales managers earn a maximum of $20,000 and, as one store manager puts it, "Those poor bastards work longer hours than the store director. But that's how you pay your dues in this business." The area sales managers are responsible for an area of the floor—for example, children's clothes or small appliances. They see that their area runs smoothly, and although they do not order merchandise—the buyer does—they are held responsible for shortages. In the retail industry, the common euphemism for stolen merchandise is "shortage."

Most store managers make their living the old-fashioned way—they sweat for it. For example, the manager at a New York store specializing in hard goods likens his job to working in a hospital's emergency room. "Once I was called out of my office for some ruckus in the camera department. Some customer had flipped out and was literally throwing cameras at the salesman. That was bad enough. But this time, my camera man was throwing them back." When another store manager is asked to describe what it is that he actually does, he replies, "Keep the store together until tomorrow." The message is that store managers have to keep their cool. They have to be able to function smoothly under pressure. And there's always pressure.

The expression "putting irons on the fire" has a special meaning to most store managers. The term "iron" refers to a store manager opening and closing his store on the same day. For a store with public business hours of 10 A.M. to 9 P.M., this means that the store manager arrives at 8 A.M. and leaves somewhere between 10 and 11 P.M. Most New York-based department store managers put in two irons per week. For an average annual salary of between $40,000 and $60,000, not including a bonus, store managers truly do earn their keep.

"The times really have changed," says an executive of a large department store in New York. "Ten years ago we had dress codes for our sales help. Today, if they can get to work without being arrested, they're okay. The retail sales industry is a mirror of society. It shouldn't be a surprise to anyone that the public with whom retail stores interact is the same public that's 'out there,' and that as society's mores change, so will our operation."

While the operations people in retailing make sure the physical plant runs smoothly, the purchasing people make sure that the store has something to sell. For the retail store buyers in our country, winter begins June 1 and Christmas is July 4. That's why most shoppers can take for granted that winter coats are usually on the racks well before the approach of winter and that bathing suits will always be there before the thermometer hits eighty. The store's merchandise seasons change because the buyer makes sure that there's product on the rack for shoppers to spend their money on. Buyers are the pulse of the industry, seen as the merchandising experts who decide which items will sell, how many will sell, and how they should be presented in the stores to ensure that they will sell. It is the buyer who decides when an item is to go on sale and for how long, and the buyer who makes decisions about the movement and replacement of inventory. And just as the buck stops with the store manager when it comes to the smooth operation of the store, the buck stops with the buyer when it comes to the smooth flow of merchandise. The buyer even has to concern himself with shoplifted merchandise. A buyer explains, "Who do you think it was who told store management to lock up the leather?" This was a reference to the practice—now the common practice in many New York retail stores—of locking the expensive soft goods to the racks so that shoplifters can't try them on and wear them home under oversized topcoats.

A toy buyer for K mart says, "The secret of buying is to find the right jobber. If you cultivate the right guy, you have a great advantage in the business." Buyers have their behinds on the line in both the buying and the selling of merchandise. As an example, consider the dilemma of a toy buyer for Macy's in New York. "You go to the Toy Fair in February and you see what you think might be this year's Cabbage Patch Doll on display. Coleco is selling 100,000 units. Should you commit to 2,000? 10,000? 50,000? If you buy 2,000 to test-market, and then Coleco sells out their 100,000, they'll sell their new run of dolls on an allocation basis and your allocation will be 2 percent. Then your boss wants to know why you didn't buy 50,000 because they're selling like potato chips at Gimbels and the Gimbels buyer bought 50,000. And now you can't beg, borrow, or steal a lousy extra 1,000. So, the next time you're in the same situation, maybe you buy 50,000 of the next Cabbage Patch Doll. Only now the little kiddies don't agree with you and Coleco has dolls up the kazoo. You've committed upwards of $250,000 of your budget. The warehouse people are screaming at you, and you're lucky if you can unload the stuff at a 50 percent markdown."

The allocation system is the buyer's roulette table. Manufacturing companies use the allocation system as a means of rewarding buyers who have supported their products. If a manufacturer has 100,000 hula hoops to sell, and buyer A commits to 30,000 while buyer B commits to 5,000, the manufacturer uses that purchase commitment as a basis for future allocations in the event that the hula hoop sells so many units that they can't meet demand. In this case, if the manufacturer's next production run of hula hoops is 500,000 units, buyer A would be in for 30 percent or 150,000 units while buyer B would be in for 5 percent or 25,000 units. With this system, buyers are really on the spot to pick the right number.

Jobbers are the buyer's insurance salesmen. Buyers will usually use jobbers as a buffer against this allocation situation. A jobber is an independent sales and distribution representative who knows the industry inside out and understands the manufacturer's role as well as the retailer's role. Jobbers have the reputation of having been in the business since most of their clients were in diapers, even if the client is sixty years old and the jobber is thirty-five. The jobbers maintain close contacts with all of the major manufacturers and often cultivate sources within the manufacturer's organization that even management doesn't have. The top-of-the-line jobbers have regular industry informants who provide them with key inside information, sometimes right from the production line itself.

A buyer for Tandy Company's Radio Shack stores remembers, "Last spring I got word that a major American manufacturer was coming out with a remote-controlled police car with a projected list price of $9.95. It had lights and sirens, could go back and forth and turn. It was going to be one hot Christmas item and the manufacturer had sunk a lot of capital into the project. I was negotiating with them for 100,000 units but two days before the deal was to have been signed I just happened to talk to a jobber friend of mine and he told me to kill the deal. It seems that the manufacturer was having a lot of trouble with the guidance system. They could get the car to do everything except turn off. To fix the problem they had two choices: to use a more sophisticated remote-system and raise the price, or to put the on-off switch on the car itself rather than on the remote-guidance device. That meant that once a kid turned his police car on and started steering it with the remote-control mechanism, he couldn't turn it off unless he picked up the car and turned off the switch. For our industry, this was a very negative feature. My friend turned me onto a company in Hong Kong that had a similar police car with all the same razzle-dazzle but this one ran on a friction mechanism which also ran the siren and flashed the lights. The friction car didn't need batteries—the other one needed four AA and one nine-volt— and I'd be able to list the friction car for $4.95. I bought 100,000 on the spot and it was one of our biggest sellers that season."

When a buyer goes through a jobber he pays 2 to 5 percent above the price he'd have to pay if he bought directly from the manufacturer, but he's getting the benefit of the jobber's experience and expertise. "It's an insurance policy," explains a buyer, "and one that my company is more than willing to let me pay for. A good jobber is like the service station you use for your car. You go to him, he doesn't come to you." A buyer for Alexander's reports, "I used to buy directly from Mattel, Fisher-Price, Milton Bradley and other manufacturers, but it was a pain in the rear. Now I have a few jobbers that I rely on to pick the cream, and now I have cream for my coffee. Sometimes I used to get skim milk." He was referring to the need for buyers to compare competing product lines from the manufacturers in order to cut the best deal. The jobber does this for the buyer. Another buyer says, "When you see ads for a manufacturer's closeout at below wholesale, it's no come-on. The prices are below wholesale. Some store buyer screwed up and a jobber bought the whole lot at a deep discount because the store had to clear out warehouse space for new inventory." In many cases, the merchandise could sell, but not in that particular store. An item may be a hot seller at Macy's but may die at Gimbels. It's up to the buyers to know whether an item will sell in their store or not. And when they're wrong, there's always a jobber circling overhead, ready to pounce.

There is no doubt that buyers are on the spot when they commit funds for a product. They could lose money for their store, and if they make too many mistakes in a row, they're looking for another store. When a jobber commits funds, he puts his reputation, credibility, and future sales on the line. Sometimes he puts his whole business on the line. For example, during the recent Cabbage Patch Doll craze, a buyer might have bought 5,000 dolls, but a jobber had to commit to at least 50,000 dolls or his margins wouldn't work. At those numbers, a jobber can wipe out an entire season because he can't recoup the loss if he can't unload the dolls quickly. In many cases, jobbers are like farmers in that they have to commit large sums of money up front for items that might not pay off until just before buyers pick up the line for a new season. In order to get the best prices and ensure that their margins will hold, jobbers have to move in early before too much interest in the product causes the price to rise. But, as an independent representative points out, if a jobber moves too quickly and demand for the product never materializes, "it's a wipeout."

For the buyer, timing may not be the only thing, but as any buyer will tell you, it's critically important. And timing to a buyer means more than the obvious planning involved in having the bathing suits ready in May and the snowsuits ready in November. A buyer is responsible for merchandise from contract to store delivery. A buyer for F.W. Woolworth recalls, "I cut the deal of my life a few years back. It was the hula hoop and the Pet Rock rolled into one. Mount St. Helen's ashes! In a little glass volcano, too. It couldn't miss. We had the biggest free ad campaign since World War II. We were all set, but my supplier ran into a production problem with the glass volcanos and the shipments were delayed one month. Mount St. Helen had slipped out of the headlines and my boss quashed the deal." Every buying contract that is ready to be signed has a cancel date and an in-store date. The time frame from contract to delivery can be anywhere from ten days to three months, depending on the item. But if the in-store date is September 1, a store may very well turn down the merchandise on September 2.

Buyers can enlist "partners" for speculative items on which, despite the projected payoffs, the downside risk is too great for one person to take on alone. In retail industry jargon, a partner is someone who is going to share the responsibility for a decision. This is an important safety net for a buyer because many times a deal may be so speculative that a buyer with any sanity will usually take a pass on it and play safe. However, the hula hoops, Pet Rocks, and Frisbees of the world—legends among retailers— didn't happen because someone was playing safe. Therefore, a buyer for a store usually has the option of calling in a partner to take the heat along with him if the product is a dud. For a buyer, that partner is usually his boss. A buyer will go to his boss with a speculative, big-ticket purchase and get an okay. Then, if it's a bust, he has a little insurance that he won't be visiting the unemployment office the next day. But as one buyer explains, "Getting your boss for a partner is like time-outs in football. You're only allowed a few a game." Buyers are hired to make critical judgement calls on new products and not to pass the decision up to their bosses. They are, above all, expected to show courage and take whatever heat necessary in order to swing the best deal for their stores. If they spend too much time running to their bosses instead of making their own high-risk decisions, their careers will be shortlived. As one buyer for K mart reports, "My boss has enough to do just making sure the store isn't stolen out from under him. If he has to be my quarterback, he might just as well hire someone who can do the job all by himself."

The entry-level position in purchasing is assistant buyer. An assistant buyer earns between $13,000 and $16,000 annually plus a percentage of

> *. . . a buyer for a store usually has the option of calling in a partner to take the heat along with him if the product is a dud. For a buyer, that partner is usually his boss.*

the buyer's bonus, which will vary depending on the situation and the relationship between the buyer and the assistant buyer. One assistant buyer says, "I went on an interview for a job in another field because I was so fed up at the time. They asked what I did and I couldn't answer because if I told them, I was sure it would sound like B.S. I did everything." And he wasn't exaggerating. The assistant buyer has the responsibility of making sure that everything happens in real life they way it is planned on paper. This means that if the buyer cuts a deal with a jobber in Hong Kong for 250,000 pairs of fireproof children's pajamas, the assistant buyer is responsible for making sure that the merchandise arrives in San Francisco on schedule, is shipped from San Francisco on schedule, arrives in the East Coast warehouse on schedule, arrives in the stores on schedule, and is priced correctly. And he also has to make damn sure that the pajamas are fireproof. As an assistant buyer gains more experience, the buyer usually lets him make increasingly independent purchases. However, when he makes his own purchases, he also has the responsibility of being sure that he's made the right choice. Assistant buyers tell horror stories of colleagues who waited for the opportunity to make their first big buy and, because they were so eager, got hooked on an item that wouldn't move even if it were piled up outside the store under a "Free! Take One" sign. And because assistant buyers often work in the shadow of the buyer, they tend to make decisions that will please the buyer and enhance his reputation. It's more likely in the industry that an assistant buyer will move on to a job as a buyer in a different store, rather than become one where he has been working. However, if another store likes him, they'll usually pay more money to hire him away from his original store.

Buyers are often required to switch product lines to stay on top of their suppliers and maximize their leverage over the industry. However, switching products can cause some real problems. First, a product-line switch usually involves a large change, for example, from hard to soft goods or from men's clothing to women's. Second, a product-line change means that the buyer will have to learn the nuances and seasons of an entirely different industry. Buyers will tell you that they must be as proficient in the industry that they are buying from as they are in their own bailiwick. Because buying is such a high-pressure job where success depends on split-second timing and every ounce of a buyer's experience, you might think that buyers and assistant buyers would be loath to switch product lines. Our research shows that this is not the case and that in fact, many buyers and assistant buyers seek to make product line switches frequently. Their reasoning is twofold: first, it usually means an increase in pay for many of the same reasons that changing store affiliations does—if the other guy wants you enough, he'll pay a little more. Second, some buyers seek to expand their knowledge of different product lines. These are the buyers who usually have their long-term sights set on positions in the higher echelons of store management. But nonetheless, a problem exists. If a buyer switches product lines, how does he compete favorably with buyers who've been in the new line for years? One assistant buyer in children's clothes became a buyer for men's furnishings in another store. "I didn't know anything. I went to school. And in this business 'school' means you latch onto a jobber, because they know everything. Jobbers are great. They want to sell, so they're happy to spend the time with you and teach you the ropes. In a week I knew enough buzzwords to get by, and in a month I was adequate at my job." A buyer who switched from hard goods to soft goods explains, "I comparison shopped. I went around to our competition, looked at the merchandise I liked, and checked the RN numbers on the labels. (These numbers identify the manufacturer.) Once I had the manufacturer,

I'd make a call, visit his showroom, and I'd be in business. Keep in mind that the manufacturers love me because I'm buying, so they are willing to give me all the time it takes for me to learn."

The top buyers can earn $80,000 annually, plus a substantial bonus. Major store buyers who are at the top of their profession and who have made the right choices during the right seasons can gross over $100,000 in good years, and report that they are lured to other stores for whopping bonuses. All stores, especially the major retail chains, realize that buyers are the lifeblood of retailing, and they train their buyers to be the trendsetters of the industry. It is the buyer who decides which of the European manufacturers will get the biggest play in the major New York markets and which styles the stores will push. "The power that fashion buyers wield in New York is enormous," one designer explains. "A smart buyer with her eye on the market and her finger on the public's pulse can set a trend that will bring millions of people into a retail chain." And because people in retail stores buy in more than just one department, key buyers making key decisions can dramatically affect the store's bottom line. Consequently, the best buyers usually move up to higher-echelon management positions and can wind up as group vice-presidents for retail chains within ten years. The buyers are truly the lifeblood of the industry and a good buyer is well worth his (and more often than not, her) weight in gold.

Currently, the retailing industry is undergoing some major realignments. Government and private analysts routinely rely on the retailers' bottom line as an indicator of both consumer spending patterns and public confidence in the growth of the economy. Their reports, based on numbers from the major retail chains, indicate that the retail industry is on an upswing that will continue until the middle of 1986. Because retailing, like residential real estate sales, is an important swing indicator in the national economy, it is highly susceptible to economic trends. In a good season for consumer spending, retail chains report handsome profits; in a poor season, retail chains wind up hurting. However, the person looking toward a career in retailing would be wise to take a look above the bottom line. When explaining their positive industry outlook, industry analysts are pointing to very specific and very divergent reasons for the industry's growth as a whole. Frequently, these reasons fall under the heading of tighter and more creative management. Although this news may bode well for stockholders, it may not necessarily bode well for employees. Alexander's, for example, has instituted a federally sponsored employment program for underprivileged people. While this is likely to reduce Alexander's 25 percent ratio of wages to sales, which is good news for investors, the impact on store operations and purchasing has already been evaluated negatively by a number of Alexander's management and purchasing personnel. Consider also that more than one-third of Alexander's new board of directors consists of real estate people and financial consultants, and that the highly successful Fred the Furrier has moved out of Alexander's. Thus, the rumors of Alexander's exit from retailing grow more plausible every day. So, the message is clear: look at the big picture. Get a feeling for what the store is like and what their priorities seem to be. These are the questions that need to be considered, and our research indicates that the answers are frequently not obvious.

In ranking our top five retailers, we looked at the position of buyer for four major reasons: First, the buyer is the true sales representative in retailing because he or she represents the store and makes decisions that bring the product to the public at the point of purchase. Second, it is the buyer more than anyone else who has a finger on the pulse of the business and can change the rate of that pulse through the types of products that are brought to market. Third, the buyer is central to the smooth flow of a product through the business, and therefore everyone else in the store is affected by the buyer's decisions and judgment. And fourth, the buyer is directly responsible for sales even though he or she is not standing behind the cash register or running the customer's charge card through a machine.

In the retailing industry, marketing and product are the keys to sales, and the buyers and independent jobbers are the true trade representatives. There is no prospecting as there would be, for example, in the medical sales industry; nor is there a presale to a dispenser of the product as there is in the pharmaceuticals industry. Therefore, because the buyer is really the individual who controls the sale in a very real way, it is the buyer who is the focus of our analysis. In ranking our top five retailers, we carefully considered their perception of their place in the market and whether their corporate decisions would register as a plus or a minus for the buyers.

With that in mind, our top spot went to Carter Hawley Hale, owners of the John Wanamaker stores, Bergdorf Goodman, and Neiman-Marcus, among others. This retail holding company is becoming increasingly powerful in the marketplace because its buyers act as trade representatives in setting important trends. Also, having sold profitable Waldenbooks and creating a marketing services division devoted almost exclusively to expanding the development of its private labels, Carter Hawley Hale has clearly defined the market it intends to pursue in retailing: the upscale, fashion-conscious customers, who consider their wardrobes as a means to advance professionally. These are among the most aggressive fashion consumers in the country, and they will become more so as their incomes grow in the middle-to-late 1980s and early 1990s.

Carter Hawley Hale has switched to a 100 percent commission-based compensation for sales personnel, and the company has become a very attractive employer to soft-goods sales personnel. What this means to the buyer is that sales personnel will be more aggressive, more merchandise will flow through the stores, and the buyer will be responsible for a larger dollar volume. In addition, we view C.H.H.'s pioneering of commission-paid salespeople as a truly unique step in an industry which has always employed minimum wage labor and accepted high turnover as a fact of existence. This step is an indication of a strong commitment by C.H.H. to pursue their markets aggressively. An executive at Bergdorf Goodman in New York reports that C.H.H. is planning to build between eight and ten additional stores by the end of 1987. All this, plus the fact that C.H.H.'s sales increased by over one-quarter of a billion dollars between 1983 and 1984, a period of gradual slowdown in the market, leads us to believe that C.H.H. is an excellent opportunity for soft-goods buyers.

Macy's, our number-two retailer, is called the superstore for a good reason. They always seem to do things right, and they enjoy a reputation of employee loyalty among the lower-paid members of the sales force that is not usually found in this industry. A grandmother whose husband's net worth is in the mid-six figure range works in Macy's New York store as a sales clerk. Why? "Because I've worked here for nearly twenty years," she says. "It's like my family." Even though Macy's, like Alexander's, is expanding their real estate interests, it is clearly not at the expense of the retail operation. A Macy's executive points out, "We've just opened a new store in Houston, and we will continue to expand our retail operation." For buyers, bigger is usually always better, and we believe that Macy's commitment to the expansion of their retail operation is a most encouraging sign for the buyers' financial well-being.

Our number-three spot goes to K mart. With an increase in sales of approximately $2 billion from 1983 to 1984, and a similar projected increase for 1985, K mart offers some excellent opportunities for buyers. K mart has also indicated a willingness to go out on a limb when it comes to carrying lines of high-tech items, such as the low-end entries in the home computer market. In addition, the diversified nature of K mart's merchandise offers additional opportunities to buyers for personal expansion into other buying lines.

F.W. Woolworth has earned our number-four spot by pursuing a direction different from most retail chains. Having sold the Woolco discount store operation and having purchased the Athletic Shoe Factory stores, Woolworth is now committed to becoming a specialty retailer. We think that their commitment to expansion and their exit from the low budget and discount retail market is a strongly positive sign for buyers. Their commitment to sprucing up their operations is evidenced by the remodeling project under way in many of the Woolworth variety stores. As with K mart, Woolworth's diversified product lines offer their buyers the opportunity to expand their product horizons, a valuable feature for buyers hoping to move toward senior management positions.

It was impossible to ignore Sears, Roebuck and Company, the world's largest retailer, but for a variety of reasons, Sears almost didn't make the list. Sales between 1983 and 1984 increased nearly $4 billion, usually a very nice sign for store buyers. However, Sears has expressed a desire to become all things to all people and this makes us question how corporate directions will impact on their buyers. Its acquisitions of Coldwell Banker and Dean Witter, and its Allstate insurance subsidiary, suggest to us that while Sears will never abandon its retail operation, they may be taking it too much for granted and turning too much of their corporate attention elsewhere. This is not the best sign for their buyers. Nevertheless, Sears is the world's largest general merchandise retailer and all indications are that they will continue to hold that position for some time to come. So although we think that there might be reasons for buyers to keep taking a hard look at changes in corporate directions, we include Sears in our top five for many of the same reasons we've included K mart and Macy's.

The median compensation for a buyer who's held that position for two years is $26,900. We did not attempt to separate any bonus from the compensation package because the compensation packages vary widely.

RETAIL		COMPENSATION	COMMISSION	SUPPORT	INTANGIBLE
1	Carter Hawley Hale Stores Inc.	4		4	+
2	R. H. Macy & Co., Inc.	4		4	
3	K mart Corp.	4		4	
4	F.W. Woolworth Co.	3		4	
5	Sears Merchandise Group	3		4	

Carter Hawley Hale [+]
Their pioneering change to an all-commission system of compensation for their sales force is a real plus for buyers because it will certainly result in increased sales.

SECTION THREE:
LIGHT INDUSTRY

MAINFRAME
COMPUTERS

MEDICAL
EQUIPMENT

OFFICE
FURNITURE

PHARMA-
CEUTICALS

MAINFRAME COMPUTERS

THE TOP FIVE:

1 IBM Corp.
2 Digital Equipment Corp.
3 Wang Laboratories Inc.
4 AT&T Co.
5 Control Data Corp.
5 Apollo Computer Inc.

U ntil recently, the mainframe and microcomputer industries were rigidly defined by the types of hardware and software delivered to the end user. Mainframes and business microcomputers were originally much larger than desktop micros and required a much higher level of manufacturer and programmer support. In addition, the type of sales representation often differs in the two markets. Over the past two years, however, this distinction has begun to blur. Both the IBM AT and the AT&T 3B2 perform more like business minicomputers than desktop micros, and the advent of network software and micro-to-mainframe connections will make 1983's market distinctions disappear by 1987.

There was once a Greek mathematician who said, "The only constant in this world is change." What was true for the ancient Greeks is true today, especially when it comes to the mainframe computer, minicomputer, small business computer, and office machine industry. According to a contemporary industry source, "Selling computers can be a very glamorous occupation, but it is fraught with the perils of change." And, change is a continuing process in the mainframe, minicomputer, and "super-micro" networked computer market. (The personal computer and business microcomputer market is covered in a separate chapter.) The differences between mainframes, minis, "super micros," and personal computers might be considered minor by people not involved in the industry, but they are major to the companies that design and manufacture them. The differences between types of computers are described more fully in the business microcomputer chapter, which contains a discussion of some basic computer concepts.

Bill Robinson, a sales rep for Control Data Corporation, a computer manufacturer and our number-five ranked company, comments on working for CDC. "For one thing, I was surprised that they even hired me. I had no computer experience whatever, other than having used a word processor when I was in college. A good friend of mine who used CDC's timesharing services told me that I'd be a natural for the sales force, so I gave it a shot." Janet Raab, an executive at Control Data's headquarters in Minneapolis, says, "Some of our old time reps came up through engineering, but we've found that our best salespeople have come from outside Control Data."

Sales managers and sales representatives for all five of our top-ranked mainframe manufacturers comment that this was one type of sales force where computer jocks need not apply. "Selling mainframes is a serious business at Control Data," Bill Robinson explains. "We train hard for what we do and get to know our product and how it relates to our customers' needs. When I go in to see a potential account, I'm prepared to learn as much about his or her business as anybody who works there. When I walk out of that office, I have to know what the potential customer's problems are, how Control Data can solve them, and how my business plan will show that client how to pay for what Control Data can sell him. Most computer jocks I know just want to talk about how slick a piece of hardware is. That's not what we do at CDC." As is the case in the business microcomputer industry, the "techies," the people who can program and who simply enjoy using the computer, are not effective salespeople because they can't get beyond the thrill of keyboard work. Janet says, "One of the strangest situations we had involved one of our software engineers who went into sales. Thom's sales figures were slightly below the average for our reps in his division, and frankly, since he was an 'old-timer,' no one really bothered him. But when we did our cost analyses of all the reps' accounts, we found that the cost on his accounts was significantly lower than the next-lowest figure. It turns out that he was servicing his accounts' technical problems."

This presented a problem to management because at Control Data, as well as at all the major computer manufacturers and business systems manufacturers, there are staff support people who exist solely to handle technical problems. Sales representatives are neither equipped nor expected to perform that function. Janet adds, "Thom's district sales manager was new and he didn't know that Thom had been an engineer, so he never thought to speak to him about the service issue. None of the other reps in Thom's group were from a computer or an engineering background, and none of them had any idea that Thom was spending sales time servicing an ongoing account."

"The bottom line," Bill explains, "is that salesmen are expected to sell. That's all we do, because if we don't, the products don't get sold. It's as simple as that, and it's what we learn in training." Bill continues. "Once I got into the training class it was pretty obvious what CDC's approach was. Every man and woman there was a sales rep hired away from somewhere else—usually not from the computer industry either." Bill had been a sales representative for a large tool and die company. "They made it clear what our role was—and it was selling. They focused a lot of attention on computer anxiety, ours and our customers'. By the time the class was over, no one felt inadequate because of a lack of computer knowledge."

Control Data is an engineering-driven company, and because of this, Bill made a choice of fields that surprised even him. "I did my homework about CDC, and I knew that no matter what kind of competition developed in the business market, the engineering market would be safe. If there was one thing that CDC had a reputation for, it was the engineering side of the business. I also knew that the engineering backup support would be superior. So I chose CAD/CAM systems." CAD/CAM stands for "Computer Assisted Design/Computer Assisted Management. It is a very specialized, very high-tech, and rapidly growing application area for computers. CAD/CAM systems can be tremendous cost cutters for businesses because the computer system can be used to simulate expensive tests.

Bill comments, "The flight simulator that the airlines use for training and for modeling in-flight 'events' is a good example of computer simulation. But there are a heck of a lot of other uses in industry that may be less dramatic, but just as economically valuable." Bill continues, "Do you know that we have a system that can simulate a dental patient? You know that most people hate going to the dentist, right? Well, how do you think people feel about going to a dental student? Students at NYU's School of Dentistry are now practicing on a 'flesh-and-blood' robot which is computer controlled to register 'pain.' It is also programmed to judge students on how well they've drilled, filled, anesthetized, and cleaned their patient's teeth. And now we're working on a simulated medical patient."

From talking to Bill, two things are clear: he is enthusiastic about his field and he is enthusiastic about Control Data. Even though he isn't knowledgeable about the "how to" of the computer operation, he is knowledgeable about the "what for" of the operation. In other words, Bill Robinson, just like any good sales representative, is an expert when it comes to explaining to his customers the features, functions, and benefits of his company's products.

Ralph Hendricks is a representative for number-one ranked IBM, the giant of the computer sales industry and the company whose representatives invented the "office automation" concept. Ralph says, "The thing I like about selling for IBM is that when I talk to a customer, he knows when it comes to support and service he's going to be treated like a king." Ralph explains that part of IBM's reputation in the mainframe and mini office computer systems market is based on the company's support of its products and customers as much as on the actual products they sell. "IBM will stay with you all the way. My accounts are sold on IBM long before I even walk into the picture."

Selling in the office minicomputer market is like coordinating a team of experts, all working on a single account at the same time. Carla Pateryn, a representative for number-two ranked Digital Equipment Corporation, agrees: "I'm as much of a group coordinator as I am a sales rep for DEC's products. After I qualify a customer, I'll meet with our support people and in many instances we'll even use outside consultants for some of our projects. The important thing is to focus our resources just like a laser beam at the point of sale, so that our customer understands exactly what we're selling and what it will do for his or her business." Bill Robinson from Control Data also brings in outside consultants when he needs to solve a customer's problem. "Some of our applications in CAD/CAM are so technically complex and highly specialized," he explains, "that not even our engineers can handle them. In those cases, we'll bring in third-party, problem-specific, consulting firms." Control Data's Janet Raab adds, "In many instances, our reputation in the highly technical areas is based as much on how well we can put together the outside consulting package as it is on the part of the package that is 'pure CDC.' Customers are interested in the final product."

"The training is extensive at CDC," Bill says, "and intensive as well. I spent five weeks at CDC's headquarters in Minneapolis. Most of the time was spent on sharpening up my selling skills, but a lot of time was also spent on looking at industry applications." Janet comments: "What we really look for in our new hires are people who understand the industries we market to. It's invaluable for us when a rep comes in knowing who the decision makers are and how to get to them. Of course it helps to have contacts in the industry too. Janet adds, "Those are the types of reps we start at the highest base salary." Bill says, "After the first five-week stint in training, they had us cold-calling from a slightly qualified customer list. We did that for a month, then it was back to Minneapolis for two weeks of sorting out and analyzing our experiences."

There are still some chinks in Control Data's armor, according to representatives who have worked at companies other than CDC. Joseph Charles, a CDC sales manager who had worked for IBM, says, "When I got to CDC I was flabbergasted at the lack of contact our reps had with the customers. At IBM, we were always reporting to management on customer

Selling in the office minicomputer market is like coordinating a team of experts, all working on a single account at the same time.

satisfaction. I started to employ some of IBM's procedures with my people, but without it being a company-wide policy, my efforts just died." Janet explains that, "CDC is an engineering-driven company. IBM is a customer-driven company." In other words, according to former representatives and other former employees, Control Data is a company that develops product to accomplish certain tasks or to do things better than other products on the market. IBM develops product it knows it can sell to a specific sector of the market.

IBM, for example, was not the first company to sell computers to small- and medium-sized businesses. It waited until other companies had established a market using word processors and small business computers and then jumped into an already heated pool. Much the same can be said for the way IBM entered the personal computer market. IBM sells to customers; Control Data sells its products. Both companies have achieved success, and the sales representatives of both companies have prospered. Yet each company approaches sales from a different perspective. An industry source reports: "Each company has its own personality. It's no easier to change a company's personality than it is to change your own. You may change traits, habits, or the way you do certain things, but a personality is a much more complex interaction. With companies it's no different. If it was just a matter of modeling a company after the most successful companies, everybody in the industry would be IBM."

Wang Laboratories, our number-three ranked company, was founded by an engineer named An Wang. It started as a small company, but soon, on the strength of its word processing technology, it became a leader in the office computer field. Wang is known for its ability to "train and retain" its salespeople so that it maintains a high level of corporate loyalty and dedication to corporate goals. "At Wang, once they have you, they keep you," says Karen Cummings, a commission rep who frequently banged heads with Wang people. "Wang was the first of the big companies that were committed to the automated office concept. They believe that satisfied customers will buy, buy, buy. And based on their performance, they're right."

George Solis, a Wang sales rep, says, "They teach us to anticipate a customer's growth. I sold a customer a system in 1980, and at the time I knew he'd be upgrading and adding some features eventually. At the time of the sale the company was in a cash-poor position, so they decided to go with a minimum configuration." We asked George why he didn't try to sell the company on an open-ended lease agreement that would allow the customer to roll over his agreement at a discount and upgrade to a more extensive hardware system. George explains, "We had a lease all worked out. Wang reps always go in with a variety of financing arrangements, but it was a private company owned by a father and his son. The father was very conservative and the son wouldn't buck him. So they wouldn't go the leasing route." But George didn't quit. "I'd drop by whenever I could to see how things were going. On average, I'd see them once every five weeks." George had become pretty good at understanding his clients. "Sales training at Wang also includes a little bit of human dynamics, and I'd been at it long enough to be able to read between the lines. I was pretty sure the son was on my side about the extent of the operation and the upgrade, and I knew the father was going to be retiring." Asked how long he usually keeps courting a customer like that, George replies, "Well, this was an unusual case. For one thing, the company was located on my route home, so it wasn't out of the way to drop in. For another I really felt strongly that I was going to make a big sale. It was obvious that the company was growing even with the father's tight reins."

And George's perseverance finally paid off. "Now, you have to remember, I'd been dropping in on this company maybe ten times a year for four years and I never once discussed business directly with the son. I'll never forget this scene. It was exactly four years and one month from the day I'd made the original sale. The son called me into his office and very casually said, 'George, we're making a few changes around here. Dad is retiring and I'm going to be running things. We need to expand our operation and I'd like you to see that it gets done right.' " This is always music to a salesman's ears, but even George had no idea what was involved. "I figured he meant they were going to buy another system and modernize the old one a little. It would have meant maybe 800 or 900 bucks to me. The funny thing was the son couldn't talk at length because he had a very important conference call scheduled so he asked me to come back in a couple of days." George was in for quite a shock. "When I came back, the son was like a different person. He looked younger and more mature at the same time. I'll never forget his exact words, 'George, you're looking at the new president of Apex International. We've gone public.' They'd bought out one of their competitors and were expanding their operation overseas, and they wanted the whole operation computerized. The son actually told me, 'George, you were a big part of the deal. I told all the principals that the computer system would be 110 percent because I knew just the man who would take care of everything.' By the way, the sale was worth over $40,000 to me personally." George sums up the whole episode by saying that the message from Wang is repeat business. Take care of your customers and they will take care of you.

Most office system sales representatives agree that the slogan "Necessity is the mother of invention" is practiced religiously by a number of computer companies who sell to the business and professional market. As one industry source says, "Who better knows what is needed in an industry than the businesses in that industry?" Wang and Digital Equipment Corporation are particularly noted for developing applications software hand-in-hand with customers. A DEC spokesperson says, "We've been criticized for our practice of relying on the customer to supply the impetus for system development, but can you think of a more logical way to identify customer and industry needs?" And a Wang spokesman says, "We expect our R&D rate to be high because the customers are telling us, in effect, 'If your system can do X, we'll buy it.' Why should we be surprised then when our new products are a big success?"

Digital Equipment's practice of using its customer base to generate new products is an important source of support for its sales representatives. "At DEC we're trained as systems analysts," says Peter Weiss, a DEC sales representative whose relationships with his accounts exemplify the two-way-street approach used by Digital Equipment to develop its product line. "Since the system will be run by people, we interview all the people who will be involved in dealing with the system from the person in charge of the company down to the person inputting the data. One of the most common and most costly mistakes made in R&D is neglecting to speak with the people who will be responsible for operating the system on a daily basis." Janet adds, "DEC has long been scorned by the industry purists for its lack of engineering-oriented R&D. But soon those purists may be at DEC looking for work. And remember," she continues, "DEC is following in a time-honored tradition; IBM's sales reps are known throughout the industry as being aggressive problem solvers."

"If it's good enough for DEC, it's good enough for us," seems to be a business philosophy followed by many consulting firms that use DEC's minicomputers, such as the VAX 11/785 in a wide variety of applications ranging from engineering to business. Tony Pussil is a consultant for such a firm and he helped to develop the accounting system used by the main branch of the New York City library. Tony says, "We've really hooked our star to DEC's equipment. It's ideal for the language." He refers to a highly sophisticated computer language known in industry circles as a "fourth generation language" because it resembles the natural language that people speak. As Tony explains, "By using the language, we can set up the system to respond to natural English commands. For example, our clients can type in requests such as 'Report all customers who fall into demographic profile A and who owe us more than $50 for more than thirty days. Also list the probability that they will pay the bill in full within thirty days if they receive dunning letter C.' " He continues, "The DEC sales reps were instrumental in working with us and creating the language. We had designed the concept and were looking for a machine that would be able to handle it efficiently.

> *"Wang is known for its ability to 'train and retrain' its salespeople so that it maintains a high level of corporate loyalty and dedication to corporate goals. 'At Wang, once they have you, they keep you.' "*

Our search was highly technical and most sales reps couldn't help us. The DEC people knew the equipment."

"We're dying to see the new VAX 8600," Tony says, referring to DEC's new entry in the supermini market, also called Venus. "We already have a backlog of orders. But," he adds, "because we have recommended DEC installations for many of our older contracts, we're grateful that DEC doesn't abandon its earlier computers as many smaller companies do." An all too common practice among less well-established companies in the office systems industry is to abandon older machines in order to sell newer ones. This leaves customers, who trusted the sales representative's advice, without the company support when the computer needs service or when a new product is made available. "The great thing about DEC is that they don't discard customers who purchased their old machines, says Tony. "We know that we'll be able to get support for our PDP-11s five years from now."

Wang's George Solis also attests to the importance of the manufacturer's reputation for support. "I know that when I made that big sale to Apex International, it was the son's belief and trust in me that got it, but you'd better believe that the other principals were happy to hear it was a Wang system that was going to be in place. I could get hit by a truck tomorrow, but their installation would be protected for life."

The rates of compensation for sales representatives in the mainframe and minicomputer industry are as diverse as the products in the industry itself. As Bill Robinson of Control Data explains, "Even the engineers can't figure out the commission schedule. Rumor has it that they have a complicated commission structure so they can pay us whatever they want to." Janet Raab comments: "Our commission schedule is flexible, but everyone knows what it is ahead of time. The schedule has to be malleable in order to keep up with a rapidly changing industry." Bill adds, "When Plato, CDC's highly sophisticated programmed learning system, went into the industrial training markets, the company was offering commission bonuses for systems we sold, so I guess the commission rates really depend a lot on what they want to sell."

As in most industries, when companies introduce a new product or make a current product available in new markets, they offer incentives to the sales representatives to make sales more valuable to them. The added incentives translate into more customer contact hours spent pushing the new product, and consequently more sales. However, even with different compensation schedules for different products, sales representatives at Control Data report that the company's quota system is unique in the industry. Janet explains, "Each district manager has a quota for the five or six reps who report to him. He sets the quotas for the individual reps." Paul Wozniak, a district manager, adds, "We usually negotiate in a friendly way with our reps. We want the reps to be content but we don't want them to get complacent." Control Data's commission structure is indeed complex, but as Bill explains it, "Two percent is a good ballpark figure for most reps." In other words, Control Data's representatives earn 2 percent on gross sales with the commission applied from the first dollar sold.

The general rule of thumb in the mainframe and minicomputer industry, as in any industry, is that commission rates tend to be lower in well-established companies and higher in start-up or newer companies. Sam Rodriguez, a sales manager for Apollo Computer, a relative newcomer in the industry, says, "Basically, we know that we're competing with the IBMs, the DECs, and the rest of the big boys for talent, so we pay better. We have a simplified commission structure which escalates up to 3 percent on gross sales over $750,000. We also offer target bonuses and stock options." Our research reveals that Apollo's target bonuses can be as high as $5,000 for bringing in a company account. An industry source says, "Apollo is going after the automated office. They are *the* up-and-coming company in work-stations, and their superminis and exceptionally high resolution graphic screens make their product a very strong competitor in the engineering, scientific, and architectural markets." The same source adds, "Apollo's sales are expected to top $250 million in '85, a half-billion in '86, and by '87 they could easily be a billion-dollar company. They know how to go after market segments, and they're willing to pay for talent."

DEC considers its sales force to be sales engineers, and they pay their people accordingly with top of the line salaries and target bonuses. Com-menting on what it takes to woo people away from other companies, Apollo's Sam Rodriguez says, "We typically aren't interested in DEC's sales force. For one thing, they're pretty content, and for another, they're en-gineers. At DEC they're expected to be problem solvers and to get their hands dirty. We don't want our sales force to approach the customer that way. We have an excellent support staff to take care of the customer's technical needs."

At Hewlett-Packard, the philosophy is similar to that at DEC, where the representatives are technically oriented. In addition, the salespeople at Hewlett-Packard are expected to supply customers with the full range of HP products, which includes microcomputers, testing equipment, and sophis-ticated plotters and laser printers. At other companies such as IBM, the rep-resentatives are expected to place the full strength of the entire product line at the customer's disposal. One IBM rep reports, "I called on an engineering company which had expressed an interest in a 308X mainframe system. After several meetings it became increasingly obvious that they didn't need that kind of computing power. At my next meeting with them I brought along some people to demonstrate the PC/AT, our new desktop 'super-micro' designed for business users. They loved it, and they loved me because I saved them a bundle." An industry source says, "IBM is famous or notorious in the industry, depending on whether you're a customer or a competitor, for selling only what the customer needs and not a nickel more."

At CDC the corporate philosophy is different. Janet says, "We're a highly segmented company, and frankly, our segments don't do a lot of talking to each other." Bill Robinson adds, "I was with the company for over a year before I knew we had retail outlets." The CDC retail outlets sell Control Data equipment as well as other business-oriented systems, including Zenith computers. Zenith Data Systems has disappointed its network of independent dealers by setting up competition from a number of sources, including Heathkit Stores, a Zenith subsidiary. Bill comments on the Zenith story: "A friend of mine was a Zenith dealer, and he offered me a Zenith Z-100 at his cost, 35 percent off list price. I told him that I could get the same computer at 50 percent off list through Control Data. The next morning, he called the Zenith Eastern Region office in Philadelphia and told them to do something with the machine which is anatomically impossible, and then he dropped the Zenith line. The irony is that the Z-100 is such an excellent machine that many CDC reps buy it instead of our own micro." And Bill adds, "The point is that we have this great resource in retail outlets and nobody has ever heard of them. I know damn well that I could have sold a shipload of micros to some of my accounts. Everybody in business is using stand-alone desktops no matter what kind of other super-sophisticated systems they have." As one industry source says, "Control Data is a good example of what happens to a decentralized company that keeps growing. After a while it winds up competing against itself."

Selling computer systems out in the field is an experience unlike selling in many other industries because sales representatives find themselves drawn into a business's deepest and most confidential problems. A good sales representative has to become so familiar with the particulars of a potential account's business that he or she often winds up being a consultant without realizing it and without ever intending to be so. Also, the nature of the product is so technical and so sophisticated that representatives find themselves in situations where potential customers know more about their products' specifications than they do. Control Data's Paul Wozniak explains: "Selling CAD/CAM systems isn't like selling potato chips or Coca-Cola. You don't take out million-dollar ads during the Super Bowl." Advertising is done primarily in trade journals and at trade shows. And who is the

> "We've been criticized for our practice of relying on the customer to supply the impetus for system development, but can you think of a more logical way to identify customer and industry needs?"

main competition in CAD/CAM systems? Who else but Big Blue. "The first trade show I went to was the Autofact show. We had a good-sized booth—it was impressive and we had a nice display of our systems. I was surprised that I didn't see IBM on the floor, because it was a pretty big show. When I asked someone about IBM's absence, they just pointed in the direction of another room. IBM had a two-story setup with a winding staircase, free refreshments, and one hell of a display."

Sales representatives in this industry get their new account leads from a variety of traditional and nontraditional sources. An average of 45 percent of the qualified leads come from industry contacts. Janet says, "That's really the main difference between hiring someone as a sales rep or as a senior sales rep. A senior sales rep comes in with an industry network of contacts in place that he can draw on to generate an immediate schedule of new accounts." George Solis of Wang adds, "We've had a lot of success selling to engineers because they tend to move around more frequently than any other segment of the industry." As George discovered, this can produce some lucrative results for salespeople. "I had just sold a system to a company where the real decision maker turned out to be the senior engineer. He maintained a low profile, but you can always tell where the power is. When you ask a question of the group, the guy who everybody looks at is the decision maker. Anyway, no sooner was the system in place than this senior engineer up and left the company for a competitor. I dropped in on him at his new employer and a week later closed on an almost identical system with the new company."

According to Paul Wozniak, selling to engineering or architectural firms which normally deal with contractors often involves going through a bidding process. Paul explains that the results of the bidding process are more than likely to be as subjective as if one person had chosen his personal preference, but at least there is a nod in the direction of a competitive benchmark test. "Many engineering companies try to maintain an appearance of objectivity in choosing their systems, and they use something like a bidding system. After a rep has the potential account seriously interested in the system, they give out a benchmark test to maybe five companies. Then a whole crew of engineers, MIS people, and management come to view the test. The engineering company will take furious notes and present a very scientific demeanor. But sometimes they still go with the heart, and that kills me."

Paul explains that it's most frustrating when a representative does everything humanly possible to sell an account, and in the end, loses out to IBM simply because they're IBM. "Sometimes I feel like the 'I' in IBM stands for Infernal. We lost a $5-million account to IBM after beating them every way possible in performance tests. My man had wooed this account for over eight months. He'd called in our senior engineers. We had flown all over the country giving demos showing these guys what we could do. And, needless to say, we were up against you-know-who. I know for a fact that we outperformed their system significantly. One of the customer's engineers even told my man, 'As far as I'm concerned, it's all yours.' Then the next thing we knew, we got a very polite, very complimentary phone call, informing us that: (a) our system is great, and (b) they went with IBM." An industry source says, "It's no secret to anybody in the industry that IBM is not a technology leader. But for some reason, people in the industry, specifically IBM's competitors, aren't able or willing to understand that IBM is a marketing leader. There are so many factors that go into a sale and many of them are simply political butt protection. Let's say an MIS manager gives the okay on a $5 million system and by some quirk it doesn't work and causes the company incredible problems. If the system is IBM's, the MIS manager can turn to senior management and say, 'Hey, it's IBM. How was I to know it wouldn't work?' But if it's not an IBM system, you'd better believe he's going to have to explain to senior management why it isn't an IBM system. The bottom line is that you can't get fired for buying an IBM, and until the competition can understand and meet that challenge, they're going to keep losing sales to IBM."

Paul adds, "Unfortunately, it's one of the ironies of the business that the engineers—those who know the system best and who have to work with it—usually have the least say in most companies. The MIS guys who cut their teeth on business systems, not on the technical stuff, love IBM and they're the ones with the say-so on the purchase."

While most of the sales representatives in the mainframe and minicomputer business systems industry agree that personal sources and internal company contacts are the best producers of qualified leads, industry analysts point out that trade shows are the second best producer of potential sales, cold calls come in third, and magazine bingo cards are the worst producer. An industry source says, "I don't even know why anybody bothers with bingo cards. They're usually filled out by tired, bored executives who have nothing else to do on a plane. My wife fills them out, however, and you'd be surprised what turns up both in the mail and on the phone."

The current debate among business system manufacturers, and consequently, among their representatives, is the distinction between communication and computing. The people at Wang have been sending the message that computing isn't enough; office automation is the wave of the future, and at the current rate of industry development, it is the biggest thing in the present as well. Office automation will include a multitude of functions, all centered around the concept of communication. As a result, the biggest head-to-head competition on the horizon is not between IBM and Wang or IBM and DEC. It will be between "IBM and the phone company," according to a reporter for a computer magazine. As an industry source says, "If you did a word association game with the American public, when you said, 'Computer,' the overwhelming response would be 'IBM.' And when you said, 'Communications,' the overwhelming response would be 'AT&T.' "

Therefore, nobody was surprised when AT&T, our number-four ranked company, burst onto the market, fresh from its divestiture, with this statement from Chairman Charles Marshall: "We're here today to take another step forward in fulfilling our commitment to provide integrated communications-based office automation systems for American business." Frank Vigilante, AT&T's division president, added: "The products we are announcing today are part of a logical evolution from our own communications-based Information Systems Architecture."

IBM, of course, is AT&T's main competition. AT&T, the folks who established the standard in telephone communications, knew that they'd have to pay technical homage to the folks who established the standard in microcomputer architecture, and so the AT&T PC is IBM plug-in compatible. Interestingly, in their press release announcing the new computers, AT&T told the public that their computer is IBM compatible without ever mentioning IBM: "It runs the same operating system and business software as other leading personal computers, and it accepts the same plug-in accessory circuit boards. It offers greater speed, more features, and a higher level of standard features than its leading competition." Their last claim was almost humorous: "It has been certified 'operationally compatible' by Future Computing of Richardson, Texas." AT&T has been in the forefront of computer technology for a very long time. However, most of the major developments at AT&T were so targeted to its proprietary automated switching systems that they never had a chance to get out of the laboratories and into the open market. As a former AT&T manager puts it, "They've been in the computer business for at least as long as IBM, but only IBM could go out and sell computers, and AT&T could only sell phones."

The techniques that AT&T developed in the telephone market were immediately transferred to the computer marketplace. After all, for many years AT&T was forced to watch from the sidelines not only as IBM, CDC, DEC, and other mainframe manufacturers dominated the business computer market and over a dozen start-up companies took the plunge and came up with seabags full of cash. Then, after the breakup of Ma Bell and after an ample opportunity to study the market, AT&T decided to take a mass market approach to personal computer sales, and a direct head-to-head sales approach to the lucrative large corporate accounts. AT&T has been very successful by using the best available sales and marketing approaches from all possible development and computer environments.

AT&T has developed one of the most extensive and well-trained sales networks among all of the service and product-oriented companies. AT&T's representatives are among the best trained and most highly motivated representatives in the world, and they believe that the products they sell are the finest. To support their entry into the business computer market, AT&T relied on several factors: the extensive data processing, communications, and programming experience of Bell Labs; a mass market approach that has proven so successful for many microcomputer manufacturers; and a service- and customer-intensive approach which is also a hallmark of IBM. In addition, AT&T was able to integrate its sales network into its penetration strategy and restructure the entire minicomputer and business systems market merely by announcing its new machines.

Each company, with the exception of IBM, has established itself in an extremely strong position within a specific market niche. Following the Henderson theory of market coexistence, each company's niche is sufficiently established to make the company an industry leader for its sales representatives. IBM is an exception to this rule in the most positive sense— instead of occupying a specific market niche, they are simply omnipresent. The IBM representative is expected to be a customer-oriented problem solver. Nine-to-fivers need not apply. IBM is a sales- and marketing-driven company that can flood a zone with sales and technical support personnel faster than its competition. Accordingly, salespeople at IBM are treated as extremely valuable human resources and are held in great esteem by the corporation. At IBM, sales is the route to advancement up the corporate ladder.

Digital Equipment Corporation used to be called the IBM of the mini-computers in the days when there was a clear-cut distinction between minis and mainframes, and IBM was associated almost exclusively with the mainframe market. But even then it wasn't true; IBM was and is IBM, and DEC was and is DEC. The two are very different companies with two very different, albeit successful, marketing and sales philosophies. DEC's marketing philosophy dictates the kind of sales representative for whom DEC is

> *"The great thing about DEC is that they don't discard customers who purchased their old machines."*

clearly the place to be. The DEC representative is a multifaceted professional. He or she must be equally capable of talking to company presidents and to engineers and software developers. DEC representatives have technical knowledge and a sales background, and in addition, they are considered an important part of the technical support staff.

Wang, like IBM, has firmly established itself in the office automation market. Wang's sales force is remarkably similar to IBM's stylistically, with one exception which is best illustrated by the following story. In 1982, Marie Brennan planned to start a word processing business. She'd worked in the office automation industry for many years and had many contacts who promised to supply her with business. Accordingly, she believed that her business had a bright future. She intended to start with two business computers and word processing software, so she set out to investigate the market. She saw demonstrations from all the major manufacturers except Wang. Marie says, "I made at least four attempts to set up an appointment. Finally I was told, 'You're too small, no one's going to waste their time with you.' " She bought two IBM PCs and started her business. She now reports, "As of now, we have eight IBM XTs, and we're looking to trade them in for IBM's new PC/ATs and go with a Local Area Network to share data among the different terminals." George Solis explains Wang's basic approach to the user marketplace, "I can see that happening. No one at Wang was willing to spend the time on a small sale. But you have to realize that we're not set up the way IBM is. There's pressure here, and they make it very clear that time is money, so we go after larger corporate accounts."

So far, AT&T is doing everything right. They're almost mimicking IBM, but on a smaller scale. They've gone after the broad, horizontal, automated office market with their mini systems; they're going after the small business market with their PC distribution through Sears, MicroAge, and other retail outlets, and they're also going through a large direct sales campaign for complete penetration of an even smaller user market. And of course, they're tying everything together with their ISN, an Information Systems Network utilizing the latest fiber optics technology, all of which has been developed at AT&T for use in their telephone switching systems. AT&T's reps must be something like DEC's; that is, they must be technically oriented. But unlike DEC, the AT&T reps have the advantage of massive support from both AT&T staff and AT&T's state of the art communications technology.

Fifth on our list of best companies to sell for is Apollo Computer, which, like DEC, employs a sales force that is technically oriented. Apollo has developed a very impressive supermini-based workstation and has made great inroads in that market. Because Apollo's name is new and they haven't been in business as long as the powerful competition, the company is offering big rewards to hire away the sales professionals in the industry.

Frankly, placing Control Data among the top five was a difficult decision, and we wish to qualify our decision. The qualification is that we are placing CDC's engineering-oriented divisions, such as CAD/CAM, in a tie for the number-five slot. We are not, however, placing CDC as a company in that slot. Our reasoning is based on one fact and one rumor. The fact is that CDC is an engineering-driven company, with a broad base of support in many facets of the engineering industry. In addition, CDC's engineering representatives have considerable resources available to them in terms of outside consulting services. This ability to put together packages, which may or may not include outside support services, is a big plus for many of the specialized high-tech applications with which CDC representatives come into contact. CDC representatives are expected to be technical because they are required to pull together the talent needed to get the job done, whether that talent is internal or outside the company.

The rumor to which we referred is that corporate CDC will be undergoing a major managerial change and that the company will be taking steps toward corporate integration. Assuming this to be true (our source was highly placed within corporate CDC), in the long run it will be a big benefit to all of the CDC sales force. The resources which are available to CDC are enormous and for a sales representative, the ability to tap those resources would be valuable sales leverage indeed.

MAINFRAME COMPUTERS	COMPENSATION	COMMISSION	SUPPORT	INTANGIBLE
1 IBM Corp.	5		5	++
2 Digital Equipment Corp.	5		5	++
3 Wang Laboratories Inc.	5		5	++
4 AT&T Co.	5		5	++
5 Control Data Corp.	5		5	+
5 Apollo Computer Inc.	5		4	+

The industry's median compensation for a sales rep with two years' experience is $30,850, but the way this compensation is calculated varies widely from company to company. DEC's representatives, for example, do not work on commission. Therefore, we have not split out commissions from the compensation package as a whole.

IBM [++]

What more can be said about the industry giant against whom

everyone else is measured? When you are a rep for a company considered to be the ultimate company, not only in its field but in the world, you truly have it made. The value of the IBM name on your business card is difficult to measure, but we think it's the best door opener in this industry.

DEC [++]

DEC's market position, their exceptional reputation, and their new Venus (a VAX supermini with the capacity to challenge many mainframes in performance) make DEC an excellent choice for sales reps over the next three to five years.

Wang [++]

Like every company ranked [++] in this section, Wang has a reputation that is clearly a door opener. Their commitment to R&D in the highly profitable office automation area makes Wang an excellent choice for reps in the near future.

AT&T [++]

Reputation, plus some of the best high-tech talent in the world in the area of communications, and a strong marketing strategy have earned this industry leader a [++].

Apollo [+]

Apollo's exploitation of their market niche plus their projected growth to a one-billion-dollar company by 1987 have earned this relative unknown company a [+].

Control Data Corporation [+]

CDC's strong engineering base, plus the rumor that the company will undergo a major reorganization, which in our opinion will greatly improve the resources available to the sales staff, have earned them a [+] as well as tying them for the fifth spot in our industry rankings.

MEDICAL EQUIPMENT

THE TOP FIVE:

1 Hewlett-Packard Co.
2 IVAC Corp.
3 TECA Corp.
4 Cordis Corp.
5 Medtronic, Inc.

The medical equipment industry has grown in complexity and importance over the past ten years. Consequently, sales representatives in the industry are becoming technical specialists in their respective fields. Not only does the medical equipment salesperson have to understand the operation and application of the product, he or she also has to understand and respect the professional dynamics of the hospital staff and the politics of hospital administration and regulations. Therefore, an experienced and savvy medical equipment sales representative is a very important link in the health care services delivery chain. And as the industry becomes more complex, the rep's role will only grow in importance.

"It was 8 P.M., and I'd been working since eight that morning. My feet ached and my face was sore from smiling. I just didn't feel like being 'up' anymore," says Bill Jorgensen, a representative of IVAC, explaining what it was like working the Metropolitan Hospital account in New York. His experience is typical of an industry in which the customer's office never closes. "It was my fifth visit to Metro, and I knew that this was the make-it-or-break-it call. I had to pitch to thirty nurses, ten on each of the three consecutive eight-hour shifts. My blood was now one-third caffeine from all the coffee I'd been drinking, and I felt that it would be closer to 50 percent before I saw the sun again. But I also knew that in two days, when I met with the nursing supervisor and Metro's purchasing agent, I'd have the account in my pocket."

Bill's particular line of equipment is infusion cartridges and pumps. Infusion equipment is a modern, high-tech, and generally fail-safe method of administering intravenous or "I.V." solutions to hospital patients. Historically, I.V. equipment has always worked on the principle of gravity feed. Everyone has seen the bottle hanging upside down alongside the hospital bed with fluid coursing through a long plastic tube into the patient's vein. This is the I.V. method still used in most hospitals today throughout the world. However, as any doctor or nurse will tell you, the traditional I.V. method is far from foolproof and, if not administered and monitored carefully, it can lead to serious complications. The infusion pump that Bill Jorgensen was selling eliminated most of the built-in hazards of the old I.V. procedure.

Bill had been in the business for eighteen months. He'd been struggling for most of those months, having earned $24,000 in his first year. He didn't like the fact that he was below the $35,000 median compensation for reps at IVAC so he decided to figure out what he needed to do to improve his performance and bring in more commissions. He spoke to his company mentor, one of IVAC's leading sales representatives. "At first I felt like an ass," Bill complains, "because I was supposed to know my business. But Al really helped. It's funny—but when he told me what I had to do to sell, I thought he was putting me on."

Bill's story continues: "Metro was a $300,000 account, of which $6,000 would be in my pocket. But what Al told me was that I had to be there for the nurses. He said the nurses had to walk off their shift and head for home knowing and believing that my infusion cartridges are the ones they need. They had to believe that I'd be around to answer their questions and they had to be able to trust me. The only good thing about those week-long days is that I really got to admire those nurses. They're dedicated, efficient, and they give a damn. And that really helped because I knew that if I did my job right, they'd go home feeling the same way about me."

Bill found out what all medical equipment salespeople know: the nursing staff plays a prominent role in the decision making process for the sale of any equipment that they use. Acting accordingly, he set out to sell to the nurses. Bill's report: it's not easy.

I'd call my wife and not know whether to say good night or good morning—it was easy to lose track. And even though she'd say she understood, her tone would say otherwise. But she's a trooper, and she wished me an easy rest of the night. At the halfway mark I couldn't believe that it was just half over, and that in four hours I'd have to start with a whole new shift of nurses; that tomorrow afternoon, instead of sleeping, I'd have still another important call to make. But I was determined to do this job the way it's supposed to be done, and that was all there was to it. So I resigned myself to the fact that at 4:00 A.M., I was going to come around with coffee and doughnuts for the nurses on the graveyard shift, the same way I did halfway through each of the other nursing shifts. And I really knew that when those nurses left for home they'd feel the way I wanted them to: that we're all on the same team. Because if they did, the word would get to the nursing supervisor and to the purchasing agent, and the Metro account would be mine."

The picture that Bill paints is common in the industry. It's not easy to establish new accounts and, since there are a lot of people, usually nurses, who take part in the decision making process, they need to be sold. Unfortunately, there are a lot of nurses, and the nursing staff is distributed across three shifts, so the sales representative's options are limited if he or she wants to pitch to all the nurses. The bottom line is that the sales representative stands watch for all three shifts.

The medical sales industry is one of the most diverse, since salespeople can sell everything from bandages costing pennies apiece to MRI scanners at $1.5 million per unit. As you would expect, the techniques employed by the representatives differ widely according to what they're selling. A sale of bandages or tape might involve filling out an order form for a purchasing agent. The sale of capital equipment such as IVAC's infusion pumps usually involves selling to the nursing staff, since they are the ones who will be using the equipment. The infusion pumps that Bill sold are some of the most important pieces of capital equipment in the industry. But even more important are the same big-ticket items that, by law, require the evaluation mechanisms of the state medical boards before any decisions can be made. Because segments of the medical sales field are so different from each other, it's necessary to organize them into three major subcategories: disposables, capital equipment, and pacemakers.

In medical sales, disposables consist of virtually anything that is not considered capital equipment. This includes the whole universe of paper and tape products, such as the white adhesive tape used for dressings and rolled paper that covers a doctor's examination table, and, on the more exotic end of the scale, it covers the disposable cartridges for infusion pumps.

The Jelco division of Johnson & Johnson provides a good example of the typical organizational structure that companies use in the sale of disposables. The national sales manager of Jelco reports to the director of sales and marketing who in turn reports to the president of the company. Typically, companies selling disposables divide the country into five or six regions, and each regional manager has six or seven salespersons reporting to him or her.

Companies like these have between twelve and forty sales representatives nationally; most have closer to forty. Compensation is based on a salary and a commission of 2 percent of gross sales over quota. Quota is usually established as last year's sales volume, in units rather than dollars, plus a fixed percentage figure of between 5 and 10 percent.

There are two common approaches used in selling medical disposables. The first is to sell in volume to distributors who have ongoing contacts with hospital purchasing agents. In this type of sale, the discounts to the distributor are high and special sales commission arrangements must be made with the parent company. There are many salespeople who use this type of approach, and unlike IVAC's Bill Jorgensen, they enjoy a comfortable and stable professional lifestyle. They can afford to be noncompetitive because once they establish a sufficient number of distributor accounts with high-volume special commissions, they become "order takers" rather than aggressive sales representatives who must generate new business to stay alive. The nature of disposables is such that replacements are guaranteed to be ordered at fixed intervals. One salesman using this approach reports that he worked an average of sixteen hours per week during most of 1984 and was more than able to support his wife and two children in a suburban New Jersey environment. He has a very easygoing manner and is quite content to be making $35,000 to $40,000 in an unpressured way each year while watching his kids spend it.

The second approach used in the sale of disposables is to deal directly with hospital purchasing agents and seek a higher percentage commission. This is the more common approach to the disposables market, and salesmen who opt for it find themselves using such traditional sales techniques as making cold calls to purchasing agents and supervisors, getting to know the nursing staff, particularly the shift supervisor, and eventually working up to seeing the purchasing agent for the entire hospital. In some cases, particularly the more sophisticated disposables such as infusion cartridges, purchase decisions are made jointly by the nursing supervisor and the purchasing agent. In the case of the less sophisticated disposables such as adhesive tape, purchase decisions are always made exclusively by the purchasing agent. In both cases, the sales representatives must be wiling to put in a lot of time per sale and a lot of legwork to see each person in the hospital's purchasing chain of command. In effect, as Bill Jorgensen

> *Another technique often used by sales representatives who work closely with hospital staffs is to assume the sale.*

finally learned, the salesperson must develop a complete empathy with the person who will be buying the product.

According to J&J's Barbara Whitlock, "When I sell disposables to hospitals, I almost feel like a part of the staff." Barbara explains that over the five years she's been in the business, she has developed an effective technique. She simply asks a lot of questions of a lot of nurses and makes them feel that their opinions are important. She tries to find the few nurses on any given shift who will go to the purchasing agent and demand that the purchases be made from her. Barbara's technique works because she becomes a coordinator of an ongoing question and answer session, and this involves her with so many of the nursing staff that the entire hospital staff eventually accepts her as one of their own. Other sales representatives also report that when it comes time to close the sale, people who feel that their opinion is valued make the surest customers. "Also," Barbara continues, "you have to give them the impression that you're responsive to their needs and will be there when they have any problems with the product. Basically, you have to know how to talk to the people you're selling to, not just as a J&J rep but as a person."

Another technique often used by sales representatives who work closely with hospital staffs is to assume the sale. They have spent so much time with the nurses and purchasing agent and have engaged in so much conversation that at the appropriate time they feel very natural saying things such as, "When you get your first shipment next month you won't believe how much time you'll save," or "Once you begin using this tape on your patients, you'll be amazed at how their attitude to your nurses will change." In many cases, if there's no objection raised, such as, "Well, we're not sure we're going to use your tape," the sales representative pulls out an order book and asks them for the numbers. According to many industry salespeople, this approach works in most instances because at this point the purchasing agent or nursing supervisor feels that turning down the company representative would be almost like contradicting a member of their own organization. It becomes a conversational rather than a sales issue. It also works because the purchasing agent or supervisor has no financial stake in the sale other than budgetary considerations. They are not paying personally for the purchase.

Although this kind of selling requires a lot of time and legwork to get started, some representatives can become monthly order fillers once they get their regular accounts established. It's not uncommon for representatives to earn $40,000 a year, working only three or four days a week on well established "disposables" accounts. However, these same salespeople would have already put in sixty-hour weeks in the first two years on the job getting accounts established by becoming a trusted member of the inner sanctum on all the hospital staffs in their respective territories.

Another important aspect of selling disposables is that the sales representative must be willing to treat women in a professional manner. "Women dominate hospitals," Bill Jorgensen explains, "not men. It's the women—the nurses and their supervisors—who are giving virtually all the feedback to the purchasing agent. And their opinion of the sales rep as a professional person is vital." Another salesperson explains how he succeeded in establishing his "sweetheart" disposable accounts because the salesperson in a competing company simply had no respect for the staff nurses: "I won over at least three major accounts because the new rep who was put on the account for our biggest competitor really believed that women should stay home and take care of the houseplants. Of course, he never said anything like that to the nurses, but they knew. You can always tell when someone has no respect for you or what you do." The ability to treat women in a professional manner is one reason why many companies are hiring women as sales representatives. One industry source pointed out that whereas there were virtually no saleswomen in the industry ten years ago, today approximately 25 percent of the company representatives are women. Companies have found that women have been consistently more successful dealing with other women than have their male counterparts, and since closing the sale is the bottom line, the companies have acted in their own best interests by aggressively hiring women.

Capital equipment is a broad category of medical apparatus that includes such large devices as CAT scanners and fetal monitoring equipment, and smaller bedside equipment such as infusion pumps. Infusion pumps are a good example of capital equipment in medical sales because they are not considered disposal items like I.V. bottles, yet they are relatively low-cost items at $1,500 per unit. Typically, only the wealthier hospitals use infusion pumps because gravity I.V. bottles are still the least expensive way of getting the job done. Infusion pumps are viewed as optional equipment, and even in wealthier hospitals they coexist with the older bedside I.V. units.

Infusion pumps can regulate the flow of medication better than traditional methods and can prevent an air bubble from entering a patient's vein, something that may happen if an I.V. bottle is not monitored carefully and is allowed to empty completely.

The typical infusion pump costs hospitals $1,500 and the disposable cartridge costs $6. A major metropolitan hospital might buy 100 pumps. The gross sale would be $150,000 with a commission of $3,000 to the salesperson. In addition, the hospital would purchase approximately 30,000 cartridges over the course of a year, resulting in a further $3,600 commission. So from a major sale to a single hospital, a representative can earn $6,600 in commissions the first year and upwards of $3,600 in succeeding years from cartridge re-orders. By selling infusion pumps to just ten hospitals in one year, a salesperson can make over $60,000 and wind up with a guarantee of about $30,000 in succeeding years from the sale of replacement cartridges. As more pumps are sold to more hospitals, the replacement orders increase, and they are just like gravy to a hard-working sales representative. Commissions are typically a percentage, usually 2 percent of gross sales and are calculated from the first sales dollar rather than on the above-quota dollars. However, the commission structure itself can vary from company to company. IVAC, the undisputed industry leader in the sales of infusion pumps, is an example of how commission structures can be changed at the whim of management. "When IVAC was an independent," a former IVAC sales manager explains, "the salespeople were raking in $75,000 or $80,000 a year. Then Eli Lilly bought them, tightened the commission structure considerably, and although none of the salespeople are starving, their average yearly take has gone down to between $45,000 and $50,000."

For some of the new, highly technical monitoring equipment, such as the evoked potential monitors which cost around $20,000, neuromyographs that vary in price from $7,000 to $30,000, and electroencephalographs or ECGs that can cost anywhere from $12,000 to $17,000, the sales commissions are 3 percent of gross sales with some companies even offering retroactive commissions. For example, a sales representative will earn a 2 percent commission on sales up to $1 million and 3 percent thereafter, so if he sold exactly $1 million he would earn a commission of $20,000, but if he sold one dollar more, he would earn $30,000.03 (3 percent applied to $1,000,001). John Iannacone, a representative for Hewlett-Packard, says, "There aren't many companies that offer the retroactive commission structure, but the ones that do are the ones that attract the real go-getters." Hewlett-Packard, an industry leader in the sale of patient monitoring equipment, pays an average base salary of $35,000 plus a commission of 1 percent on everything sold. As one industry source says, "HP is the Cadillac of the industry. Sales reps stay there forever."

Capital equipment sales attract some of the industry's best sales-people. Often, because a piece of highly technical equipment involves the sale of support equipment, the total ongoing commissions over a five-year period can be very handsome. Multiply this by five hospitals, and you can see why medical equipment sales in this area of the market generate so much money. But the commissions don't come easily; much time is spent initially establishing the credibility of the representative and the company to the satisfaction of the hospital's medical staff. As a result, the purchase of any capital equipment by a hospital can often be a long, drawn out process. Joelle Goodman, an EKG saleswoman in New York, describes her first big sale to Metro Hospital in Brooklyn: "I had really done my homework. I knew the total purchase would be around half a million, so I had two leasing companies all lined up to take care of the financing. I knew they'd already been using a competitor's echocardiogram that had some minor problems, so I

"There aren't many companies that offer the retroactive commission struture, but the ones that do are the ones that attract the real go-getters."

was going to sell them one of ours. I'd worked out all the numbers, showing them how they could write off the old echocardiogram using the loss-on-disposal provisions of the investment tax credit. I was really prepared. Then, as my luck would have it, they'd had a staff turnover in the purchasing department, and somehow their certificate of need had never been filled out. I had to start all over again."

The certificate of need requirement is an important factor in the sales of highly technical or expensive capital equipment in an industry as tightly regulated as medicine because it can delay a transaction for up to six months. Salespeople in the industry must prepare for this by knowing which hospitals in their territories have filed certificates of need, which ones are thinking about filing, and in which ones the chief of medicine is looking at the newest capital equipment with a twinkle in his eye. Simply stated, the certificate of need is a document that justifies a hospital's need for a piece of expensive equipment. Before a hospital even puts out a proposal for bids on capital equipment purchases totaling over $100,000, it must obtain the certificate from the state medical board. Every hospital, public or private, is required to file this industry-standard document. In the certificate of need application, the hospital justifies the medical and institutional need for the particular pieces of equipment and establishes the basis for an independent evaluation.

After the certificate is submitted to the medical board, the hospital may be visited by investigating doctors, who will do an on-site medical evaluation of the hospital's application. Even if the investigatory visit is waived, the institutional evaluation must take place at the state medical board, and the usual turnaround time for this, including subsequent approval or rejection, is two or three months. Salespeople who sell such big-ticket capital equipment as CAT scanners or the new MRI scanners always find out about the certificate of need first. And they don't stop there. By spending time on the floor and talking to nurses and shift supervisors, they also find out what doctors are eyeing what equipment, whether a doctor can get the support of a department head for a new device, and what exactly is on the chief of cardiology's wish list. A good sales representative can also learn about the funding mechanism within the hospital, establishing which doctors can influence the members of a hospital board to support a major purchase. Joelle Goodman learned the hard way that there are many more aspects to doing your homework than just researching the financing.

Financing is another critical issue for capital equipment salespeople, especially in an industry in which most forms of funding are open to professional and public scrutiny. Because financing arrangements for capital equipment can be extremely complex, many companies routinely give their representatives seminars in financing. Also, representatives who have already seen the need for an on-going financial resource have struck private deals with commercial leasing companies in which the salesperson opens up a new market for the leasing company and the leasing company kicks back between 3 and 5 percent of the purchase price of the lease to the rep. This practice is more common in sales to doctors' offices rather than in sales to hospitals. One representative, who specializes in sales of EKG machines to doctors, explains, "I made over $3,000 last year from lease companies alone." Some medical equipment companies, recognizing that the practice is common and also recognizing that some lease companies are fly-by-night operations, have set up independent leasing companies themselves that service their prospective customers. Their representatives get a flat 3 percent from the leasing company for every lease-sale they make. And although the medical equipment company doesn't make any money on the lease itself, they make their money from the sale of the equipment, and they're satisfied that the leasing company is reputable and that their client will be properly serviced on the financing end of the deal. It goes without saying that the hospital or doctor purchasing the equipment will not be informed of this aspect of the financial arrangement.

Other companies will just issue the credit themselves and assume all the risk. Although the individual credit terms are quite varied, the standard arrangement requires the buyer to pay 20 to 30 percent of the purchase price up front, with the balance due in three-month installments over nine months. In deals of this type, no interest is charged directly to the buyer, although the buyer does pay top dollar for the equipment. This kind of arrangement is particularly useful to hospital purchasing departments that want some equipment below the certificate of need level and have to roll over the funding into the budget for the next fiscal year. For example, if Metro Hospital's fiscal year ends August 31, and they want to take August 1 delivery of three evoked potential monitors at a total cost of $60,000, the purchasing department will find itself in an awkward situation. The funding is not available in the current fiscal year, but it will be in the next. Accordingly, they cut a deal with the manufacturer to take delivery of the equipment on August 1, pay a premium price, but fund the equipment as of September 1, the beginning of their new fiscal year. Everybody makes out in this arrangement. The hospital gets its equipment, the company makes a sale it might not otherwise make, and Joelle Goodman, who has spent five months structuring the deal, gets her commission as well as a continuing account at Metro. In summary, capital equipment sales in the medical business are, at least from the financial end, no different from sales and credit arrangements in other industries. The one notable exception is that those hospital administrators in charge of making purchase decisions usually do not have a direct financial stake in the transaction.

Although some analysts might consider pacemakers to be a type of capital equipment, selling pacemakers has so many aspects specific to cardiology that pacemaker sales warrant a separate category. Pacemakers require the most aggressive sell in the medical industry and currently command one of the most active markets. As you might expect, this makes pacemakers the single most lucrative sale in the industry. The major pacemaker manufacturers, such as Medtronic, Cordis, Intermedics, and Pacesetter each manufacture a device which has the same basic quality components. In general, when dealing with equipment like pacemakers, whose function is vital to the preservation and maintenance of human life, one often finds that the quality of an item produced by competing manufacturers is essentially the same. Because quality is a given, sales representatives must rely on other selling points when approaching doctors with their product. And these other selling points come under the heading of perks.

Perks operate most effectively in a market with lots of dealer and manufacturer markup. Normally this is where the negotiation takes place between buyer and seller. However, the real pacemaker buyer is an unconscious patient who's hanging between life and death, wide open on an operating table, and completely at the mercy of the cardiologist. The patient, therefore, is in no position to do comparison shopping when it comes to pacemakers, and more often than not, he is covered by a medical plan that will pay the freight. In this market, pacemakers, which cost the manufacturer between $100 to $200 to produce, are sold to hospitals for about $3,000, and finally are tacked onto the patient's bill at around $6,000. Consequently, there is a lot of room for all types of perks, consulting fees, paybacks, and, above all, profit in pacemaker sales.

The most common, and entirely legal, form of perks is investigatory fees. A typical scenario looks like this: Medtronic's ace pacemaker salesman, Bill Griffin, makes a cold call on Metro Hospital. He visits the cardiology department, talks to the nurses, and quickly learns the names and memorizes the bios of all of the staff cardiologists and up-and-coming residents. If he's really done his homework, he has already committed this information to a notebook before he even visits Metro for the first time. Bill has been selling pacemakers for five years and appreciates the fact that, unlike the purchase of other capital equipment in the medical field which is typically done by committee, cardiologists purchase pacemakers as individuals, and it is not unusual for four different cardiologists to use two or even three different brands of pacemakers.

After many attempts, frequently seven to ten, Bill Griffin gets Dr. Mar-

> *"Pacemakers require the most aggressive sell in the medical industry and currently command one of the most active markets . . . this makes pacemakers the single most lucrative sale in the industry."*

vin Lappin to listen to his pitch for a solid seven minutes—an above-average time for an interview during a cardiologist's day. Since both salesman and cardiologist know that quality of the equipment is not at issue because the pacemaker is one of the "name" brands, the discussion centers around the investigatory fees. Dr. Lappin agrees to file a report analyzing the performance of each pacemaker he implants. In exchange for filing the report, he receives an investigatory fee of $400 to $500. The fee is paid by the company distributing the pacemaker which might be, but is not necessarily, the manufacturer. As you might imagine, the reports which the doctors must submit require a minimal effort, usually no more than a simple signature on a preprinted form. For the company paying the investigatory fee, the fee itself is tax deductible as a cost of doing business; for the cardiologist, especially one starting out and shouldering huge bank finance charges and malpractice insurance premiums, the investigatory fee is often the first pocket money he or she can lay hands on. The sales representative has made a commission, and the patient doesn't care because he hands the bill over to his insurance carrier.

Dr. Marvin Lappin is a typical cardiologist working in a typical major metropolitan hospital. He might implant 100 pacemakers per year. This means that the hospital will be billed $300,000 by the pacemaker distributor; the patient and his insurance carrier will be billed $600,000 by the hospital; the doctor will receive $40,000 to $50,000 in investigatory fees from the distributor, and the salesperson will receive upwards of $6,000 in commissions, based on a typical commission of 2 percent of gross sales. And these figures represent the production of one cardiologist in one hospital for one year. The top salespeople in the field earn well over $100,000 in commissions annually.

There is also a very lucrative market for middlemen in pacemaker sales. A number of former pacemaker salesmen have formed companies which stock and distribute the pacemakers from one or more of the major manufacturers. Because they established good doctor and hospital connections as salesmen, they can now sell the pacemakers much more easily than some of the manufacturers' own representatives. And sometimes the manufacturers are willing to part with their profit just to get the steady sale. Some of the middlemen-distributing companies have found the business so lucrative that they spend millions of dollars annually entertaining for the doctors. It is not uncommon for these companies to own one or more yachts which they use for entertainment. Both doctors and salespeople admit that the profit margin in the pacemaker industry and the heavy demand for units make these types of perk arrangements run of the mill. As Dr. Lappin explained, "The bottom line is the welfare of the patient. When I install a pacemaker, I know damn well it's going to work and I know how to do my job. Before I operate, a patient and his family would be willing to sell their souls to the devil in exchange for a guarantee of success, so the patient and his family are happy as long as the operation is a success. If some people make a buck in the process, who gets hurt? Do you think that there's a patient alive today because of his pacemaker and my skill who'd complain if he knew how all of it came about?"

But the life of a pacemaker sales representative is not all roses, and they don't spend all their time partying on yachts and buying villas on the Mediterranean. Salespeople are frequently required to be immediately available during the actual pacemaker implantation operation to adjust the device to the required specifications. The salesperson will not actually touch the patient, but he's there during the entire operation and comes as close as any nonmedical person to being a part of the surgical implant team. As one pacemaker salesperson explains, "I'd only done outpatient pacemaker adjustments during all my years in the business. Outpatient adjustments are pretty simple, at least for me, because I just sit behind my black box and adjust the signals. No big deal. The first time I was involved in an open heart procedure I thought I was going to faint. Here's this guy's chest wide open. You hear bones cracking as they cut into his chest cavity. Blood is everywhere. The cardiologist is cursing at no one in particular, and then everyone turns to me and tells me to do my thing. I've never been that scared in my life."

Most pacemaker implants are done on an outpatient basis. It is when the patient's heart problems are complex, and the cardiologist wants to be able to make adjustments on the spot that the pacemaker sales representative must stand by in the operating room ready to join the surgical team.

What kind of individual makes the best medical equipment sales representative? Joseph Stevens, the national sales manager for TECA Corporation, says, "When I'm hiring a sales rep I look first for a rep who has a good track record selling capital equipment in any industry. I've hired copy machine sales reps to sell high-tech monitoring equipment and they do quite well." Joseph admits that he is reluctant to hire a sales rep who has made a career of selling disposables, even if the disposables are in medical sales. "I'm looking for aggressive salespeople, and traditionally, sales reps who concentrate on disposables do not fit that bill. Of course, there are exceptions." Joseph says he looks for evidence that the prospective salesperson is a committed individual, and although paper credentials are not important to him, he tends to view college degrees as an indication of commitment. For the salespeople under him, Joseph has structured bonus plans based on the principle of "selling at the top," which means that the company is much more likely to increase its overall sales by getting the top salesmen to sell more, than by getting the bottom salesmen to sell more. For this reason he offers bonuses for selling at least one piece of equipment per quarter from each of his company's product lines. He explains that his top salesman had been selling two of the company's products as if they were being given away, and ignoring the rest of the line. It wasn't that he couldn't sell the other products; he just didn't concentrate on selling anything other than his two most successful products. When the new bonus policy went into effect, this same salesman increased his gross sales dollars by 12 percent while the average company increase was 7 percent.

If there's anything that will instantly create companywide anxiety, uncertainty, and confusion in any industry, it's U.S. government intervention. And the effect of the Diagnostic Related Groups (DRGs) on the medical industry has been exactly that. The government's motivation in establishing the DRGs—468 groups of possible patient diagnoses and related treatment recommendations—is to reduce health care costs. The logic behind the DRG concept is that for all patients with a given diagnosis, the costs of treatment should fall within a given price range. This attempt to control health care costs by trying to look at health care as a product and determining what it should cost the consumer is a drastically different approach from the original Medicare plan. Under the old Medicare rules, hospitals were reimbursed for all reasonable costs, as long as they could be justified. The new rules, based on the DRGs, were introduced in 1983 and are expected to be fully implemented by 1986. In the interim period, hospitals receive payments based on a formula whereby they are paid 50 percent of what they would have received under the old rules, and 50 percent of what they would receive under the new rules. Although private insurers are not required to use the DRGs in reimbursing hospitals for patient care, some do. Industry analysts believe that most private insurers will follow suit, and that doctors offices and private laboratories will soon be using the DRGs.

In addition to the cost cutting introduced by the government, hospitals themselves, in response to the critical escalation of health care costs, have begun to pare their budgets by following standard business practices. They are reducing inventories, calling for sealed bids from suppliers, and discharging patients earlier. The general atmosphere of the entire medical profession has become one of cost consciousness. Employers are requiring employees to pick up more of their health insurance tab and in some cases are even offering employees cash bonuses if they don't exceed the deductible amount on their medical insurance. The net result is that hospital admissions have been dropping, and industry analysts think that this trend will continue for at least the next three years.

What this means for most of the medical sales industry is reduced profits. Industry analysts believe that there will be a general belt-tightening among the medical suppliers. In addition, many salespeople are reporting that hospitals simply aren't purchasing anything beyond bare essentials, choosing instead to wait and see how the DRGs will affect major equipment purchases. For these reasons, we raise the "caution" flag for representatives. In any industry where there is a significant degree of uncertainty regarding the factors which impact on sales, the prudent salesperson will investigate the specifics closely before jumping in. We are not saying "Hands off," but we are saying, "Take a close look."

One notable exception to this rule is in the area of high-tech advances in diagnostic and treatment equipment which result in overall cost savings. For example, the Gruntzig balloon catheter, produced by C.R. Bard, eliminates the need for bypass surgery for many patients by compressing fat deposits in clogged arteries. This procedure, called angioplasty, is much easier for the patient, involves a much shorter hospital stay, and is, therefore, much more cost effective. In addition, follow-up studies are beginning to indicate that bypasses have a tendency to clog up again after just a few years. So, although Bard is being hurt by lowered sales on most of their staples, the Gruntzig balloon catheter is picking up the slack.

Hospitals are also finding that highly technological diagnostic tools such as the evoked potential monitors manufactured by TECA are invaluable in the diagnostic process, and often eliminate the need for more expensive testing. Their initial costs are recovered over the long run by reductions in expenditures for laboratory time and hospital support staff, and the elimination of certain nonrecoverable patient care costs.

Industry analysts believe that sales of high-tech diagnostic equipment, due to its long-term cost efficiency and effectiveness, will be a strong part of the industry for the balance of the 1980s. Because of this and other favorable company information revealed by our research, we have taken the somewhat unusual step of including TECA Corporation among our top five companies. An industry source advises, "They should be included in the top five. Their new management is dramatically more dynamic, and their equipment is excellent. The only caution for potential salespeople at TECA is that it is not a company for soft-stepping individuals. The TECA people will not provide much in the way of pre-job evaluation or training, although their technical support and general on-the-job training for sales representatives is excellent. Overall, I'd say that if a sales rep is a true self-starter and really wants to work for a living, he or she can do quite well at TECA."

We felt it necessary to call a tie between the two top companies: Hewlett-Packard and IVAC. Both are industry leaders by performance and by reputation. Representatives can do extremely well at either company, and the overall organizational structure of the corporate parents places both IVAC and Hewlett-Packard's Patient Monitoring Division in favorable positions within their respective corporations as a whole. Because these companies are comparable in overall strength and offer similarly favorable outlooks for their reps, we could not justify ranking one ahead of the other.

The industry median salary for a two-year rep is $32,100, and the industry median commission is 2 percent on gross sales from the first dollar and not on after-quota dollars. This alone should be an inducement to anyone who feels that he or she can succeed within the pressure-cooker environment of selling medical equipment.

MEDICAL EQUIPMENT		COMPENSATION	COMMISSION	SUPPORT	INTANGIBLE
1	Hewlett-Packard Co.	5	2	5	+
1	IVAC Corp.	5	3	5	+
3	TECA Corp.	5	5	4	+
4	Cordis Corp.	5	5	4	−
5	Medtronic, Inc.	5	4	4	−

Hewlett-Packard and IVAC [+]

Most of the reasons for the [+] ratings have already been listed, but to summarize the strong points: excellent equipment, excellent reputation, excellent support, and excellent compensation packages have earned HP and IVAC shared billing as the number-one companies.

TECA Corp. [+]

TECA so impressed us with their operation and so impressed our industry sources with their potential, that we have moved them right up in the ratings among the larger, more established companies in the industry. But remember, TECA is an assertive, growing company, and representatives who do not fit their fast-paced profile should stay away.

Cordis and Medtronic [−]

Because both are industry leaders in pacemaker sales, and because pacemakers are the industry's most lucrative area at present, we feel that these companies earn their spot in our top five. The [−] is not a reflection on either company per se, but is an indication that these companies are more vulnerable than any of the other top five to the DRGs, as discussed earlier. Simply put, the effect of the DRGs will be to trim some fat, and pacemaker sales are a lot fatter than any other area of medical equipment sales.

OFFICE FURNITURE

THE TOP FIVE:

1 Steelcase Inc.
2 Herman Miller, Inc.
3 Haworth, Inc.
4 GF Corp.
5 Westinghouse Electric Corp.

O ffice furniture is more than just an obvious necessity: it can be the critical component in making a sale, landing a client, starting a successful practice, or closing an important contract. In a business that involves contact with the public within an office environment, the correct office furniture can generate sales where a poor design with inferior furniture will turn potential customers away. Originally office furniture was designed for durability and for the protection of files and equipment. However, with the recognition that the layout of office space, the comfort and design of furniture, and the color of walls, carpets, and cushions can affect the way people think and behave, the office furniture industry has taken on even greater importance.

Office furniture is a Cadillac industry for its representatives, with a median industrywide compensation figure of $41,250, including salary and bonus. However, this figure reflects the fact that a typical office furniture salesperson has had five or six years' sales experience prior to joining this industry.

"Designers design from the top down," is the lament of one representative for a major floor-covering company. "By the time I make my pitch to a designer or an architect, they've already blown the budget, and I wind up selling my cheapest lines," he says, pointing to the fact that in the office furniture industry, architects and designers are hired to design the bigger jobs and must work within a strict budget figure. And as it turns out, designers do traditionally and literally design from the top down, factoring in ceiling coverings and lighting requirements before the wall coverings, and factoring in the wall coverings before the office furniture or floor coverings. As one industry source puts it: "The bottom of the design is also the bottom of the industry."

Office furniture was a $4 billion industry in 1984, and according to industry sources, it is expected to be a $10 billion industry by 1990. A representative for Herman Miller, our number-two ranked company, says, "With the explosion in office technology in high gear, office furniture has to be right alongside." He adds, "Every time the IBMs, Wangs, DECs, and AT&Ts come out with new automated office equipment, we in the industry have to be there with the furniture for it." An industry analyst agrees: "The furniture people talk quite a bit to the equipment people, and although they're not married, they're certainly dating."

Rudolph Freehan, a dealer in New York City, comments, "We have a very close relationship with our suppliers, particularly Steelcase, our furniture supplier." It's quite common for large dealers to have only one major furniture supplier. Steelcase, our number-one rated company, insists on an exclusive arrangement for its dealers. A Steelcase spokesperson says, "We offer our dealers the best support by far in the business, and we have the best product. One of the things we expect in return is loyalty." Rudolph adds, "The fact that we are Steelcase dealers opens quite a few doors for us. I can certainly understand why Steelcase wouldn't want to be the ones who opened the door only to have a competing line get the sale." In general, Steelcase products are regarded as the best value for the dollar in the office furnishings industry. Steelcase has worked hard at developing a standard office "look" to its furniture that appeals to most business owners and to managers in public and private administrative positions.

Rudolph continues, "Although some office furniture companies do sell direct, dealers do most of the selling in this business." Manufacturers such as our top five—Steelcase, Herman Miller, Haworth, GF Business Equipment, and Westinghouse—all sell through dealers. GF Business

Equipment, however, sells directly to the customer as well.

The biggest money in the industry is in being a dealer's rep, according to Rene Moscoli, a dealer representative selling Herman Miller's product line. "Most dealerships are working on a 20 percent margin, and dealer reps typically earn a straight commission of around 30 percent of gross profit." Rene continues, "For a good-sized sale, let's say outfitting a branch office of

> *The sales representatives have adapted their "features, functions, and benefits" approach to encompass the new management matrix that exists in today's office.*

a major corporation, the total tab might come to $100,000, and my cut would be $5,000 or $6,000, depending on the details." The dealership would then make $14,000 to $15,000 in gross sale dollars after subtracting the representative's commission.

A representative for Westinghouse, our number-five ranked company, says, "I was in dealer sales for awhile, and even though the really big bucks are there, it just wasn't for me." He explains that the demands of representing a dealer are very different from the responsibility of working directly for the manufacturer. "You have to be super-organized and really get out there and hustle up a storm, and that's not my cup of tea." He quickly adds, "I have no objection to hard work; I work fifty or sixty hours a week now. It's just a different style, that's all." Karen Stevenson, a representative for Haworth, our number-three ranked company, agrees. "We, as manufacturers' reps, are involved in a very different kind of selling from the dealer reps. The biggest difference is that the dealers have to be closers; in other words, they have to close a final sale, and this means that they have to get down to the nuts and bolts of what it takes to make the close. They have to bid against many other dealers and they have to be price sensitive. They have to contend with all aspects of furnishing an office from the lighting to the floor covering, and everything in between. The manufacturers' representatives have an entirely different, but related, role. Our main function is to sell to and support the dealers. Although there is certainly competition among manufacturers' reps to sign up dealers, it's not the same kind of sale as a dealer trying to close a sale with a point of purchase client."

In the beginning, the office furniture business operated much the same as it does today. However, back in 1912 when Steelcase was founded, clients' needs were a bit less complex than they are today. John says, "Steelcase's first product was a wastepaper basket made of wood. In fact, all office furniture was made of wood until the introduction of metal furniture." And the impetus for metal furniture, according to John, was fire safety and the need to protect vital documents from being burned in a building fire. Jeff Boyle, a representative for GF Business Equipment, our number-four ranked company, adds, "Our first product was a fireproof safe. In fact, the company was originally known as General Fireproofing." John explains that when the market responded to fireproof steel office furniture, "Steelcase responded in turn when it manufactured steel desks in 1915 for a skyscraper in Boston. Prior to that, fires were rampant in office buildings for two reasons: buildings were being constructed higher than the early municipal fire departments could reach, and the buildings themselves were stocked with flammable furniture such as wooden filing cabinets, desks, and chairs. The advent of steel furniture not only controlled early fires and protected the documents stored inside, it also saved lives.

"When steel furniture was first introduced," John continues, "it had to look like wood because wood was what people were used to seeing in the office." He adds, smiling at the recollection, "After the 'wood' look was abandoned, office furniture was either battleship gray or mist green, and it wasn't until the '50s that attractive colors began to appear. Then, in the late '60s, technology began to impact on the industry. Prior to the late '60s, office furniture consisted of freestanding pieces: a desk, a file, a credenza. But when the term 'information processing' became much more than a technological buzzword and the proportion of white-collar to blue-collar workers started to increase, the office furniture industry began to change dramatically. As the need for information processing grew, the office workforce grew along with it, and it became obvious that the workforce was having a greater and greater effect on the bottom line of business in general. And so," John continues, "it became apparent to the decision makers in corporations that any efficiencies gained in the area of office productivity would impact on their company's bottom line." And that's when the office furniture industry entered a new, technologically conscious stage of design. John says, "The basic question we asked at Steelcase was, 'How do you make people more productive?' And the answer was, 'By giving them better tools.' By 'tools' we mean anything from a ballpoint pen to a word-processing unit."

Steelcase and the other major manufacturers have been responsible, in part, for a new look to offices. The sales representatives consistently refer to the "new office environment" as a workplace where management, administrative staff, and clerical support people share a common space, share information over a networked electronic data communications system, and even share in the responsibilities for processing company information. John adds, "The term 'office environment' was probably coined in response to the focus on new productivity tools. The word 'desk' has been replaced by 'work station.' What good would a word processor be if the work surface on which the equipment rested was too small for it, or too low or too high? If the people operating the equipment get fatigued after four hours because their working environment is inefficient, how much of an effect will that have on their performance, on the total productivity of the office staff, or on the entire operation of the company?" He points out an example: "Typewriters used to be placed on twenty-inch returns, but now with word processing equipment and data terminals, the surfaces have to be twenty-five inches deep."

The industry had to understand the real meaning of the word "ergonomics." John says, "The hardware manufacturers came to understand that detached keyboards were desirable; they studied the relationship of the eyes to the CRT, and of the hand to the positioning of the keyboard." Karen Stevenson adds, "And with more than one worker using the same equipment, all those relationships change from hour to hour or shift to shift." John continues: "The bottom line was that the work stations had to be dynamic. They had to be designed so that the components could be moved to make them comfortable for any size worker who would be using them and also for all the different types of equipment that could be used." And in each case, once one of those problems was solved, the task was still incomplete because each solution uncovered a new problem the manufacturers had to solve. John adds, "Then the seating had to be adapted to fit the different constructs of the work stations." And to illustrate his point, he changed his own Steelcase office chair to a series of different heights and seating positions in a matter of seconds as he spoke. John adds what probably best sums up the Steelcase approach to the office environment: "User-friendly has taken on a new meaning at Steelcase."

The term "user-friendly" has become an almost hackneyed expression as it is applied to the computer software business. When software is said to be user-friendly, it means that the software is very easy for a non-technical person to understand and to use. At Steelcase, the corporate philosophy is that the entire working environment ought to be user-friendly. John comments, "That's true. By making the office environment as flexible as possible, people can be themselves while they work. When people can do things the way they want to do them, they'll be more motivated, and there's an excellent chance they'll be more productive." It isn't surprising to learn that at Steelcase, each office worker participates in the design of his or her office environment to make it more productive. John concludes, "When office workers feel a part of the design, they are more motivated, more productive, and more involved." And this is the sales perspective he uses when he represents the Steelcase design philosophy to prospective dealers.

We questioned John about how Steelcase keeps up with the changing technology. He explains: "Our marketing and R&D departments at the home office in Grand Rapids are constantly looking into that question. For example, some of the computer equipment in use in offices generates quite a bit of heat. Our R&D people examined the issue to decide whether the panels that divide the offices could carry air conditioning to the various locations." Karen Stevenson adds, "It certainly would not be the least bit obvious to the casual observer of the office furniture industry that the specifications of a computer sitting on a desk could influence the design of the paneling between offices." But those are the kinds of issues that need to be addressed by the manufacturers who expect to stay on top of the industry. In addition, John points out, "Our home office is frequently in touch with hardware manufacturers such as IBM, DEC, Wang, and Prime, to see what's coming down the road."

Thus, by remaining sensitive to the changing office landscape, an industry that began by manufacturing wastebaskets and safes has turned into an ultrasophisticated, technology-conscious manufacturing and service industry. The principle that unifies the office furniture industry of fifty years ago with the office furniture industry of today is that the manufacturers who are staying on top continue to address the needs and desires of their clients as those needs and desires change. By any standard financial measurement, it can be seen that the office furniture manufacturers have been extremely successful at what they do. They have remained competitive with one another, yet the top companies have remained at or close to the positions they have occupied over the past five years. Those companies which have been strong historically remain strong today. And at the same time, the entire manufacturing industry has been able to adapt to a brand new set of office technologies and to a change in the social psychology of office manangement as well. The sales representatives of this industry have also adapted their "features, functions, and benefits" approach to encompass the new management matrix that exists in today's office. And, as a group, they point to a rosy future in this sales industry.

If there were a common denominator besides the obvious corporate financial measuring tools that one could use to compare companies on an interindustry basis, it would be an intangible one such as corporate style or management culture. Using this common denominator as a gross measuring tool and applying it across the broad spectrum of American corporations, one would find that some companies have no unifying conceptual theme in their approach to business and that other companies are aggressively motivated by a central idea which guides everything they do, from manufacturing to sales to customer support. Such central themes are very evident in most of the companies in this book. IBM has such a theme, and it is represented by their salespeople, their customer support personnel, and their product developers. Chrysler has such a central theme to its business approach, as does McGraw-Hill, Apple Computer, and Century 21. The themes may differ from company to company, but to the people who do business with the various divisions of these companies, it is evident that all the representatives seem to represent their company's ideals as well. That company personality is also evident at Steelcase, and in the opinion of Steelcase sales representatives, it is what makes it so easy to sell the product. As Peter Jeff, a spokesman for Steelcase, explains, "Steelcase leads the industry with the most extensive dealer network, the most consistent on-time delivery record, the most manufacturing assembly sites in the world (twenty plants in nine countries), and over a billion dollars in annual sales volume, more than double that of Steelcase's nearest competitor."

An industry source says, "Steelcase is a real rarity among companies because it has a personality, and this personality emerges in every aspect of the company's operation." To illustrate this point, the same source tells a story that he often uses to describe the impact that Steelcase has on the industry. "Imagine that you're the vice-president of a large corporation. Your main New York office is being moved from one part of Manhattan to another, and the company has decided to outfit the new location from top to bottom with new office furniture. You've heard that Steelcase is the largest manufacturer of office furniture, and you've decided to pay a visit to their New York showroom. When you walk in, you notice two things: a simple elegance and an articulate presentation of Steelcase's product. You see a reception area that is a showroom and a showcase. The lighting is subdued, and the only way you can describe the color scheme is with the word 'warm.' You might have been tense as you came up in the elevator. There are a million things you need to do just running your business, and you don't really want to be bothered buying furniture. But you know that the furniture is very important, so you've decided to take a direct hand in the purchase. By the time you've walked to the receptionist's desk, you find yourself smiling. You're more relaxed. The receptionist offers you coffee or tea. You find yourself relaxing even more. You really can't believe that in the middle of a series of very frenetic, crazy days, you're sitting in a peaceful, elegant reception area on the twenty-fourth floor of a Manhattan skyscraper, sipping tea and thoroughly enjoying yourself."

Perhaps walking into the New York sales office of a company and having the receptionist offer you a cup of coffee isn't important in a strict business sense. Perhaps having the company logo adorning the coffee cup and paper napkin, albeit a nice touch, isn't important either. After all, most potential clients are a lot more concerned with whether the right furniture will be delivered on time. But potential Steelcase clients know that the company that puts such thought and consideration into its reception area is going to do even better with service and product performance.

One industry analyst says, "Steelcase is a company with 8,000 employees that is run, from the point of view of employee relations, as a family business. They never lose sight of the individual. They even have an 1,100 acre campground not far from company headquarters in Michigan, and it's there for all Steelcase employees." He adds a truly amazing statistic: "Approximately 5,000 Steelcase employees participate in some form of company-sponsored recreation such as a softball league. The turnover rate at Steelcase is less than half the national average."

Steelcase scored a 5 on our compensation scale, indicating that a prototypical industry rep earns more than $45,375, including bonus, which is more than 10 percent above the industry median of $41,250. All Steelcase employees, including sales representatives as well as factory workers, receive a bonus each year, and although the percentage of the bonus is confidential, it is the highest of any of the top hundred companies in our survey. In addition, Steelcase has an uncommon approach to merit raises. Most companies have fairly rigid salary structures for specific positions within the company, making it necessary to promote an employee to increase his or her compensation. Often the employee accepts the new position reluctantly in order to receive the additional compensation. At Steelcase, this is not the practice. Employees in the same functional position within the company can be on significantly different compensation schedules. In this way, excellent performance is rewarded without forcing an employee into a position he may not want, and more important, from the company's point of view, may not be as qualified to perform.

Sales manager John Munroe, who greets prospective customers in the reception area of Steelcase's New York showroom, exemplifies the hiring, training, and employee policies at the company. John has been with the company for fourteen years and does not hide his pride in that fact. He

> *"The main thrust of the industry today is in open plan systems and furniture which supports the advances in computer technology."*

has the kind of quiet assertiveness that comes with knowing that he is very good at what he does, and the relaxed demeanor that comes with knowing that the people with whom he works are very good at what they do. In many cases, according to the independent representatives interviewed in our survey, when prospective customers meet the sales representatives of a supplier, they are sometimes left with the feeling that the person-company match was the proverbial square peg in a round hole. This will almost always have a negative impact upon that person's ability to sell the product. However, the hiring and training policies at Steelcase are such that when potential customers meet John Munroe, they understand why John chose Steelcase, and why Steelcase chose John.

With very few exceptions, according to John, Steelcase does not hire from within the office furniture industry. He explains the company's rationale: "We feel that if we're going to be on the leading edge of the industry, we're going to continuously need people with new ideas and new blood." He adds, "The typical sale in the industry today is no longer a concrete sale: it's a conceptual sale. You're no longer selling a desk, a chair, and a file; you're selling the concept of an office environment. You're selling a system." So what kind of people does John try to hire? "People with exceptional learning abilities," he explains, "and people who have had between three and ten years of very successful sales experience either with major corporate accounts, the end users, or with the architecture and design community. I also want the people I hire to be able to assimilate new ideas into their daily sales activities. And although we hire from the outside, we promote from within, so I want the person we hire to be committed to doing an excellent job for himself as well as for the company. I also want the people we hire to be committed to growing into positions of greater responsibility within the company."

Since Steelcase hires from outside the industry, its training program for new representatives is intensive and thorough. John explains that the Steelcase training program has five phases. During phase one, the new representative spends a mimimum of six weeks in a regional office learning about the company, the industry, and the products. He becomes oriented with the dealers and travels with the district manager. Phases two through five are held at company headquarters in Grand Rapids. Phase two lasts approximately eight weeks and includes further product training as well as training in selling and presentation skills. Phases three, four, and five each last a week. Steelcase has given considerable thought to its training and has continually refined the program through the years. After completing phase two and before beginning phase three, the employee works in his or her territory for three months. The employee also returns to work in his territory before entering phases four and five. By the time phase five is completed, the employee has worked for Steelcase for between sixteen and twenty months and has spent between fourteen and sixteen weeks of that time in formal training and on full salary. Clearly, this company leaves absolutely nothing to chance. And if you're still not convinced, the following story involving a large Steelcase sale gives a very clear indication of why this company is as big a force in the industry as it is, and why it's not only going to stay that way, but will become an even greater force in the future.

A major New York City bank had been buying all its office furniture from a Steelcase competitor for many years. Steelcase, along with all the other manufacturers, found out that the bank was moving its major corporate operation into lower Manhattan, and that the figure budgeted for the interior design and furnishing of the office complex was eight million dollars. This figure was to include furniture as well as floor and wall covering, lights, and other nonfurniture products. John says, "Everyone at the bank was new, and we had no idea who were the main players in their organization. We really had to start from scratch. But we kept at it and we pursued them very aggressively. After finding out who the decision makers were, we flew them out to Grand Rapids to see what we are all about." John continues, "A lot of companies can put up a good facade in their showrooms and field locations, but we want our customers to see what's behind our facade. In Grand Rapids, they met the chairman of the board, Robert C. Pew, who invited the bank's representatives to his house for cocktails and conversation. In addition, they saw our facilities, our obvious financial strength, and our employees in action."

Even with this exceptional presentation and expression of interest, John explains that Steelcase left no stone unturned. "We also made contact with the designers of the bank's project and established a professional relationship with them. We wanted to make sure they were fully aware of the quality of Steelcase products. And last but not least, we also introduced them to a group of our local dealers, one of whom would be chosen to install the furniture." Were there any problems with making the sale? "No, but the bank had a problem in the timing of the move. Their computer system had to be fully operational at their old facility until 5 P.M. Friday and had to be up and running at the new facility by 9 A.M. the following Monday. It couldn't be operational unless all the furniture and interior installations were in place. The installation people worked the entire weekend and the job was finished around 11 P.M. Sunday." John explains that, to his mind, the most impressive part of the entire operation was the involvement of the company's chairman in the sale. John reiterated that although the company made its money on the transaction, the central office went beyond the call of duty in supporting the local New York representatives financially as well as personally. This type of operation is not unusual at Steelcase, he explains, and he points with pride to the fact that all the furniture in the Sears Tower in Chicago was sold by Steelcase. Steelcase not only belongs at the top of our survey in the office furniture industry, but it belongs near the top of any list of the best companies to work for in the United States.

Herman Miller, also based in Michigan, is our number-two ranked company. It was a close race with Haworth for the number-two spot, but Herman

Miller won out because of its reputation for a top-of-the-line product, excellent service, and their new office environment concepts, Action Office and Ethospace. An industry source describes Herman Miller: "In any other industry, they would be the creme de la crème, but going head to head with an outfit like Steelcase, they're just damn good." Herman Miller earned a 5 on our compensation scale, indicating that the prototypical industry rep at Herman Miller earns more than $45,375, or 10 percent above the industry median figure of $41,250.

Rick Harman, a representative for Herman Miller in Connecticut, comments on the interaction between dealers and manufacturers' sales reps: Most manufacturers' reps have between ten and twenty dealers they're responsible for. Dealers usually handle their own sales, but when there's a big sale, particularly in the case of a national account, they call us in." He adds, "We also call dealers in when we're contacted directly by a national account. For example, we were contacted by Wang Labs a while ago. They were looking to make a major purchase on a national scale. We called in a few of our dealers and worked with them as well as with the people at Wang, and hammered out an arrangement which was quite beneficial for us, our dealers, and for Wang."

Because our research in the microcomputer industry revealed that the manufacturers themselves frequently compete directly against their dealers on national accounts, we asked Rick whether that kind of competition exists in the office furniture industry. He says, "Not to my knowledge. Certainly, if we were going to do something like that, we would have done it with a sale like Wang. But this industry is based quite a bit on good will, both between manufacturers and dealers, and between dealers and clients. If a manufacturer starts to play games with his dealers, it won't take long for his dealers to give a call to the competition." He adds, "In the computer business, dealers don't have the product loyalty that exists in the furniture industry. It's not uncommon for a computer dealer to be selling IBM, Apple, and Compaq computers. It's unheard of in this industry for a dealer to carry two major competing brands of office furniture."

With the company's plans to increase manufacturing capacity to the tune of $100 million in the next two years, and with the company's focus on their open plan systems, we consider Herman Miller a very good bet for reps. Sales have been rising steadily since the leveling off in 1983 and were up by over 25 percent in 1984, and they are projected to increase by another 25 percent to $500 million by the end of 1985.

Haworth was referred to by one industry source as the "Avis of the industry. They try harder." Company sales for 1984 were in the $400 million range, and the company was in close competition with Herman Miller for the number-two spot. The same industry analyst reports, "They're also hoping to attract some high-powered reps by upping the compensation ante, but in situations like this, when a company attempts to move up the industry ratings ladder, these compensation bonuses can often be temporary."

Haworth's Karen Stevenson says, "The way to sell in the office furniture industry is to establish positive business relationships with your clients. The industry is extremely service sensitive." She continues, "A good example occurred about a year ago. We got a call from one of our dealers who was pitching an account with a small bank." Dealers usually deal directly with clients, but in the case of a major presentation, a dealer will call on the manufacturer for sales support. "The bank told us that they were opening up three branches in lower Manhattan, and wanted to know what we could do for them. The actual sale was relatively small for a manufacturer to be called in: only around $80,000 to $90,000. But the dealer had a feeling about it. He'd seen one of the bank's corporate VPs around the branch one day, and he just had a feeling that there was more going on than just furnishing a few branches." So he called in Karen. "Basically, he wanted me to let them know what we at Haworth are all about. The sale was pretty straightforward, but when I left, the bank knew that we were a quality company and that this particular dealer had enough regard for their account to bring us in at the very earliest stage."

Manufacturers' representatives do not work on a commission basis, but receive a salary and performance bonus instead. As Karen says, "Our job is to sign up quality dealers and to keep dealers informed of changes in our product line. We train dealers, hold seminars and, as I indicated, we also support dealers on sales calls when we are needed." And what did happen with the bank? "Just recently, they moved their corporate headquarters uptown, and they called our dealer to handle the whole job. The sale was in the six-figure range, and for a sale of this size, companies usually ask for bids from a number of manufacturers. But they were so pleased with the service our dealer had provided, they just said, 'You do it!' "

Haworth earned a 5 on our compensation scale, indicating that the prototypical rep at Haworth earns more than $45,375, or more than 10 percent above the industry median figure of $41,250.

Ohio-based GF Business Equipment, which originated as a manufacturer of fireproof safes, has earned our number-four rank because of its professional commitment to its representatives and to the quality of its product. GF earned a 5 on our compensation scale, indicating that the prototypical industry rep at GF earns more than $45,375, or 10 percent above the industry median figure of $41,250.

Sales at GF increased by more than 30 percent in 1984, and the projection for 1985 is for an additional increase of 13 percent to just over $200 million. This, in addition to the fact that GF is increasing its high-ticket wood furniture operation, bodes well for GF representatives who are seeking to penetrate the executive office market with quality products.

Ken Woods, a GF representative, comments about selling for the company, "I like the way the organization is run. It's almost like working for a large dealership, but the management organization and the company's resources are, of course, far superior to that of a local point-of-purchase dealer." He adds: "The main thrust of the industry today is in open plan systems and furniture which supports the advances in computer technology. It makes my job a lot more interesting. I'm on the cutting edge of an office systems revolution." Ken agrees with our sources in GF management who report that the office furniture industry is expected to triple in size by 1990. With the obvious commitment to growth exhibited by GF's directors, we believe that the company will provide a very lucrative opportunity for its representatives.

Westinghouse has earned our number-five rank in the office furniture industry for a number of reasons, not the least of which is that it's Westinghouse. It's hard to imagine a company so large that a segment of its business can generate $200 million in sales annually and represent only 2 percent of total annual sales for the company, but that's the position of Westinghouse's office furniture division. One Westinghouse representative says, "I sometimes have the feeling that Westinghouse corporate doesn't even know we exist." Yet Westinghouse has earned a 5 on our compensation scale, meaning that our prototypical rep at Westinghouse earns more than $45,375.

Bernice Kantor, a Westinghouse representative based in Connecticut, says, "We at Westinghouse just quietly go about our business. Corporate seems pleased with what we do, and we're right there competing with the Steelcases and Herman Millers of the industry, and quite often winning." Bernice adds, "The Westinghouse name is a corporate door opener, and we frequently use our credit arm to help dealers set up floor plans." An industry source reports, "Westinghouse seems to be content with its slice of the office furniture market pie, but if they ever decide to turn full corporate attention to the office furniture market, the rest of those guys had better watch out."

Westinghouse furniture is an enigma of sorts in that its $200 million annual sales in 1984 is a respectable share of the office furniture market, yet the figure represents only a small percentage of total sales for the parent corporation. Nevertheless, the company is doing quite well and is well respected in the office furniture industry. Westinghouse should continue to supply its reps with a very comfortable living in the foreseeable future.

The industry as a whole gets a [+]. As mentioned earlier, this is a Cadillac industry for reps. The industry is growing at a phenomenal clip, and all projections indicate that it will continue to do so. It is primarily a relationship-based sales industry, which augurs well for long-term individual growth for sales reps.

The median industrywide compensation figure is $41,250, but keep in mind that our prototypical rep has had five or six years prior sales experience before entering the office furniture industry.

OFFICE FURNITURE	COMPENSATION	COMMISSION	SUPPORT	INTANGIBLE
1 Steelcase Inc.	5		5	+ +
2 Herman Miller, Inc.	5		5	+
3 Haworth, Inc.	5		5	+
4 GF Corp.	5		5	
5 Westinghouse Electric Corp.	5		5	

Steelcase [+ +]

There's not much more that we can add about this company except that based on all their strengths, they have certainly earned a [+ +].

Herman Miller [+]

In addition to being an excellent and well-respected company, HM's expansion plans have earned the company a [+].

Haworth [+]

A close third behind HM, Haworth's aggressive pursuit of reps and their expansion plans have earned them a [+] in our intangible category.

PHARMACEUTICALS

THE TOP FIVE:

1 Merck & Co., Inc.
2 Eli Lilly and Co.
2 Pfizer Inc.
3 Squibb Corp.
4 The Upjohn Co.
5 G. D. Searle & Co.

P harmaceutical sales are inherently different from most of the other industries in our *Selling at the Top* survey because the sales reps don't sell directly to the consumer. In fact, most sales reps don't even sell to the retailer; they promote their product to the physician, dentist, or veterinarian who will in turn prescribe it for the patient. This indirect selling places added pressure on the field representative to get his or her product to the point-of-purchase buyer. Through courtesy calls to doctors at their offices, meetings with staff physicians and hospital pharmacists, and occasionally through meetings with independent retail druggists, the reps try to squeeze their pharmaceuticals to the consumer.

"Don't look back for a year." That was the advice that kept Janet Lyons going at Pfizer during the most trying months of her sales training program in the company's Roerig Division. The rigorous sales intern programs, she reports, are common to all drug companies because of the high-risk nature of the products that are sold. Selling at the top in the pharmaceuticals business means working at Merck, Lilly, Pfizer, Squibb, Upjohn, or Searle—the top companies in our survey—and knowing the indications and contraindications of every single drug in your book. That's why training is critical, and it forms a common bond among the sales representatives in all of the major pharmaceutical companies.

The drug industry is one of the most regulated industries in the United States. Not only are its products tested, but even the testing procedures themselves are subject to a harsh public and professional scrutiny. "Products can be on the market for years and then pulled off the shelf within a month," an industry specialist reports. "And the sales people have to keep on top of every product they represent." Also, the threat of lawsuits—both government and private—hangs over all the companies like a sword. "This is a tremendous responsibility," the industry specialist continues, "because the slightest mistake at any level, from research and testing through sales and distribution, can cost a company millions of dollars." And the responsibility of making sure that the right product gets sold for the right reasons falls squarely upon the shoulders of the pharmaceuticals representative. That's why the Janet Lyons experience at Pfizer is typical of most beginning sales trainees in pharmaceuticals.

Janet is bright, intent, and communicates the kind of quiet self assurance that is typical of seasoned executives who have been in business for many more years than Janet. After thirteen months as a Pfizer representative, she is finally able to look back on her training with a professional objectivity that she didn't have when she was completing Pfizer phase three testing. "I'd been sleeping about three or four hours a night for two weeks," she says. "I was stretched further than I thought possible, and I was really thinking seriously about quitting. I couldn't see the light at the end of the tunnel, and I didn't even have enough sense of humor left to joke about the headlights of the oncoming train. I happened to be in a coffee shop near Pfizer headquarters in New York when I bumped into Bruce Stevenson. Bruce had been with Pfizer over twelve years. I didn't really say much to him—just chit-chat. But as he left, he said, 'Don't look back for a year.' I didn't know what he meant until 3 A.M. that night. I was finishing one of my phase three quizzes. I was simultaneously happy, because I knew I was learning the pharmaceutical business when at last, and exhausted, I thought of what Bruce had said. I knew then that he had gone through this too. That was the precise moment I knew for sure that I was going to make it."

Pfizer's training program is common among the top pharmaceutical companies such as Lilly, Upjohn, and Merck. A member of Merck's training staff says, "Selling drugs is one business where nobody screws around in training. You either learn or you're out. To say that the potential for lawsuits is a ticking bomb in the drug industry is an understatement. It's an atom bomb." The director of training at a large pharmaceutical company says, "We can't have our people misinformed. Top management has made that extremely clear."

At Pfizer's Roerig Division, training consists of four phases. Phase one is a two-week training class held at one of Roerig's five regional offices. There are typically five to ten people in a training class. Janet describes the training she received. "I was very impressed. Everyone there was nice, and also extremely professional. They made it quite clear that you were there to learn, but also that they (the training staff) were there to help. The worst part for everybody was seeing themselves on videotape." Although Pfizer's phase one training consists mainly of product training, the trainees were required to run through mock sales presentations as well. Another mem-

> "To say that the potential for lawsuits is a ticking bomb in the drug industry is an understatement. It's an atom bomb."

ber of the training staff says, "The videotaping is invaluable. Most people have no idea how they look or sound to others. It's one thing to have someone tell you that you wet your lips too often when you speak. It's quite another when you can see it for yourself. You can experience yourself as another person might."

Pfizer increases the pressure on its new sales trainees in phase two of its program, where the emphasis is placed directly upon the face-to-face selling which includes presenting the product, speaking to doctors, and speaking to pharmacists. "You wind up doing a lot of role playing, and of course everything is on videotape," Janet says. But the real pressure starts in the third phase. "Even though the training we got in phases one and two was extremely valuable, to a large extent we were insulated. We were learning, but we were still playacting. Phase three is the real thing." Here, the Pfizer trainees are expected to absorb a tremendous amount of product information. They undergo an intense, programmed learning course in presentation and product that's based in part upon thoroughly digesting the company's voluminous sales and product manuals. In this phase, the trainers are relentless. As if all this weren't enough, the trainee is also working a territory. "You get to go out with your district manager some days, but for the most part, you're on your own." In some cases the trainees also go on calls with an experienced salesperson.

In pharmaceuticals sales, as in most industry sales, it's common for a sales representative to work from home. This can place an additional burden on a new employee because there is no constant office environment to relate to. Janet Lyons remembers that it was disorienting at first. "It was an unusual feeling waking up that first morning and knowing that if I wanted to, I could go to the movies at one o'clock and no one would know." But she found out early that the apparent freedom was deceiving. "Needless to say, you don't start a new career by going to the movies your first day, but it was just a strange feeling knowing you could. What I did do was schedule my first few calls with doctors who had open calling hours spread across a few hours." Open calling hours refer to a doctor's setting aside a specific time—eleven to one, for example—as the period when pharmaceutical salespersons can drop in and make a presentation. "I knew that some doctors are impossible to get in to see, so I thought this would be a good way to start, and I thought that a doctor with open calling hours would be 'sales-rep conscious.' " For Janet, this was the first of many mistakes. "I've always prided myself on being punctual. I was there at eleven-thirty on the dot (the start of open hours). The place was jammed with reps. There were at least five when I arrived, and I know that at least three others showed up later, and then left when they saw the crowd. I think that every rep there was brand new. You never saw a more self-conscious looking group in your life—including me."

Can you imagine a sales rep in any industry spending hour after hour pitching a product to someone who he knows will absolutely never buy it? And what's more, picture this same salesperson begging a doctor to take a free sample. That's what selling is like in the pharmaceutical industry when the sales representatives from all the major companies visit the doctors in their territories. While the people who eventually buy pharmaceuticals are the patients, the intermediate buyers are the pharmacies. In a normal "non-prescription" industry, the sales representatives would sell directly to pharmacies. And in fact they do, but the role of the the pharmacist is literally one of filling orders for the doctors who prescribe the drugs for their patients. Therefore, the role of the doctor is pivotal because although he or she doesn't buy directly from the drug company, prescriptions that the doctor writes form the basis of what the pharmacist will buy. And the structure of the entire drug sales industry in the country is based on the fact that even though the pharmacies order products from the pharmaceutical companies, it is the doctors who actually make the ordering decisions for the pharmacies and the purchase decisions for the patients according to the prescriptions they write. A Merck sales representative, who has been selling in the industry for eight years, says: "It's not as strange as it sounds if you view the pharmacies and doctors as a large corporation with different departments. Looking at it that way, the doctors are the decision makers, the patients are the messengers, and the pharmacies are the ones who provide the product. And in the sales industry, as anyone can tell you, the pitch is always made to the decision maker."

If you can only sell to the doctor and if the doctor orders the drugs from the pharmacy, how do you know who's making the commission? A sales representative from Princeton-based E.R. Squibb & Sons reports, "Like every drug company doing business in this country, Squibb uses zip codes to assign commissions." Because there is no way to track a representative's sales to a pharmacy—remember the pharmacy's order was placed by a doctor who's dealing only with the patient directly—the industry, by common consent, divides a sales representative's territory into zip codes. And the salesperson gets credit for any sale made to a pharmacy within his or her zip codes. This can result in some strange sale situations. For example, assume that a patient visits a doctor in representative A's territory. The representative has sold the doctor on using Glucotrol, an oral drug produced by the Roerig Division of Pfizer for the treatment of type-two diabetes. The patient has gone to a doctor near home. The next day, the patient goes to work and during lunch hour, takes the prescription to a nearby pharmacy where the company has a drug prescription plan. However, the pharmacy where the patient works is not in the zip code of the representative who made the "sale" to the doctor, so another Roerig representative gets credit for the sale. It seems unfair at first, but the problem in assigning a commission is handled the same way by all the drug companies. As an Upjohn executive explains, "It usually balances out for the salespeople in the end. For every sale that one person loses to the zip code system, I'm sure there's one he gains right back from it two weeks later. But in view of the unusual selling structure of the industry, can you think of a fairer way to credit sales?"

Although the drug companies claim that the zip code system, is fair for their salespeople, it does create problems for the doctors, however. First of all, doctors tend to have many different styles for dealing with drug company salespeople. These styles range from an absolute refusal to see the representative to a reliance upon their salesperson's current knowledge of the drug industry as a means of keeping abreast of the new developments in pharmacology. Dr. Sheila Feinstein, an internist in Connecticut, explains, "I really used to count on the reps for information. I tried to be fair and give them a hearing. And in exchange for sales, I used the reps as teachers to learn about the new drugs on the market. I had regularly scheduled rep hours and I thought the setup was fair and efficient for both the reps and myself. Then I moved my office and everything changed. I could hardly pay a rep to come see me. It took me a while to find out, but the reason was that my office was located on the boundary of two zip codes, and I was no longer simply ordering drugs within one territory. Most of my former salespeople began avoiding me like the plague because every prescription I wrote gave them a headache rather than a clear commission." It turns out that what happened to Dr. Feinstein is not unusual in the industry. As is the case in virtually every kind of sales, people see time as money, and they're not as inclined to spend time with a doctor when half of the doctor's patients are likely to be creating sales for another representative.

Pfizer's Janet Lyons recalls sitting in the doctor's waiting room on her first call. She says: "After twenty minutes, a rep about my age came out of the doctor's office, crying. I couldn't believe it. Everybody was shocked. If I'd been nervous before, I was going crazy now. Fortunately, I never got in." Janet describes how the doctor cut off the young woman in mid-sentence, jumped up, said, "Time's up," and pushed her through the door without so much as an "I'll call you back." But undaunted, Janet returned. "The next time, I got there at eleven—half an hour early. I was the second representative to see the doctor. When I walked into his office I was flabbergasted. He had an hourglass on his desk, and instead of greeting me with 'Hello, I'm Dr. Smith. How are you today?' or some other such pleasantry, this bozo turned his hourglass over and said, 'You have ten minutes. Make your case.' " Did Janet make the sale? She says, "Who knows? Remember, doctors don't buy, so you usually don't know if you've 'sold' them or not. Some doctors— the ones who didn't fail 'Works and Plays Well With Others' in med school— will give you some indication of how they feel about your product. In the best case, they'll say 'This is great. I'm going to use it.' But usually, they're non-committal."

Alan Bloom, a salesman for Merck, explains what it's like selling for his company: "First thing in the morning I go through my appointment book and map out a route. The company expects us to see between six and eight doctors a day, which means I have to try to see ten or twelve, since half the offices I call on won't see me. The rejection rate is 50 percent."

Lunch for Alan means slowing down to fifty. "There are no business lunches in this business," he says. "Who ever heard of a doctor going out for lunch? It doesn't happen. So what you have to do if you want to make your daily quota is grab a sandwich and coffee. More often than not I slow down to fifty, pull into the right lane and eat my lunch between appointments." Alan continues, "Usually I end my last call at eight in the evening. I get home around nine, and then I have to plan tomorrow's schedule." Janet Lyons adds, "And remember, the trainees at Pfizer also have to fit in study time while they are on the road."

Compensation in pharmaceutical sales is based on a salary and bonus structure. The bonus structure varies, not only from company to company, but also according to a salesperson's length of service within the company. The general or industrywide structure of the bonus is based on a weighted value of the products sold by the company. The "weight" placed upon any given product varies according to how much value management places on the product. The value of a product is calculated on such issues as its development costs, the amount of research that it entailed, its patent status, and its popularity in the professional market. An official at Pfizer reports that the average starting salary for a sales representative is "between $18,000 and $25,000 a year depending on experience and background, and an average first year bonus of around $3,000." A salesman for Merck claims, "We have the best salary structure in the industry. A first-year rep can easily make $30,000 if he hustles." There are also incentive bonuses. For example, a sales manager at Pfizer reports, "Last year there was a $1,000 bonus for making quota on all products."

Pharmaceuticals salespeople consider selling directly to hospitals to be a promotion because those are the most lucrative sales in the industry. Robert Cody, a district sales manager for Merck, says, "Representatives usually need at least five years' knocking on doctors' doors before they're considered for hospital positions." The hospital sale structure is two-tiered, based on the size of the hospital. "The large hospitals such as New York City's Mount Sinai have a sales representative who just calls on that account and that account alone. However, any salesperson can call on a smaller hospital that happens to be in the representative's territory."

Most pharmaceuticals companies hold new-product lunches at major hospitals—especially teaching hospitals—across the country. Do staff residents and their chiefs come to these presentations only because of the free-lunch aspect? Drug sales reps and doctors alike say that the lunch seminars allow company representatives to present new products in a strictly professional atmosphere. Dr. Leslie Coopersmith recalls, "When I was a fourth-year medical student at Rutgers in New Jersey, it was an excellent learning experience, not only for me, but for doctors as well. The pharmaceutical companies usually had a speaker who was a leading specialist in the field, and the presentations were always first-class." Janet Lyons, who has been involved with a number of luncheon seminars, elaborates: "The Pfizer salespeople get doctors on the cutting edge of their field." When asked about what the doctor gets for taking time away from his practice to speak, she replies, "Money. They get an all-expenses-paid trip, and the going industry rate for doctors is approximately $500 per talk. A doctor we brought east from Stanford gave three talks in two days. That's $1,500. Another thing that interests the doctors is that they get to talk about the thing they love. Remember, these are doctors who are involved in research—and usually also in teaching—so they're anxious to talk to other doctors. These doctors are usually in love with what they're doing." When asked about the propriety of having a doctor pitch a company's product, she said, "They don't. There's sort of an unwritten rule. They won't agree to speak to your hospitals if they don't like your product, but there's an understanding that any selling comes from the rep. The doctor talks only about his or her specialty."

The sales representatives set up the conferences. Janet smiles and points to herself. "I have to be a caterer, a production specialist, and above all, a diplomat. When I get frazzled, and I do, I have to keep my cool. I have to give the clear impression that I do this every day of my life."

Getting a drug into the hospital pharmacy involves a lot more than being a caterer. Representatives have to sell their product to the hospital's pharmacy and therapeutics committee, which consists of members of the hospital staff—doctors and pharmacists—whose job it is to evaluate new pharmaceuticals. Bill Collingsworth, a sales representative, explains, "Most of the people on the P&T committees are pretty decent sorts, but there's always one guy in every hospital with the charm and deportment of Darth Vader—and that's the infectious disease specialist. These guys act like Zeus descending from Mount Olympus with bolts of lightning flashing around them. I don't think anyone ever gets within ten feet of them when they walk down the halls." The infectious disease specialists usually head the P&T committees and usually have the final say on which drugs will be added to the hospital's formulary, the official list of approved drugs. The formulary is the sales representative's pot of gold, and of course, every salesperson tries to get his company's drugs placed on the formulary. Some salesmen, after encountering the infectious disease specialist and failing, try to introduce their drugs through the formulary's back door by selling to the residents. As Merck's Alan Bloom comments, "Residents are people after all, and they write prescriptions." And usually if the resident recommends a drug, it will be placed on formulary.

Upjohn's Geoffrey Allen, whose territory includes New York's Beth Israel Hospital, says, "Hospitals are where the big bucks are. If you can get a few of your biggies on formulary, you'll be in good shape." A moderately successful hospital representative can make $40,000 to $50,000 the first year, and usually 25 percent of that income comes from bonuses.

Another representative for Pfizer labs says, "After ten years on the job, doctors know you. So for those doctors, I'll send literature and cover letters once a month, and maybe I'll drop in to say hello once every three or four months. Some kind of contact is important because with doctors, 'Out of sight is out of mind.'" Janet adds, "I send out over thirty letters a week to doctors." Asked about her company's office support for her correspondence, she laughs. "You're looking at my office staff. Everything that gets done, I do. The company is great with technical support. Whenever I have a question—and that's probably twice a week—I get it answered with one phone call. But when it comes to secretarial help—well, each rep is also a secretary. But at least I can touch-type." When asked about computerization, she explains, "The industry is completely computerized on the business end—R&D and certainly accounting—but for the field sales force, the companies are only just looking into it." Merck's Lester Holtzman mentions that Merck has given IBM PCs on a trial basis to its reps in one district for doing correspondence, company reports, and scheduling, but for the present the industry hasn't really computerized its field salespeople.

The pharmacies represent the bottom line for most sales representatives. Because it is the pharmacies who actually buy the drugs, the representatives have to keep in touch with the pharmacies in their territory to stay on top of drug sales figures and to determine where their products stand in relation to their competition's drugs. In some rare cases, reps try to convince pharmacists to use substitute drugs; that is, to use their company's product rather the competition's drug which the doctor has prescribed. Pharmacists are understandably reluctant to do this because they can go straight to jail for switching a prescription, so the salespeople try to get the pharmacists to call the doctor and convince him to make the switch over the phone.

Some representatives use pharmacies in order to get to the doctors. As Wendy Tollifero, a saleswoman for Eli Lilly, recalls, "When I started, I had terrible luck getting to see doctors; it was really frustrating me. Then I had a great idea. I went to some local pharmacies and got a list of which doctors were ordering which drugs. I picked the doctors who were using antibiotics I knew weren't as good as what we had, so when I pitched to the doctors I would start out with 'I see you're using Brand X. Did you know that Nebcin is just as effective and is less likely to result in stomach upset?' This approach worked wonders. Not only did I get in to see more doctors, but many began treating me as an expert—and in a way, I am."

Another change affecting the pharmaceutical and medical sales industry is the declining consumer interest in generic drugs. Generic drugs are becoming a thing of the past. We've seen the drug exposés on TV news during the past few years which center around the reporter's purchase of a name-brand drug for $11.95 while its generic equivalent sells for $6.95. Moral: drug companies, doctors, and pharmacists are conspiring to gouge prices. Actually, many drug salesmen used to use the generic drug concept to get the pharmacies to use their drugs instead of the ones that the doctor recommended. For drugs which do have generic equivalents—and legitimate ones do exist—the pharmacist can make a substitution without the doctor's okay. Virtually none of the newer drugs have generic equivalents, however, because the newest products represent specific types of disease research, and consequently, the drugs have very specific functions. And they are patented. Because of this, if Pfizer patents a new antibiotic and Lilly has one which does the same thing, they will not be considered generic equivalents. "Generic equivalents" means that two drugs have the same chemical composition, but because of the patent laws, this is virtually impossible.

There are two ways in which drugs can become generically equivalent to one another, but both ways involve the marketing of the identical drug under a different name. An Upjohn manager explains how two manufacturers can produce the same drug and how their sales representatives can freely convince pharmacists to replace one drug with another without consulting with the prescribing doctor. The Hoechst-Roussel company of Germany, the world's largest drug company outside the United States, had developed an oral diabetes drug called Micronase. They didn't believe they could successfully market it in the United States, so they licensed it to Upjohn, whose representatives were so successful in selling Micronase that when Hoechst-Roussel underwent a management change, the new leaders decided that it would be a good idea for them to market the drug in the United States also, selling head-to-head against Upjohn. Of course, they couldn't market Micronase because of the licensing agreement with Upjohn. So they manufactured a new drug called Diabeta, which had the identical chemical

> *If you can only sell to the doctor and if the doctor orders the drugs from the pharmacy, how do you know who's making the commission?*

composition as Micronase and became, in fact, its generic equivalent. Representatives of both companies were able to convince pharmacists to interchange the two drugs.

The second way that generic equivalent drugs can appear in the marketplace occurs when the patent on a drug runs out. For example, McNeil produces a drug called Haldol, which is used for the treatment of certain mental disorders. At present it is the best-selling drug of its kind. Once the patent runs out on Haldol, other drug companies can manufacture it under a different name and sell their drug as the generic equivalent of Haldol.

"The patent process is murdering the drug companies," says an executive at Merck. He is referring to what happens after a drug is patented.

Although the patent is valid for seventeen years, during this period the drug company must test the drug—which usually takes two years—and then submit it to the FDA for approval. And once the FDA gets a product, approval takes an average of nine years. The net result is that the effective patent life for drugs has been six years, not seventeen. Considering that the industry's estimated cost for bringing a new drug to the marketplace is $70 million, it is clear why an effective six-year patent hurts the drug companies. The recently passed Patent Restoration Bill has partially alleviated the patent problem by extending the patent life of a drug to ten years on the marketplace regardless of the actual patent status. However, as an industry source explains, "It's not enough. The consumer still has to bear the brunt of the FDA's politics." He is referring to the fact that the drug companies must pass the tremendous R&D costs on to the consumer. Our industry source also believes that the FDA policies on drug testing are hindering the overall effectiveness of the industry.

Another major trend operating in the pharmaceuticals industry is the shift away from a "men only" club among drug sales personnel. As is the case in the entire medical industry, the ratio of women representatives to men is increasing. A member of Pfizer's training staff reports, "In my last class there were seven women and three men." Nurses who have become disenchanted in their nursing careers are turning to the pharmaceutical industry in greater and greater numbers, and because of their extensive knowledge of the field, they're being welcomed by companies who must rely heavily on a product-competent sales force.

Pfizer's reaction to this shifting trend was to send one of its trophies back to the shop. The Pfizer "Man of the Year Award," given to the representative with the best sales performance at the end of the year, was no longer appropriate. Because the award was won by a woman—and a woman with only three years' experience in the company—Pfizer executives ran back to the engravers to change the inscription on the trophy. Janet Lyons is particularly fond of this story, but comments that although the phenomenon seems brand-new, it's grounded in real practicality. "Sex is an issue," she says, "but not in the bedroom sense. It seems as though doctors are more comfortable with women and respond better to the female representatives. You can see it in their zip code sales at the end of each quarter. For one thing, women tend to be better listeners and doctors love to talk. All I have to do is shut up and listen. At the end of fifteen minutes, the doctor is asking me for recommendations."

Cost containment is becoming the name of the game in pharmaceuticals, and this is beginning to have a serious impact not only on the industry sales but on product development and manufacturing throughout the health care industry. The new cost containment policies outlined in the diagnostic related groups (DRGs) have squeezed the drug industry from two directions. On one hand, hospitals are tending to purchase less expensive drugs and are avoiding, wherever possible, the expensive top-of-the-line brands. Eli Lilly sales representatives report that this has had a schizophrenic effect on the company's recent sales performance. Lilly, the nation's leading supplier of antibiotics, has reported significant reductions in sales of Keflin and Mandol: the two big-ticket antibiotics in the company's drug book. At the same time, however, sales of Kefzol and Keflex, two of the company's bargain-basement antibiotics, are on the increase. "You can win and lose at the same time," the Lilly representative says. "I'd just rather be winning with Keflin than with Kefzol."

Any drug which tends to reduce hospital stays will gain an increased market share when all things are equal in terms of patient care. A good example of this is Pfizer's Feldene, an anti-arthritis medication which does not involve the use of steroids. The steroid drugs frequently have side effects, such as swelling of adjacent muscle tissue, which need to be monitored in the hospital, thereby increasing the total cost of the patient's bill. Feldene eliminates this problem, resulting in shorter hospital stays and lower bills. The result, Janet Lyons explains, is that Feldene is now the number-one anti-arthritis drug in use in the country, and Janet is able to promote it effectively at all of her sales calls to doctors' offices. She points out that this was a case where her company got behind a growing trend in health care—reducing the cost of a patient's hospital stay—with the right drug at the right time. "Pfizer supports its representatives," she comments proudly.

The Patent Restoration Bill, which was designed to extend the effective patent life of a drug and improve the companies' returns on their investments, also had a provision which has been evaluated negatively by most drug companies. Prior to passage of the bill, in order for drug companies to obtain approval from the FDA for the production of drugs on which post-1962 patents had expired, the companies first had to go through a long testing program. The Patent Restoration Bill enables the FDA to approve the marketing of these post-1962 drugs by new companies with no additional testing, thereby enabling the new generic equivalents to reach the marketplace much more quickly and with virtually no significant R&D overhead. This, the major companies claim, is unfair because they might have invested millions of dollars in required FDA testing to obtain the marketing rights and now see their only protection—the patent—compromised by the new legislation. However, the sales representatives claim that there is an up side to this as well. Companies such as Merck and Upjohn, which are expected to be hit the hardest by this change in procedure, can also elect to go the generic route and market drugs whose patents were originally held by other companies. Upjohn's salespeople indicate that this will allow them to make more inroads at the pharmacy level, which might offset the challenge of new generic equivalents to their big-ticket items. Their instincts are corroborated by industry analysts who agree that the provisions of the bill create a double-edged sword. However, it's not clear at this time which companies are likely to be the winners and which will be the losers, or even if there will be winners and losers within the same company. One industry source says, "It may well turn out that the effects of the bill will be a wash. It may well depend on marketing strategy, not R&D support, to create profits within the provisions of the bill."

As a whole, the industry looks promising to qualified reps. Keep in mind that there is increasing competition in the job market from health care professionals such as nurses, who are abandoning the health care field for the greener pastures of pharmaceutical sales. Also keep in mind that pharmaceutical sales require extensive technical product knowledge, perhaps more extensive knowledge than any industry in our survey. One industry source says, "The ideal sales rep in this field is an R.N. with an MBA in marketing." And he isn't kidding.

Company support of sales representatives in the pharmaceutical industry is spotty and varies according to the company and the type of support or computer-based management provided. Representatives usually work out of their homes where they must perform many office chores for themselves. Because of this lack of office and clerical support, none of the major drug companies listed in our survey's top five received a support rank of 5.

Support is also spotty in the critical area of on-the-job training. Such training is standard in the industry, and each company listed in our survey does train its new representatives. However, in some cases the support is really a catch-as-catch-can situation in which the rep is left to his or her own devices because scheduled rounds with other reps or managers are canceled. This is not to imply that the companies, managers, or representatives are lax. It is simply a reflection of the fact that the bottom line is the sale—as it is in all industries—and that if the district manager must make a choice of helping to close a potentially large sale or training a new sales representative, the new representative loses out on that particular day. In the area of compensation, Merck, with an average compensation of $30,000 (including bonus), stands out above all of the others, and for that reason it is ranked at the top of the industry. Although Merck received a [−] in the intangibles category, we believe that the problem, as we explain below, will be short-term, and that Merck will continue to warrant the high regard of its reps, just as it has in the past.

The remainder of the companies all fall within the same general compensation range of $28,000 to $30,000. However, Eli Lilly and Pfizer are tied for the number-two ranking because of their reputations for excellent training. Squibb is ranked next because of its [+] in intangibles, and G.D. Searle is ranked fifth because of its [−] in intangibles.

PHARMACEUTICALS	COMPENSATION	SALARY	BONUS	SUPPORT	INTANGIBLE
1 Merck & Co., Inc.	5	5	5	3	−
2 Eli Lilly and Co.	4	4	4	4	
2 Pfizer Inc.	4	4	4	4	
3 Squibb Corp.	4	4	4	3	+
4 The Upjohn Co.	4	4	4	3	
5 G. D. Searle & Co.	4	4	4	3	−

The industry median compensation for a second-year sales rep is $27,700, which includes a salary of $22,000 and bonus of $5,700.

Merck & Co., Inc. [−]
The Patent Restoration Bill is likely to affect Merck negatively in the short term because other companies are likely to manufacture generic equivalents of some of Merck's biggest selling drugs such as Aldomet. However, we believe that any diminished sales resulting from this situation will be short-lived and that Merck will continue to be the industry standard for sales reps.

E.R. Squibb & Sons [+]
The parent company, Squibb Corporation, has taken—and is in the process of taking—steps to enhance the corporate position of their pharmaceutical arm, E.R. Squibb & Sons. Increased spending in R&D, the willingness of management to look favorably upon acquisitions, and the recent favorable FDA ruling regarding Capoten, one of their top-selling drugs, are among the factors that make the outlook for Squibb sales reps quite favorable.

G.D. Searle & Co. [−]
As much as Squibb Corporation is favoring the pharmaceutical side of the corporation, Searle seems to be losing interest in theirs. It appears that management wishes to further diversify the corporation, and there are even rumors of a buy-out of the company. None of this extracurricular news is likely to have the sales force sleeping any better at night.

SECTION FOUR:
HEAVY INDUSTRY

AEROSPACE

BUILDING

INDUSTRIAL
CHEMICALS

HEAVY
MACHINERY

PAPER

PRINTING

AEROSPACE

THE TOP FIVE:

1 The Boeing Company
2 McDonnell Douglas Corp.
3 General Dynamics Corp.
4 Lockheed Corp.
5 Grumman Corp.

L ike the automobile industry, the aerospace industry is a product of the 20th century. Beginning with the first powered flight in a heavier-than-air craft in 1903, the aerospace industry has changed just about every facet of life on this planet. The dream of powered flight has so inspired inventors and developers that only 65 years after the first flight from the sand dunes at Kitty Hawk, pilots were navigating over the craters of the moon. The aerospace industry has also changed the way war is waged. And as this chapter shows, the combined aerospace and defense industries, while not as large as some of the other industries in our survey, tend to involve a greater percentage of national budgets than any other single industry in *Selling at the Top.*

Selling an F-15, even last year's stripped-down model without the Electronic Countermeasures package, or a brand spanking new ready-to-launch cruise missile topped off with the latest in neutron warheads, is not quite the same thing as moving the last '85 Chevy off the showroom floor. The process of selling in the defense industry is heavily dependent on regulations and procedures supplied by the Department of Defense. These are codified in the Defense Acquisition Regulations (DAR), supplied by the Pentagon, which establish the procedures to be followed in the process of bidding on defense contracts. The volumes of the Defense Acquisition Regulations are measured not in pages but in pounds; and are specific, precise, and meant to cover every possible contingency that might arise when a weapons development proposal is prepared and submitted to the United States government. The DAR is the defense industry's bible and a must for any representative of a company involved in the manufacture of weapons systems. The breadth and specificity of the DAR point to the fact that the Department of Defense not only is concerned about how it acquires new weapons; it also must worry about how company representatives use their influence in the United States military and in the houses of Congress, and how weapons development deals are negotiated and pushed through the swamps of administrative and legislative committees. This process of weapons acquisition is also designed to protect United States military technology and all the associated classified information. As a result, the Defense Acquisitions Regulations make the sales of aerospace products and weapons a complex and sensitive issue.

As anyone might imagine, the defense segment of the aerospace and defense industry is shrouded in secrecy and politics. A representative selling weapons systems simply doesn't call on the Saudis, in the same way a magazine salesman might knock on the door of a ranch house in Shaker Heights. There are layers upon layers of clearances needed just to be able to bid on certain projects, and the complexity doesn't end there, since virtually all bids are subcontracted out many times. Donald Westervelt, the president of a small technical consulting firm in the Midwest, says, "In order to even be eligible to bid on subcontracting work, I personally had to get Top Secret clearance. The process is very complex and very time consuming. It appears designed so that only those who really need it will persevere long enough to get it." How did Donald get his? "I was sponsored by one of our client firms. We've done quite a bit of technical consulting for this particular engineering firm, and they knew we were excellent at what we do. They needed us on a contract they were creating for General Dynamics." So Donald applied for Top Secret clearance and was given the DOD's clearance check. Donald reports: "I have a grandfather who is eighty-nine years old and is in a nursing home in a small town in Illinois. When he was younger he had a few minor skirmishes with the law. Although they didn't talk to my grandfather, they did visit the nursing home and talk to the staff." In researching Donald Westervelt's background, the DOD's security people examined every aspect of his life and the lives of his family.

Regarding Top Secret clearance, an industry source says, "You have to understand that the government takes those things relating to national defense very seriously. If you had a bedwetting problem when you were five they'll find out about it, and some psychiatrist will be given that information for analysis as part of the applicant's personality profile." Donald adds, "After I got clearance, my company then had to comply with a slew of federal regulations, some of which were related to security and some to federal employment laws." How difficult was compliance? "Not very, since we were quite small at the time, with only ten employees, and the federal

> *"In this business, you frequently have to shoot from the hip. And Lockheed has a pretty good hipshot."*

employment laws tend to focus on large companies. The most amazing part of the regulations was that we had to purchase a specially constructed file cabinet for all documents related to the project." The file cabinet costs $1,000 per unit and is manufactured by only one firm in the country which is based in Washington, D.C.

"Sometimes 'Top Secret' gets misused," according to Allen Tryock, the general manager of a technical consulting firm in Cambridge, Massachusetts. "When I was working as an engineer for a major defense contractor, we all had Top Secret clearance, which meant that we could classify documents as being Top Secret so only another person with Top Secret clearance would be able to see the contents. When an engineer was rushed on a particular writeup he was doing, he would classify the project Top Secret so that no one but another engineer would be likely to see that he screwed up." Our Washington analyst agrees. "Sure these kinds of minor abuses go on, but who cares? No one gets hurt by the practice. The main issue with regard to Top Secret documents is that the ones that should legitimately have Top Secret designations do." And Donald adds, "We had so much stuff marked Top Secret, that if a spy broke in and stole all the Top Secret documents, he'd never know in a million years what was important and what wasn't. The system engineers who were inappropriately classifying documents Top Secret actually worked as a pretty effective scheme to protect the real thing."

The health and financial strength of the aerospace and defense industries are directly related to the political climate of the moment. And, as any student of national affairs knows, the political climate can change faster and more often than the physical climate. On the positive side, however, industry analysts in general agree that there is reason to expect greater than usual stability in the industry. This is due in large part to a strong grassroots movement nationwide supporting a philosophy of a strong defense. Analysts believe that this grassroots support will be sufficiently powerful to maintain a stable political environment for the industry as a whole through at least the next presidential election. It's been pointed out that even with all the pressure placed on the candidates in the last presidential election to cut defense spending, the DOD received budget approval at an increase of an adjusted 6.9 percent over the preceding year.

Selling in the defense industry is quite different from most other kinds of selling in that the seller usually does not have a product to sell when the buyer—in all cases the government—is interested in making a purchase. For example, at General Dynamics, our number-three ranked company, all three branches of the military are customers. The typical scenario involving the sale of a product is explained by Kevin Kendall, a company representative and spokesman. "The Air Force will decide that in twelve to fifteen years they will need a new fighter aircraft. They put out a Request For Proposals (RFP) to defense contractors. The defense contractors submit preliminary proposals, and based on these, the DOD narrows the field to two or three competing companies." Kevin adds, "This is when the money really starts rolling in." The preliminary proposal submitted by a defense contractor explains how the company will respond to the government's specifications—the weapon's mission as defined by the RFP from the Department of Defense—including what the proposed weapon will accomplish relative to the specified mission, a preliminary production cost schedule and line analysis, and a preliminary production timetable. An industry analyst remarks, "Much of what a defense contractor submits as a preliminary proposal may contain more fiction than a romance novel, but it serves an important purpose. First, it focuses DOD thinking about a weapons system, and second, it lets the DOD know how many companies can play in the ballpark. The top companies—and this, too, may be a political decision—get their preliminary development funding. And believe me, if you're a defense contractor and you can get past the preliminaries, you may not win big, but you won't lose."

Another industry source points out: "Getting past the preliminary proposal is no guarantee you'll actually get the bid. And even if you do win it, you may wind up working on only 20 percent of the project." She was referring to the DOD policy of having companies bid against each other and then awarding portions of a contract based on the submitted bids. As is anticipated with the Army's massive LHX helicopter project, it's not uncommon for two or more companies to be working on the same project.

Peter Phelan, a technical adviser with General Dynamics' Electric Boat Division, points out another aspect of the bidding process: "You know, we don't just go and submit a bid to build a Trident submarine." An industry source emphasizes, "A company may have over thirty bids under consideration at one time, and if all the bids are awarded, they may not build more than 40 percent of their project, whether it's the Trident or the B-1 bomber."

Because the nature of defense products is so highly technical, it's not at all unusual to have over 100 manufacturers and subcontractors contributing to the construction of a final product. One exception to this is one of the largest defense contractors and our number-three rated company, General Dynamics.

Boeing, the Seattle-based industry giant, has earned our number-one spot in the survey primarily due to its strong position in both the military and the commercial areas. One industry source estimates that in the decade beginning with 1982, Boeing will deliver over 3,600 commercial jetliners, with a value of $120 billion, as measured in 1982 dollars. The same source says, "Boeing is truly a remarkable company. They have managed to maintain a strong position in the development of military aircraft and weapons systems, while developing into the number-one commercial jetliner manufacturer on earth. They have outshone their competition time and time again."

Richard Thompson, a Boeing engineer, says, "The company is extremely market conscious. They work very closely with their customers." And it's not at all unusual for the top engineers to be moved from military to commercial projects. "It's one reason why I love working at Boeing. I get to work on a very wide range of things. At other companies, I'd be on the same project for three years." At Boeing, Richard found himself shuttled between two different projects. "As an example, I worked on the E-3 AWACS project for six months, and then I was pulled off to help with the 767." By using groups of engineers in this manner, Boeing is able to indirectly use some of the military funding from the government for commercial development projects such as the 767.

"On my next trip to Seattle, I'm going to buy every damn engineer in the place a drink!" So said a passenger on a TWA Boeing 727 that ran into some mechanical difficulty on a flight to Detroit. The plane was cruising at an altitude of 39,000 feet when suddenly the pilots noticed a strong vibration coming from the tail section. They immediately flashed the "Seat Belt" sign when, according to a TWA spokesperson, "The aircraft nosed down and started plummeting." The plane had done two complete rolls along its longitudinal axis and went out of control in a dive, which, said the TWA spokesperson, "very few people ever live to tell about." In a frantic effort to control the plane, which by then was traveling at better than 700 miles per hour, the captain engaged the air brakes, which were promptly sheared off. With the plane now diving at more than 1,000 feet per second, he frantically lowered the flaps in an attempt to slow down the plane and gain control. Another TWA pilot said, "It was like spitting into the wind," and not only did the flaps rip right off the wing, they landed on a farm in Tennessee, hundreds of miles away. By this time, the plane had blasted through the sound barrier and was losing altitude at a rate of 1,100 feet for every second this nightmare lasted. Richard Thompson comments: "That was completely incredible. We test our aircraft well beyond any condition that the aircraft is ever going to encounter, and I can tell you that a 727 simply can't go that fast without disintegrating, even though I know it didn't." In a last-ditch, desperation effort, the captain lowered the plane's landing gear. The gear held firm and the friction produced by the lowered landing gear assembly slowed the plane sufficiently for the captain to regain control. Before the plane was stabilized, it had fallen 12,000 feet in twelve seconds. After the captain landed the plane safely and the passengers were deplaning, one woman was heard to say: "Thank God we're all safe." To which one of the

> ". . . one of the crew members was heard to respond, while pointing to the captain: 'Yeah. Thank God, thank him, and thank Boeing. And not necessarily in that order.' "

crew members was heard to respond, while pointing to the captain: "Yeah. Thank God, thank him, and thank Boeing. And not necessarily in that order." Wendell Simpson, a consulting aeronautical engineer based in St. Louis, comments on the TWA story: "I spoke to a few engineers about what happened, and I'll tell you this: I'm never flying in anything but a Boeing aircraft again."

A spokesperson for American Airlines, which flies Boeing's 727 and 767 aircraft, says, "They are super marketeers. When they were pitching their new aircraft, the 767s, we mentioned in passing that one of the things we had to put on the negotiating table was financing arrangements. One week later they showed up with a banker from Citicorp." Commenting on the American Airlines deal, an industry source explains that most carriers lease rather than purchase their aircraft because it ties up less cash and makes the carriers less vulnerable to fluctuations in the economy and in the price of jet fuel. "It was Boeing," he explains, "that was instrumental in developing and arranging the commercial airlines lease project."

Boeing's position on the military side of the aerospace/defense industry is also very strong, with contracts to manufacture such diverse military items as the CH-46 and 47 helicopters, the E-3 AWACS and E-4 Command Post surveillance and fire-control aircraft—the type that was recently sold to the Saudis and is on station in the Persian Gulf—Minuteman ICBMs, and portions of the Titan III booster rocket used on the space shuttle.

The future also looks good for Boeing's marketing representatives, as the company's abilities and influence in the domestic and foreign defense and weapons procurement community continue to grow. Boeing is being considered for the $20 billion Pentagon contract for an advanced bomber. In addition, on the commercial side, carriers such as Delta, American, and United have long-term contracts with Boeing. These are carriers which in 1983 flew 86 billion passenger miles, and which, according to industry projections, will be flying a quarter-trillion passenger miles by 1995. And they'll be looking to Boeing to supply the aircraft. Offering further testimonial to Boeing's domination of the commercial jetliner industry, at the end of 1983, Boeing's backlog of commercial aircraft orders worth over $10 billion to Boeing represented nearly 80 percent of the backlog for the whole industry.

St. Louis-based McDonnell Douglas, which reported total 1984 sales figures of nearly $10 billion, has earned our number-two rank primarily for their demonstrated excellence in the military arena, supplying McDonnell Douglas with more than two-thirds of its sales. Although McDonnell Douglas is certainly a major manufacturer of commercial jetliners, they are not in Boeing's league in this segment of the market. Boeing derives more than two-thirds of its sales from the private or commercial sector of the aerospace industry, providing aircraft to most of the world's major carriers. McDonnell Douglas, while a major player to be sure, has lost ground to Boeing over the past twenty-five years.

An industry source, commenting on McDonnell Douglas's history in commercial aviation, says, "The DC-10 is a good example of 'What do you call a horse designed by a committee? A camel.' " He is referring to the fact that the DC-10 was originally designed as a medium-range aircraft with the ability to take off and land on shorter runways than the other jumbo jets would need. This meant that DC-10s could, for example, fly into New York

City's La Guardia Airport, while the 747 could not, and thus had to be routed to the harder-to-get-to JFK. However, on the way to becoming a horse, something happened. Boeing released the 747, and the powers that be at McDonnell Douglas decided to capitalize on the similarities in load capacity—approximately 450 on the 747 and approximately 350 on the DC-10, depending on specific internal configuration.

With the fuel crisis of the early and mid-1970s, the major aircraft manufacturers' attention turned to smaller, more fuel-efficient aircraft. McDonnell Douglas has been in the thick of the race for a share of the 150-seat jetliner market which, according to an industry source, could reach 2,000 by the mid 1990s. McDonnell Douglas' MD-80 series is very popular with both American and TWA. American, in particular, having expanded its short-haul operation considerably in the Southwest, is using the MD-80s extensively. The same industry source says, "McDonnell Douglas had to cancel their plans for the MD-100 because the players, the major domestic carriers, wanted a different type of aircraft." The MD-100 was designed as a replacement for the DC-10, which McDonnell Douglas is phasing out of the commercial production picture, although they are continuing to produce the military version of the aircraft.

Mainstays of McDonnell Douglas' military fleet include: the F-15 fighter, quickly becoming indispensable to the Israeli air force; the F-18A Hornet, the attack aircraft of the United States fleet; the venerable F-4 Phantom, which dominated the skies over Vietnam and the Middle East for over fifteen years; and the AV-88, C-9, and KC-10 (the military version of the DC-10). The company has a strong history of designing military aircraft, marked by such classics as the C-47/DC-3, which saw action throughout World War II. Currently, MD is a leader in the development of the V/STOL, or vertical/short take-off and landing aircraft, which, according to Wendell Simpson, "will keep MD real busy for some time to come." Wendell adds, "MD is an engineering-driven company. They don't make engineering mistakes." We believe that MD has earned our number-two spot on merit, although as will be indicated in the rankings, we would have ranked the company higher if they had a stronger position in the commercial segment of the market.

St. Louis-based General Dynamics, with 1984 sales reported at $7.8 billion, has earned our number-three ranking for a variety of reasons, all of them centered around a very aggressive management committed to doing things right. GD is known for an extreme dedication to secrecy. One industry source said jokingly: "If you call their main switchboard, you're likely to be greeted by a 'Good morning. May I help you?' without the usual mention of the company name. If you then think you may have a wrong number and inquire, 'Is this General Dynamics?', it's not unusual for the voice on the other end to say, 'And who would like to know?' " A representative for Boeing says, "It's not only GD, it's everyone. This industry only hires people who test out as somewhat paranoid on the personality profiles."

"The strategy at General Dynamics when approaching the defense industry is to hire technical advisers who are familiar with the branches of the armed services to which GD is selling," according to Charles Retton. Charles was an engineering test pilot who was wooed by GD after serving over twenty years in the Navy. When GD decided to make the Navy version of the Air Force F-111, they were looking for men like Charles for a number of reasons. "At that time, in 1963, there were no true sales representatives.

> "This industry only hires people who test out as somewhat paranoid on the personality profiles."

We didn't even have a marketing department." Charles explains that he was hired by General Dynamics because, "I knew the Navy. I knew how the Navy operated and how the system worked. And I knew a lot of people in the Navy."

An industry source comments: "That procedure may sound political to a lot of people, but you need to understand that the aerospace/defense industry must necessarily be political. Although the contracts are awarded by the military services, the purse strings are controlled by Congress and the President." Our source explains that military projects are political not only for their own sake, but for the sake of the subcontracting industries within the congressional districts. If a B-1 bomber or a new class of nuclear submarines is approved by Congress, there may be over fifty different districts affected by the levels of subcontracting that will take place. Because money will be spent on defense projects regardless of the administration, members of the House and the Senate will want the money spent in their states and in their districts. And, our source continues, if the administration wants to put pressure on members of Congress to approve defense packages, it knows how to apply it by dangling money.

This past year has seen a clear lesson in the political nature of the defense industry, with the DOD cutting back its 1984 budget request by $10 billion, from $284 billion to $274 billion. The appropriations committee actually granted a budget sum of $251 billion, less than the increase requested by the DOD. However, there were enough poker chips in the

DOD budget to allow the allocation to be cut back without seriously undermining any new weapons systems development. And the administration was still able to put enough pressure on individual members of Congress to squeak the MX missile through both houses.

General Dynamics has positioned itself very strongly, with its main sales coming from F-111 parts, the F-16 fighter, the Tomahawk cruise missile, the Atlas and Centaur booster rockets, the Trident submarine, and the Phalanx shipboard defense system. GD, according to one source within the industry, was able to demonstrate the value of the Phalanx by pointing to the Falklands war, in which single Exocet missile hits were able to take out the British destroyers which were not protected by computer-controlled radar defense systems. After the British were able to throw their shipboard defense system around their fleet and landing parties, the Exocet missiles were no longer as effective. In addition, GD is the exclusive builder of tanks for the Army.

Charles explains that his role as a company representative is to introduce the company to the system of defense procurement and to introduce his contacts in the Defense Department and the Navy to the people at General Dynamics. It is a normal business relationship. "There is certainly nothing shady about the operation. I am able to open doors for them that they wouldn't be able to open themselves." Charles points out an irony in GD's dealings with the Navy. "They might not have needed me had they not ceased their dealings with the Navy after World War II." GD's Convair Division, based in San Diego, built the PBY Flying Boats, but after the war, they became primarily an Air Force contractor, and as Charles says, "They subsequently lost track of how to do business with the Navy. By the mid to late '60s, General Dynamics had approximately thirty ex-Navy people in important positions in the organization. Some were strictly engineers, but most were in operations."

Charles's job became a de facto sales position. "After a while it became clear that what I was supposed to do was sell to the Navy." And as any military officer can tell you, "That can be a very sticky situation because it's against the law to become involved in any direct sales work involving the military." What did Charles do? "My thinking was, and still is, that I don't sell. The company sold the aircraft. I didn't receive any remuneration for my efforts; that is to say, no commissions and no bonus beyond my salary. I had nothing to do with contractual arrangements." A General Dynamics spokesperson says, "The Company is quite careful not to place anyone in a compromising position. It is made emphatically clear that the ex-Navy people were not to sell so much as a rivet to anybody."

Robert Poole, a retired GD engineer, says, "The ex-Navy guys that GD hired were able to talk about the technical stuff to the guys in the Navy's technical bureaus and operational areas. How was the company going to be able to sell a plane without having technical representatives call on the buyer?" An industry source explains: "There are a lot of rules that get bent, and not only in this industry. Anybody with an IQ greater than his shoe size has got to realize that in any industry, selling has to be done by the people who know the buyers. In the defense industry, that's ex-military men." However, as Charles says, "You have to be very careful not to step on someone's toes, because if anyone makes an issue of ex-officers working in a quasi-sales environment, the result can be loss of military pension." Robert agrees: "It also puts the ex-officers in an uncomfortable position. They tend to be very direct individuals who are not given to subtlety. They tend to run into trouble when politics get in the way."

If the ex-officers who made the contacts with the military were not actually selling or closing a sale, who was? Charles says, "The engineers who were involved with the actual development and design of the aircraft were the real market people." And Robert adds: "Today, as you might expect, General Dynamics—as is the case with the other large defense contractors—has a very large marketing department." And not surprisingly, "with a very knowledgeable political arm."

Domestic weapons sales are only one side of the picture. Most of the major defense contractors make a sizable portion of their money by selling approved weapons to foreign governments. And in many cases, the weapons sales to friendly governments support development of weapons in the United States. Foreign governments buy American weapons that they know will be supported by purchases of those same weapons by the American military. One industry analyst says, "Foreign sales are a very lucrative aspect of the aerospace/defense industry." But Charles remarks, "It wasn't always that way. In the mid '60s, we sold twenty-four F-111s to the Australians, and that was a big sale at the time." As Robert Poole points out, General Dynamics led the industry in some very innovative marketing concepts when it came to overseas sales. "When GD developed the F-16 fighter, they approached England and France with a proposal for a joint production agreement." Of course, the Air Force and the State Department had to first give their blessings, and as Robert says, "They did so with glee. It reduced the development costs for the aircraft tremendously."

The joint production concept, which was later jumped on by virtually every major defense contractor, was quite a bonanza for all concerned. "The Air Force got their F-16s at a lower cost per unit because the foreign governments were picking up part of the tab. The foreign governments were tickled pink because they were getting a very sophisticated aircraft that they would never have been able to develop themselves. And GD was happy because they had the widest possible market for the aircraft, at a reduced cost per unit." According to Charles, "Congress was also very happy with the concept. Congress congratulated the Air Force for the cost savings, and General Dynamics really had favorite son status with a lot of politicians, both military and non-military." An industry analyst thinks the kudos are insufficient. "The F-16 project was one of the only projects I know that came in under budget, on time, and met all the performance requirements. It was a magnificent feat of project management."

The joint venture concept is quite common in the industry today because it minimizes the up-front R&D costs. Robert Poole says, "The F-16 program is really a milestone in the industry. The Air Force has very strict requirements on aircraft performance and very strict rules governing procedures of development and testing. GD, in effect, said, 'We'll do it.' And they did: better, faster, and cheaper than anyone ever dreamed, and in the process came up with a new marketing concept which is still used today." An Air Force spokesperson says, "Not only was the project a reflection of outstanding project management, but the aircraft is to this day the best single-engine fighter in the world, although it has been modernized with some very sophisticated computer guidance systems."

Although General Dynamics' current procurement controversy, drops them from an unchallenged number-one position to number-three in our rating, we think, nevertheless, that the future looks bright for GD's marketing representatives. There is no product competing against the Air Force F-16 fighter in the near future or against the Trident missile-launching submarines. Foreign purchases of the F-16 are expected to remain high, especially in light of Israel's highly successful deployment of the aircraft

> "... the aerospace/defense industry must necessarily be political. Although the contracts are awarded by the military services, the purse strings are controlled by Congress and the President."

against the Soviet-supplied Syrian air force in the skies over Lebanon. As an indication of the trend toward increased foreign sales, GD announced that Greece recently contracted to purchase forty of the aircraft at a price close to $2 billion. In addition, eleven other nations have agreed to purchase the

F-16 as their front-line attack aircraft, and the Air Force is still taking delivery on 2,000 F-16s. GD has also built up its tank division, acquired from Chrysler in 1982, and looks forward to supplying the Army with its main battle tank well into the 1990s.

As is customary in the industry among the large defense contractors, GD's marketing representatives work on a salary basis, with performance bonuses. However, the aerospace/defense industry is not a commission-based industry for marketing reps.

California's Lockheed Corporation has earned our number-four ranking primarily because of its very strong position with the military and its recent efforts at expansion into electronics. Lockheed derived over 80 percent of its 1984 sales figure of $8 billion from U.S. Government contracts.

Roy Ward, a Lockheed marketing representative, says, "This business of defense contracting is not for the weak of heart. It's very easy for a company to get hurt very badly through no fault of its own." The defense budget system is one problem with which Roy has learned to live. "Plans for a five-year defense program are reviewed and updated each year," he reports. Does that pose a problem for defense contractors? "Not in and of itself. It's the review process that can be maddening. The three branches of the armed services, the President, and the Congress all contribute to the decision making process at various stages."

And the process, particularly in election years, can be extremely complicated. The budget process begins with the Defense Resources Board, which is composed of members of the three branches of the armed forces and the office of the Secretary of Defense. Roy explains: "Their job is to present an overview of the defense structure—you might call it the 'concept of defense.' After the overview at this policy-study level, the recommendations go to the Office of Management and Budget, the Treasury, and the President's Council of Economic Advisers. The job at this level is to make modifications before the final budget goes to the President, who then modifies the budget requests further before passing them along to the Congress." An industry analyst adds: "The process is not unlike one of Rube Goldberg's contraptions." After the administration has finished its work, Roy explains, the real politics begin. "Hearings are held with the House and Senate budget committees, the Armed Services Committees, the Joint Chiefs, the OMB, and the Secretary of each branch of the military." And what finally comes tumbling out of each administrative and legislative committee is a budget resolution to which the armed services are committed as a ceiling for the authorization bill.

The authorization bill is a piece of legislation which sets the level of what's called total obligational authority or TOA. TOA, it turns out, is the authority to issue funds for specific projects, but not all funds issued are necessarily spent. At the end of all this negotiation and allocation of funds, one might well ask: where does this leave Lockheed? Roy Ward answers, "In the same place it leaves all the major defense contractors. They take on the monumental task of having to guesstimate what the hell is going to be going on politically and how that is going to impact on the various programs." In other words, just because a contract has been awarded to Lockheed and a budget amount has been allocated to develop a specific weapons system, that doesn't mean the weapon will ever reach final development stages. The project will be inserted into the administration's budget, funds will be deleted by one House committee, reinserted by a Senate committee, and pushed back and forth across the table by a joint congressional committee meeting to iron out the differences between the House and Senate versions of a funding package. At some point during the legislative process the marketing representatives from the different defense contractors will get to make their pitch before the committee, and representatives from the different branches of the armed services who are desperate for this particular weapons system will get to make their pitch. Finally, if the administration is willing to turn up the heat and admit that it really wants the allocation, it will trot out the Secretary of Defense himself to make the pitch. If the particular allocation can survive the political process, it will make it to the House and Senate floors, where it will eventually be voted on for passage.

As an example, Richard Wohl, a planning engineer at a New York-based advanced technical multiple systems firm and a writer for *Defense Science 2002+*, has indicated that the Soviet nuclear submarine fleet may be more sophisticated than has been assumed by United States defense strategists and Soviet specialists. This kind of research, from one of the most respected journalists in the field, can and often does influence budgetary decisions. Roy Ward says, "That is exactly right. As a matter of fact, Lockheed was recently awarded a contract to speed up the development of the Trident II." The Trident II is a strategic fleet ballistic missile which is the grandson of the original submarine missile, the Polaris. Roy continues, "We have no way of knowing whether research of the kind that Richard Wohl does has an effect on the budget process, or if it does, how much. In this business, you frequently have to shoot from the hip. And Lockheed has a pretty good hipshot."

The future for Lockheed's representatives looks quite rosy. On performance alone, they are putting themselves in a very strong position as a versatile manufacturer of basic as well as more elaborate computer-managed military weapons systems. Even if the political climate should change after the 1988 presidential election, we feel strongly that Lockheed would still be in a strong position. The Milstar communications contract is just one indication that the company is being recognized as an industry leader in high-tech communications, and the fact that Lockheed's backlog of negotiated contracts at the end of 1984 stood at somewhere over the $20 billion mark bodes quite well for the company's continued growth.

Grumman Corporation, a Long Island-based defense contractor with 1984 sales at just over $2.5 billion, is the number-one supplier of carrier-based aircraft. As one industry analyst says, "Carrier-based defense is usually a well-regarded segment of the military budget." Most analysts see an increased role for carrier-based aircraft, especially in situations like the Lebanese civil war, in which a United States military presence was deemed necessary but for which no land-based fortification was available. The Falklands war also demonstrated the continued importance of carrier-based aircraft for support of landing operations. Grumman's sales, demonstrating the reliance the United States military has placed on naval

> *"My thinking was, and still is, that I don't sell. The company sold the aircraft. I didn't receive any remuneration for my efforts; no commissions and no bonus beyond my salary. I had nothing to do with contractual agreements."*

aircraft, have increased by nearly $250 million from 1982 to 1983; over $400 million from 1983 to 1984, and are projected to increase by nearly $750 million in 1985.

Regina Gonda of Grumman comments on military contracts: "There are basically two types: cost-reimbursement and fixed-price." And the type of contract chosen can make all the difference in the world to the contractors. "With cost-reimbursement contracts, the contractor is paid for costs plus a fee for performing the services." Grumman got burned with overruns on their X-29A project. "We had a fixed-price contract with the Air Force for the demonstrator model of the X-29A, which is used to demonstrate ultrasophisticated guidance systems. However, in the development of this type of aircraft, what we've really done is invest in the future." An industry analyst agrees: "When they supply a big chunk of R&D money like that, the armed services committees tend to smile at you when the next big projects come along." Grumman's strong position is due largely to the mainstays of its fleet: the F-14 supersonic fighter, the EA-6B Prowler, the EF-111, and the A-6E Intruder. Grumman is expanding into electronic component systems, and this creates a stronger base for the company in an increasingly sophisticated and automation-oriented marketplace.

In the aerospace/defense industry, our prototypical marketing representative has three years' experience instead of the usual two years assumed in other industries. Our research indicates that three years is the minimum time for a representative to become fully established in this industry because of its myriad complexities.

AEROSPACE	COMPENSATION	COMMISSION	SUPPORT	INTANGIBLE
1 The Boeing Company	4		5	
2 McDonnell Douglas Corp.	4		5	–
3 General Dynamics Corp.	4		5	–
4 Lockheed Corp.	4		5	–
5 Grumman Corp.	4		5	

The median compensation figure is $32,100, and this includes salary and bonus. There is no commission paid in the aerospace/defense industry.

McDonnell Douglas and Lockheed [−]
As mentioned earlier, both companies are heavily dependent on military contracts, and we feel that their position in this area could be stronger. For example, Grumman has a market niche—carrier-based aircraft—which is a favorite of the armed forces budget committees. We feel that McDonnell Douglas and Lockheed are excessively vulnerable to politically motivated budget cutbacks, and this is something that marketing reps need to investigate closely.

General Dynamics [−]
We had previously ranked General Dynamics number one in the industry, but due to the negative publicity surrounding their contract problems with the DOD, we had to drop them two positions in the rankings.

BUILDING

THE TOP FIVE:

1 Blount, Inc.
2 Koger Properties, Inc.
3 Pulte Home Corp.
4 U.S. Home Corp.
5 Kaufman and Broad, Inc.

T he demand for housing and office space has not only fueled the real estate industry over the past three years, it has fueled the building industry as well. As interest rates have dropped and more and more businesses have started up, the need for office and light industrial buildings has almost doubled on both coasts. And as light industrial parks have sprung up out of the soybean and corn fields, so have housing developments, townhouses, and apartment complexes. There is a whole generation of growing families now on the move for larger homes and apartments, and the current boom in new construction is partly the result of this growing affluence. While the flow of money is supported by the market and the interest rates, this is a good time for the construction industries.

Can you imagine going into your local department store and ordering a couch, a TV, and a new condominium apartment? That sounds far-fetched, even for science fiction, but according to one industry source, there are people in California who are doing just that. Barrett Developments, a homebuilding company based in Great Britain, has contracted with Sears to sell complete condo packages in selected California retail outlets. "Now," according to one Barrett representative, "you can shop for your furniture and your condo while you have your muffler checked and your tires rotated."

"I've heard of one-stop banking, but this is crazy," a Sears shopper remarked upon seeing the Barrett display. Jillian Baxter, a Barrett representative in California, explains, "The concept is going over quite well. Granted, many people stare at us in disbelief, and we've heard more than a few chortles, but we're also selling our packages." Barrett has packaged the condo, the furnishings, and the financing into a tidy one-stop package. Another industry source says, "It's not that crazy an idea when you consider how many builders have gotten into the financial package or mortgage market in order to sell their buildings and houses. They have to move product just like the car dealers, and if GM can offer financing as part of the inducement to buy, why can't the building developers?" He adds: "These guys have just taken the concept a few steps further. And it's obvious they've done their homework because they're using Sears and marketing in California." He was referring to the fact that Sears, our number-five ranked company in the retailing industry, seems to be determined to sell everything that can be packaged as a unit from within its department store or catalog retail operation. Bob Crenna, a Sears manager in California, says, "It's now theoretically possible for a customer to come in, buy a furnished condo, arrange for the financing, insure their new property at the Sears Allstate booth, and before leaving the store, set up a solid financial planning portfolio at our Sears Coldwell Banker offices." Jillian remarks: "Sears was a natural for us because of their eagerness to expand their operation." And Bob Crenna smiles and says, "And of course, the furnishings for the condo come from our catalog."

While the Sears department store concept of selling residences is certainly unique, the concept of packaging all the ingredients which go into a housing unit sale is not. Ken Rutledge, a builder located in Houston, says, "The homebuilding market is becoming extremely competitive. With interest rates jumping all over the place, it can be a very nerve-racking experience trying to build and furnish a house." He adds: "The builders who are successful are the ones who make it as easy as possible for the customer." Karen Maxwell, a sales representative for U.S. Home, our number-four ranked company, agrees. "For the first time, small builders are competing with us on an equal footing. A small builder can make a nice profit if he's willing to be a broker in order to work with the banks and the home furnishings people."

"I'm as much a middleman as I am a builder," says William Roberts, a builder in Dallas. "My business was going right down the toilet in '82, and I thought I'd be selling used cars within the year." But William had the good fortune to bump into a marketing specialist. "Talk about fate. He overheard me at a party complaining about business. He called me aside and told me that he specializes in solving business problems like mine."

William's problems were not unique in 1982, when builders nationwide found themselves in a crisis situation. The money spent on the construction of new, single-family homes dropped by 25 percent from 1979 to 1980 ($60.8 billion to $45.7 billion), and another 23 percent from 1980 to 1982 ($45.7 billion to $35.7 billion). One industry analyst says, "The bottom fell out for a lot of these builders. Many of them had mortgaged themselves to the hilt in the boom years from 1975 to 1977, and the bubble not only

> "Someone coming to us for a home could take care of all his needs right on the spot. And business really took off."

burst, it damn well exploded!" Construction was a boom industry in the mid '70s, with the dollars spent on new, single-family homes doubling from $27.4 billion in 1975 to a 1977 high of $55.3 billion. The same analyst adds: "What happened in the construction industry was not too much different from Black Friday in 1929. Everybody and his uncle were buying equipment and expanding, and newcomers were mortgaging their own homes and starting construction businesses. Anybody who could lift a hammer was jumping into the construction business. And most of the new players didn't last even a year. The construction market collapse was the most dramatic in memory. Annual sales were nearly cut in half in the bear market of 1978 to 1982." A spokesman for the National Association of Homebuilders confirms the industrywide disaster: "Membership in the association dropped by 20,000 in that period." So in 1982, having managed to hold on "by the grace of God and some understanding banks," William was ready to call it quits when he bumped into his "guardian angel" at the party.

It is generally agreed among psychiatrists that moving generates a high level of stress. Thus it was not unusual that William and his guardian angel found that people wanted someone to handle the whole moving business for them, from soup to nuts. So it was back to the bank. "I'd been there so often in the last few years that some people thought I was an officer," William said. But this time, he had a marketable idea. "I sold the bank on entering into a partnership with me and a few builder buddies of mine. The bank would handle the mortgage on the property and the house, and we would take care of the building. We contracted with plumbers, electricians, and architects, so that we offered a complete package for people. Someone coming to us for a home could take care of all his needs right on the spot." And business really took off. "We started doing so well that we expanded both the operation and the concept. We started offering furnished homes. We contracted with two local furniture outlets to furnish our homes at a nice discount off their list prices. People felt like they were getting a bargain, and we were getting 5 percent on every piece of furniture we sold." And the bank even got into the act. "They had the idea of offering mortgages to the people who were buying the homes that our buyers were selling, thereby making it easier for our buyers to unload their present homes. So the bank was into the mortgage market on both ends: buying and selling."

After a while, William Roberts and his partners had become so successful that the banks themselves started competing with one another in offering financial packages. "Things got so good that we were approached by other banks to work with them, and we wound up getting between two and five points on the mortgages." William explains that it was the financial packaging that seemed to have made the difference to the prospective home buyers. He points out that most individuals and young families view getting the first mortgage package as the biggest hurdle to buying a house or condominium. Once that hurdle is past, the housing unit itself is the investment that often induces banks to offer the next mortgage, and the mortgage after that.

Dave Doman, a manager at Citicorp, our number-one rated banking and finance institution, says, "The Southwest, particularly Texas cities like Houston and Dallas, were real hotbeds of activity. A lot of the state banks there were in some hot water due to their oil-backed loans, and they really jumped at the opportunities that the builders were presenting." He adds, "It was not at all uncommon for the banks to offer the builders some points on the mortgages they brought in." And some banks became very creative. "They also got into leasing. With the building boom getting into full swing, many small builders were undercapitalized for the kind of operation they wanted to run, so the banks held leases on their equipment, and the builders were able to maintain a more liquid cash position." He concludes: "The banks became very aggressive and really helped fuel the building boom down there." And as a consequence, William reports, business became very strong. "We had to hire a full-time staff just to handle the paperwork. We added four people to show demo houses, and we bought a $40,000 computer system."

The residential and commercial construction industry, more than most industries, is affected by the economy and swings wildly according to fluctuations in the interest rate. With a prevailing mortgage rate of 14 per-cent, new home construction suffers, but when rates dip below 13 percent, there is a resurgence. Commercial building is also affected by interest rates, but there are enough government-backed programs and state-administered office and plant construction programs in existence that the most damaging effects of spiraling money rates is mitigated somewhat. Nevertheless, because of the extreme dependence of the construction industry on the cost of money, our ratings of the top building and construc-tion companies took into careful consideration the company's ability to withstand the cyclical fluctuations that have become a natural part of the construction industry. Each one of our top five companies—Blount, Koger, U.S. Home, Pulte, and Kaufman and Broad—has earned its position by being able to protect itself from the gyrating market.

While the building and construction industry, according to one analyst, "was being slapped silly," and builders were faring as well as ski shops in Miami, it was no accident that Blount, Inc., an Alabama-based company, saw annual sales rise at a 2 percent clip. A modest increase to be sure, but far superior to the havoc that was being wreaked on the smaller companies in the industry. In part, Blount succeeds by being big enough to compete in the lucrative municipal and large commercial construction market. Even in the slowest of economic cycles, the fact is that cities, count-ies, and states still put out bids for construction projects, if only to provide jobs. Therefore, a company's ability to bring down these major government building contracts is a natural insulator against slowdowns in the private construction market. Blount has demonstrated that it has this ability.

The primary requirement for any company wishing to compete for government construction is the ability to respond to the request for bids. "Just for openers, the bidding process itself is really complex," according to Bryan Dundee, a representative for Blount in Houston. Blount was recently awarded the bid for the Houston Convention Center, and Brian explains the bidding process for this project: "The first step is that the city of Houston puts out a pre-bid for the proposed convention center. The purpose of the pre-bid is so that the people who are funding the project, whether it's a municipality such as Houston or a private group, will have an idea of what the cost of the project will be. Our people, along with about two dozen other outfits, take a long, hard look at the plans for the project, and we submit a pre-bid. It's a tentative bid, and no one is locked into a final number at this point. After that, things can get very hectic. The bids are sealed so you know that you have to give it your best shot. There will be no negotiation." Bryan explains that Blount follows standard industry practices and assembles its pre-bid from the bids it has already put out to subcontractors who want to be hired for the project. "The subcontractors supply quite a bit of the inside work, such as the windows, doors, partitions, the frames around the work of the plumbing and electrical subs, and pretty much the whole interior of the center." And then? "After we get the bids from subcontractors, we put our bid together, including the subcontracting costs."

Even for large subcontractors, the bidding process can be difficult and subcontractors are often in a more precarious position than the contractor. While the contractor can sometimes find another sub to handle a specific job, the subcontractor has to be sure of his labor supply and labor costs down to the last dollar before submitting the bid. If the subcontractor's bid is too low, he may be locked into a final figure that guarantees him no profit. His only options might be to forgo the profit and perform the work, or back out of the project and lose credibility; neither of which he wants to do if he plans to continue doing business with major contractors. The subcontractor also has to prepare his bid quickly if he wants to stay competitive, especially if the contractor is facing considerable pressure in putting together a bid for a major civic landmark project like the Houston Convention Center.

When the time frame for new building construction contracts is very narrow, as it often is in municipal or state projects that must have legislative

Even in the slowest of economic cycles, the fact is that cities, counties, and states still put out bids for construction projects, if only to provide jobs.

or bond authority approval, subcontractors must have a way to develop their bids quickly and change those bids if the specifications of the project change. Gary Cummings, one of the subcontractors bidding on the center, explains how it's done. "We've developed a computer software program to help us with the bids. Before we got on the computer, bidding used to tie up our office for days at a time. Now we can crank out a bid in three hours from start to finish." Bryan adds, "Computers are invaluable in doing bids. For one thing, the computer records all costs and prices, labor rates, contract specs, the whole ball of wax." He explains that in the past, as a construction company representative, he often had to wait for days while the company put together the bid. He couldn't respond as quickly as he would have liked, and often, if the building authority changed the specifications, the entire set of financials had to be redone from the bottom up. More often than not, submission deadlines were met by the fastest companies, and they were even flying blind. "In the jobs I had before I came to Blount, we did it all manually. That meant that when a bid had a few minor changes, the whole thing had to be redone." Bryan points out that Blount's ability to seize on a new technology and utilize it in the sales process has made it easier for him to sell the company's services to its major buyers.

In addition to bidding on major domestic projects such as the Houston Convention Center, Blount has a significant overseas operation with 1984 overseas sales of nearly $90 million. One of the most significant of these projects has been the building of King Saud University, which has been worth over $2 billion to Blount since the project began in 1980. For U.S. markets, Blount is developing small power plants which will be capable of burning garbage and producing electricity. One industry analyst says, "This kind of power plant would be ideal for small municipalities. It could definitely be the wave of the future."

Architects are the boss, according to Gary Cummings. "That's where a lot of the marketing gets done. You call on the architects and convince them that your products, whether they are partitions, windows, or concrete footings, are topnotch." The architect sells for the contractor or the subcontractor in much the same way that a doctor sells for a pharmaceutical company. "The architects don't sell in the real sense of the word; what they do is put out a book with the plans for the project. They'll specify a certain kind of concrete, or windows, or partitions, and if you're listed in the book as a specified bidder, you just submit a bid." Selling to architects in advance, Gary points out, is also a way of letting the state's architectural firms know who is producing what kinds of products. Once they are made aware of the availability of specific types of construction and building components, they are more likely to include those components in their bid specifications. Gary suggests that selling in this way is much like putting one's foot in the door before the door is really opened. In the bid, the contractor is required to state that he's bidding, in industry lingo, "per the plan." This simply means that the construction company has reviewed the plan and is submitting its bid according to the plan's specifications.

Bryan adds, "With the Convention Center contract, there were twenty-four bidders at the outset, but only five submitted final bids." What happened to the rest? "In a few cases they just couldn't meet the requirements. For one thing, when you bid on a job like the Center, you have to put up a performance bond, which, in this case, was $106 million." And insurance companies—being the suspicious sorts that they are—"do not trip over each other trying to write performance bonds for companies that do not have a very strong track record," Ken Rutledge explains. "The performance bond literally guarantees that the contractor will complete the job. For example, in the case of the Convention Center, if the bid on the job is $106 million, and if after receiving a draw against completed work of $50 million, the contractor disappears, the insurance company is obligated to ante up the balance of $56 million so that the Center can be completed by another contractor." This, according to Ken, "is exactly why the Convention Center bid was awarded to a company like Blount."

Bryan continues, "Some builders will submit preliminary bids, knowing full well that they are going to drop out. They do this because it's good advertising in the industry. The principals of other projects will see their names associated with a major contract like the Convention Center, and possibly keep those names in mind for future work."

"The reps are paid a straight salary with bonus," according to Bryan. "It would be nice," he admits, "to receive commissions from sales, but the bonuses amount to what most sales representatives would make on a straight commission. I wouldn't mind having a piece of the Convention Center pie." Gary adds: "Typically, reps for the big companies like Blount are on straight salary, but reps for small companies may sometimes be on a commission basis." Blount's compensation rating is a 5, which means that the average compensation for Blount reps is above $28,930, which is more than 10 percent above the industry median of $26,300, and of course, bonuses for particularly large sales are extra.

Koger Properties has earned our number-two ranking because, in addition to having a top rating in the compensation category—a prototypical Koger representative earns more than $28,930—Koger's versatility in the commercial building market offers their reps a very stable working environment. Koger actually consists of two principal businesses: Koger Properties, Incorporated (KPI) and The Koger Company (TKC). KPI's specialty is building lower cost, very large office parks, mostly in suburban locales. TKC is principally a management company which was formed by KPI. TKC manages buildings built by KPI as well as buildings constructed by others.

Like Blount, Koger has the versatility of a highly successful property management arm complementing their growing building operation, and these factors have contributed to our ranking Koger number-two in this industry. In the very lean years of 1981-1982, the dollars spent on new construction fell by 3 percent, from $239.4 billion to $232.1 billion, but Koger's sales rose by an incredible 25 percent, from $54 million to $67.3 million. The company has continued to grow at an electrifying pace, with 1984 sales reported at $83.5 million and the projection for 1985 at $95 million. The numbers do more than add up to a 76 percent increase in sales since 1981; they also offer Koger representatives considerable peace of mind and have helped earn the company our number-two ranking.

Carl Sawyer, a Koger representative, says, "The company is very cost conscious. We handle the architectural, the building, and the leasing ends of the business." Because Koger is responsible for so much activity at each

> "Architects are the boss . . . 'That's where a lot of the marketing gets done. You call on the architects and convince them that your products, whether they are partitions, windows, or concrete footings, are topnotch.' "

stage of the construction contract, it must be in a position to cover its costs from either side. This puts a lot of pressure on the representatives to keep new business flowing. Jim Rogers, an independent contractor who subcontracts to Koger, says, "Frankly they make me nervous. They are my only business." Jim has worked with no other builders since 1982. He adds, "I know in practice it's not a good idea to tie yourself to one company like that, but they're so good. There's never even a problem with the draw." (The term "draw" refers to the partial payments received by the general contractor and the subcontractors during the completion of a job.) Carl says, "I've been in the business a long time, and subcontractors are really at the mercy of the general contractors for payments. Frequently the general contractors are stretched pretty thin. They'll have more projects on the fire than they really should, and their cash flow is tight. As it turns out, this situation is pretty common in the industry. To compensate for their poor cash flow, the general contractors press the subcontractors to get their part of the job done as quickly as possible to push toward an optimal completion date. The general contractor gets paid by the owners as the job is completed, so the more they finish, the more they get, until at completion, the full contract price is paid. In the situation that Carl describes, some general contractors are getting paid 100 percent of their contracted fee after having completed

90 percent or less of the work, and they hold off paying the subcontractors until the job is complete. This is also a standard industry practice because it allows the general contractor to cover immediate expenses to keep the administrative portion of the job flowing toward completion, even though the actual job itself is only 90 percent done. The subcontractors who complete their jobs must still wait to get paid, however, and this puts financial pressure on them to finish as quickly as possible so they can get onto the next job. Jim Rogers says, "A lot of subcontractors are pretty small operators and have a very hard time doing business that way. But in many cases, if they want the business, that's the way it has to be." He adds, "That's why I love working with Koger. When I finish my job, I get my money."

Subcontractors' subcontractors are even smaller companies that are hired to complete a portion of the job. For example, in the case of a large convention center in which the plumbing, heating, and air conditioning systems will require a substantial amount of pipefitting and ductwork, the plumbing, heating, and air conditioning subcontractors may let out bids for independent pipefitters and ductwork people to run the water and vent lines. A plumbing subcontractor for a particularly large project may let out three or four subcontracts for toilets, sinks, hot water or steam conduit pipes, drain-waste vent lines, and water supply lines, rather than attempt to manage every discrete stage of the installation job himself. The same is true for the electrical contractor handling a modern office building construction contract.

With so many different types of power supply, backup supply, and dedicated lines for computers or word processors, it makes more sense to sub the job out to independents. Moreover, no matter what the funding authority for the project—whether public or private—there are so many state construction, insurance, zoning, and fire prevention codes in operation that the general contractor has his hands full just making sure that the inspections, paperwork, and approvals are in place before moving on to the next stage. A scrupulous contractor does not want to find himself in the position of having to undo construction work or cut into a finished wall surface so that a hidden junction box can be inspected.

In many cases, a modern, large construction project resembles a medieval feudal state in which each level is directly responsible to the level above. Jim says, "There are sometimes four and five levels of subcontracting for really complex jobs." All the general contractor can do in these instances is make sure that the controlled riot proceeds in the right direction.

Carl Sawyer adds: "The big money in the subcontracting business is in being an independent rep." Independent building and construction representatives frequently handle four or five lines, but never competing products. Carl says, "Independent reps are frequently used for their contacts. If a subcontractor wants to get an in with a big job like one of our office parks, but he knows he doesn't have the contacts, he might work through an independent subcontractor—some call themselves consultants—who has an in with one of our subcontractors. The consultant typically gets 5 percent of the fees he passes along, but individual deals are frequently cut, and for the really large jobs, the percentage is usually more like 1 or 2 percent than 5 percent." It is sometimes worthwhile for the subcontractor to pursue a lower commission. This will happen, according to Jim, when the lower commission is applied to "a really humongous job like a $90 million industrial park a buddy of mine got involved with in Phoenix. He took care of the partitions and the windows. He was in for 2 percent, but the total tab for the partitions and windows was nearly $2 million. In this way, he cleared $40,000 on the one job."

Pulte Home Corporation, a Michigan-based company, has seen sales increase by over 125 percent in the 1981-83 market while the rest of the industry was in a 20 percent decline. Pulte has earned our number-three rank in the building industry because they have selected their markets carefully and successfully, and have expanded into financing through their wholly owned subsidiary, the ICM Mortgage Corporation, which allows them to offer a complete financing package to buyers.

Barry Lockwood, a Pulte representative, comments on the financing available through Pulte: "The financing makes all the difference in the world when it comes to selling the properties. Sellers were, in effect, telling buyers, 'Sure, we'll sell you our house, just come up with $150,000.' The buyers would then go to banks who would say, 'Sure, we'll give you a mortgage, but you have to put $30,000 down and then be able to make a monthly payment of $1,711 not including property taxes.' Is it surprising that the industry went into a tailspin?" Barry is referring to the peak of the interest-rate escalation of 1980 to 1982 which saw mortgage rates top out at 18 percent. He adds, "Nobody was buying homes with conventional mortgages."

Barry started his career in the industry by selling vacation home construction packages in Michigan's lucrative resort industry. "We sold packages which included land, a vacation home, and rental management. Some people bought the homes for their own use and others for investment purposes." Barry's company expanded as the market grew. "There was a tremendous market in Michigan for this kind of development, and we were involved in the business pretty early on before it got too crowded." The rental management was also quite lucrative. "If the company handled the rental of one of the vacation homes for the whole year, they'd get between 20 and 25 percent of the rental fee for the service. For weekly rentals, the cut was 30 to 40 percent plus the fees charged for cleaning the property between tenants." And the operation expanded still further. "We eventually had a service for everyone. Some people didn't want to rent, but would come up to their vacation homes a few times a year and leave the home unattended the rest of the time. For these people we ran a security service which watched over their homes and did normal maintenance."

The financial arrangement that Barry had with the developer was also standard. "I got fees in two ways. If I brought in the client, I got 40 percent of the developer's fee on the sale and the rental. For walk-ins I got 10 percent of the developer's fee." During peak vacation times the rental money could be quite good. "We charged between $150 and $200 a night for the rentals." The owner of the home would get 60 to 70 percent of the rental money, and the developer and Barry would split the remaining 30 to 40 percent. "So, on the low end, I'd get as little as $4.50 per night for a rental, and on the high end I'd get $32." How much of a living could someone make this way? "I averaged between $9,000 and $12,000 a year in rental income. And of course, there was income from sales as well. For sales, the percentages were the same." Barry earned an average of an additional $25,000 to $35,000 per year from selling vacation homes. He says, "I didn't earn all that much compared to some of the really heavy hitters in the business. I could have earned much more if I wanted to pursue it, but "because I wanted to see my kids grow up, I worked an average forty-hour week, and I always

> " I think everybody in building sales cuts their teeth by selling either building construction materials or real estate. . . There's no real training in this business. You have to know the business in order to be hired."

scheduled time for my kids during the week. I had to work at least one weekend day during the peak vacation seasons."

According to Barry, the heavy hitters in the industry were able to make much more money as sales representatives. "They're pretty much workaholics. This is a percentage business. If you're going to sell to 10 percent of the people you see, it follows that for every additional ten presentations you give, you're going to make one more sale. I had somewhat different priorities." When asked how much a top representative in the industry was able to make during that period, Barry replies, "That's a hard one to answer because it can vary quite a bit, but when I was making around $35,000 or $40,000 a year, the top guys in the company were making over $100,000.

Vacation home construction and sales was a lucrative industry, but it was heavily dependent on market conditions, the number of companies selling to the public, and the interest rates on land purchases and construction loans, so the bubble was bound to burst. "What happened to the industry?" Barry asks. "What didn't happen! First of all, the competition became outrageous. Most people don't know that Michigan is the number-five state in the nation for vacation and leisure-home construction." An industry source adds, "In 1956 there were exactly six developers of vacation and leisure homes in the state. By 1975, there were 840." Barry continues: "When I first started in 1970, it was a real sellers' market. Mortgage rates were low and people were buying vacation homes like there was no tomorrow. By 1975, the market was generating $10 billion annually, but the slices of the market share for each company were a heck of a lot smaller. Finally, the interest rates caught up with the sellers. When the interest squeeze set in, my company was really hard hit. We didn't realize how dependent we'd been on the auto industry. We knew that a lot of the people who were buying from us were involved in the auto industry, but everyone took it for granted that it would always be the way it was." But that was not to be the case. "When the interest rates started escalating, people stopped buying. When the economic crunch hit the auto industry, a lot of people had to sell their vacation homes because they were moving or they simply needed the bucks. And the whole vacation and leisure home industry crashed." Barry continues: "The prices of vacation homes plummeted, and there were still no buyers. My company went out of business, and so did over 300 others. Nobody used the word, but in Michigan we were in the middle of a depression." But Barry managed to survive, although not in Michigan. He was hired by a developer in Arizona and came to Pulte five years ago.

Pulte Corporation took a different path to mortgage financing so that it would not be squeezed as the other builders were in the 1981 to 1982 depression in the new home construction and building sales market. Barry explains: "We started offering mortgages through our own company so that our buyers weren't at the mercy of the banks. We also used buydowns quite a bit." A buydown is a payment made by the seller (Pulte in this case) to the buyer in order to reduce the buyer's mortgage rate. "We also have a very long-term view of the industry. We're set up to deal with just about any eventuality in the economy." This versatility, along with the fact that the company received a 5 in the compensation ranking, has earned Pulte our number-three spot.

Although revenues fell by $50 million from 1983 to 1984, and the company has done some belt tightening, Houston-based U.S. Home Corporation has earned our number-four rank in the industry for a number of reasons. It would be difficult to ignore what one industry source calls, "the big guy on the block." U.S. Home is the largest on-site manufacturer of single-family homes and is among the industry leaders in retirement communities, condominiums, and multifamily housing.

Stanley Kendall, a U.S. Home representative, says, "I've been up and down more times than a yo-yo in this business. I decided to go with a company like U.S. Home for the security." U.S. Home, with 1984 sales of $1.1 billion, has positioned itself well in the building market. The company is a manufacturer of concrete and wood building materials, and like many large builders who must guarantee their sources of supply in order to stay competitive and bring in the contracts on time, U.S. Home has a mortgage subsidiary. Stanley says, "U.S. Home is like the IBM of the industry. You know they're going to be here tomorrow." And to Stanley, that's very important. "I had my fill of the speculative end of the business. I sold condos in the Florida boom market, and I sold retirement homes in the Arizona boom market." But Stanley adds, "If you'll pardon a cliché, what goes up eventually comes back down, and the 'downs' were too down for my taste, so I went with a nice, stable organization that knows how to build houses."

Commenting on training, Stanley says, "I think everybody in building sales cuts their teeth by selling either building construction materials or real estate." Stanley took the real estate brokerage route into the building industry. "I paid my dues selling real estate for a local agency in Ohio. You can make a living, but I was looking for a little more excitement." He adds: "There's no real training in this business. You have to know the business in order to be hired." The main attraction for Stanley is traveling. "I love to travel and see different parts of the country," he explains, "and U.S. Home is all over the place, so I get to move around." Stanley also points out that the compensation at U.S. Home is among the highest in the industry. The company has earned a 5 on our compensation scale, meaning that the prototypical representative at U.S. Home earns over $28,930 annually.

California-based Kaufman and Broad, with 1984 sales of $600 million, has earned our number-five ranking because, like the other companies in this industry, it has a strong, versatile position in the very volatile building market, and it maintains a stable atmosphere for its representatives. Kaufman and Broad's diversification into areas such as life insurance and general mortgage banking, although good news to company stockholders, actually lowered the company's position in our rankings for this industry. The reason is fairly simple, and is in no way a negative reflection on the company. Our research indicated that K&B's nonbuilding-related operations are growing to the point where the building aspects of the business are likely to generate less than half the total revenues. Consequently, the company may choose to give less support to the building side of the business than a company whose entire operation is devoted to building and building-related construction activities.

Rose Woo, a K&B rep in San Francisco, says, "I think that manufactured housing is going to be the wave of the future in this business." K&B is currently one of the top producers of manufactured housing in the United States, while still constructing on-site housing. One industry source says, "Manufactured housing used to mean mobile homes. But now many more units are being used at permanent sites." Rose adds, "The manufactured-home industry is now in the $4 billion range, and estimates are that it will be $10 billion by 1990. Manufactured houses are substantially less expensive than on-site homes." An industry source agrees with this assessment and points out that the price range for a manufactured home is $10,000 to $40,000, while a new on-site home is approximately $87,000, and a previously owned home is approximately $70,000 to $90,000, depending on the location. Rose says, "Here in California, with the price of land and construction going through the roof, I really believe that manufactured housing will become very popular. And I intend to be here when it does."

	BUILDING	COMPENSATION	COMMISSION	SUPPORT	INTANGIBLE
1	Blount, Inc.	5		4	
2	Koger Properties, Inc.	5		4	
3	Pulte Home Corp.	5		4	
4	U.S. Home Corp.	5		4	
5	Kaufman and Broad, Inc.	5		4	+ −

The median compensation package for our prototypical two-year rep is $26,300, including salary, bonus, and commission. Because the individual compensation packages were quite different across the industry, and even within individual companies, we did not split the individual parts of compensation.

Kaufman and Broad [+ −]
The company's position in the manufactured-housing market, particularly in the housing-hungry California market, has earned K&B a [+]. We

agree that manufactured housing will be an increasingly popular alternative to high priced on-site housing, especially in the growing warm-weather areas. K&B has earned a [—], indicating a yellow caution flag for its reps: examine how K&B's obvious interests in non-construction areas, such as their insurance business, will impact on K&B sales support. We stress that we have no reason to believe there will be a negative impact. However, it is our policy to caution reps in every industry to take a second look when their company shows signs of expanding into areas which would not benefit the rep directly.

INDUSTRIAL CHEMICALS

THE TOP FIVE:

1. Air Products & Chemicals, Inc.
2. Monsanto Co.
3. American Cyanamid Co.
4. The Dexter Corp.
5. Big Three Industries

I n this heavy industry, the sales representatives have to be part engineer, part problem-solver, and part project manager. They have to know exactly how their particular product will perform, how it must be handled and stored, how it must be delivered, and how it will satisfy their customer's needs. There is very little room for error here because of the toxicity or volatility of some of the products and the strict regulations that govern the sales of chemicals and gases. Therefore, the sales reps in this industry are true experts who have spent years on the job learning about the nature of the industry as well as chemicals manufactured by their companies and their companies' competitors.

"This is an industry where there's absolutely no bull. If you want to be a successful sales rep, you'd damn well better do your homework." So says Sam Carter, a top-of-the-line sales manager for Big Three Industries, our number-five ranked company. "I came to Big Three with a strong technical background but virtually no sales experience." Sam had a degree in chemical engineering when he applied at Big Three. "Frankly, I wanted a job as an engineer, but they turned me onto sales," he says.

"Establishing yourself in this industry is tough," Sam explains, "because in the industrial chemicals field, technical expertise is considered to be the number-one factor in hiring sales representatives." An industry analyst adds, "The industry's management feels that they can teach somebody to sell a lot easier than they can teach them to be chemical engineers." Sam's district manager agrees. "I look for somebody with the ability to listen. Then I let him try to sell me—on himself. I'm a tough SOB, and I figure that if my reps can sell me, they can sell my product." He adds that he rejects nine out of every ten job applicants he sees, and he denies interviews to nine out of every ten requests he gets, so becoming established as a representative in this business is not easy. He recalls how he hired Sam: My buddy, who's the manager in engineering, couldn't use him. Sam failed their water test on his interview—he couldn't walk on it. But the engineering manager saw something in Sam and thought I might want him for sales." Sam chuckles at his boss calling himself an SOB. "That's probably the nicest thing that's been said about him in five years. When he interviewed me I thought he wanted to fight me or something. He asked me a question about the liquefication of nitrogen and when I answered, he just stared at me and told me I was full of horsespit." Sam's boss smiles, "I've toned down my act since then, but I still like to see how a guy will stand up under pressure. Because when he's selling in this industry, he's going to be selling to guys whose businesses are going to rise or fall on what the gas can do, and you'd better believe they're going to be a lot harder on him than I am."

An industry source comments on tough interviewing: "Everybody has his or her own style of interviewing, but it's true that many of the folks you sell to in this industry are rough-and-tumble types. About ten years ago there was a crazy case. One of our reps called on a small account in Colorado, and in the process of making his pitch, quoted an incorrect number for the boiling point of liquid oxygen. The owner of the business threw him bodily out the door—and I mean literally—and has refused to deal with that company ever since."

There is much that can go wrong if the chemicals and gases are handled improperly, or if the wrong chemical is used for a particular job. The same industry source emphasizes this point: "If you want to know the worst that can happen in this business—and you can rest assured that the people at the top in senior management do want to know—just say 'Union Carbide.' " He is, of course, referring to the tragedy in India, where leakage of deadly methyl isocyanide gas at a Union Carbide plant resulted in over 2,000 deaths. In every industry, any situation that can potentially result in loss of life is obviously going to be handled with extreme caution. However, in the industrial chemicals business, extreme care is required. As one industry source puts it, "If we screw up here it's worse than when a doctor screws up. I don't mean for this to sound callous, but a doctor can only kill one person at a time if he makes a serious medical error; we can kill a million." Every single one of our top five companies: Air Products, Monsanto, American Cyanamid, Dexter, and Big Three Industries, emphasize the serious nature of the chemicals business. The leaders of this industry are extremely careful when it comes to hiring. As is the case in the pharmaceuticals industry, above all else, the sales reps must be technically competent.

Of all the industries we researched, this is the most diverse. To be as consistent as possible, we have considered the chemical and gas industry vis-a-vis industrial, rather than consumer sales, and for our purposes we have defined the industry as consisting of those companies that supply industrial chemicals and gases to other businesses. We have therefore excluded companies that derive a significant portion of their gross rev-

> "In those days we thought 'high-tech' was a local college. We sold gas door to door . . . sometimes the weather could get pretty hairy."

enues from peripheral areas. The excluded companies include Allied Corporation and W.R. Grace, which are involved in oil and gas exploration and sales; Millipore and other companies whose major products include pharmaceuticals; and Du Pont and Hercules, whose major products include fibers and plastics. The companies we did include derive the lion's share of their gross revenue from the sale of gases such as liquid nitrogen, used extensively in frozen food processing, and chemicals such as diammonium phosphate (DAP), used in phosphate-based fertilizers.

The Allentown, Pennsylvania-based Air Products and Chemicals has received our number-one ranking in the industry for a number of reasons. David Leibrock, a district manager for Air Products, says, "We pay our reps well and they earn every dollar." An industry source agrees: "Air Products is the end of the search for many reps. The management at Air Products takes care of their people, and they keep them." He adds: "In an industry that is very engineering and high-tech conscious, Air Products is one company that is marketing-, as well as engineering-driven." David, who has been with the company almost since its inception, describes what it was like at the beginning. "In those days we thought 'high-tech' was a local college. We sold gas door to door. The company gave us a car and gasoline—they still do—and we drove through the back roads of industrial states and sold gas. My territory back then included North and South Dakota, and sometimes the weather could get pretty hairy."

One prospecting technique that David used is still common in the industry. "I looked for a certain type of company, specifically one that was using a gas such as nitrogen stored in metal cylinders." Metal cylinders are the most expensive way to store gas on a per-volume basis, but for small companies just starting out, a sufficiently small volume makes the cylinder method of storage the most cost effective. However, as David found out, that can soon change. "What I saw was that some companies were growing quite fast and had reached a point where they could really use liquid storage for their gases." Liquid storage is the way larger volumes of gas are stored. Tanks are installed at the customer site and huge tanker trucks make scheduled deliveries of the liquefied gas, which is stored in the large pressurized tanks. As you might expect, it's a much more cost-effective way to transport and store gas because, as David explains, "Any gas is denser in its liquid form. It's pretty much the same concept as boiling water. In liquid form, the water fills a particular container—for example, a pot on your stove. But when you boil the water, and it becomes steam, the steam will fill whatever container is available. And how big is the available 'container'? Would you believe it's as big as a house? Your house?" Thus, because gas in liquid form is much denser, more of it can be stored in a smaller container. Therefore the per-volume cost of liquid gas is much lower than the per-volume cost of gas in the gaseous form. "

"So I traveled around and became a sort of de facto inspector, checking industrial gas installations and giving management reports on their gas volume relative to their needs. It was time consuming, but as I discovered, it was well worth the effort. Pretty soon I had the reputation of being the local 'gas man.' I was probably doing energy audits for companies long before the utility companies ever thought of the concept. This is a very bottom-line business, and once I showed company management how much they could save by using liquefied gas, they'd switch to our gas."

Today, Air Products sells over 150 specialty gases, including mixes and blends of their more standard gases such as argon, nitrogen, oxygen, hydrogen, and helium. By the end of 1984, gross sales from their gas distribution business alone had reached $937 million, including industrial pipeline sales. An executive at Air Products says, "Just as liquefied gas is much cheaper per unit volume than gas stored in cylinders, so is pipeline gas cheaper per volume than liquefied gas. Now it is quite common in the industry to have gas piped to the major corporate users."

"60 Billion Frozen" is a sign that will never appear over any McDonald's outlet in the U.S., but just as the fast food giant is proud to display its signs proclaiming "60 Billion Served," so too, could Air Products proclaim, "60 Billion Frozen." Most McDonald's hamburgers and those of other fast-food chains, are flash-frozen by liquefied nitrogen gas at 300 degrees below zero. A source at Air Products, says, "The process is 100 percent safe. It's not used just at McDonald's; the liquefied nitrogen flash-freezing process is quite common in the entire food industry." Although industrial gases are an important part of fast-food processing, their role is almost unknown to the consumers of the food.

Nitrogen is an ideal gas for many industrial processes, including the freezing of food, because it provides a suitable non-oxygen atmosphere. "All life on our planet is oxygen dependent, and that includes most disease causing agents, so where oxygen gas might cause various problems in industry, either with combustion or with bacteria growth, nitrogen gas is used." Air Products sells liquid nitrogen, and consequently, it has become an aggressive giant by servicing the fast-food makers.

One of the questions we asked the sales representatives during our survey was: "What sale, in your opinion, best describes the nature of selling in this industry? " David laughs as he recalls an experience he'll never forget: "I was calling on a scrap iron plant in North Dakota that was using liquid nitrogen in the process of recycling the scrap. They were using a competitor's gas, but I didn't mind dropping in on them because they were friendly, and one of my best accounts was just down the road. I don't know if you know what the weather is like up in that part of the country, but let me tell you it can change pretty fast." And for David, the weather predictions bode well one January day. "There was a forecast of light snow, not unusual for a January day in North Dakota. I dropped in on my account, and afterwards dropped in on the company I'd been trying to sell for over a year. It had started to snow by then, so they invited me into the office for some coffee. We couldn't have been there for more than an hour, but it snowed like I had never seen it snow before or since. There had to be half a foot on the ground and you could barely see your hand in front of your face. They'd been expecting a gas delivery that afternoon which was obviously not going to get there. Kidding around, I said, 'See? If you were dealing with us, you'd have your gas today.' The president of the company overheard me and he said, 'Son, if you can get us gas today, the account is yours.' " And in the middle of a North Dakota blizzard, the sun shone for David. "I knew he was serious because he was that kind of guy—sort of a riverboat gambler type.

Now, I knew that my other account was taking delivery right at that moment, and it was just up the road, so I called them and asked if they'd be willing to take half the shipment if I cut the price and promised they'd have the balance within a day after the snow stopped. They agreed, and you should have seen the look on the company president's face when our truck came lurching out of the storm into his yard!" David got the account.

"Features, functions, and benefits" is a basic training term describing a common sales approach across all industries. Name your product's features, show its functions, but above all, be sure the client understands the benefits. This approach is critical to selling industrial chemicals and gases. Janet Simmons, one of the few women reps in a male-dominated industry, says, "My sex isn't much of a factor in how I'm judged in this industry. Sometimes I run into guys with an attitude about women in business, but I have a degree in chemical engineering, and I usually straighten them out in about a minute and a half." As she explains, "We do a lot of cold calling on accounts. It's really a qualifying technique. You find out what your competition is up to, and you also establish a rapport with a company for possible future business. Once in a rare while, you can spot a glaring deficiency in one of their processes and by offering a correction, you can make a change on the spot." In fact, she once saved a company substantial money, almost against her better judgment. "I made a call on a plant where they were melting scrap iron and forming iron sheets which were going to be used even-

> " '60 Billion Frozen' is a sign that will never appear over any McDonald's outlet in the U.S., but just as the fast food giant is proud to display its signs proclaiming '60 Billion Served,' so too, could Air Products proclaim, '60 Billion Frozen.' "

tually for fuel tanks. They were using a relatively old-fashioned combustion technique, and I pointed out to the chief engineer that if he used oxygen gas in the combustion process he'd probably increase the rate of combustion by over 10 percent." But for her efforts, all Janet got was a lesson in human nature. "The guy started screaming at me. He told me I didn't know anything and that he'd been in the business thirty years and therefore he was smarter than I was. I said that just makes you older, not smarter, and I walked away." When Janet told her sales manager of the incident, she found out her mistake. "I was so interested in being right, I didn't let the guy save face. His whole crew was listening to us, and I backed him into a corner. I realized that I should have spoken to him privately." And if he still didn't bite? "I could have gone over his head to the plant manager, but I'd have told him first." However, as it turns out, the story has a happy ending. "The chief engineer called me a day later and apologized. He said that I was right, and if I'd come back he'd see to it that I got an order. Not only did I get an order, but six months later, he became the chief engineer for another company in the field, and I wound up with all their business."

Air Products is well known in the industry for high-level technological support. Fred Short, an Air Products representative in California, says, "My territory included Silicon Valley, and I used to call on some of the big chip manufacturers. It turned out that they were having a problem in their production process and were losing over 10 percent of their chips due to a static discharge problem. The chief engineer told me that if I could come up with a way to beat this, I'd make a lot of money." However, Fred was at something of a disadvantage: "I didn't know what the hell he was talking about in his technical description of the problem." So Fred called on Air Products' excellent engineering support staff. "I described the problem to them the same way it had been explained to me. I felt like I was reciting some weird litany in a foreign tongue." Three days later, Fred met two Air Products' engineers at the San Francisco airport. "They had come up with a solution using hydrogen gas. Somehow, using a hydrogen atmosphere, the static discharge simply didn't occur and the problem was solved. Everybody was happy, including me. I got a nice bonus."

Air Products' sales representatives are on straight salary, but performance bonuses are commonplace. The representatives are not only highly trained and highly motivated, but they must have excellent qualifications, especially in the related fields of chemistry and chemical engineering. As Air Products' manager Sam Carter reports, "Because the industry is so refined and specific now, and because we're so highly regarded, I can be a lot more selective than I used to be. Although there are exceptions, I look for someone with a strong three-year-plus track record as a successful sales rep in the industry. He or she must be technically qualified. We do very little technical training except with the development of our new products. Because selling is very often problem solving, and because problems must come from customers, we rely heavily on our sales reps to report to the engineers. The reps are out there. They see what's happening and they know what's needed. It would be putting the cart before the horse to train our reps on what to expect. We expect them to tell us what to expect.

This market-reaction approach to selling, which Air Products relies on, is a common marketing theory applied in many industries. Products are developed or improved according to the needs of the marketplace. Therefore, the sales representatives have a double mission: besides selling the product, they must evaluate the marketplace for what products are needed. The dominance of IBM in office automation equipment is a result of years of evaluating of the needs of the clerical office marketplace. In addition, the company paid serious attention to the reports of IBM's representatives who had been selling typewriters and other devices to that market for over a quarter of a century. Air Products and IBM are among many companies using the market-reaction technique. In fact, companies that employ this theory are usually the most aggressively sales-oriented companies within their industries. Some examples are highly successful companies in diverse lines of business: Caterpillar in road building; DEC, in addition to IBM, in office and business computer systems; and John Deere in tractors and other farm and agricultural equipment. In one way or another, these companies use customer and market input as a means of determing the products to develop and the improvements to be made in existing products. This approach to marketing products is in contrast to engineering-intensive companies such as Texas Instruments and Control Data, which tie product development to research more than to market response. It is a difference in marketing philosophy: pro-active versus re-active.

Another major area of concern, according to industry spokesmen, is foreign competition. An industry analyst says, "The strong dollar has hampered the export business, but with economists forecasting a decline in the dollar, I expect the export business to increase." Air Products has already taken steps to protect itself in the foreign arena via an investment and technology agreement with Daido Oxygen, one of Japan's top industrial gas companies. The willingness of management at Air Products to consider a variety of solutions to problems of competition and to proceed with steps such as the Daido accord bodes well for Air Products' representatives.

The financial future of Air Products looks strong. Expanding markets in fertilizers accounted for nearly one-half billion dollars of gross sales for Air Products in 1984, and their newly formed engineering services division accounted for approximately $200 million. With the domestic farm market expected to expand substantially from 1985 through 1987, these segments of the business look strong for the foreseeable future. In addition, the identification of Air Products as an engineering-intensive company, one that is being strengthened by the new engineering services division, can only add to the company's esteem, and therefore increase the sales in the industrial gas division of the company.

Because we see Air Products as a strong and growing company, establishing a strong, yet diversified base in both domestic and foreign markets, and because we see it as a "rep-conscious" organization offering strong field-sales representative support and compensation, we have selected it as the number-one company in the industrial gas and chemicals industry.

Fifty-year-old St. Louis based Monsanto registered gross sales of nearly $7 billion in 1984. It has earned our number-two ranking for several reasons: its tremendous commitment to R&D—a half-billion dollar budget for 1985 to develop new products that Monsanto's representatives will eventually be selling, its carefully chosen diversification, its commitment to its representatives, and its commitment to manufacturing and selling

> " 'Features, functions, and benefits' is a training term . . . Name your product's features, show its functions, but be sure the client understands the benefits. This approach is critical to selling industrial chemicals and gases."

quality products. A spokesman for Monsanto says, "After the industry shakeup in 1982 and 1983, we have taken the necessary steps to protect ourselves." Monsanto, which has seen sales increasing at a rate of one-half billion dollars annually since 1983, had, along with the rest of the industrial chemicals industry, suffered through a belt-tightening situation in some of its major markets, such as domestic farms. In addition, the strong U.S. dollar hurt Monsanto's foreign trade, which accounted for nearly $2 billion in sales in 1984. With the dollar's highs against foreign currencies projected to fall off during the latter part of 1985, Monsanto's foreign sales are expected to pick up.

Managers at Monsanto explain that the company aggressively supports its field representatives in two specific ways beyond the normal compensation and bonus packages. First, Monsanto believes that a sales representative's credibility with his clients depends largely on the quality of the product and the ability of the company to bring new products to the market quickly and continuously. Second, Monsanto stresses excellent training. According to one sales manager, "This training places our reps on a much higher level than any other rep visiting that same customer. When a Monsanto rep talks about what a product can and can't do, his customers believe him because they're confident he knows what he's talking about."

"Commitment to state-of-the-art technology has long been Monsanto's credo," according to James Rivers, who described the primary objective of Monsanto's R&D division. "We pride ourselves on always staying on top of the industry when it comes to R&D," he says. An industry analyst agrees. "As an example of their commitment to high-tech advances, right now they're racing ahead with genetic research to improve their herbicide line." The analyst describes how the introduction of a product line that resulted from research in recombinant DNA rather than the traditional toxin-based approach will accomplish two of Monsanto's primary marketing goals. "It will demonstrate that Monsanto's technology is truly state of the art, and it will establish Monsanto's field sales force as representatives of an environment-oriented, high-tech, twenty-first-century approach to developing products that solve customers' problems."

Robert McAnn, a veteran sales representative for Monsanto, comments on the training that new people receive when they join the company: "Here, product training is intensive. The atmosphere is very professional and you are expected to know your stuff backward and forward." Robert explains what can happen if a representative doesn't really know the product. "One of our reps wrote a big order for Roundup, our best selling herbicide. The problem was that it wasn't ideal for the area it was going to be used in. Certain herbicides and pesticides work best under specific climatic conditions. In the case of Roundup, the ideal conditions require a moist soil environment, and the rep in question sold the herbicide for use in a particularly arid environment. "The customer complained to us because he noticed right away that he wasn't getting the results he expected, so we gave him a full refund." And the representative who sold the wrong product? "He caught hell. The company is very committed to the idea of making sure that

> *The industry picture is one in which finding the right corporate outlook is more important than finding the right market niche.*

the chemical products are used properly. Even though there is no danger in using Roundup in an arid environment, the company will not sell it for use in those areas." A company spokesperson says, "We are very protective of the way in which our products are used. The sale is not necessarily the bottom line here—long-term commitment is."

Monsanto has earned our number-two rating for support of field representatives, stress on product development, and extensive training program. However, they might have edged out Air Products for the number-one position had they not run into some technical and legal problems with patents for a number of their products, most significantly Roundup, the best selling herbicide in the industry. Our research has revealed that there is a chance that Monsanto will in fact lose the Roundup patent, in which case a number of companies will rush to market the same product under a different name. According to one industry source, "Some of those companies could be delivering product in the marketplace within sixty days of a ruling favorable to them." We believe that when a company's representatives are in danger of losing the exclusive market rights to the industry's biggest seller, the company simply can't be ranked number one in that industry. There is too much uncertainty for the representatives. However, from another point of view, the fact that Monsanto is ranked number two despite the patent disputes should be an indication to potential sales people that we believe the company is strong enough to weather the problem.

American Cyanamid, the New Jersey-based industry giant with 1984 gross sales of $3.9 billion, has earned our number-three ranking for a number of reasons, not the least of which is its apparent commitment to pursuing the high sales growth areas of the industry. An industry source says, "They're already one of the industry leaders in the type of R&D that supports their entire sales force, and with the additional cash, they are likely to be even more aggressive." The cash to which he refers is entering the company coffers from the sales of its titanium dioxide and Formica operations—manufacturing and sales operations that have been hugely successful for the company.

Medical and chemical sales accounted for over 75 percent of sales in 1984, and the same source says, "Their research facilities are awesome. They operate a very well integrated and product-oriented research environment, and some of the high-tech research really overlaps different product areas." He is referring to American Cyanamid's ability to take genetic engineering principles developed in their medical operations and apply them in their agricultural product R&D. Like Monsanto and many of our other sales-oriented companies, American Cyanamid tends to conduct its research with a weather eye on its customers' needs and its marketplace. This means that the company can feed its field representatives the product information they need to maintain ongoing dialogues with their accounts about their future needs as well as their current orders. "Any field rep who can do that," our industry source reports, "virtually assures himself a long-term relationship with his accounts even if there are no current orders."

The engineering backup is impressive at American Cyanamid, according to Russ Priel, a sales representative for the company. "When we pitch to a major account, we'll fly a team of engineers across the country for demonstrations and meetings, or if that's not practical, we'll fly the account's principals to our facilities." Russ describes a first-class operation which is very technology conscious. "When the guys from our medical division are pitching a new drug, they'll fly in world-renowned doctors, but the focus is strictly on the business and the product. To be sure, there's wining and dining, but nothing at all outlandish. Everybody is very focused on the product. And the same technique is used in the agricultural chemicals division." It is this focus on the product in all of American Cyanamid's divisions that has made the company a representative-oriented manufacturer that backs up the people in the field with product development, new product information, and engineering support for whatever is being marketed. Consequently, the style at American Cyanamid is very definitely in keeping with what our research has revealed is this industry's standard: a direct approach to the customer, a forthright presentation of the product, and a commitment to long-term relationships.

Connecticut-based Dexter Corporation, which has the distinction of being the oldest company listed on the New York Stock Exchange, is ranked number four in our industry survey. This is due in no small part to their commitment to the same type of high-tech R&D support of new product sales that has been a feature of the number-one, two, and three ranked companies in the industry. Dexter, long known for taking care of its own people, has been engaged in major acquisition and product licensing ventures, such as the recent deal negotiated with Boots-Celltech Diagnostics for the exclusive North American rights to sell interferon-based immunoassay kits. We feel that this commitment to get product to the marketplace through acquisition is a positive indicator for Dexter's field representatives. Interestingly enough, however, Dexter has not chosen to pursue the acquisition path exclusively, as witnessed by the retainer agreement recently created with a group of Stanford University scientists who will be working in the area of genetics.

Dexter's sales have been increasing annually by approximately $70 million, to a projected 1985 total of approximately $750 million. This growth, plus their market and R&D orientation, recommends Dexter as a company with excellent growth potential for its field sales people.

Houston-based Big Three Industries barely lost out to Dexter for the number-four position in our survey. Dexter earned the extra points because of their dual commitment to the present market through acquisition of new products, and to the future market through high-tech research and development. Big Three Industries is substantially smaller than Air Products, our number-one ranked company, but Big Three's sales have been increasing by over $100 million annually for the past two years, and they are projected to close in on the billion-dollar mark by the end of 1985. In short, they are more than holding their own. The company utilizes an extensive pipeline service in Texas and the Southwest to boost sales in its industrial gas division to the $400 million mark in 1984, with further growth expected in 1985. In addition, Big Three shows signs of backing off from its oil-field operations, manufacturing and supplying oil field equipment, in favor of increasing their industrial gas business. Ted Grogan, a manager in the industrial gas division at Big Three, says, "We're committed to increasing our market share, and we're offering our reps substantial bonuses when their efforts are successful." And who are Big Three's reps? "People who have a proven track record of sales within the industry. We're in a growth cycle and we're looking for reps who are committed to growing.

The industry picture is one in which finding the right corporate outlook is more important than finding the right market niche. The nature of the industrial chemical and gas industry is such that it is subject to many economic influences ranging from foreign politics and the price of the dollar, to the weather, in the case of fertilizer, pesticide, and herbicide producers. The big guys, such as American Cyanamid, Monsanto, and Air Products have looked toward diversification for overall protection and the guarantee of a stable market. And some companies, such as Dexter and American Cyanamid, are pouring funds into R&D, particularly in the area of genetic research.

INDUSTRIAL CHEMICALS		COMPENSATION	COMMISSION	SUPPORT	INTANGIBLE
1	Air Products & Chemicals, Inc.	4		5	+
2	Monsanto Co.	4		5	
3	American Cyanamid Co.	4		5	
4	The Dexter Corp.	5		4	+ −
5	Big Three Industries Ind.	5		4	+ −

The industry median compensation figure for a two-year sales representative is $28,850.

Air Products [+]

In an industry with much uncertainty, we believe that Air Products, with its proven growth record, strong support of its sales force, and commitment to diversification within the relatively narrow area of its expertise, offers reps an unusually stable environment. For this reason, we have given Air Products a [+].

Dexter Corp. and Big Three Industries [+ −]

These companies have earned our "good news [+] and bad news [−]" awards. The good news is that they are each in their own way going out on a limb. Dexter is moving heavily into high-tech research, and Big Three is concentrating on a major expansion of its industrial gas operations. But with the good news also comes the bad news. Because of the relative risks both companies are taking, reps are offered the potential for growth and success, but also the potential for some significant readjustments if the repective ventures are not as successful as present indications suggest. In summary: only risk takers need apply.

HEAVY MACHINERY

THE TOP FIVE:

1 Cincinnati Milacron Inc.
2 The Stanley Works
3 Ingersoll-Rand Co.
4 Caterpillar Tractor Co.
5 Barber-Greene Co.
5 CMI Corp.

The sales representatives in the heavy machinery and construction industries are also technical specialists and sometimes financial advisors as well who help their customers comply with the financing and legal requirements of construction bidding and contracting. There is a need for this expertise because large road grading equipment, cranes, and earth movers are usually sold or leased for specific types of construction projects. Often, the companies making the purchases have to conform to strict bidding procedures and comply with a variety of local, state, and federal laws governing work on public projects. It is here that the heavy industrial equipment sales rep can offer advice and guidance as a part of closing the sale."

George Kendrick reminisces: "Driving along I-40 from Henryetta, Oklahoma, to Little Rock, Arkansas, certainly makes for some good thinking time. I remember as a kid how much I liked maps, and now I spend a big part of my day inching along a map I know almost as well as my house. Fortunately for the company and their car, I've lived in this part of the country all my life. Most people don't know that you need to change the oil and all the filters after each trip. Dust is a way of life here, and you'd better learn to accept air you can see and taste. More than one of our road equipment reps has been stranded for a lot of unpleasant hours just because no one told him about how cars hate dust." Before being hired as a sales rep for an independent Caterpillar dealership in the southwest, George Kendrick had worked as a service engineer for six years. And before that, he'd been a truck mechanic. "When they told me they wanted me to be a service engineer I was pretty excited. 'Engineer' is an impressive word. Then I found out that the difference between a service engineer and a mechanic is that a mechanic gets to go home at five o'clock." If George were a dog, he'd be a mutt: he is a little bit of everything. He is self-educated, working his way up from mechanic's helper to mechanic on ability and a firm handshake. He also loves what he does. When his company asked him to become a sales rep, he was more than a little surprised.

"I thought they were going to promote me to foreman. When they said they wanted me to sell, I really thought they were kidding. But what had happened was that they'd developed a new line of road-building equipment and the only guys who knew anything about it were guys like me, service engineers. It was funny. We always used to put down salesmen as city-slicker types, the kind of used-car salesmen you'd see in the movies. Boy, did we get educated in a hurry!" George attended a two-week sales training course, after which he and three other service engineers parted ways and hit the road. "At first I thought there had to be a catch. I got a $5,000 raise, a company car, an expense account, and a commission." George would fantasize about the commission. "If I sold just one dual-lane slipform paver, I'd make $1,250. If I sold a million dollars of equipment in the year, I'd get $6,000. Catch or no catch, I was ready."

The heavy equipment industry has gone through a metamorphosis, and George Kendrick has been a part of it. He explains that he sees himself in the evolutionary stages of an industry that is vital to the growth and economy of the nation. It is an industry that has seen its level of sales representation evolve in less than a decade from a back-road, fly-by-the-seat-of-your-pants environment to a sophisticated, high-tech, jet plane and satellite operation. "The one thing that had me worried was the selling part. I'd always thought salesmen were polished, slick types who were very glib. That wasn't me and never would be. But I figured that there was nobody who knows this equipment better than I do and nobody who can give a road contractor more reasons to buy it than I can." George's bosses knew that the presidents of the contracting companies were guys who started out just as he did—by getting their hands dirty. Their strategy was simple: use sales representatives who speak the language, and use service engineers, not city-slickers.

George Kendrick's territory includes eastern Oklahoma, eastern Kansas, and all of Arkansas. George's sales manager, Ernest Aronson, explains that representatives like George make $25,000 per year plus an escalating commission which begins at .5 percent after $250,000 and increases to 1.4 percent after sales over $5 million. "My boss was the one who set the commission schedule," Ernest says. "He'd sold corporate insurance at one point and had been pretty unhappy with the descending commission structure typical of the insurance industry. He knew a lot of insurance reps who stopped pushing after awhile because they didn't have a big enough carrot

> "The training of sales reps used to consist of a slap on the back, a puff of cigar smoke, and a 'Go get 'em kid.'"

dangling in front of them. He's a great guy to work for. He's actually proud of the fact that his people can get rich on commissions. You don't run into many people with that kind of attitude." Tim Boswell, the director of sales and Ernest's boss, says, "I want to see my salesmen get rich, because it means that the company does also." Ernest does receive a cut on what his reps sell, but he gets a performance bonus based on his group's sales performance compared to the average of all groups. Tim Boswell is paid on a straight salary basis plus bonus.

Road-building companies typically start out by having their sales reps sell directly to road contractors. Then, as product lines become more complex and sophisticated, they evolve into a distribution arrangement with local dealers. CMI of Oklahoma City is an example of a small company which began with a direct sales approach to the road-building industry and local sales reps who traveled the back roads of the Southwest. Today they sell to distributors all over the globe. One of the most significant elements that propelled CMI was their engineering. CMI has developed some road-building equipment which actually revolutionized the industry. One such piece of equipment is their spreading machine, which is used to spread base material—rock, concrete, or asphalt—for the roadbed. CMI's spreader can handle a forty-foot subgrade with a one-eighth-inch tolerance. This means that the road contractor knows exactly how much material is needed, and that highway officials can determine that a roadbed is of uniform consistency. Prior to this equipment breakthrough, it was not uncommon for roadbeds to be inadequately thin in spots, and for them to crack as a result. However, building the better mousetrap wasn't enough for CMI. Even convincing the presidents of the road-building contracting companies that they had a better mousetrap wasn't enough. They had to convince the state highway officials who in turn had to approve the use of the new technology. Their strategy worked, and once the highway officials at the state and municipal level, and the county engineers who were responsible for validating the tolerance specifications of state and federally funded highways were convinced that CMI could do the job, the company was on the way.

Other road-building equipment developed by CMI includes dual-lane slipform pavers, dual-lane autograde machines, and scarify machines. The list price to contractors for the equipment typically runs between $50,000 and $300,000. All of CMI's equipment is designed for maximum efficiency from both an engineering and a cost perspective so that it stands out against the competition in the very aggressive construction industry. Contractors jump at CMI's equipment because it enables them to tender lower bids for road-building contracts with the states.

Not long after the introduction of this equipment by CMI, other manufacturers started producing machines with the same technology. These manufacturers are quick to point out that in road-building equipment, quality not price, is the primary sales feature. The potential expenses that could be incurred through inadequate road construction are astronomical, not to mention the possibility of damages, liability, forfeited construction bonds, and whopping fines. However, as the industry and the associated technology evolved and the typical industry shakeout occurred, quality was no longer such a competitive issue or strong selling point because the equipment provided by the core number of road-building companies was assembled from the same suppliers, represented the same technology, and was basically of the same high quality.

Suddenly the road-building and construction industries found themselves with a select group of heavy-equipment manufacturers who could supply them with high quality for all of their contracts. This industry evolution effected an important change both in the methodology of selling in the industry and in the sales force itself. Where previously sales representatives had been calling on the presidents of road-building companies to sell them on the new technology, they now had to call on the contractor's purchasing agent, or more often they found themselves selling to local area distributors. A representative for Ingersoll-Rand, our number-three ranked company, who's been in the business over twelve years, says: "It's not as much fun now that the industry is civilized." He really misses the rodeo atmosphere of the early days of the industry, when salesmen traveled the dusty Southwest and contractors were hundreds of miles apart. Today the rodeo has been replaced by a fashion show and the dusty back-road circuit has been replaced by chrome-and-glass showrooms.

Andrew Wheat, an executive of Caterpillar Tractor Company, our number-four ranked company, says, "The training of sales reps used to consist of a slap on the back, a puff of cigar smoke, and a 'Go get 'em kid.' Today sales reps attend regularly scheduled company sales seminars, and many companies send their reps to AMA seminars in New York once a year." Today's heavy-equipment sales representative must also be aware of the levels of political approval in state, county, and local administrations that are responsible for construction programs. Andrew explains that his salespeople must learn how to work within the guidelines of government approval. Also, technological progress in the road-building and construction industries almost always involves state and local officials, even when federal approval is not necessary for funding. Andrew points out, "When the industry began using recycling machines, it took some state highway departments a full year to approve their use. Recycling machines have been incredibly valuable because they enable the contractor to use a mixture consisting of between 65 percent and 75 percent old materials in the construction of the roadbeds. This has reduced costs dramatically." Prior to the development of recycling machines, when road-building contractors repaired roads, they would discard the old concrete and asphalt. Today those materials are recycled and the enormous savings are passed on to the states. Andrew adds, "California has the toughest highway construction standards, so manufacturers know that when they have the okay from California, they have the industry equivalent of the Good Housekeeping Seal of Approval nationwide and often worldwide."

There is another, equally lucrative aspect to the heavy-equipment industry, and that's foreign sales. American construction companies are among the most technologically advanced and highly skilled in the world, and even though they are among the most expensive, their expertise is in great demand in Asian, Middle Eastern, and Third World countries. Because much of the major construction in the Third World is funded through either the U.S. State Department, Aid to International Development, or international banking sources, the contractors must satisfy strict performance standards and usually must post large performance bonds. The same is true for construction projects in the Middle East. There, funded by the huge resources of oil revenues, oil-exporting countries have embarked on major construction programs. Each quarter, a variety of newsletters circulating through the international construction and service industries announces major new projects and requests for proposals to bid competitively on contracts to be written for the construction of entire cities. The companies that win the bidding for these projects have to rely on their equipment, and American-manufactured heavy equipment is among the best in the world. As one analyst explains, "Americans have spent so much

> *"California has the toughest highway construction standards, so manufacturers know that when they have the okay from California, they have the industry equivalent of the Good Housekeeping Seal of Approval nationwide and often worldwide."*

time building and rebuilding, they've just gotten good at it. And they don't play around with second-rate equipment."

Selling internationally is quite different from selling in the American marketplace, according to industry spokesmen. James Creighton, a director of sales whose territory includes Japan and China, says, "Foreign sales strategies are almost completely unrelated to domestic sales strategies. For openers, the sales rep has to know the language of the country." But as many an unhappy sales rep has discovered as he innocently butchered the Japanese language and more than a few Japanese customs, it's not at all difficult to thoroughly offend foreign clients. James points out, "Many companies have learned the hard way and now send their foreign reps to AMA seminars where the reps are taught those aspects of foreign culture and society necessary for them to conduct business overseas. After I started the AMA programs in my company, our Far East sales increased approximately 12 percent." Most foreign sales representatives indicate that what they have learned in two business quarters spent on the road in foreign countries could fill an encyclopedia. James explains, "The Chinese and Japanese negotiate from an entirely different perspective than Americans. Once you try to sell to the Hong Kong and Taiwan markets, all bets are off." Other representatives from companies doing business in the Middle East report that the sales etiquette is so strict that one missed cue is enough to send a multimillion-dollar contract to a competitor.

A former director of foreign sales reports that he would hire only an engineer to be a sales representative overseas. His logic is the same as it was in the early days of the industry, when the salespeople were service engineers, and most of the buyers were road-building contractor presidents who had also started out as mechanics. It turns out that the buyers of road-building equipment overseas typically have an engineering background. Therefore, logic dictates that the salesperson who is hired should be the one who speaks the language. In other words, hire the engineer.

But there's a lot more to foreign sales than just "hiring the guy who speaks the language." James Creighton reports, "Obviously, when we travel overseas it's not too practical to bring along a twenty-ton piece of equipment." So demonstrations are handled in two ways. One is by the use of slide presentations. Some companies have a full-time staff person whose job it is to put together polished and sophisticated presentations. The second way is to bring Mohammed to the mountain. Companies typically hold road shows to which they invite all interested parties. And the truly amazing thing is that usually the buyers and government officials who attend these road shows pay their own way. According to one show coordinator, the atmosphere at the shows is very much all business, and even the after-hours entertainment is sedate—usually dinner and sometimes a local show.

Jeanette Lee is a road show coordinator for a major manufacturer of heavy construction equipment. She worked with an advertising agency in New York City before she was hired away by the equipment company. "When I compare my office in a converted railroad car with what I had on Madison Avenue, I just shake my head." Jeanette's story sounds like a Hollywood script. Her company was attempting to sell some equipment to the Soviet government. The Soviets were to send five engineers to what amounted to a private road show at the company plant in Kansas. Jeanette says, "The potential sale was very large so everyone was on edge, and the prospect of having 'Russkies' in Kansas didn't help calm anyone down either. No one really knew what to do or what to expect. When the big day came, the five Russians were introduced to us by a State Department official with the kind of pomp and circumstance Kansans never see. It soon became obvious to the company executives that the Russian engineers were not here to buy, but rather had been sent to learn how to build the equipment themselves. The company executives were mildly amused because they knew that it was impossible to do that in the four weeks which had been allotted by the Russian government. The Russian engineers soon realized this also. Therefore, without ever having discussed the issue explicitly, everyone seemed to suddenly adopt an attitude of 'What the hell, at least let's have a little fun.' And what ensued was a round of zany partying, with the Russians learning how to square dance, and the company executives practicing those boisterous Russian dances on some tables. By the time the four weeks ended, there were some friendships formed. One of the Russians had taken a strong interest in a vice-president's cowboy hat, and on saying goodbye, the VP gave it to him. Russian citizens simply do not have the material possessions that we do, and those possessions that they are able to buy are very few and far between. So giving up a valued possession is a very big thing. The Russian engineer had a wristwatch. He took it off and handed it to the VP, and when the plane took off there wasn't a dry eye in the house." Unfortunately, Jeanette's story has an unhappy ending. A year later the VP traveled to Russia on another business deal and decided to look up his engineer friend. He discovered that the man had become a nonperson, just like in the movies. Apparently, the Russian engineer's superiors felt that he had become too westernized. No one ever found out exactly what happened to him, but State Department officials said that he was most likely sent to a rehabilitation camp. As a postscript, it became common knowledge some years later that when Russian groups, such as the engineers, travel outside Russia, at least one member of the group is a KGB agent.

As is the case with domestic sales of heavy industrial equipment, foreign sales have also undergone a metamorphosis. Mike Warren, an executive of one of the smaller equipment manufacturers competing in the international marketplace, freely admits that today there is no way he would ever hire himself as he was when he started his company's overseas export business. Laughing, he recalls, "My responsibility was to open markets in Central and South America. I didn't even speak Spanish. And by the time I'd learned enough Spanish to get by, I'd covered every country except Brazil. I figured that at least I was going to one country with all the bugs worked out of my presentations. Of course, I didn't realize at the time that Brazil's national language is not Spanish but Portuguese."

Mike describes how he visited libraries and telephone companies in cities such as Caracas and Bogota to look up the locations for dealers of equipment sold by International Harvester, Caterpillar, and other major suppliers of heavy equipment. He then called on the dealers and tried to convince them, in his own gesture-laden dialect of pidgin Spanish, to include his company's equipment in their line. "I looked for hungry dealers. I stayed away from dealers who appeared to be doing so well with their present lines that they weren't likely to aggressively sell ours." He also stayed away from dealers who carried competing lines of his type of equipment. "My goal on each trip was to come away with four dealers located in one or more major cities of each country I visited. After reviewing the dealership, I'd choose the one dealer I believed would do best by our product line and offer him an exclusive national territory." Typical dealer discounts were 15 to 20 percent on the equipment, and that meant that the dealer would make somewhere between $7,500 and $60,000 per sale, depending on the type of equipment sold.

Financing the equipment can also be a problem for foreign construction companies or companies working in a foreign country who do not have their own independent sources of cash. It is not uncommon for U.S. equipment companies to arrange loans for foreign dealers through the Import-Export Bank or U.S. domestic banks. In some cases, U.S. dealers eager to develop overseas business will back part of the loan or will provide a variety of third-party leasing arrangements to carry the cost of the equipment until the final payout. These types of arrangements are becoming common as more American banks, seeing the lucrative nature of international construction loans, are vying with each other to capture a share of the market. Thus, the sales representative, even a rep for a small company that is not a major international player, often finds it an easy matter to structure a deal in advance and sell the entire package, including financing, to a construction company. Mike Warren explains, "In many cases it was my ability to arrange for creative financing that closed the deal, not my selling ability."

In some cases, U.S. companies are selling directly against foreign governments who support manufacturers in their own countries. This usually means that the U.S. companies aren't selling because they don't

> *The early road show has been replaced by a modern version in which a full-time company manager with a full-time staff contacts dealers and appropriate government officials from around the globe and sets up transportation to these shows.*

have the financial flexibility to move money in at the same interest rates and terms of repayment that foreign governments can offer. In one instance, a sales representative had been cultivating a deal for his company to construct an airport in Indonesia. He'd made many trips there and spent considerable time and effort, not to mention the money he had charged against his company expense account. At the last minute, right before he expected to close the deal, the French government stepped in and offered to loan Indonesia all the money needed for the construction if Indonesia agreed to purchase the equipment from French companies. The Indonesians accepted the French offer on the spot, and the American sales representative was left out in the cold. He complained later that because many European

> " At our last road show, a considerable number of invitees came disguised as empty seats."

governments are anxious to pull the lucrative construction contracts away from U.S. companies, they will bankroll their own people and float what in this country would be called giveaway terms to the buyer. The sales representative can only go back to the company's bank for a competitive offer, but since the Europeans are playing with their own revenues and the Americans have to rely on private funds, the deck is usually stacked against them. Even a realist such as Mike Warren explains that the international marketplace does not play by the same rules that govern American transactions. Because the stakes are so high, he points out, and the gains to be realized by foreign manufacturers and their governments are so great, it is often worth it to a government to invest their limited tax revenue resources in grabbing a share of the international market away from the Americans who are the major players.

The picture in international sales today is a testimonial to the technological advances which are taking place in communications, computer equipment, and travel. The early road show has been replaced by a modern version in which a full-time company manager with a full-time staff contacts dealers and appropriate government officials from around the globe and sets up transportation to these shows. Although the foreign buyers and government officials are wined and dined, they still pay for their own transportation.

New computer technology has prompted some companies to design software which is capable of animated engineering displays showing the effectiveness of new equipment from an engineering as well as a cost-effectiveness perspective. Industry analysts expect that by the late 1980s it will be commonplace for a foreign equipment dealer to receive, via satellite transmission, updated materials from manufacturers worldwide. One industry source speaks of the changes that are going to affect the way trade representatives do their jobs: "Right now there are people working on holographic imaging to use in the presentation. With holography, the people will think they're operating the equipment. The industry has become so competitive that you're going to see a lot more high-tech glitter in the selling process."

A leading industry analyst, commenting on the industry as a whole, says, "Because exports are such a large part of the market, the industry is extremely sensitive to the fluctuating strength or weakness of the dollar in the world money markets." When the dollar is especially strong against foreign currencies, it creates a particularly difficult economic environment for American manufacturers, suppliers, or distributors in which foreign buyers trip over each other to get out of the way of U.S. products and their sales representatives. Executives from a number of heavy-equipment manufacturers complain that the foreign governments can score gains against American competitors because the value of the dollar works against the American products themselves. As international representative Jeanette Lee puts it, "At our last road show, a considerable number of invitees came disguised as empty seats."

When this happens, especially in the current international financial environment, companies that rely on international sales make reductions in their expenditures, and that usually means layoffs. Another industry source says, "The ax has been taken to employment rolls industrywide." Payrolls have been cut by over one-third. Industry giants like Ingersoll-Rand and Barber-Greene have seen the part of their market that is tied to oil and gas cut substantially. Barber-Greene, a major supplier of road-building equipment to the Arab states, has had orders canceled because the Arab countries are having their own troubles with dramatically falling oil prices, and their surplus revenues are dwindling fast. When this happens, it is the large construction projects that are usually the first to go because they are the most labor and capital intensive and because they can be a continuing drain on the countries' economies. As contract after contract is either postponed or suspended, the sales representatives in the different construction and equipment supply companies down the line start to feel the ripple effect. Eventually, construction in the area dries up, and the companies have to sell the equipment elsewhere. Production falls off to compensate for the new and unexpected growth in unsold inventory, and the responsibility falls upon the shoulders of the sales reps to move the equipment out. Caterpillar, the largest earth-moving machinery producer in the world, has been forced to close plants, and the rumors of the impending takeover of International Harvester are growing louder every day. Sales representatives, especially those who sell International Harvester's construction equipment, are particularly vulnerable to takeover rumors because new customers are reluctant to sign contracts for equipment that is manufactured by a company undergoing a management reorganization. After a merger, when people are being reassigned at the uppermost echelons and when middle management heads are rolling down the office aisles, sales representatives spend more of their time reassuring current accounts than selling new equipment. Their commissions and bonuses fall off, and they become vulnerable to the comptroller's ax.

Currently, in the heavy equipment industry, profits are being squeezed, and as indicated earlier, competition for market share is intense. Because exports account for approximately 50 percent of the market, the strong dollar has hurt the heavy equipment industry by making exports financially unattractive, and conversely, by making imports financially attractive to the U.S. market. Best able to withstand these forces are smaller, more flexible companies such as CMI, and diversified companies such as Ingersoll-Rand, which can swing more smoothly with market fluctuations. Companies such as Caterpillar and Barber-Greene are more susceptible to political repercussions in their main area of operation, earth-moving equipment. In the case of Barber-Greene, a backlog of U.S. interstate highway contracts should help to boost the company's position.

The major corporations in the heavy-equipment manufacturing industry are currently looking into creative financing arrangements to stay current with their debt and with their production capacities. An industry source reports, "With corporate debt on the rise, a number of companies are turning to financial markets for help. They are also following Exxon's lead in bond issues." Exxon recently issued a series of long-term zero coupon bonds, the funds from which were immediately invested in enough U.S. government securities to pay off the zeroes. Because of the difference in interest rates, Exxon realized a profit of $20 billion.

Although the machine tool market is not export sensitive, as is the case with the heavy machinery industry, the strong U.S. dollar has resulted in machine tool imports increasing their 1984 market share nearly 10 percent over 1983's, and nearly 20 percent over 1982. The good news for the industry is that major automobile manufacturers such as GM, who are committed to the "buy American" proposition, are expected to account for over three quarters of a billion dollars in sales in the next five years. For sales representatives, however, the competition from foreign sources is expected to grow more intense. One industry source says, "Imports supposedly make up 40 percent of the market, but there are a lot of small manufacturers who never make it into the statistics. The difference in the cost of labor alone between the U.S. and foreign countries will drive some U.S. companies out of the market, if not out of business altogether.

There are, of course, exceptions to this trend, such as Stanley Works, the world's largest hand-tool manufacturer, and Snap-On Tools. Stanley has been able to price itself successfully in areas of greatest foreign competition and make up the slack in other areas, most notably automatic garage-door openers. Mechanics' hand tools account for over 85 percent of their business, and with the boom in auto sales, Snap-On is well positioned in the market. Their marketing strategy has been unique to the industry. Snap-On Tools has over 3,000 dealers in the U.S. who sell out of walk-in vans. The vans travel to user locations and sell the tools at retail. One industry source says: "There's only one way the machine tool industry is going to survive in the U.S. and that's through the use of FMS—flexible manufacturing systems." Cincinnati Milacron, the largest manufacturer of machine tools, has already begun to do just that. An executive at CM reports, "We're the only tool company in the country with the robotics technology necessary to create FMS." Industry sources believe CM has already installed between five and ten FMS systems and has increased sales in the last fiscal year by approximately 15 percent. A newly hired rep for CM, who previously sold heavy equipment, says, "I was nervous about making the transition to selling machine tools. The people here have been great. The atmosphere is so much more relaxed." An executive at CM says, "We know what it takes for our reps to do the kind of job we want. Our attitude is: 'You're a professional and you know how to do your job or we wouldn't have hired you.' So, we let our reps do their thing and we stand behind them with all the support they need."

The outlook for sales representatives in the heavy equipment and machine tool industries cannot be generalized. Although both industries

> ". . . buyers of road-building equipment overseas typically have an engineering background. Therefore, logic dictates that the salesperson who is hired should be the one who speaks the language. In other words, hire the engineer."

will be facing major challenges in the next five years, there are companies with the demonstrated ability to move product. But the prospective sales representative will have to be cautious. These are not boom industries where sales are waiting to be picked off a bush. As an industry analyst says, "The successful rep will have to be creative, flexible, and innovative. Opportunities abound, but they will have to be made; they won't be found."

In choosing our top five, we looked for companies with a special philosophy of approaching the marketplace. Attention to the rapidly ex-panding benefits offered by high-tech implements, flexibility in approach-ing the market with diversified product lines, and ability to deal with the political influences that can potentially hurt overseas operations were the main issues we examined.

Cincinnati Milacron earned our number-one ranking for their strengths in all the areas indicated earlier. Their commitment to high

> *Snap-On Tools has over 3,000 dealers in the U.S. who sell out of walk-in vans. The vans travel to user locations and sell the tools at retail.*

technology makes them an excellent candidate for future expansion, and their willingness to be on the cutting edge of the industry bodes well for their reps. Sales at CM are on the upswing, having increased by 46 percent in the past two years, and the development of their highly successful flexible manufacturing systems promises continued growth. In addition, CM is known industrywide as an organization which takes care of its own, and that enhances their number-one ranking. In addition, with overseas sales rep-resenting less than one-fifth of CM's gross sales, they are less vulnerable to the problems mentioned earlier.

Stanley Works narrowly beat out Ingersoll-Rand for the number-two position in our survey. Although we feel that both companies offer excellent opportunities for sales reps, SW's preeminent position as the world's leader in hand tool manufacture and their less vulnerable position with regard to the vagaries of the foreign markets have earned them the nod. In addition, SW's recent acquisition of Ingersoll-Rand's Proto line indicates to us that they are in a growth cycle; a position favorable to the sales force.

Ingersoll-Rand edged out Caterpillar for our number-three rank on one issue: diversification. A representative for Ingersoll-Rand says, "The com-pany will always find a place for you. As long as they know that you do your job, you'll be okay." Although foreign sales account for nearly half of IR's gross sales, we feel that their diversification in areas as disparate as bearings, tools, gas rigs, and air compressors offers a cushion to sales reps against the kind of difficulties International Harvester is experiencing.

Caterpillar, as the world's largest producer of earth-moving equip-ment, simply could not be ignored. Projected sales during calendar 1985 are $7.5 billion, an increase of nearly $1 billion since 1984. And 1984 sales increased by $750 million over 1983's figures, so the numbers say that Caterpillar is on the upswing. Although sales have failed to meet company projections, we feel that the expectations may have been somewhat inflated. In addition, Caterpillar is recognized as the industry leader in marketing expertise.

For our number-five spot, we had a tie between David and Goliath. CMI, playing the role of David, earned their place through their commitment to engineering and high-tech advances, and through their support of sales representatives. CMI is in many ways an anomaly in the industry in that it is both engineering- and sales-driven. Representatives at CMI are very well compensated for producing results. In addition, precisely because CMI is David-like when compared to the industry behemoths, it is able to maintain enough flexibility to move quickly into more lucrative markets when old standbys falter.

Barber-Greene, playing the role of Goliath, is sharing the number-five spot. Although many industry analysts see Barber-Greene as being in trouble, we don't agree. The issues usually cited as negative in evaluating the company, such as the federal government's cutback of highway funds and a vulnerability to foreign political influences, we see as positive. We say this because B-G has weathered the worst of the storm. During 1984, a year that saw them faced with a number of unexpected obstacles such as the highway cutbacks, Barber-Greene's sales were less than 1 percent under the sales figures for calendar 1983. With the likelihood that federal highway funds will soon be flowing once again, and with the severe cost-cutting measures a thing of the past, we believe that Barber-Greene is positioned well for a big increase in sales.

	HEAVY MACHINERY	COMPENSATION	COMMISSION	SUPPORT	INTANGIBLE
1	Cincinnati Milacron Inc.	5		5	++
2	The Stanley Works	4		5	
3	Ingersoll-Rand Co.	4		5	
4	Caterpillar Tractor Co.	4		5	
5	Barber-Greene Co.	4		5	
5	CMI Corp.	5		5	

The industry median figure for our prototypical two-year rep is $28,700. Because the structure of compensation packages varies so widely in the industry, we have included only the compensation figure; this includes commission, if any.

Cincinnati Milacron [++]

The company's strong commitment to their employees, and their strong position in the high-tech area of flexible manufacturing systems has earned CM our [++].

PAPER

THE TOP FIVE:

1 | International Paper Co.
2 | Great Northern Nekoosa Corp.
3 | Champion Int'l. Corp.
4 | Hammermill Paper Co.
5 | The Mead Corp.

In an economy that is driven by the printed word, the paper industry is all important. But beyond print, paper and paper-based products play key roles in the construction and manufacturing sectors of the economy as well. As new technologies emerge and paper manufacturers find new markets for their goods and products, the industry will grow even further. Paper is a very high-volume, high-consumption industry, and the product typically flows from manufacturer to distributor to repackager to wholesaler to retailer. Most sales reps for the large paper manufacturers, therefore, deal directly with the large distributors or OEMs such as Xerox who repackage the product and sell it under their own brand names. Thus, it is usually only the high-volume end user that will recognize the identity of a major producer.

"When people ask me what I do for a living, and I tell them that I sell paper, they just sort of look at me blankly, smile politely, say something like 'that's nice,' and change the subject." So said John Thorsen, a former sales representative for Mead Paper, our number-five rated company. John's experience sums up one aspect of our research into the paper industry: it's an industry which the consumer hardly notices. One industry source says, "In a way, it's a tribute to the industry that people outside take it for granted. People take the Rock of Gibraltar for granted too. It's always there." But to the people who run the paper mills, and to the company representatives who sell paper, the industry is not one to be taken for granted.

Roger Erickson, a sales representative for Champion International, our number-three ranked company, says, "Paper selling is more of a public relations job than a true sales job. My job really amounts to wining and dining my large accounts and establishing a personal relationship." George Dunphy, a representative for number-four ranked Hammermill, agrees. "There are probably ten or even fifteen paper manufacturers that will all deliver excellent quality and excellent service. The rep's job in this situation is to make sure that his accounts are kept happy and that his company's product is kept in the client's mind."

In the paper industry, as in the office-furniture industry, manufacturers' representatives usually sell to franchised dealers—called merchants in the industry—who in turn sell to end users. There are exceptions where a paper manufacturer might sell direct to a very large account, but John Thorsen explains, "The manufacturers never try to cut out the merchants by selling direct." Another similarity to the office-furniture industry is that manufacturers rely heavily on their merchants for end user sales, and they simply do not take any actions that could possibly jeopardize that relationship. George Dunphy comments on merchant sales: "The merchants can sell to anyone from Time-Life and AT&T on down to the local corner copy shop."

He describes some of the problems a mill representative can have selling to merchants. "The issue always boils down to warehouse space. Merchants typically stock paper from ten or fifteen primary mills, and maybe five secondary mills. There's just so much warehouse space that a merchant has, so you've really got to be pretty convincing if you want these guys to change their stock around for your paper." And what would prompt a merchant to do that? "Personality issues—convincing a merchant to carry your line because he likes you. Or showing him how he could move more tonnage of your paper than one that he's already carrying. One way to do that is to show him that you have a new product that will sell. For example, when carbonless forms were first introduced, some were better than others. There was a problem with the pressure needed to cause reproduction. On some forms, the pressure exerted by the weight of someone's hand resting on the form was enough to produce a reproduction of the hand, which of course caused a smudge." And so? "In a situation like that, if your mill has developed a product that defeats that problem, you can push it because your merchants have been getting plenty of complaints from their customers that the forms aren't doing the job and they're afraid of losing business." He adds, "In the particular case of carbonless forms, there is additional competition from Moore."

Moore, our number-two ranked printing company, recycles forms and makes their own carbonless forms. Since carbonless forms have been around as long as grass has been green, we asked if there are any situations in today's market that involve the same quality-oriented competition. George says yes. "The latest form-oriented development is carbonless

> *"Produce" didn't mean "produce now," it meant "produce yesterday."*

forms that can reproduce in color. One copy might have red writing, the next might be green, and so on. It's a brand-new technology and there's going to be some competition among the mills for the business." He hastens to add, "Forms are not where the money is in paper sales, however; specialty paper is." Specialty paper is coated paper which is used in catalogs, magazines, and books. The coating on the paper holds ink at the surface so that it doesn't run unevenly across the paper or into the fibers. This is the kind of paper used in four-color printing and is most often sold to printers for magazine and advertising work.

Warren Royce, a direct sales representative for Mead, comments on selling to book and magazine publishers: "The rep's contact at the big publishing houses is usually the production manager or the director of production. These folks are always bombarded with sales reps so when you call on them, you've got to make it good." He smiles and adds, "Of course, having Mead behind you does tend to open a few doors." Commenting on being a part of the direct sales force, Warren says, "I like it, but it's not for everybody. I like to get involved in the whole production process right down to finished products, and as a direct rep I can do that. The merchant reps usually do more hustling, and they tend to solve technical problems such as which kinds of papers or coatings are best for certain kinds of processes.

I like to solve problems that are more involved with the direct production of finished products, such as books."

Although Warren likes to get involved in problem solving, he wasn't quite prepared for what turned out to be his most unusual sale. It took place during the recent computer book boom, and Warren recalls: "I personally have never seen an explosion of such enormous numbers of books or publishers hit the marketplace before or since. One of my large publishing accounts came to me in a state of panic. They were trying to put together a package consisting of a book, a few computer cassette tapes, an operations manual, and they wanted the entire package boxed. It was a project the likes of which I'd never seen before. At that time book/software packages were quite new to the publishing scene. I had dealt with these people for many years, and I'd never seen them in such a state of terror. They were acting as if their jobs depended on finding a solution to their production problem, but I knew their jobs were secure." The phenomenon Warren describes was very common during the great computer book boom. Due to the nature of the computer business, it was imperative that new products got to the market immediately. New computers were being announced and released with incredible speed, and the sheer volume of updates of existing computers won adjective-of-the-year award for the word "obsolete."

The problems of the computer and software manufacturers became the problems of book publishers. An industry that was used to being very laid back and esoteric was being told that it had to produce in a way it had never done before. "Produce" didn't mean "produce now," it meant "produce yesterday." There were some very qualified people in publishing who simply had never had to do the kind of things that were being asked of them, and although they eventually learned, the experience was something they'll never forget. The computer industry became a very large rock that got dumped into a lake. The result was more of a tidal wave than a ripple effect, and more than one boat overturned. After the wave crashed into the publishing industry, it roared through the paper industry with equal force, aided and abetted by the cries of frantic production managers who were under the gun from top management to "do it." And the buck stopped in the laps of people like Warren. "As you can imagine, we have a great number of resources at our disposal, so I was in a good position to help. I set the publisher up with a packaging house for the box and the interior holders for the cassettes. I was even able to put the publisher's production people in touch with a cassette copying service I'd heard of through another one of my contacts." But even with Warren and all his contacts at the helm, the ship foundered. "We found a printer who could handle printing the box covers, the book covers, and the manual cover, but not the cassette box covers." Adding to the problem was the fact that this book/software project represented the publisher's entrance into the high-tech market and they understandably wanted everything to be 110 percent. "Little did they know," laughs one of our computer representatives, "that the rest of the computer industry hasn't quite made it to 75 percent."

So here was Warren and his band of crazed and desperate assistants still struggling with the problems inherent in coordinating a whole new production endeavor. "It got truly bizarre. By the time we coordinated all the printers and all the packagers, we found out that some of the printers didn't have the inks that the publisher was going to use on the book cover. We had inks flying all over the country, and box covers, boxes, book covers, and manual covers all criss-crossing each other all over the United States in an attempt to pull the project together." The printers had a field day. "Printers love it when a customer, especially a new, rich customer, tells them, 'I need it yesterday.' After the printer bitches and moans about press time, scheduling, and overtime, and after he says that the best he can do is the middle of the twenty-first century, he always pauses." Warren laughs. "For every second the customer lets that pause go on, the printer jacks up the price. On this project, the publisher paid exactly one arm, one leg, and his first-born son to get the job on a priority status." Having had some experience with the kind of problem Warren describes, we are impressed that it got solved so easily. But we are wrong. Warren chuckles at the memory. "There was one tiny complication. After all the wheels of production were set into motion, the publisher got an urgent call from one of the software reviewers. And what did the reviewer have to say? He said that while the cassettes may have some value as kindling for starting campfires, the programs on them were essentially worthless."

Now what was the publisher to do? "It turns out that the concept of the programs was okay; it was the cassette tape medium that was wrong. What was needed were computer disks. They hired a team of computer jocks and the programs were done and humming and the manuals were adjusted within a week." Great, we say, relieved that they finally did it. "Not so," says Warren. "They had all the guts in place—the book, the manuals, the disks—but the packaging was all wrong. It was designed for cassette tapes, not disks, but they were able to salvage most of it, and they finally got it all together." But he adds, "No one thought of the assembly problem. They were going to have 25,000 books, an equal number of manuals, box bottoms, box tops, and box inserts, plus 50,000 computer disks. How was it all going to get put together?" Well, how did it get put together? "One of the printers had a brother who worked in a home for retarded adults. To earn money for the residents of the home, they would hire out the residents to assemble all kinds of packages. Usually they did envelope stuffing, but they were eager to do our assembling, and they did a good job. The final chapter came when a truck pulled up to the home and they loaded 25,000 boxes into it and sent it off to be shrink-wrapped."

One interesting aspect of the paper industry is that in addition to direct sales from the major mills such as Mead, there are some OEM operations, the most notable of which involves the great copy giant, Xerox. Kent Ayella, a representative with Great Northern Nekoosa, our number-two ranked company and the world's largest producer of uncoated paper, says, "We make all of Xerox's copy paper. They just put their name on it." According to Kent, "Xerox, as you might imagine, is a corporate account. I'm sure the account was signed at the senior management level, and if there are any reps on the account now, they are there strictly to dot the *i*'s and cross the *t*'s."

For paper representatives, the first priority in choosing which mill to work for isn't the quality of the training or the product support, or even company prestige. Cash is ranked first of all factors and everything else is tied for last. This is decidedly different from other industries where the representatives often indicated that there were important factors beyond compensation, but not so paper reps. We were so surprised at this response that we asked a sales manager point blank, "Do you know what all the industry reps are saying is their number-one criterion for going with one mill over another?" He said, "Sure. Money. In fact, when I interview some kid fresh out of college and I ask him why he wants to be a sales rep, if he says anything besides, 'I want to make money,' I won't hire him." Before you get the impression that paper reps and mills are a bunch of dollar-chasing cutthroats who care only for their income, listen to the rest of the explanation. "You have to keep in mind that there are probably a dozen mills in the country and all are producing a high-quality paper, all are giving adequate-to-good training, all are supporting their reps, and all have an excellent

> *"Buying the wrong paper for a job is not unlike buying the wrong fuel for your car. But it can be a hell of a lot more expensive."*

reputation. So, why would a rep choose one over the other?" Clearly, the answer is money.

Probing the issue of compensation a bit further, we uncovered two interesting facts: First, there are other issues besides money that count in the eyes of the industry representatives. It turns out that our top five mills— International Paper, Nekoosa, Champion, Hammermill, and Mead—enjoy a superior reputation for training and supporting their salespeople. Second, expense accounts in the paper industry are quite high. A sales manager says, "Expense accounts range between $15,000 and $35,000. The whole industry is based on wining and dining merchants. Of course, the companies build this into their budgets, and frankly, if one of my reps is eating in diners instead of good restaurants and pocketing the money, I'd fire him." But the sales manager's reason is quite interesting: "I'd fire him not for stealing, but for short-changing the merchant rep. We're a first-class operation, and I want our reps to communicate that."

One of the best ways to judge the outstanding company in the paper industry is to look at sales history. When we examined the sales history of International Paper, the New York-based industry giant, it came up number one on sales performance as well as for a number of other reasons. They scored a 5 on our compensation scale, indicating that our prototypical two-year industry rep at IP earns more than $23,210, a figure which is more than 10 percent over the industry median compensation figure of $21,100. Sales at IP have climbed steadily since 1982, with 1983 figures up by 9 percent, 1984 sales up another 8 percent, and projections for 1985 indicating another rise of 6 percent to $5 billion. In addition, IP is the world's largest paper manufacturer and the largest industrial landowner in the United States with over seven million acres of timberland.

An industry source says, "It's not unusual for paper reps to help out in the overall production process. The good reps have usually been around all aspects of the industries in which the paper gets used, plus they have great contacts. They also know paper very, very well. Buying the wrong paper for a job is not unlike buying the wrong fuel for your car. But it can be a hell of a lot more expensive." Daniel Thornton, a representative for IP, agrees. "When I started out in this business, I did a lot of cold calling. In one case I called on a small publishing house and tried to sell them a special coated paper for a children's book they were doing. They were printing the book in four colors and were planning to use a grade of paper that was not only inadequate for the job, but also more expensive than what I had to offer." Daniel doesn't like what he calls "nickel and dimers." "I can appreciate the fact that a company has a budget. But there are places where you just can't cut corners." He continues, "They really yanked my chain. First they placed an order for the paper, then they changed it, then they canceled it. Finally, I went to the production manager and I told her point blank that they couldn't print a four-color book on toilet paper." The coating on paper for four-color printing is very important, since if the coating is inferior, or not there at all, the pages of the book can easily end up resembling a surrealistic rainbow that is very hard to read. Daniel knew his paper, but the president of the company didn't. "He was a real know-it-all guy. I'd heard that he'd made his editors switch from Federal Express to one of the lesser-known air carriers when they sent important manuscripts in order to save fifty cents per package, and as a result lost a quarter-million-dollar book contract when a manuscript arrived three days late."

But by the time Daniel went to see the president, he said, "I was in no mood for baloney. I asked him if he wanted to publish a quality book or a piece of garbage." He gave me a fifteen minute lecture on the paper industry and how smart he was, and then he told me I could have an order for an uncoated paper or I could leave." And? "It was my first job and one of my first sales, so I took the order." Daniel says, "I don't usually like to see other people have misfortune, but in this case, I loved it. The book was a mess—the colors bled, and with children's books especially, the quality is very important to the sale and I knew the book wouldn't sell." So, what did Daniel do in this case? "I marched right back up to the president's office, showed him the book, and asked him if he was satisfied." Daniel chuckles at the recollection. "He was livid. He threw me out and canceled the account. He even demanded a refund on the paper he had ordered but he had as much of a chance at that as I do of being elected president. I learned not to compromise standards to make a sale. If I had it to do all over again, I would walk away from the sale if I couldn't convince them to take the right kind of paper."

An industry source says, "IP has a reputation for doing things right. They take care of their reps, both in terms of compensation and of support, and it's not surprising that they have the lowest turnover rate in the industry." We agree fully, and as a result have rated IP as the number-one company in the industry.

The industry giant with the unusual name of Great Northern Nekoosa has earned our number-two ranking, just a notch ahead of Champion, our number-three ranked company. For one, they scored a 4 on our compensation scale, indicating that at Nekoosa our prototypical two-year industry representative earns between $22,155 and $23,210, a figure which is between 5 and 10 percent above the industry median compensation figure of $21,100. For another, Great Northern Nekoosa, formed in 1970 from the merger of the Great Northern Paper Company and Nekoosa-Edwards, is the largest manufacturer of uncoated paper in the world. It is so large that Xerox has found it profitable to OEM their copy paper from GNN. Also, sales at GNN have been increasing nicely with 1983 figures up 9.5 percent, 1984 sales up another 20 percent, and projections for 1985 indicating another increase of 7 percent to a nice, round $2 billion.

Another reason Nekoosa received our number-two ranking is that, in the words of a merchant rep, "Nekoosa supports their merchant reps better or at least as well as any company in the industry. Mills like IP will sell paper, particularly forms, directly to end users." And how does a merchant rep deal with that? "I'll order small quantities, say five or ten rolls at a shot from IP. But for the really big orders, I'll switch over to Nekoosa's forms division."

Rodney Rogers, a GNN rep based in New York, comments on selling in the highly competitive New York market: "New York has well over 5,000 printing businesses of all sizes and shapes, and the owners of the businesses are constantly being bombarded with sales reps for all manner of things ranging from equipment to supplies to paper." Carlton Taylor, one of Rodney's merchant reps, describes how Rodney has helped his territory grow in revenues by over 50 percent in the last two years. Carlton explains: "Rodney holds seminars in which he and his support people keep us up to date on the latest developments in paper. Frequently, he'll hear of a new application from one of his merchants and he'll pass it along to us." Rodney adds, "I also like to use the seminars to keep the merchant reps' blood circulating, to keep them enthusiastic. It's nice for them to know that the mill cares enough to do a lot more than just fill orders." Carlton chuckles and replies, "Yes, and let's not forget that there are a lot of mills out there that would really love to sell their paper to us." Rodney acknowledges Carlton's friendly dig. "The competition is very tight, particularly for the merchants who are stocking paper." Rodney explains that a growing number of merchants have simply become order takers, and they don't stock paper. He says, "Obviously it's a heck of a lot cheaper to be able to do business without carrying inventory. These merchants who don't stock paper just take orders and call up the mill on an as-needed basis." He adds, "Of course, the merchants who do stock paper get preferential treatment, as well as first crack at supplies. Having a merchant stock your paper in inventory is pretty much a guarantee of continuous orders since you know they're going to push their stock paper whenever possible rather than make special orders, and if the stock is depleted, and therefore moving, they'll order more."

An industry source comments on the inventory issue: "More and more merchants are not carrying inventory, and instead are acting almost as mill agents or middlemen. These merchants secure business with end users and simply place orders with the mills. The problem is that pretty soon the mills are going to be asking themselves why they need the merchants. Why not sell direct and cut out the merchant's percentage?" Either way, long-term prospects for GNN are excellent, and that's just one of many reasons why the company with the unusual name earned our number-two rank.

The recent acquisition of the newsprint-rich St. Regis Corporation boosted Champion International a notch above Hammermill, into the number-three spot. Champion has long been known in the industry as a leader in general paper sales, and the acquisition of St. Regis' newsprint expertise can be nothing but good news for Champion representatives. Champion's sales figures have also been quite impressive with 1983 sales up 17 percent, 1984 sales up another 22 percent, and 1985 sales projected to be up yet another 41 percent. Champion earned a 4 on our compensation scale, indicating that at Champion our prototypical two-year industry rep earns between $22,155 and $23,210, which is between 5 and 10 percent above the industry median compensation figure of $21,100.

John Thorsen says, "The operating margins in the paper industry are probably the tightest of any industry in the country, if not the entire world. The margin that a large merchant company makes on a carload of standard grade paper is between 3½ and 6 percent over cost." Roger Wilhite, a Champion rep, adds, "Paper is a high-volume industry. Even though the top-notch merchant reps are making between 20 and 40 percent of the merchant company's net profit, the actual percentage on the sale is quite low." He adds, "They have to sell quite a few tons of the stuff to make a living. But, of course, they do." In an industry situation like this, salesmen sometimes have to appear unique to remain in a merchant's mind. Roger explains what he did to convince a particular merchant to become an account: "I'd been calling on one particular printer for almost a year. He was near a large account of mine, so I didn't mind dropping in. The guy would never talk to me. Something always 'came up.' Finally, after a year of visits like this, I stopped in and asked to use his bathroom. He just grunted at me in reply. Then I had an idea. I left one of my cards in the bathroom wedged into the mirror. I walked around his place and I left cards in all sorts of crazy places, so that they would keep turning up at odd times." And how did the strategy work? "After three weeks I got a call. He said 'Okay, I'll buy, I'll buy. Just come get your cards.' "

Hammermill is known as the largest producer of fine writing-grade papers. This Erie, Pennsylvania-based company has earned our number-four ranking for its commitment to long-term growth, as evidenced by the new paper-producing equipment it is acquiring. One industry source estimates that by the late 1980s Hammermill's paper production will be increased by over one-third just as a result of technological advances in equipment. We think this is good news for reps, since with more product there are likely to be more sales. The company also earned its number-four ranking by scoring a 4 on our compensation scale indicating that at Hammermill our prototypical two-year industry rep earns between $22,155 and $23,210; between 5 and 10 percent above the industry median compensation figure of $21,100.

Bob Green, a Hammermill rep, comments on selling to merchants: "There is a growing trend in the industry for merchants to act more as middlemen than as dealers for the mills. I think these merchants are eventually going to experience a falling out, and the ones who will remain will be the ones with the best contacts." He continues, "The merchants who are the true mill representatives, who stock paper, will become even more sought after. At least they will by me." Bob is commenting on a phenomenon in the industry mentioned by a number of mill reps, which makes it more profitable for the merchants to drop their warehousing costs and let the mills worry about it. But Bob Green and a number of other representatives agree that eventually more and more mills are going to be selling direct. "They can make an additional 5 percent on a sale by cutting out the merchant, and with margins being as tight as they are, if the merchants aren't going to assume warehousing responsibility, it will become a very attractive proposition for the mills to simply cut out the middlemen."

Mead Paper Corporation of Dayton, Ohio, has earned their place in our sun for a number of reasons, not the least of which is their sales of $2.7 billion, which makes them one of the industry giants. Mead's ranking was not higher for two reasons. One, they scored a 3 on our compensation scale, indicating that at Mead our prototypical two-year industry rep earns between $20,045 and $22,155, which is between 5 percent below and 5 percent above the industry median figure of $21,100. Two, Mead seems to be in somewhat of a transitional phase in its corporate development, having divested itself of most of its nonforest products, while simultaneously expanding its information retrieval business.

Monte Nesbitt, a former Mead representative now working for a New York merchant house, comments: "Mead is a great stepping stone in the industry. They teach you everything you need to know, both from a technical as well as a sales point of view. I worked for Mead for two years, and they really provided me with my entry into the big money market." John Thorsen, another former Mead rep, agrees. "The training is excellent. Before they let you out on the street to sell, they make very sure that you know your business." We asked John why he is no longer with Mead. "Money," he replies. "Mead is a great company to work for, but there's a lot more money to be made in independent—merchant—sales." How much more money? "A number of people I know who are merchant reps are earning six figures a year and I don't know any merchant reps personally who are grossing under $50,000." With these figures being bandied about, we wondered why every mill rep in the country didn't quit and go to work for merchant reps. Monte had an answer: "For one thing, not every merchant rep makes the kind of money I've described, and not every merchant outfit can provide its reps with the opportunities that I've had. For another, there's a lot more long-term security at a company like Mead than there is working for a merchant rep. Mead is a $3 billion company and they own two million acres of forest land. The point is that they're not going to be leaving town in the near future. They're around to stay. Even with the top merchant reps, you don't have that kind of foundation." John Thorsen agrees. "If you want to have a house in the suburbs, two cars, and send two kids to a good college, Mead will be able to supply you with the income to do that. If you want to be a wealthy man, you can't stay at Mead." Nor, as former sales representatives explain, can you stay with any mill if riches are your goal. However, this financial dichotomy between working for manufacturers and working for dealers is very common in the industries which are organized by manufacturers and dealers. As one example, in the office-furniture industry, which was the Cadillac industry for manufacturers' representatives with a median compensation schedule of approximately $41,000, the dealer representatives still had the potential to earn considerably more, frequently in the six figure range. And, in the office-furniture industry, it was also true that the greatest security was in working for the top manufacturers.

Mead's reputation as a first-class organization which offers excellent training to its reps helped place them among our top five companies, but their compensation figures, which were slightly lower than those of our other four companies, contributed to our ranking Mead no higher than number five.

PAPER		COMPENSATION	COMMISSION	SUPPORT	INTANGIBLE
1	International Paper Co.	5		5	
2	Great Northern Nekoosa Corp.	4		5	
3	Champion Int'l. Corp.	4		5	
4	Hammermill Paper Co.	4		5	
5	The Mead Corp.	3		5	

The industry median compensation figure for our prototypical two-year industry rep is $21,100 including salary and bonus.

PRINTING

THE TOP FIVE:

1 R.R. Donnelley & Sons Co.
2 Moore Business Forms Inc.
3 Pandick, Inc.
4 Bowne & Co., Inc.
5 Deluxe Check Printers Inc.

For people in the industry, printing is more than just a business or even a skilled trade; it is almost a way of life. Even the first industrial and commercial printers in the 16th century were considered master craftsmen whose reputations rose or fell on the beauty, quality, and accuracy of their work. This hasn't changed. Our most successful printing companies stand behind the aesthetic quality of their work as well as behind their reputation for turning large and complicated jobs around quickly and without errors. And in this industry, as in so many others, the sales representatives who respond to their customers' needs first and sell solutions rather than product are the ones who are most successful.

The printing industry encompasses a wide range of activities. At the consumer and small business end of the spectrum there are storefront operations like the small "ma and pa" local offset print shop. At the commercial and corporate end of the spectrum there are huge four-color magazine and book printing factories that are completely mechanized with word processing input, integrated typesetting, high-speed web presses, and automatic binders. Printing is one of the most diverse and loosely structured industries in the United States, as well as being one of the largest and most important. And because the commodity of information is a vital component of our gross national product, the industry will continue to grow and gain in importance throughout the rest of the century.

Printing is unlike any of the other industries in our survey because it spans a very wide set of related technologies that do the same thing—graphically recording and duplicating messages on paper—in different ways. Storefront "quick-print" franchises in many shopping centers and business districts can run their entire operation from a single photocopier or offset press. The financial printers, such as our third- and fourth-ranked companies, Pandick and Bowne & Company, use mammoth presses which can crank out 50,000 prospectuses in four colors in the twinkling of an eye. They can take a job from inception to completion in twenty-four hours and can be paid over $1 million for a day's work. In between these extremes, there are book and catalog printers such as our number-one ranked company, R. R. Donnelley and Sons; and forms printers such as our number-two ranked company, Moore Corporation. There are also check printers such as our number-five ranked company, De Luxe Check Printers, which work almost exclusively with banks.

Printing is one of the oldest and most protected industries in the world, among the first to have sales representatives and to be organized into skilled labor and trade unions. Printing is also one of the world's most durable industries, having evolved through a series of technological advances over thousands of years, beginning with the invention of writing and culminating in the recent development of laser imaging.

The industry began over three thousand years ago in the early Mediterranean civilizations, thrived during the Middle Ages, flourished in Asia after the invention of block printing, and became a formal skilled trade in Europe after Gutenberg developed his moveable type and press apparatus. The first press arrived in America in 1640 with the early groups of colonists. It was from this press that the *Bay Psalm Book*, the first mass-published book in the American colonies, was pulled at a private shop in Cambridge, Massachusetts. Eventually the press was moved to Harvard College where it became one of the first presses of the Harvard University Press, the oldest continuously operated printing facility in the United States.

Early printers were considered publishers, and it was during this period that many of America's publishing traditions were started. The most famous early printer-publisher entrepreneur was Ben Franklin who, despite all of his inventions and accomplishments, described himself as simply a printer until the end of his life. Because printing has flourished in North America for over 350 years and because its accompanying traditions of free speech are woven deeply into the fabric of our society, the printing industry has become emblematic of American enterprise. But beyond that, the printing industry has always been at the center of the great social enterprises that affect people's lives. It was the printed bible, the first official bestseller, that allowed the population of Europe in the sixteenth century to read the gospels for themselves. This, in turn, helped fuel the fires of the Protestant Reformation. It was a network of printers and their presses throughout the American Colonies that spread the news of the Revolution

> *Asked if he or Bowne had ever messed up, he answers, "No, and I can prove it—I'm here talking to you."*

and helped the individual colonial legislatures to remain in contact with one another. And even today, in Warsaw, Gdansk, and other Polish cities, it is a network of underground presses that keeps the members of Solidarity in touch with one another as a counterpresence to the official government news agencies.

For as long as printing has been an industry, printers have been selling their wares. Printing today is an aggressive business which spends millions of dollars a year on promotion and marketing. Just as the kinds of printers vary widely, so do the sales techniques. The financial printing industry is by far the most lucrative, for companies and for representatives, but the competition is fierce. It is not unusual for financial printers to hire famous sports and entertainment personalities as "sales reps." They are, of course, door openers. O.J. Simpson works for Pandick, our number-three ranked company. Is O.J., who also teams up with Arnold Palmer to pitch for Hertz, as knowledgeable about the printing industry as he is about renting cars? A Pandick rep says, "Who knows? If O.J. Simpson calls the president of a corporation who is putting together a large stock offering, and he invites the president to lunch, what's the president going to do?" He's going to have lunch with Mr. Simpson. This public relations technique has been growing at a rapid clip, according to an industry source. Fran Tarkenton has also been involved, and according to the same industry source, Pete Gogolak, a former place kicker with the football Giants, signed a contract with a $1 million bonus to sell printing.

Jim Wynanch, a representative for number-four ranked Bowne & Company, says, "Financial printing is not for amateurs or lightweights. If you get involved in this business without knowing exactly what you're doing, it's like going shark fishing—with you as the bait." An industry analyst agrees: "The companies that use financial printers often have hundreds of millions of dollars at stake in a stock offering. Everything that the printer does has to be 100 percent right, and it has to be exactly on time. A delay of one day for a book printer is considered good service. The same delay for a financial printer is considered a 'code-red bombs-are-falling' disaster and would probably be the death knell of the printer." As Jim explains, "The SEC regulations for stock and bond offerings are very specific and very strict. It's literally true that if one word in a prospectus is not correct, it can void the entire offering. In addition, these offerings are based on the stock price at market closing on a given day, so the whole production has to be completed between the time the market closes on Monday, for example, and in the hands of the SEC Tuesday morning."

Jim describes some of the all-night sessions he's attended. "In a way, they remind me of some of the all-night study sessions in college. But there's an important difference. Nobody screws around. Everybody involved in the process, from the client company lawyers to our proofreaders, is a professional. Everyone knows what has to be done, and we do it." He adds, "I know the whole process sounds very dramatic and mysterious, with huge financial deals being turned over in the middle of the night, but the fact is, it's all pretty routine. Obviously the financial aspects of the stock offering deal are already completed, and the act of putting together the prospectus or printing the actual stock is a pretty straightforward operation." But the aura of mystery and suspense, Jim suggests, still exists because the entire process is collapsed into one painfully exacting night's work. "Probably because printing is usually considered a pretty mundane profession, the thought of all this happening overnight, and with so much at stake, makes it exotic. We know what we're doing and we know what's at stake if there's a screw-up, so we make damn sure everything works to perfection." Asked if he or Bowne had ever messed up, he answers, "No, and I can prove it—I'm here talking to you."

Because selling financial printing is the most competitive area of print sales, the techniques used by sales reps are the most elaborate. Besides the employment of name personalities, sales representatives are expected to provide their clients with entertainment. One industry source says, "Entertainment can range from dinner at the Four Seasons for you and the missus, to some Hollywood-style scenarios." He elaborates: "Let me put it this way. For the high-end printing deals, where we're talking about high six or even seven figures, if you tell a rep that you'll deliver the deal, you can have just about anything you want in return." He explains that sales representatives at the most competitive companies can receive "anything from a nice, comfortable living, on up to the low-to-mid six-figure range, plus any perk you can imagine."

Other areas of the industry, such as book printing, are not as melodramatic, or as lucrative. According to Henry Goldstein, a production manager for a computer book publisher during the computer book boom, "I didn't buy my own lunch for two years. I almost had to buy a baseball bat to give to my secretary so she could keep the salesmen away. I used to dream that I was trapped in a room with a hundred salesmen banging at the door, and one would climb in the window. Then I'd wake up shaking." Those were the days when everybody from McGraw-Hill, our number-one publishing company, to Far Out Press, since gone out of business, was producing computer books. Henry says, "Look, I used to sell printing to publishers so I was sympathetic to those salesmen, but it got insane. I had guys offering me perks. I didn't want perks. I wanted books—well-made books done on time and at a good price."

The recent expansion and contraction of the computer book market illustrates, in a microcosm, the problems that printers have with book publishers. As an industry source explains, "Computer books, unlike most other books, could be obsolete really quickly. If you don't believe that, just ask all the publishers who are selling Texas Instrument computer books at 75 percent to 90 percent off list." Texas Instruments pulled out of the home computer market two years ago, causing many computer publishers to cancel the remainder of their TI books as a knee-jerk reaction. The same industry source adds, "Many book publishers were caught with their proverbial pants around their ankles, and with TI books up the wazoo. They rushed to dump them on the market." But not all publishers took such a short-range view of the TI problem. Jane Rafal, the production manager for Hayden Books in New Jersey, says, "Our thinking was that the TI market would actually expand. We didn't rush to dump our TI books." And it turns out that she made the right decision. "TI had to unload a lot of their home computers at very low prices, and a lot of people bought them. Our reasoning was that if one million new TI computers were going from warehouses to homes, a lot of people were going to be buying TI books." And indeed they did. Fran Teitelbaum, a spokeswoman for *Publishers Weekly*, says: "Some of the publishers who didn't panic at the TI crisis made out like bandits."

However, Henry Goldstein wasn't pleased with the TI developments. "That was the whole damn problem with computer books. Companies were coming and going all the time. It was like watching a tennis match. Apple serves. IBM returns. Osborne leaves the stadium. Back and forth. How the hell are you supposed to make plans that way?" Sam Fenty, a sales representative for Banta, laments, "I lost at least three big deals when publishers canceled orders, either because the hardware manufacturers went out of business or because the hardware manufacturers changed plans and that in turn changed the publisher's plans for the books." Henry adds: "And what made it even worse was that there were reps selling electronic printing services that could get your book from copy-edited manuscript to bound book in six weeks—supposedly. How were the production managers supposed to judge something like that? All that newfangled stuff was a start-up operation, even for the major printers." An industry source agrees: "One major publisher got burned badly on a book because they contracted to have it done electronically. They spent some serious cash on ad space to pitch the book, and the printer guaranteed them six weeks. The printer supposedly had equipment that could read text from any kind of word processor except, that is, from the one that this author used. But they assured the publisher not to worry because they had a backup system—an optical scanner. And so the day was saved, right? Wrong! The optical scanner was able to read text from a printed page and dump it on a computer disk which the printer would then use for typesetting. Nice system, expensive system—no typos, no proofing. There was one problem: the optical scanner read typed text—text produced from a typewriter. The author, being a computer jock, used a dot matrix printer." According to Henry, any-

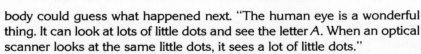

> " *Financial printing is not for amateurs or lightweights. If you get involved in this business without knowing exactly what you're doing, it's like going shark fishing— with you as the bait.* "

body could guess what happened next. "The human eye is a wonderful thing. It can look at lots of little dots and see the letter *A*. When an optical scanner looks at the same little dots, it sees a lot of little dots."

As production manager for a computer book company, Jane Rafal had a particularly stressful job during the flurry of computer book publishing. She reports that printers, more than most fulfillment operations, are held captive by a series of internal schedules, many of which are not of their own creation. They have to rely on camera-ready material from typesetters, stats from the photographer, and firm print-run orders from the publishers. Once press time is scheduled, it can be changed only at a significant cost. Therefore, changing schedules and last-minute cancellations caused serious problems for the book printers who were trying to serve their publishing clients. "Everybody was in a new situation. Computer books were as new as the computers, and just as the hardware and software companies had to make adjustments, so too did publishers and printers." But some printers, such as Donnelley, our number-one ranked company, didn't have too much adjusting to do.

Simply put, R. R. Donnelley and Sons is the largest commercial printer in the world. Sales have been booming right along, up 10 percent in 1983, up another 15 percent in 1984, and projected to rise another 14 percent, to $2 billion, in 1985. Donnelley has earned our number-one ranking for many reasons, but the main reason is best expressed by one of their competitors: "Donnelley is a class act." Donnelley earned a 5 on our compensation scale, indicating that at Donnelley our prototypical industry rep earns more than $31,900, over 10 percent above the industry median of $29,000.

Tim Stenson, a Donnelley representative in New York, says, "They are great to work for. Before I ever made a sales call, I felt like I knew the printing business inside out." Tim spent two years at one of Donnelley's printing plants, learning the business as a printer. And as any skilled printer will tell you, you have to experience what printing is like before you can sell it. Says Tim, "They expect you to work hard, and they take care of you when you do." John Carnes, a Donnelley representative for five years, affirms, "They teach you the business. On some sales jobs, you get product training or you get sales training. Here, you get both. The sales seminars are excellent. They're motivating as well as informative. The seminars are very tight."

Henry Goldstein comments about Donnelley representatives. "They're professionals. They're what I imagine the IBMers are like. They come prepared. They know what a publisher is doing and they know what books he has in the works. They always do their homework." Sharon Samuels, a production manager for a book publisher in New Jersey, agrees: "I've actually learned more about book production through the years from Donnelley reps than I have anywhere else." John Carnes is proud to be a Donnelley sales rep. "It's very nice to know that I'm respected, and I get that on first calls because my business card says 'Donnelley.'" An industry source remarks, "At Donnelley, they treat their reps as if they count. They fully expect that they will keep each of their reps for life, and they treat them that way." Whom do they typically hire? The same source says, "Usually they hire their reps right out of college. The thinking is that if they take someone who's worked in the industry, he'll have a passel of bad habits. By hiring reps fresh out of college, they can train them and have them learn the business 100 percent the Donnelley way.

While the computer book boom spelled trouble for many printers who had problems adjusting to the level of technology, it didn't for Donnelley because the company had already made its commitment to the new environment of electronic text processing. Tim Stenson explains, "In a lot of ways the mistakes that were made in the industry at large were the result of having people trying to jump into something new without adequate preparation. Maybe some of the smaller printers had no choice, but at Donnelley, things aren't done that way." An industry source adds, "They are expanding into the high-tech end of printing. They're doing some really sophisticated composition by computer. They use satellite transmission to send materials all over the world. They are a state of the art operation. And we haven't had the growing pains that have been common in the electronic publishing industry."

"In addition," a Donnelley spokesman points out, "we are going to be pursuing the electronic catalog market." Electronic catalogs are computer-based systems which can display merchandise on a computer screen. Donnelley's expertise at handling color images electronically gives them a clear edge in the perfection of this technology. The same Donnelley spokesman adds, "There are quite a few systems out there, but I don't think that any will be able to generate the kind of color resolution that is so critical to the merchandising concept. We've already solved the imaging problems that the other folks are still working on." And another industry source says, "Electronic imaging is not a new concept. It ties in with the idea of the shrinking planet, the idea that electronic communications are bringing distant parts of the world closer and closer together. I read a story a while ago about the first intercontinental bank card cash transfer made by a customer using a teller machine. A woman traveling in Australia, whose funds were deposited in her hometown bank in Iowa, went into a Sydney bank. She inserted the card in the machine and punched the buttons. This set into motion a chain reaction of electronic events and messages. The signal was relayed from the bank branch in Sydney to another Sydney location via telephone lines. From there it was beamed by satellite to Hawaii. From there it was relayed over cables to San Francisco, and from there, by telephone lines to her bank in Iowa. Finally, the pass codes were recognized at her home bank and the transaction was approved electronically, the signal giving the okay was sent the other way: Iowa, San Francisco, Hawaii, Sydney one, and Sydney two. The cash machine in Sydney spit out the woman's money and she was on her way. Incredibly, the whole transaction took about six seconds." The message is that the age of electronics and satellite communication is here, and Donnelley, because it utilizes electronic telecommunications devices in much the same way the correspondent banks between Sydney and Iowa do, is right in the thick of it.

Donnelley has earned our number-one spot in the printing industry for many reasons. They're big, they're good, and they take care of their people. If all this isn't enough, their client portfolio includes a couple of magazines you may have heard of—*Time* and *Newsweek*.

Moore Corporation is to business forms what Donnelley is to magazines and books, and what IBM is to computers. And that's one reason why this $2 billion-a-year industry giant received our number-two rating in the

> *"Those financial printing reps are very well taken care of, and the financial printers can certainly afford it."*

industry. Moore's sales have rebounded by 12 percent in 1984 after a three-year leveling off which saw sales fall from $1.85 billion in 1982 to $1.81 billion in 1983. According to Harvey King, a Moore representative based in New York, part of the reason for Moore's leveling off is due to "the computer venture." He elaborates: "The company felt that with our name being a household word, we had a natural market for branching out into other office-related areas." Specifically, Moore moved into the office automation field as a systems integrator: putting hardware and software into problem-solving packages and selling them to business. Moore's reasoning, according to Harvey, was that, "The doors were open for Moore sales reps. Why not bring in something besides forms?" But, as many companies who have tried to crack the office automation market can tell you, it just ain't that easy. However, Moore learned from the mistake. And they learned fast. Harvey says, "We got killed with the price competiton. So we got out of the systems business and into the computer store business." Moore utilized the staff and expertise it had built up during their venture into office automation, and turned their attention to computer stores with the purchase of a major chain.

Harvey comments on the frenetic New York printing market. "Care to take a guess as to how many printers there are in New York? Five thousand at last count, and the number keeps growing." He points out that with competition in such large numbers, a New York printer has to be doing something very right to keep growing. Moore, he explains, is doing it right.

"Moore is a great name to have engraved on your business card. It opens a lot of doors that would otherwise stay shut." And of course, this is another reason that Moore earned the number-two spot in our survey. "Sometimes it can almost get embarrassing. I don't do any true selling. I take orders." Harvey recounts one situation: "I'd heard that a major broadcasting company was having a problem with forms coming in from their printer. The printer had been late a few times, and the executives were leaning on the purchasing people to get the problem solved." So Harvey paid a visit. "I walked up to the purchasing agent and said, 'I heard you're having a delivery problem. I can solve it for you.'" Harvey laughs at the recollection. "Apparently the guy had some kind of deal with the printer rep—either he was getting a kickback, or maybe the guy was a friend. Anyway, he was pretty nasty to me and basically told me to get lost." But Harvey had done his homework. "I knew which execs were really hot about the work bottlenecks that had resulted from the delivery delays." So Harvey turned the screws a little bit. "I said to the purchasing agent, 'Okay. But when your

> "We're heading for a paperless society. Electronic banking is here to stay. It's popular with banks and consumers . . . People are going to stop using checks, ultimately, and the bank printers are going to be in trouble."

delivery gets screwed up the next time, I'm going to call Bob McFadden and tell him that he could have all the forms he wants right in front of him instead of in a warehouse somewhere.' I got a call later that day and wound up with a $5,000 annual account. The purchasing agent still hates my guts, but he'll be buying Moore forms for as long as he's in the company."

Kickbacks, according to Harvey, are a factor that sales representatives have to face within the industry. "Printing is really incredibly competitive, so it goes on a lot. Keep in mind that there are a hell of a lot of independents out there." An independent is a rep who works either on his own or for a printing representative company. "They are middlemen between businesses and the printers. Those guys work on straight commission, and I know for a fact that some of them make six figures. I'm not saying that all independents give kickbacks, but I am saying it's a lot scarier working on a straight commission and flying by the seat of your pants than it is working for somebody like Moore." And would Harvey ever give kickbacks to get a job? "Never have and never will. We don't do business that way. Period." Moore earned a 5 on our compensation scale, indicating that at Moore, our prototypical industry representative earns more than $31,900.

Pandick, rapidly becoming known in the industry as the O. J. Simpson Company, earned our number-three spot for a lot more reasons than the fact that they are employing one of our all-time favorite football players. However, the fact that Pandick is interested in the kind of public relations that Mr. Simpson can provide indicates that they are marketing conscious, and they are willing to pay for it. That does say something about their commitment to selling their product.

Lowell Lewis, a Pandick representative, comments on today's market: "All the financial printers are obviously very dependent on the financial markets, and right now things are pretty slow." However, he matter of factly reports that Pandick's sales have been thundering along at an impressive clip, having increased by over one-third in 1983 to $120 million, by another 30 percent in 1984 to $158 million, and 1985 projections are for still another jump of 20 percent, to $190 million. "The financial printing market is incredibly competitive, and all the signs are pointing to a quiet period." One industry source assesses Pandick reps. "They're known in the industry as a bunch of real go-getters who are very aggressive. I'm not surprised that 20 percent growth is not getting them excited." As Lowell points out, "It's not only a deceleration of sales that's bothering me, it's also that the most lucrative instruments—new debt and equity offering—aren't there right now. And in a flat market like the one we're now in, a lot of companies are sitting tight."

In fact, Pandick is apparently so concerned with the volatility of the financial markets that, according to an industry analyst, "they are moving into the office services business." Lowell says, "We are able to open a lot of doors, get in to see a lot of people, and we've found that there's a pretty big market out there in office management consulting and equipment." We point out that many companies have been burned by the glamour of the high-tech industries, but Lowell is quite confident. "We've been around a long time, and we have our eyes open. Before we dive off the board, we always make sure the pool is filled to the top."

Lowell comments on some of the hectic all-night sessions for which the industry is famous: "There's no feeling quite like it. You're living in the middle of some of the largest financial transactions taking place in the world. There are batteries of lawyers, accountants, and executives, and incredible as it seems, the whole thing can go blooey if we don't do our job right." But obviously they do their job right. Pandick is also very well known throughout the printing industry for taking good care of their reps.

Pandick's representatives are among the highest paid in the industry. They earned a 5 on our compensation scale, only because our scale doesn't go any higher.

Although Bowne & Company has been slowed somewhat by the same negative market forces that have put a bit of a crimp in Pandick's sales, we feel that this financial printer has earned our number-four position in the ratings. They instill a sense of loyalty in their representatives and pay them

> *"I didn't want perks. I wanted books—well-made books done on time and at a good price."*

well for the business they bring in. In the highly competitive printing industry, we feel that instilling good feelings among your representatives is extremely important.

Jim Wynanch, a typical Bowne representative, is in love with his company. "We're treated like royalty," he explains. "They expect a lot of us and we deliver. They get their two days' work for two days' pay." One industry source confirms this: "Those financial printing reps are very well taken care of, and the financial printers can certainly afford it." They demand and receive huge contracts for the detailed, exacting, overnight work that they do. Bowne's sales, for example, though not as spectacular as Pandick's, have increased steadily in the last few years, with 1983's figure up 3 percent to $109 million, 1984's figure up another 5.5 percent to $115 million, and the projection for 1985 is an increase of 17 percent to $135 million.

Jim describes his experience with the now famous all-nighters to produce the financial prospectuses. He denies that there is any real melodrama; it is simply like working the night shift. "All of the people there know their jobs, and they've all been there before." The work is so precise, however, that the rules of professional behavior do not allow for any deviation from the job at hand. "Once an employee of the company—I think he was an accountant—on the evening before a major offering was to be printed and distributed, ordered a drink with dinner and was summarily asked to leave." He wasn't fired from the company; he was merely relieved from duty for that night for having one drink with dinner. When you're working the night shift at a financial printer, not even a comma can be out of place. "That's what you sell when you sell for Bowne," Jim explains. Bowne responds by paying their representatives very well; so well, in fact that their 5 rating for compensatation does not indicate that their salaries are actually higher than the $31,900 for the prototypical two-year salesperson.

De Luxe Check Printers is a leading bank printing house. According to reps, selling printing to banks is little more than taking orders. Banks, they explain, run on paper and forms, and for the printers who can service the banks' needs, the market is almost limitless. One industry source explains that bank printing is a very easy market to service. Most of the business involves forms that rarely change from order to order. In fact, he says, "The bank printers are to the printing industry what 747 captains are to the airline industry." And flying a 747, according to some of the pilots on the L.A.-New York red eye, is about as tricky as playing your stereo, but not nearly as exciting.

Representative Steve Mowatt defines De Luxe's truly astounding market share statistics: "We *are* the check printing industry." De Luxe owns over half of the bank market outright. In addition, nine out of every ten banks in the United States deal with them, and no one bank accounts for as much as 2 percent of their sales. Steve continues, "Frankly, I don't sell. I take orders. The only innovations we come up with are different styles and colors of checks." With such a large market, one wonders how the De Luxe representatives cover all the banks and service the large volume. "A lot of selling is simply done over the phone and by mail," Steve explains, "and a lot of selling is done through third-party reps." He also points out that repeat check-printing orders are sent directly from the banks and include a punched tape that has all of the typesetting and printing instructions already coded. He explains that the machines can simply read the tape, cue the printing job, execute it, package it, and send it directly to the customer with little or no human intervention.

But events are changing and new economic factors on the horizon could hurt the entire bank-printing industry, including De Luxe Printers. "We're heading for a paperless society," Steve explains. "Electronic banking is here to stay. It's popular with banks and consumers, and as more and more people purchase home computers, the home electronic banking market is just going to grow. People are going to stop using checks, ultimately, and the bank printers are going to be in trouble." No one is ready to ring down the curtain on the printed family checkbook yet, he admits, because a paperless society is still a long way away. Nevertheless, De Luxe, as has consistently been the case with all of our top companies, has prepared for all eventualities. "We have a subsidiary, Data Card, which manufactures the plastic bank cards that people would use in a paperless system." And Steve adds, "With our penetration into the banking market, we're not too worried about paperless systems. We'll do just fine." De Luxe also has moved into the computer forms market, and a company spokesman reports that this infant market accounted for 15 percent of sales for De Luxe in 1984 and is expected to grow considerably in the next few years.

De Luxe's sales have increased steadily, albeit not spectacularly, in the last few years, up 13 percent in 1983 to $620 million, up another 10 percent in 1984, to $680 million, and are projected to increase another 10 percent in 1985, to $750 million. With the company's entrance into the computerized banking business, all indications are that the company will continue to grow. De Luxe earned a 4 on our compensation scale, indicating that at De Luxe, our prototypical industry rep earns between $30,450 and $31,900.

	PRINTING	COMPENSATION	COMMISSION	SUPPORT	INTANGIBLE
1	R.R. Donnelley & Sons Co.	5		5	+
2	Moore Business Forms Inc.	5		5	
3	Pandick, Inc.	5		5	+
4	Bowne & Co., Inc.	5		5	+
5	Deluxe Check Printers Inc.	4		5	

The median compensation figure for our prototypical two-year industry rep is $29,000, including salary, bonus, and commission.

Donnelley [+]
The folks who are the biggest are not always the best, but in this case they are. The company earned our [+] for its commitment to electronic communications and diversification into that field. We feel it's good news to Donnelley reps who should already be used to lots of good news.

Pandick and Bowne [+]
These two companies have earned a [+] as our way of indicating that their compensation figure should really be a lot higher than a 5. There's a lot of money to be made in the sale of financial printing.

Advanced Systems, Inc. 37, 40, 51
Advertising Industry 3-20
    compensation in 9, 12, 20
    competitive nature of 7, 9
    computer applications 15
    direct-response 14-16
    high-tech 7-8
    top-ranked companies in 3, 20
Aerospace Industry 241-256
    compensation in 253, 256
    Defense Acquisition
        Regulations' effect on
        242
    foreign sales in 251
    nature of selling in 242, 244,
        250-51
    top-ranked companies in 241,
        256
    Top Secret Clearance in 242-43
Air Products and Chemicals, Inc.
    273, 275-78, 279-81,
    284, 285, 286
Alexander's 164, 167, 171-2
Allied Corporation 275
Ally & Gargano, Inc. 3, 12, 13-14,
    19, 20
Allyn & Bacon 113, 122
Allstate Insurance Co. 53, 63, 64,
    65-66, 67, 68, 258
Altos Computer Systems 143, 159
American Airlines 28-29, 246-47
American Booksellers
    Conference 106
American Cyanamid 273, 275,
    283-84, 285
American Express 14, 17
American Renaissance School 44-45
AT&T 16-17, 34, 42, 177, 190-91,
    192, 193, 194
AMREP 72
Apollo Computer Inc. 177, 185-86,
    192, 193, 194
Apple Computer, Inc. 7, 8-9, 51, 109,
    110, 120, 143, 151, 153,
    154, 159, 217, 319
Arco Books 106, 114, 122, 124
ASK MICRO 116
Atari Computers 34, 153
Automobile Industry 85-103
    changes since 1950s in 86-87
    commissions in 92, 95, 101
    effect of Japanese imports
        on 89, 93

federal government support
    of 89, 93, 98
top-ranked companies
    in 85, 102
training in 101
BankAmerica Corp. 21, 22, 24, 26,
    27, 32, 33, 36
Banking Industry 21-36
    compensation in 25, 33
    computerization of 25, 31, 34,
        145-46
    diversification of services
        within 22-23, 24, 31-32,
        33, 35
    lease packaging offered by 28
    top-ranked companies in 21, 33
    training for a career in 24-25
Barber-Greene Co. 287, 297, 298,
    301
Barrett Developments 258
BASIC BASIC 108
BBDO Inc. 3, 12, 13, 18-19, 20
Beatrice Foods 128
Bell & Howell 37, 40, 41, 42, 46, 47,
    51-52
Bergdorf Goodman 172
Better Homes and Gardens 9
Better Homes and Gardens agencies
    70, 72, 76, 79-80, 81, 82
Big Three Industries Inc. 273,
    274-75, 284-85, 286
Black & Decker 19
Bloomingdale's 164
Blount, Inc. 257, 261-63, 271
Boeing Company, The 28-29, 241,
    245, 256
Book Publishing Industry 103-126
    book/software packages
        produced by 111, 306
    college sales in 105, 111-12,
        113
    compensation in 112, 117, 122,
        123, 124
    computer book boom in 106-11,
        116-17, 119, 306,
        319-21, 322
    educational sales in 112
    role of book distributors in 113
    top-ranked companies in 103,
        125
    trade sales in 113-16, 118
Boots-Celltech Diagnostics 284
Bowne & Co., Inc. 315, 316, 318,
    326-27, 328

Building Industry 257-272
    bidding process in 261-264
    compensation in 264, 270, 271
    computer applications in 262-63
    financial packages offered
        by 258, 259-60
    independent reps in 266-67
    top-ranked companies in 257,
        271
    training in 270
Byte Books 117
CAD/CAM computer systems 179,
    187
Caldor retail chain 163
Calvin Klein 14, 27
Car & Driver 90, 92
Carter Hawley Hale Stores Inc. 161,
    172-3, 174
Caterpillar Tractor Co. 280, 287, 288,
    291, 294, 297, 298,
    300-01
CBS 15, 119, 120
Cencor, Inc. 37, 41, 51
Centex Corporation 69, 72-73, 81
Century 21 Real Estate Corp. 69, 71,
    72, 75-76, 78, 79, 81,
    82, 217
Champion International Corp. 303,
    304, 308, 311-12, 314
Chemical Bank of New York 34
Chrysler Corp. 85, 86, 94, 98-100,
    102, 217
Cincinnati Milacron Inc. 287, 299,
    300, 301, 302
Citicorp 21, 22, 23, 24, 25-26, 28-29,
    32, 33-34, 247, 260
CMI Corp. 287, 289-90, 298, 301
COMDEX conferences 106
Commodore computers 151, 153-54
Compaq 143, 155, 159
Computer Assisted Instructed
    (CAI) 41
Computer Curriculum
    Corporation 42
Computer-generated graphics 5-7
Connecticut Center for Continuing
    Education, The 40,
    48-49
Connecticut General Life Insurance
    Co. 53, 56-58, 64-65, 66,
    67, 68
Continental Illinois Bank 30
Control Data Corp. 37, 41, 42, 47,
    51, 52, 177, 178, 181,
    185, 186-87, 192-93,
    194, 280
Cordis Corporation 195, 204, 210
CP/M 151-52

CYMA 116
Dalton's Bookstore 110, 115
Daniel and Charles, Inc. 10
John Deere 280
Della Femina, Jerry 4, 9-12, 13, 17,
    19
Della Femina, Travisano & Partners
    3, 7-8, 10, 12, 13, 19, 20
Delta Airlines 247
Deltona Corp. 72-73
De Luxe Check Printers, Inc. 315,
    316, 327-28
Dexter Corp. 273, 275, 284, 285, 286
Digital Equipment Corp. 177, 180,
    183-85, 191-92, 193,
    194
Dodge 19
Donnelley, R. R. & Sons, Co. 315,
    316, 321-23, 328
DuPont 275
Education Products Industry 37-52
    compensation in 51
    continuing education 47-49
    educational sales in 40-44
    personal and career
        betterment 49-50
    private schools 44-45
    sales reps' role in 38, 40, 50
    structure of 38, 39
    top-ranked companies in 37, 51
Esquire, Inc. 113
Export Trading Act 34, 35, 36
Exxon 298
Fairfield 72
Farmers Group Inc. 53, 67
Federal Express 14
Federal Reserve Board 34
Fleming Companies, Inc. 126, 128,
    131-33, 139, 141, 142
Food Industry 127-142
    compensation in 133, 136,
        140-41
    computer systems for 134-35
    fast-food industry's role in 128
    nature of selling in 133, 136,
        137
    restaurant industry's impact
        on 128-31
    top-ranked companies in 127,
        141
Ford Motor Co. 24, 85, 91, 94, 95-98,
    100, 102
GEICO 64, 67
Glamour 9
Glass-Steagull Act 29
General Dynamics Corp. 241,
    242-44, 245, 248-53,
    256

General Foods 11, 128
General Motors Corp. 85, 88, 94, 100-01, 102, 298
GF Corp. 211, 212, 213, 222, 224
Gogolak, Pete 318
Gourmet Dining Club 138-39
Grace, W.R. & Co. 275
Great Northern Nekoosa Corp. 303, 308, 310-11, 314
Grumman Corp. 241, 255-56
Gulf & Western 106, 113, 122-24
Hammermill Paper Co. 303, 304, 308, 311, 312-13, 314
Harper & Row Publishers, Inc. 103, 116, 117-19, 123
Harris, Richard 23
Haworth, Inc. 211, 212, 221-22, 224
Hayden Book Company 16, 108-10, 111, 156, 319
Heathkit Stores 148, 186-87
Heavy Machinery Industry 287-302
    compensation in 289, 300-01
    financing as an aid to sales in 295-96
    foreign sales in 291-97
    future prospects in 299-300
    machine tool sector of 298-99
    nature of selling in 288
    recent changes in 288-89, 290-91
    top-ranked companies in 287, 301
    training in 291
Hercules 275
Herman Miller Inc. 211, 212, 220-21, 223, 224
Hewlett-Packard Co. 186, 195, 201, 209, 210
Holt, Rinehart & Winston 103, 116, 118, 119, 120, 125
Honda Motor Co., Ltd. 85, 88-89, 90-93, 102
Horizon Corp. 72
Houghton Mifflin Company 103, 116, 120-22
Hornick, Mel 40, 48-49
Iacocca, Lee 95, 98-100
IBM Corp. 7, 15, 42, 110, 118, 120, 143, 148, 159
    creation of sub-market by 155-57
    domination of mainframe computer market by 188-91, 193
    domination of microcomputer market by 146-47, 151, 154-57, 159

marketing techniques of 181, 216, 280
    reputation of 180
Industrial Chemicals Industry 273-286
    compensation in 279, 285
    experience required to sell in 274, 279
    foreign competition in 280
    market reaction approach to selling in 280
    nature of selling in 277-79
    top-ranked companies in 273, 285
    training in 279, 281, 282
Ingersoll-Rand 287, 291, 297, 298, 300, 301
In Search of Excellence 91
Insurance Industry 53-68
    brokers role in 64-65
    commissions in 55, 58-59, 61, 64, 68
    computer applications in 60-61
    future role of reps in 67
    innovations in 59-60
    service intensive nature of 63-64
    training in 54-55, 57-58, 60
Intermedics 204
International Harvester 294, 297-98, 300
International Paper Co. 303, 308, 309-10, 314
IVAC Corp. 195, 196, 201, 209, 210
Jobs, Steve 160
Johnson & Johnson 198, 199
Kaufman and Broad, Inc. 257, 261, 270, 271-72
K mart Corp. 161, 166, 173, 174
Koger Properties, Inc. 257, 261, 264-66, 271
Ladies' Home Journal 9
Life of Virginia 64
Eli Lilly and Company 201, 225, 226, 227, 236, 238
Lockheed Corp. 241, 253-55, 256
Logo 109, 120-22
Lotus 7
Macmillan 119
R. H. Macy & Co., Inc. 161, 174
Mademoiselle 9
Mainframe Computer Industry 177-194
    changeable nature of 178
    compensation in 185-86, 193
    future trends in 189-90, 193
    IBM's domination of 188-91
    nature of selling in 186, 187-88

skills required to sell in 178-79, 180

top-ranked companies in 177, 193

training in 180, 182, 185

Marcus, Dr. Glenn 44

MasterCard 17

Mays 163

McAllister, Peter 24

McDonald's Restaurants 277

McDonnell Douglas Corp. 241, 247-48, 256

McFadden Act 31, 34

McGraw-Hill, Inc. 16, 41, 103, 105, 108, 109, 110, 116-18, 122, 123, 124, 217, 319

MCI 14, 17

Mead Corporation, The 303, 304, 305-07, 308, 313-14

Medical Equipment Industry 195-210
capital equipment sales in 200-03
compensation in 196, 198, 201, 202, 206, 209, 210
disposables sales in 197-200
experience required to sell in 207-08
future trends in, 208-09
nature of selling in 196-97, 202-03, 205-06, 207
pacemaker sales in 204-07
role of financing and leasing in 203-04
top-ranked companies in 195, 210
U.S. government intervention in 208

Medtronic, Inc. 195, 204, 205, 210

Merck & Co., Inc. 225, 226, 227, 229, 230, 231, 233, 236, 238

Meredith Corp. 69, 72, 79, 81

Merrill Lynch & Co., Inc. 21, 23, 25, 29-30, 32, 33, 34-35, 36

Metropolitan Life Insurance Co. 53, 54, 58, 60-61, 62, 63-64, 66, 67

Microcomputer Industry 143-160
applications to banking 145-46
compensation in 149, 157, 159
growth of 144, 152
IBM's domination of 146-47, 151, 154-57, 159
skills required to sell in 146, 149, 150, 157-58
top-ranked companies in 143, 158

MicroSoft 7, 154-55, 157

Millipore 275

Minnesota Educational Computing Consortium (MECC) 41

Monsanto Company 273, 275, 281-83, 285

Moore Business Forms, Inc. 305, 315, 316, 323-24, 328

National Board of Realtors 77, 79

Neiman-Marcus 163, 172

New American Library 110

New Century Education Corporation 39, 41-44

Newman, Paul 48

Newsweek 323

New York Times 50

Northwestern Insurance Co. 56

Office Furniture Industry 211-224
compensation in 212, 213, 218, 222, 223, 224
dealer reps' role in 212-13
experience required to sell in 219
future trends in 223
history of 213-14
manufacturers' reps' role in 213, 222
new office environments created by 214-16
top-ranked companies in 211, 224
training in 219

Official Airline Guide 17

Ogilvy & Mather International, Inc. 3, 4, 6, 8, 12, 14, 15, 16, 17, 18, 20

Ogilvy, David 14

Osborne, Adam 108, 116, 319

Pacesetter 204

Palmer, Arnold 317

Pandick, Inc. 315, 316, 317, 325-26, 328

Paper Industry 303-314
compensation in 308-09, 310, 312, 313, 314
expense accounts in 309
manufacturer-dealer relationship in 304
merchant reps' role in 313-14
nature of selling in 304-05
top-ranked companies in 303, 314

Pascal 109

PC Magazine 7, 8, 156

Pepsi 19

Perdue, Frank 7

Pfizer Inc. 225, 226-28, 231, 232-33, 236, 238

Pharmaceutical Industry 225-238
  company support of reps
    232-33, 237, 238
  compensation in 229-30, 231,
    237-38
  generic drugs in 233-34
  hospital sales in 231-32
  Patent Restoration Bill's effect
    on 234-35, 236-37
  top-ranked companies in 225,
    238
  training in 225-28, 237
  working environment in 228-29,
    230
Pharmaceutical Media 4, 8
Pierson, Dr. Lee 44, 49-50
Pisaturo, Ron 23-26, 27
PLATO 41
Prentice-Hall, Inc. 103, 104, 105-06,
    107-10, 111, 113, 115,
    123-24
Prescription Learning 41, 42
Printing Industry 315-328
  compensation in 321, 325, 326,
    328
  history of 316-17
  future trends in 327
  independent reps' role in 324
  nature of 316
  top-ranked companies in 315,
    328
  training in 321
Prudential Insurance Co. of America,
    The 53, 54, 59, 63, 64,
    66, 67
Publishers Weekly 111, 319
Pulte Home Corp. 257, 261, 267-69,
    271
Radio Shack 167
Rafal, John 22, 23, 31, 57-58, 65, 66,
    67
Real Estate Industry 69-82
  commissions in 70-71, 76, 81
  computer applications in 76
  duality of agent's role in 77-78
  financing in 71, 73, 80
  psychology of 78-79
  referral systems in 71, 76
  top-ranked companies in 69, 81
  training in 79
Redbook 9
Reed, John 25-26
Reston 106, 116, 123
Retail Industry 161-174
  building a career in 164, 169
  buyers role in 165-66, 168-71,
    172
  changes in 171-72

  compensation in 165, 169, 171,
    174
  jobbers' importance in 166-69,
    170
  sales managers' role in 162,
    164-65
  security in 162-64
  top-ranked companies in 161,
    174
Road & Track 92
Ryan Homes, Inc. 69, 74, 81
Rykoff-Sexton, Inc. 126, 128, 136-37,
    139, 141, 142
Ryland Group, Inc. 69, 71-72, 74-75,
    81
St. Regis Corporation 311
Sales Recruiters International 23
G. D. Searle & Co. 225, 226, 230
Sears Merchandise Group 30, 161,
    173, 174, 258
Security Pacific Corp. 21, 23, 26, 32,
    33, 35
Sexton Educational Centers 49-50
Shearson Lehman Brothers, Inc. 21,
    23-25, 30, 32, 33, 35-36
Simon & Schuster 111, 113, 122,
    123, 124
Simpson, O. J. 317-18, 325
Skinner, B. F. 42
Snap-On Tools 298-99
SPRINT 17
Squibb Corp. 225, 226, 229, 238
Stanley Kaplan Centers 50
Stanley Works, The 287, 298-99,
    300, 301
Steelcase Inc. 211, 212, 214-20, 223,
    224
Super Valu Stores, Inc. 126, 128,
    140-41, 142
Sysco Corp. 126, 128, 130, 133, 136,
    139, 141, 142
Tandy 151, 152-53, 154
Tarkenton, Fran 318
TECA Corp. 195, 207, 209, 210
TeleVideo 143, 159
Texas Instruments 280, 319
Time 9, 323
Toyota Motor Corp. 85, 93, 101-02
TWA 28, 72, 76, 245-46
"21" Club 128, 138, 139
Union Carbide 274-75
United Airlines 28, 246-47
United Grocers 131
Upjohn Co., The 225, 226, 227, 231,
    236-37, 238
U.S. Home Corp. 257, 258-59, 261,
    269-70, 271
USLIFE Corporation 60

VisiCalc 153
VisiCorp 7
Vogue 9
Volkswagon 86, 87
Von Nostrand 124
Walden Books 114
Wall Street Journal 123
Walther, Charles 42-44
Wanamaker Stores 172
Wang Laboratories, Inc. 148, 177,
　　182-83, 185, 189, 192, 193,
　　194, 221
Washington Post 50

Westinghouse Electric Corp. 211,
　　212, 213, 223, 224
Wetterau Inc. 126, 128, 139-40, 141
WICAT Systems 39, 41, 42
Williams, Tennessee 48
Wood, Evelyn 49
Woodward, Joanne 48
F. W. Woolworth Co. 161, 173, 174
Xerox Corp. 37, 41, 45-46, 47, 51,
　　308, 310
Young & Rubicam, Inc. 3, 4, 15, 16,
　　19, 20, 48
Zenith 146, 147-48, 156, 186-87

■■■■■ INDEX OF THE 100 TOP COMPANIES ■■■■■

Advanced Systems, Inc.
　155 E. Algonquin Rd.
　Arlington Heights, IL 60005
　(312) 981-1500
　Vice-Pres., Sales: Bette Tomaszewicz

Air Products and Chemicals, Inc.
　P.O. Box 538
　Allentown, PA 18105
　(215) 481-4911
　Vice-President, Employee Relations:
　　James O. Boyce

Allstate Insurance Co.
　Allstate Plaza
　Northbrook, IL 60062
　(312) 291-5000
　Vice-President, Sales:
　　William V. Henderson

Ally & Gargano Inc.
　805 Third Ave.
　New York, NY 10022
　(212) 688-5300
　Chairman, President and
　Chief Executive: Amil Gargano

Altos Computer Systems
　2641 Orchard Parkway
　San Jose, CA 95134
　(408) 946-6700
　Senior Vice-President, Marketing &
　Sales: Phillip White

American Cyanamid Company
　One Cyanamid Plaza
　Wayne, NJ 07470
　(201) 831-2000
　Vice-Pres., Personnel: W. D. Brown

American Telephone & Telegraph
　550 Madison Ave.
　New York, NY 10022
　(212) 605-5500
　Sr. Vice-President, Personnel:
　　H. Weston Clarke Jr.

Apollo Computer Inc.
　330 Billerica Road
　Chelmsford, MA 01824

　(617) 256-6600
　Dir. of Personnel: Robert Giroux

Apple Computer, Inc.
　20525 Mariani Ave.
　Cupertino, CA 95014
　(408) 973-2433
　Employment Services

BankAmerica Corporation
　Bank of America Center
　San Francisco, CA 94104
　(415) 622-3456
　President: Samuel H. Armacost

Barber-Greene Co.
　400 N. Highland Ave.
　Aurora, IL 60507
　(312) 859-2200
　Vice-President, N. American Sales:
　　W. E. Putz

BBDO, Inc.
　383 Madison Ave.
　New York, NY 10017
　(212) 415-5000
　Sr. Vice-Pres. & Dir. of Administrative
　Services: Charles Buck

Bell & Howell
　5215 Old Orchard Road
　Skokie, IL 60077-1076
　(312) 470-7100
　Vice-President, Human Resources:
　　John Kambanis

Big Three Industries Inc.
　3535 W. Twelfth St.
　Houston, TX 77008
　(713) 868-0333
　Admin. Vice-President: James Fry

Blount, Inc.
　4520 Executive Park Dr.
　Montgomery, AL 36116
　(205) 272-8020
　Vice-President, Human Resources:
　　Joseph McInnes

The Boeing Company
P.O. Box 3707
Seattle, WA 98124
(206) 655-2121
Personnel Department

Bowne & Co., Inc.
345 Hudson St.
New York, NY 10014
(212) 924-5500
Vice-President, Human Resources:
Allen D. Marold

Carter Hawley Hale Stores Inc.
550 S. Flower St.
Los Angeles, CA 90071
(213) 620-0150
Director of Executive Recruitment &
Placement: Barbara Helstrom

Caterpillar Tractor Co.
100 N.E. Adams St.
Peoria, IL 61629
(309) 675-1000
President: Peter Donis

Cencor, Inc.
P.O. Box 26610
Kansas City, MO 64196
(816) 474-4750
Personnel Director: Larry Levret

Centex Corporation
4600 Republic Bank
Dallas, TX 75201
(214) 748-7901
Vice-President, Corporate
Communications: Sheila Gallagher

Century 21 Real Estate Corp.
18872 MacArthur Blvd.
Irvine, CA 92715
(714) 752-7521
President: Richard J. Loughlin

Champion International Corp.
One Champion Plaza
Stamford, CT 06921
(203) 358-7000
Manager, Professional Recruiting:
Anita Wheeler

Chrysler Corp.
12000 Chrysler Dr.
Highland Park, MI 48203
(313) 956-5252
Vice-President, Personnel &
Organization: G. E. White

Cincinnati Milacron Inc.
4701 Marburg Ave.
Cincinnati, OH 45209
(513) 841-8100
Vice-President, Human Resources:
Theodore Mauser

Citicorp
399 Park Ave.
New York, NY 10043
(212) 559-1000
Chairman: John S. Reed

CMI Corp.
I-40 & Morgan Rd.
P.O. Box 1985
Oklahoma City, OK 73101
(405) 787-6020
Vice-Pres., Sales: Stu Murray

Compaq
20555 FM149
Houston, TX 77070
(713) 370-0670
Human Resources

Connecticut General Life Insurance Co.
900 Cottage Grove Rd.
Bloomfield, CT 06002
(203) 726-6000
President: Hartzel Z. Lebed

Control Data Corp.
P.O. Box O
Minneapolis, MN 55440
(612) 853-8100
Vice-President, Personnel &
Administration: Frank R. Dawe

Cordis Corporation
P.O. Box 025700
Miami, FL 33102
(305) 551-2000
President, Marketing Division:
Richard T. Spencer

De Luxe Check Printers, Inc.
1080 W. County Rd. F
St. Paul, MN 55112
(612) 483-7111
Sr. Vice-Pres., Sales: W. N. Hansen

Della Femina, Travisano & Partners
625 Madison Ave.
New York, NY 10022
(212) 421-7180
Chairman: Jerry Della Femina

The Dexter Corp.
One Elm St.
Windsor Locks, CT 06096
(203) 627-9051
President: Worth Loomis

Digital Equipment Corp.
146 Main St.
Maynard, MA 01754
(617) 493-7243
Vice-Pres., Personnel: John L. Sims

R. R. Donnelley & Sons Co.
2223 Martin Luther King Dr.
Chicago, IL 60616
(312) 326-8000
Vice-Pres., Marketing: R. D. Missimer

Farmers Group Inc.
4680 Wilshire Blvd.
Los Angeles, CA 90010
(213) 932-3902
Vice-Pres., Sales: W. H. Braddock

Fleming Companies, Inc.
6301 Waterford
Oklahoma City, OK 73118

(405) 840-7200
Exec. Vice-President, Human Resources: Richard D. Williams

Ford Motor Co.
Sales Operations
P.O. Box 43331
Detroit, MI 48243
Recruiting and Placement:
Ron Pettay

General Dynamics Corp.
Pierre Laclede Center
St. Louis, MO 63105
(314) 889-8200
Corp. Dir. of Personnel Planning & Placement: Edward C. Bruntrager

General Motors Corp.
3044 West Grand Blvd.
Room 7-220
Detroit, MI 48202
(313) 556-2633
Vice-Pres., Marketing & Product Planning Staff: Robert T. O'Connell

GF Corporation
4944 Belmont Ave.
P.O. Box 1108
Youngstown, OH 44501
(216) 759-8888
Sr. Vice-Pres., Sales & Marketing:
Richard S. Strong

Great Northern Nekoosa Corp.
75 Prospect St.
P.O. Box 9309
Stamford, CT 06904
(203) 359-4000
Director of Industrial Relations:
Ronald J. Rakowski

Grumman Corp.
1111 Stewart Ave.
Bethpage, NY 11714
(516) 575-0574
President: George M. Skurla

Hammermill Paper Co.
P.O. Box 10050
Erie, PA 16533
(814) 456-8811
Dir., Corp. Personnel: Daniel A. Moss

Harper & Row Publishers, Inc.
10 E. 53rd St.
New York, NY 10022
(212) 207-7107
Vice-President, Personnel:
Chester S. Logan

Haworth, Inc.
One Haworth Center
Holland, MI 49423
(616) 392-5961
Staffing and Placement, Human Resources

Herman Miller Inc.
8500 Byron Rd.
Zeeland, MI 49464

(616) 772-3300
Vice-Pres., Sales: Philip Mercorella

Hewlett-Packard Co.
3000 Hanover St.
Palo Alto, CA 94304
(415) 857-1501
Professional Employment: Ann Anton

Holt, Rinehart and Winston
383 Madison Ave.
New York, NY 10017
(212) 872-2000
Vice-President, Marketing and Sales: Joseph M. Krassner

Honda Motor Co.
1-1, 2-chome, Minami-Aoyama
Minato-ku, Tokyo, Japan
03-423-1111
President: Tadashi Kume

Houghton Mifflin Company
One Beacon St.
Boston, MA 02108
(617) 725-5190
Vice-President, Personnel:
Joan P. Bowman

Ingersoll-Rand
200 Chestnut Ridge Rd.
Woodcliff Lake, NJ 07675
(201) 573-0123
Vice-President, Human Resources:
Robert G. Ripston

International Business Machines Corp.
Old Orchard Rd.
Armonk, NY 10504
(914) 765-1900
Vice-President, Personnel:
Walton E. Burdick

International Paper Co.
77 W. 45th St.
New York, NY 10036
(212) 536-6000
Vice-President, Human Resources:
David W. Oskin

IVAC Corp.
10300 Campus Point Dr.
San Diego, CA 92121
(619) 458-7000
Sales Personnel Supervisor:
Mike DeAngelis

Kaufman and Broad, Inc.
11601 Wilshire Blvd.
Los Angeles, CA 90025
(213) 312-5000
Dept. of Human Resources:

K mart Corp.
3100 W. Big Beaver
Troy, MI 48084
(313) 643-1000
Manager, Personnel: H. C. House

Koger Properties, Inc.
P.O. Box 4520
Jacksonville, FL 32201

(904) 396-4811
Personnel Dir.: Dianna Payne

Eli Lilly and Company
Lilly Corporate Center
Indianapolis, IN 46285
(317) 261-2000
Pres., Pharm. Div.: Eugene Step

Lockheed Corp.
2555 Hollywood Way
Burbank, CA 91503
(818) 847-6121
Vice-President, Marketing:
Charles de Bedts

R. H. Macy & Co., Inc.
151 W. 34th St.
New York, NY 10001
(212) 560-3600
Vice-President, Exec. Recruitment:
R. Barry Lyons

McDonnell Douglas Corp.
P.O. Box 516
St. Louis, MO 63166
(314) 232-7595
Mgr. of Employment: Jack Boatman

McGraw-Hill, Inc.
1221 Avenue of the Americas
New York, NY 10020
(212) 512-4258
*Vice-President, Staffing and
Development:* Walter F. Whitt

The Mead Corporation
Courthouse Plaza, N. E.
Dayton, OH 45463
(513) 222-6323
Director of Exec. Recruiting:
J. C. Bramlage

Medtronic, Inc.
3055 Old Highway Eight
P.O. Box 1453
Minneapolis, MN 55440
(612) 574-4000
President: Dale R. Olseth

Merck & Co., Inc.
P.O. Box 2000
Rahway, NJ 07065
(201) 574-4000
Director of Exec. Employment:
Frederick Siepert

Meredith Corp.
1716 Locust St.
Des Moines, IA 50336
(515) 284-3000
*President, and Chief Executive
Officer:* Robert A. Burnett

Merrill Lynch & Co., Inc.
165 Broadway
New York, NY 10080
(212) 637-3070
Manager, Employment Department:
Johanne Reid

Metropolitan Life Insurance Co.
1 Madison Ave.
New York, NY 10010
(212) 578-2211
Vice-President, Human Resources

Monsanto Company
800 N. Lindbergh Blvd.
St. Louis, MO 63167
(314) 694-1000
Professional Employment Director:
G. E. Wiley

Moore Business Forms, Inc.
1205 Milwaukee Ave.
Glenview, IL 60025
(312) 480-3000
Human Resources

Ogilvy & Mather International, Inc.
2 E. 48th St.
New York, NY 10017
(212) 907-3400
*Sr. Vice-President, Personnel
Director:* Fran Devereux

Pandick, Inc.
345 Hudson St.
New York, NY 10014
(212) 741-5555
Personnel Director: Eileen Stewart

Pfizer Inc.
235 E. 42nd St.
New York, NY 10017
(212) 573-2323
Vice-Pres., Personnel: Bruce R. Ellig

Prentice-Hall, Inc.
Englewood Cliffs, NJ 07632
(201) 592-2000
Vice-President, Human Resources:
Joseph F. Kelly

The Prudential Insurance Co. of America
745 Broad St., 16th Floor
Newark, NJ 07101
(201) 877-6000
*Sr. Vice-President, District
Agencies Sales:* Pellegrino P. Porraro

Pulte Home Corp.
6400 Farmington Rd.
West Bloomfield, MI 48033
(313) 661-1500
*Exec. Vice-Pres. and Chief
Operating Officer:* Robert K. Burgess

Ryan Homes, Inc.
100 Ryan Ct.
Pittsburgh, PA 15205
(412) 276-8000
Vice-President, Human Resources:
Tom Ford

Rykoff-Sexton, Inc.
761 Terminal St.
Los Angeles, CA 90021
(213) 622-4131
President: Roger W. Coleman

Ryland Group Inc.
10221 Wincopin Circle
Columbia, MD 21044
(301) 730-7222
*Vice-President, Corporate
Development:* James B. Webel

G. D. Searle & Co.
Box 1045
Skokie, IL 60076
(312) 982-7000
*Chairman and Chief Executive
Officer:* Donald H. Rumsfeld

Sears Merchandise Group
Sears Tower
Chicago, IL 60684
(312) 875-2500
*Vice-President, Personnel &
Employee Relations:* Con F. Massey

Security Pacific Corp.
333 S. Beaudry St.
Los Angeles, CA 90071
(213) 613-6211
*Vice-President, Employment
Division:* Nancy Bergmans

Shearson Lehman Brothers, Inc.
2 World Trade Center
103rd Floor
New York, NY 10048
(212) 321-6000
Vice-President: Joseph Haberman

Squibb Corp.
P. O. Box 4000
Princeton, NJ 08540
(609) 921-4000
Director, Human Resources:
Anthony Archer

The Stanley Works
1000 Stanley Dr.
New Britain, CT 06053
(203) 225-5111
Dir., Marketing: F. E. Hummel

Steelcase Inc.
P.O. Box 1967
Grand Rapids, MI 49501
(616) 247-2710
Employment Mgr.: Jim Wittig

Super Valu Stores, Inc.
11840 Valley View Rd.
Eden Prairie, MN 55344
(612) 828-4000
Vice-Pres., Sales: Thomas L. Dekko

Sysco Corp.
1177 West Loop South
Houston, TX 77027
(713) 877-1122
*Vice-President, Management
Development:* Lawrence H. Pete

TECA Corp.
3 Campus Drive
Pleasantville, NY 10570

(914) 769-5900
National Sales Manager:
Joseph Stevens

TeleVideo Systems, Inc.
550 East Brokaw Rd.
P.O. Box 6602
San Jose, CA 95150-6602
(408) 971-0255
Personnel Department

Toyota Motor Corp.
1-Toyota cho
Toyota, Aichi, Japan 471
0565-28-2121
Managing Director, Personnel:
Masami Iwasaki

The Upjohn Co.
7000 Portage Rd.
Kalamazoo, MI 49001
(616) 323-4000
Employment

U. S. Home Corp.
1800 West Loop S.
Houston, TX 77027
(713) 877-2311
Dir., Personnel: Nancy Nobles

Wang Laboratories Inc.
One Industrial Ave.
Lowell, MA 01851
(617) 459-5000
*Sr. Vice-President, Sales &
Marketing - U.S.:* Robert L. Doretti

Westinghouse Electric Corp.
Gateway Center
Westinghouse Building, Rm. 1053
Pittsburgh, PA 15222
(412) 642-3337
Manager, Career Development:
Patricia Shields

Wetterau Incorporated
8920 Pershall Rd.
Hazelwood, MO 63042
(314) 524-5000
*1st Vice-President, Human
Resources:* Andy Levy

F. W. Woolworth Co.
233 Broadway
New York, NY 10279
(212) 553-2000
Vice-President, Public Affairs:
J. F. Carroll

Xerox Corp.
Xerox Business Sys. Group
Rochester, NY 14644
Vice-President, Personnel:
Ms. D. K. Smith

Young & Rubicam Inc.
285 Madison Ave.
New York, NY 10017
(212) 210-3000
*Sr. Vice-Pres., Manager of
Client Services:* Marie Mandry